'*Cartier, qui fait tenir, magicien subtil,*
de la lune en morceaux sur du soleil en fil'

JEAN COCTEAU

HANS NADELHOFFER

Cartier

JEWELERS EXTRAORDINARY

HARRY N. ABRAMS, INC., PUBLISHERS,
NEW YORK

For Ralph Esmerian

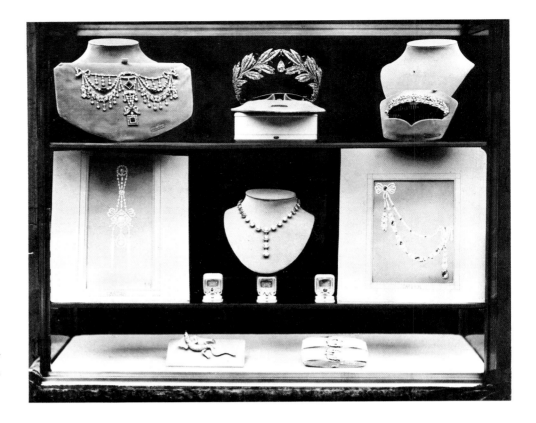

On the half title: Delivery van from Cartier's New York, 1911

Cartier's window display on the occasion of the marriage of Princess Marie Bonaparte in 1907. The various pieces of jewelry were commissioned for the event.

Library of Congress Cataloging in Publication Data
Nadelhoffer, Hans.
    Cartier: jewelers extraordinary.
    1. Cartier (Firm)   2. Jewelers—France—Biography.
    I. Title.
    NK7398.C37N32 1984   739.27′092′2 83-26646
    ISBN 0-8109-0770-4

Published in 1984 by Harry N. Abrams, Incorporated, New York. All rights reserved. No part of the contents of this book may be reproduced without the written permission of the publishers.

Printed and bound in the Netherlands by Royal Smeets Offset b.v.

Notes to the Illustrations

Numbers in the inside margins refer to colour plates.

Except otherwise stated, the provenance of all pieces illustrated is Cartier's Paris.

All colour illustrations are actual size unless measurements are indicated. Black and white illustrations of jewelry are half-size, unless otherwise indicated.

When the archives do not permit exact dating of a piece, either no date is indicated or reference is made to similar datable pieces.

Dates following the description of items refer to the year of manufacture.

Around 1900 the carat weight for precious stones was not yet unified and varied in different parts of the world between 0.1885 gr. and 0.2135 gr. The old carat gave subdivisions as fractions from $\frac{1}{2}$ to $\frac{1}{64}$ and the weight was expressed as a series of fractions, i.e. $1, \frac{1}{2}, \frac{1}{4}, \frac{1}{32}$ and not as a unit and unreduced fraction. A first attempt to standardize the carat at 0.205 gr. made by Paris merchants in 1871 did not gain international recognition. In 1907 the 'Comité International des Poids et Mesures' proposed a metric carat of 200 mg which was accepted. Switzerland legalized it in 1909, Italy in 1910, France in 1912, the United States in 1913 and England in 1914.

The Cartier archives give the metric carat as from 1911. Earlier weights used the old confusing system which in France varied at subsequent times between 205.9 and 205.5 mg. These old carat weights were therefore in excess of corresponding metric weights. The present work leaves early carat references unchanged.

All mounts unless otherwise stated are made in platinum.

All pearls are natural and not cultivated.

Photographic Acknowledgments

Messrs Christie's; Messrs Sotheby's; Diamond Information Center, New York; Condé Nast Library, New York; Metropolitan Museum, New York; Musée des Arts Décoratifs, Paris; Photothèque Kahn, Paris; Smithsonian Institution, Washington; Roger-Viollet, Paris; Royal Archives, Photograph Collection: By Gracious Permission of Her Majesty the Queen.

Most of the colour photos were taken by Mr Tjerk Wicky, Lausanne.

Photos from the Cartier archives were developed by Mr Frédéric Proust, Paris; Mr Hubert Salmon, Paris; and Mr Georgios Hadjigeorgiou, London.

Contents

1. Louis-François Cartier (1819–1904)

2. Louis Cartier, aged 29 (drawing: Emile Friant)

3. Jacques Cartier (photo: Boissonas & Taponier)

E. Friant
30 avril 1904

Introduction

WHEN LOUIS-FRANÇOIS CARTIER established his first, somewhat modest business in 1847, there were few indications that future greatness lay ahead. The period between the abdication of Louis-Philippe and the setting-up of the Second Empire was fraught with difficulties for all the luxury trades: competition was severe, and the district around the Eglise Saint-Eustache in Paris was scarcely one to encourage the growth of any future business. Half a century later, however, Cartier's name was to be found in resplendent letters adorning the world's leading shopping street, drawing within its orbit the wealthiest of international customers. Branches in London and New York soon became the fixed points in a strategical game of international business politics. Cartier's was now a firm of worldwide reputation; it had become an Institution.

Following the industrialization of the nineteenth century, the years between 1900 and 1915 witnessed a period of unprecedented economic growth. Communications were opened up, the wealth of the colonies flooded into Europe, and technical inventions strengthened men's faith in an optimistic future. Like the great industrialists, international bankers built up their empires, becoming the confidential advisors of governments and kings. Those business tycoons who had acquired their wealth through speculation and a spirit of pioneering enterprise chose the court etiquette of an aristocratic élite as the model on which to base their own lifestyles. Although they were deprived of the aristocracy's genealogical antecedents, their financial dealings were sufficient to ensure them access to the highest circles of court society.

It was in the service of this as yet unspoilt consumer society that Cartier's scored its most triumphant successes, though commissions from royalty were certainly not excluded: between 1904 and 1939 the firm received fifteen letters patent appointing it official purveyor to various royal households, from those of King Edward VII and King Paramindr Maha Chulalongkorn of Siam, to the court of King Zog of Albania.

From a sociological point of view, one of Cartier's jewels might well guarantee entry into a society which depended for its survival upon imitation and plagiarism. On the eve of society weddings the firm would deliver its *corbeilles de mariage* — and one thinks of the extravagance lavished on that of Marie Bonaparte — as characteristic status symbols which complemented the trousseaux of the great fashion houses.

For all their varying backgrounds, Cartier's clients had one thing in common — unlimited wealth, which justified the firm's keeping in stock what, by today's standards, must seem an inconceivably costly range of gemstones. As the stock attracted clients from all over the world, language barriers often gave rise to situations of subtle humour, attested to by countless anecdotes:

The interpreter of the King of Siam said that the King wished to see some bracelets, whereupon the sales assistant Jules Glaenzer showed him one tray after another, glittering with precious stones. But the King simply shook his head. Finally Glaenzer went over to the safe and brought out a tray containing the rarest and costliest bracelets. The King gave his interpreter a sign, and the latter turned to Glaenzer, 'His Majesty has chosen this one.'

'Which one?' asked Glaenzer. 'The whole tray,' was the haughty reply.

Thus the King of Siam became the owner of bracelets to the value of $450,000. (Two years later, by way of comparison, the Hope Diamond was sold for $180,000.)[1]

Coming as it did from a prewar era of luxury and affluence, the name of Cartier, like that of the Ritz, was divorced from its context and turned into one of the few lasting symbols of a lifestyle and a philosophy that was acted out with exemplary taste. 'Dickens in a Cartier setting' was how Edward VIII described Christmas at Sandringham, conjuring up the glittering atmosphere which illuminated the house like a precious jewel.[2]

But exemplariness provokes imitators. Cartier's ideas, which were to have such an impact on twentieth-century jewelry design, were eagerly snatched up by competitors, robbed of their value and beauty and often reintroduced on to the market in the form of mass-produced trivia.

The Cartier phenomenon was the achievement of three brothers, who built an empire and divided it up among themselves, between New York, Paris and London. Preeminent among them — and not only for reasons of age — was the eldest of the three, Louis (1875–1942). Born four years after Marcel Proust, he was nineteen when the later Dreyfus Case first burst upon the world, and forty-two at the outbreak of the First World War.

In Louis Cartier we meet that rare combination of aesthete and highly instinctive market tactician. As an aesthete he became a collector, influenced by the taste of a *fin-de-siècle* aesthetic whose interchangeable standards embraced every age and every culture. In this he found a kindred spirit in his friend, the eccentric *bon vivant* Boni de Castellane, who for years officiated as a social observer in Cartier's service.

Louis Cartier admired the France of the eighteenth century, with its painting and elegant craftsmanship. Not content, however, with the role of a mere arbiter of elegant taste, he developed an understanding of Islamic and Far Eastern art, incorporating their refined ideas into his firm's range of products. It was thanks to Louis Cartier that the Orient came to play so important a role in the firm's art deco designs.

Also typical of the *fin-de-siècle* mentality was his personal interest in contemporary ideas of philosophy and science — theories about matter, the atom and radioactivity which were by no means irreconcilable with his poetic awareness of the infinite. 'The grandiose contemplation of our planet's remotest past, this proof of God's existence in the structure of an atom, fills me with a sense of awe,' he wrote to his father in an undated letter.

Pierre Cartier (1878–1965), on the other hand, was a born businessman who might have achieved much of value in any field of activity. That he felt the need, as a man of great pragmatic skills, to go to the United States and run the firm's New York branch according to the rules of the New World, was in itself entirely typical

4. Pierre Cartier with King George VI and Queen Elizabeth of England

of him. Whereas Louis cultivated links with the old aristocracy of Europe, marrying Countess Almassy of Hungary *en secondes noces*, Pierre grew up dreaming of a career as an ambassador, surrounded by the leading families of America who opened their doors to him following his marriage to Elma Rumsey, the daughter of a rich industrialist from St Louis, Missouri. Many of Pierre's important decisions were reached in consultation with Jules Glaenzer, the son of an antique dealer, who was in charge of the firm's Fifth Avenue branch, entertaining Hollywood artists to dinner and contributing to Cartier's image in America in the same way that Jeanne Toussaint contributed to that image in Paris.

The youngest member of the family, Jacques (1884–1942), was only fifteen when the firm moved to the rue de la Paix. He was probably the most sensitive and introverted of the three brothers. When his father Alfred divided up the family empire, it was the London branch which fell to Jacques. After it broke away from the parent company in 1919, and the political conditions of the 1930s obliged it to adopt a more independent policy in artistic matters, it was Jacques who provided increasingly valuable suggestions for the design studios and whose purchase of gemstones showed a sure understanding of what he was doing. Together with his wife Nelly Harjes, a member of the well-known banking family which had connections with Morgan in America, he built up his social contacts so that by the time he died they had come to include all the leading princes of the Indian subcontinent.

The triumvirate of brothers was joined in Paris by Jeanne Toussaint (1887–1978). According to the English court photographer Cecil Beaton, she was a woman 'of small bird-like stature' – one thinks of the countless allusions to birds in the descriptions left of the American socialite Emerald Cunard. Beaton was struck by her 'almost male contempt for trivialities' and by her sixth sense of taste, the famous 'goût Toussaint'. It was an acid test to which the firm's most sophisticated products were mercilessly subjected. She never designed anything herself. 'My inability to draw qualifies me to assess the work of others'; and from the distance of this self-imposed limitation she watched over the firm's designs for four decades, offering splendid suggestions and brilliant analyses.

Jeanne Toussaint saw jewels as an aspect of fashion. The most sophisticated creations of Elsa Schiaparelli, Christian Dior, Coco Chanel and Cristobal Balenciaga provided endlessly changing backgrounds for her jewelry. Painted by Helleu, Boldini, Sem, Iribe and Bérard, she conveyed the impression of a sorceress even in her daily routine. 'You who perfume diamonds!' Princess Bibesco cried out in amazement.

Although she was committed to the aesthetic taste of the 1930s and 1940s, Jeanne Toussaint was one of the first to recognize the originality of Cartier's products from earlier periods, and in 1934 she advised a return to 'the sources of inspiration', namely the ideas that had been formulated around 1906.

Cartier's most original creations stopped short at nothing, especially during the Cocktail Age of the 1930s: tin-openers with a crowned monogram, gold yo-yos (W. K. Vanderbilt bought ten of

5. Jeanne Toussaint (1887–1978)

them), and a diamond belt for the actress Polaire, not to mention gold toothpicks made for King Farouk, and a silver shoe which it took Cartier's master craftsman Ferdinand Albouze 180 hours to complete in the firm's workshop. It was an amusing line of work which helped to tide the firm over at a time when, because of the economic situation, major commissions were relatively few in number.

At the end of the 1940s Pierre Cartier handed over the New York branch to Louis' son Claude, devoting himself from then on to the parent firm in Paris. He died in 1965, the last surviving member of the Cartier brothers. The New York branch had been sold three years previously, and the firm was fragmented and sold off in a series of further transactions, before passing into the hands of a financial syndicate organized by Joseph Kanouï and headed by Robert Hocq in 1972. With the reunion of the three Cartier branches foremost in his mind, Hocq once more built up the firm to international preeminence. Apart from carrying on its reputation in gems and jewelry, Cartier's in 1972 witnessed the birth of 'Les Must de Cartier', a worldwide marketing concept selling high-fashion items of jewelry and gifts which, under changed social circumstances, once again carry the name of Cartier to every country on earth.

6. Silhouette showing the Cartier brothers: Pierre, Louis and Jacques

From apprentice to court jeweler

THE HISTORY OF CARTIER'S begins with an incident which, according to family tradition, took place in 1808 in Saragossa at the time of the Napoleonic Wars in Spain: Pierre Cartier (1787–1859), a young and inexperienced infantry soldier, had just been taken prisoner but was saved from the immediate threat of being lined up and shot along with other soldiers by the bravery of a baker's wife, who hid him in the baker's oven before helping him to escape, dressed as a woman. Wellington's English soldiers, however, soon saw through his disguise and he was transported by ship to Plymouth. It was much later before he saw his homeland again, and not until 1815 that he married Elisabeth Gérardin, a washerwoman,[1] and began to earn an honest living as a manufacturer of powder-horns. He had scarcely known his father Louis-François (1755–93/94), who had worked as a metal turner in a small workshop in the Louvre, producing items for the royal household. Suspicion fell upon him at the time of the Revolution, as it did on so many others, forcing him to abandon Paris. He died at the early age of thirty-nine on his small property near Saint-Denis.

It was Pierre's son (1819–1904), christened Louis-François after his grandfather, who was to point the way to his family's later calling. He was employed in the workshop of the jeweler Adolphe Picard,[2] at 29 rue Montorgueil, close to the huge oyster market in the Saint-Eustache district. Louis-François was a capable assistant, and when in 1847 Picard moved to 29 rue de Richelieu, he consigned his business to the younger man. Louis-François' entry in the Trade Almanac described him as the 'successor to M. Picard, manufacturer of jewels and bijouterie, fancy decorations and novelties'.

The quarter where, in addition to the rue de Richelieu, the first jewelers had taken up residence, where fashionable society went shopping and where the beautiful women of Paris were to be seen driving around *en calèche*, was the Palais-Royal. Louis-François' ambition to settle in the neighbourhood of the vast palace of the Orléans family was achieved in 1853; with Picard's help he set himself up in 5 rue Neuve-des-Petits-Champs, as a manufacturer of jewels and *bijouterie*, which he also sold to the public. The thirty-four-year-old Cartier not only produced his own jewelry but, in accordance with contemporary practice, received supplies from a number of other workshops, including that of Picard, to whom he remained contractually bound.

The business quickly prospered. Cartier's first pretax profits amounted to Fr9,252 and the firm's proximity to the Palais-Royal began to pay handsome dividends. But how was he to succeed in drawing the attention of the imperial family and its circle to his activities? Emperor Napoleon III had married Eugénie de Montijo, Comtesse de Teba, in the same year that Cartier had transferred business. The jeweler Ouizille-Lemoine in the rue du Bac was among those whose workshops supplied Cartier; and it was this firm, together with those of Lemonnier, Baugrand and Mellerio, that the emperor had chosen to rework various pieces of jewelry. Couturiers and jewelers hoped that the arrival of the beautiful Spanish countess would bring an increase in business; after all, the Paris city council had agreed to spend Fr600,000 on a necklace with a 23-carat heart-shaped diamond as a wedding present. The empress, however, wisely foreseeing malicious criticism, declined the generous gift, much to the disappointment of the Parisian jewelers.

But Cartier was to achieve his goal by indirect means. His first important female customer was the Countess of Nieuwerkerke, who bought some fifty-five items between 1855 and 1858. The time was not yet ripe for large pieces of jewelry: it was a transitional period during which the prevailing fashion was determined by the puritanical bourgeois taste of the Age of Louis-Philippe. The great fashion for cameos, which had started under Napoleon, had not yet died out, and so the countess began by ordering a cameo necklace, together with six buttons set with antique cameos. The Count of Nieuwerkerke was well known in his day as a sculptor in bronze: he had produced an equestrian statue of Napoleon III which had won the emperor's approval. More important, however, as far as Cartier was concerned, was the count's friendship with Princess Mathilde, through which he had attained his appointment as Superintendent of Fine Art. The princess, who was the daughter of Napoleon's brother Jérôme, had left St Petersburg in 1845 in order to settle in Paris, following the failure of her marriage to the Russian Prince Demidov di San Donato. She maintained a salon, first in the Palais de l'Elysée and later in the rue de Courcelles and on her estates at Saint-Gratien, which attracted scholars, politicians and artists and which formed a striking contrast with the frivolity of the Tuileries court. It was through Nieuwerkerke that Cartier received commissions from the princess and an imperial eagle which Nieuwerkerke ordered in 1857 was undoubtedly destined for her jewel casket. The commissions which Princess Mathilde herself placed, whether they were intended for her own use or as gifts, included four Medusa-head cameos, seven amethyst plaque brooches, a turquoise scarab brooch, an opal bracelet, a ruby and pearl necklace, earrings in the Egyptian style and a parasol. All in all there were more than two hundred items, which fill several pages in Cartier's sales ledgers.[3] Louis-François' most ardent wish was to be fulfilled in 1859 when the empress herself, possibly at the instigation of the princess, ordered a silver tea-service.

The rue Neuve-des-Petits-Champs had definitely become too small for the purveyor to the imperial household. His eye was caught by the business of the jeweler Gillion at 9 boulevard des Italiens, for which offers were being invited. Louis-François took over the lease in 1859 and paid Fr40,000 for the existing stock.

Over the years, the area around the Palais-Royal had lost some of its splendour, but this was more than made up for by the bustle of the boulevard des Italiens, which took its name from the nearby Théâtre des Italiens: barouches, landaus and omnibuses jostled their way along the shady tree-lined street, crinolines billowed over the pavements, flower girls offered their wares to passers-by and the crowded coffee-shops of Tortoni, Du Grand Balcon and the Café Anglais attracted regular customers and tourists alike. At an earlier period, No. 9 had housed the confectioner's 'Au Fidèle Berger' and it was later the site of the fashion-house 'Aux Bayadères', before the above-mentioned Gillion took over the premises in 1847, to be followed by Cartier twelve years later. We do not know how Cartier designed the interior of the shop, but in 1873 the marble interior was renovated; the front of the building was faced with marble in 1891 and at the same time electric lighting was installed; a telephone followed in 1898.

At the new address, the stream of eminent customers continued unabated. They included Prince Bibesco, Prince Saltikov and Prince Belgiojoso, a member of the family of Princess Cristina Belgiojoso, who was politically active in support of her Italian homeland.[4] Cartier's jewels remained of modest size – small emeralds, amethysts, pearls and garnets set in silver and gold. The firm also offered everything from simple silver objects, ivories and bronzes, to the varied bric-a-brac of an antique-dealer. The business was run on patriarchal principles, with Louis-François enthroned 'like Zeus in Olympus', while his son Alfred (1841–1925) looked after the gem-stones and a general factotum by the name of Prosper was employed both as a designer and to arrange the displays. Louis-François had the refined taste of a man who enjoys life: both father and son ordered their shirts from the exclusive firm of Charvet, their cellar contained the finest French wines, and the pastry-cook Boissier provided them with a regular supply of *marrons glacés* and similar delicacies. Louis-François also found time to play a musical instrument, which he did immediately on rising; and in later life, following his retirement, he became an expert in ancient and Oriental languages. The garden of his country-house at Roanne revealed him to be a modest disciple of Jean-Jacques Rousseau, whose shining example enticed him to the Swiss Alps in 1869. Ever since 1729, when the doctor-poet Albrecht von Haller had praised them in verse, the once-feared Alps had become the shrine for a picturesque and poetical communion with nature. Louis-François' brief account of his journey is full of the magic of an unspoilt tourism, as when he was rowed across Lake Brienz to the Giessbach Falls and came unexpectedly upon Frédéric Boucheron and Jean-Paul Robin from Paris, with whom he marvelled at the natural wonder of the Falls. In Fribourg he trembled beneath the waves of sound produced by the cathedral organ, and completed his journey by setting out on the back of a mule for the traditional ascent of Mont Blanc.

The previous year he had travelled to Germany, a visit which may have taken him to the gemstone dealers in Idar-Oberstein. As for the important trip to England in 1871, he entrusted that to his son Alfred. Following the French defeat at Sedan in 1870 and the abdication of Napoleon III, the disruptive policies of the Commune had undermined all hopes of a trade revival and economic recovery. The couturier Charles Worth, who was important for Cartier's future survival, temporarily closed down, while Alfred sought refuge in England, as the empress herself had done. The exodus to England, which lasted until 1873 and brought Cartier's their first letters patent as purveyor to the court of St James, had, however, a much more concrete basis. The celebrated Italian courtesan Giulia

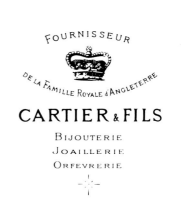

FOURNISSEUR
DE LA FAMILLE ROYALE d'ANGLETERRE

CARTIER & FILS

BIJOUTERIE
JOAILLERIE
ORFEVRERIE

Beneni, better known as La Barucci, had died of tuberculosis in Paris in 1870/71, like the *dame aux camélias*. During the Second Empire *cocottes* had enjoyed all the material advantages of a socially ambiguous reputation. The example set by the emperor or the Duc de Morny raised this Parisian *demi-monde* into spheres where, on the arm of some wealthy admirer, these women exercised an equal influence on fashion and on politics. La Barucci's jewel case was famous for its separate compartments of coloured stones and diamonds.[5] Alfred Cartier was assigned the sale of these jewels, including a ten-row pearl necklace. In London he raised the huge sum of Fr800,000 for La Barucci's heirs, who were of simple Italian peasant stock, and he himself kept 5 per cent of the proceeds.

A further episode dating from this period in London was his meeting with Léonide Leblanc (1842–94), a latter-day Ninon de Lenclos, who had been a great success both as a courtesan and as an actress at the Paris Odéon. In 1870/71 she appeared in various English theatres giving benefit performances for the French prisoners-of-war, and momentary financial worries brought her into contact with Alfred Cartier. It was a debt of gratitude which, upon her return to France, she was never to forget, and as the mistress of Henri d'Orléans, the Duc d'Aumale, she became one of Cartier's leading patrons, comparable to the later Mrs Keppel, who came from a different social background, and Lady de Grey.[6]

Circumstances were difficult in 1874, when Alfred Cartier took over his father's business in Paris. Whereas in 1866, for example, when Napoleon III had been at the height of his power, the year's profits had amounted to Fr48,244, it was only by dint of considerable effort that, following the economic decline which had set in with the Commune, Alfred was able to maintain profits at Fr39,200, the figure recorded for 1875, when the Third Republic was proclaimed. On the other hand, liquid capital at that time amounted to only Fr186,630, a sum which increased by 1890 to Fr500,000.

Cartier's continued to sell all manner of things: fans, bronze busts of Louis XV, Wedgwood medallions, ivory statuettes, silverware, Sèvres porcelain and, of course, jewelry and watches. The firm's clientele was made up of the well-to-do families of France, including the Prince de Wagram, the Comtesse de Montesquiou and even the Comte de Paris, who bought six silvergilt frames adorned with the fleur-de-lys. But the sales ledgers were becoming increasingly filled with the names of well-off members of the middle classes, including bankers and industrialists, all of whom had acquired their wealth in often risky speculations during the Second Empire. Their patronage of Cartier and the ostentation with which they flaunted their jewelry were intended to sanction their social respectability. One new customer which Cartier's acquired at this time and which they were able to keep for many years to come was the city of Bordeaux; from 1878 onwards hundreds of bronze medallions were ordered which bore the city's coat-of-arms and which were handed out on numerous occasions, including the university's commemorative celebrations.

Following the economic upheaval of the 1870s, which witnessed the growth of trade unions under a socialist government and which were characterized by constant power struggles between royalists and republicans, and clerical and anticlerical factions, there was a brief period of economic prosperity from 1880 until 1882. Banks were liberal in offering credit, new companies were founded and the French railway network grew; but this was soon followed by a collapse of the market, spectacular bankruptcies and renewed economic uncertainty. Forces hostile to the parliamentary republic banded into the phalanx of General Georges Boulanger, who used the Wilson scandal of 1887 for his own political ends. Alfred Cartier enjoyed the patronage not only of this popular general but also of the latter's life-companion, the Vicomtesse de Bonnemain, who festooned herself with Cartier silver and Cartier jewelry. The diamond aigrette which she received in 1887 must be one of the earliest recognizable Cartier jewels in a contemporary photograph. Daniel Wilson's fraudulent dealings in counterfeit decorations led to the fall of the cabinet. It was an affair whose progress may be charted in Cartier's records, for whereas the profits for 1882/83 still amounted to Fr93,365, they fell in 1886 to Fr63,904 and did not return to their former high levels until 1888/89, when profits of Fr93,725 were recorded (total sales in 1888 amounted to Fr399,529). In 1890/91 the figure of Fr100,000 was passed for the first time, and in 1899/1900, following the move to the rue de la Paix, the million-franc barrier was crossed (Fr1,776,785).

The sales ledgers for 1886/87 contain insignificant entries, as well as numerous purchases from private individuals who found themselves in financial difficulties: Prince Friedrich von Sachsen-Coburg bought miniatures, whereas a certain Mr Brunswick sold diamonds weighing 95$\frac{7}{8}$ carats.[7] From 1890 onwards Cartier's enjoyed the patronage of the family of the former Brazilian Emperor Dom Pedro II, who had abdicated in 1889 and now lived in exile in Europe. Although the ex-emperor died in 1891, his grandson Prince Pedro continued to visit Cartier's shop in the boulevard des Italiens.

The stock of a business like Cartier's brought together the products of three different professional groups which, ever since the Middle Ages, had jointly formed one of the most distinguished of guilds: the goldsmith who made silver and gold vessels, the *bijoutier-orfèvre* who manufactured gold and enamel jewelry and snuff boxes, and the *joaillier* who restricted himself to working in gemstones. It is difficult to gain a clear overall picture of these individual specializations since, following a long-established tradition, the individual firms employed workshops which were scattered across Paris, and which in their turn handed on work to subsidiary workshops. Jules Fossin the Younger, who worked for Cartier's in the rue de Richelieu, was himself in charge of three other workshops, with the result that a single commissioned item was often produced in collaboration with several workshops.[8] What is additionally confusing is the fact that firms which to an outsider appeared as rivals supplied each other with the items produced in their respective workshops. Not only did the workshop of Alexis Falize produce items for Boucheron and for Cartier's, but Boucheron himself supplied Cartier's in 1858 and 1863, as did Gideon T. F. Reed, who was in charge of the Paris branch of Tiffany's.

Colour plates 1 – 15

1. Hydrangea, the umbel in pink opaline glass, leaves in aventurine quartz, stalk in oxydized metal. Agate tub with gold and diamond mounts, on ivory ground, with wooden base. A similar hydrangea is dated 1926

2. Desk clock, the arched mount in purple sunray enamel over silver-gilt. Applied gold laurel wreath. 1904

The Tsar Nicholas II egg, in purple and white *guilloché* enamel over gold, with applied cipher for Nicholas II, and pearl and diamond crown. On fluorite cushion. Tapered enamel base. 11.60 cm. 1906 (See p. 92). The Metropolitan Museum of Art, New York

3. *Left:* Desk clock, the rectangular ivory panel with enamelled column and applied vase. Laurel-leaf and floral swag gold motif. 18 cm. 1904. Sold to J. P. Morgan

Right: Desk clock-cum-barometer, the cylinder with two dials in blue *guilloché* enamel over silver-gilt. On fluted column with berried laurel-leaf wreath motifs and two enamelled plaques. Acanthus-leaf feet. 17.5 cm. 1906

4. Vanity case, in pink *guilloché* enamel over gold. White enamel border. Rose-cut diamond motif. Inserted pencil and thumb-piece with cabochon moonstones. On chain. Cartier's New York

Pendant watch, in pink *guilloché* enamel over gold. Green and white enamel festoon border. Rose-cut diamond centre. On tubular enamel and pearl platinum chain

Propelling pencil, in pink *guilloché* enamel over gold. Green and white pellet border. Rose-cut diamonds. 1906. Sold to Baron Henri de Rothschild

Repeater desk clock, in pink sunray enamel over gold and silver, with applied rose-cut diamond motto 'Time Passes and Thoughts Remain'. Cabochon sapphire push-piece and initial 'H' on top. On agate base. 1909. Sold to Mrs Marshall Field, Chicago

5. Lorgnette, in blue and white *guilloché* enamel over gold. Rose-cut diamond floral motif. 1906

Belt-buckle, in waved lilac enamel over silver-gilt. Rose-cut diamond and blue enamel paterae. 1906

Desk set, comprising tray in grey sunray enamel over silver-gilt; two circular inkwells in mauve *guilloché* enamel, with green wreath borders and cabochon sapphire finials; rectangular clock with rose-cut diamond cipher; and a pen on its rest. 1908

6. Desk clock, in blue *guilloché* enamel over silver, with green enamel wreath borders. The face with green and white pellet rim over gold. Rose-cut diamond rosace motifs and hands. Agate and cabochon sapphire finger-ring. On agate base with rose-cut diamond cipher. 1909

Perpetual calendar, in greyish-green *guilloché* enamel over gold, with green enamel wreath border. The mechanism manually adjustable, by means of a moonstone knob, to cover the years 1908–18, showing day of the week, date, and month. 1907

Photograph frame, the slanting mount in purple, white and green enamel over silver-gilt. Rose-cut diamond corners (transformed from a desk calendar). Portrait of Countess de Zoubov. 1907

7. *Above, left to right:* Lady's bracelet watch, the gold and platinum case with diamond surround. Rose-cut diamond winder. On two-colour pearl bracelet with *deployant* buckle.

Lady's bracelet watch, the gold and platinum case in diamond surround. Semicircular diamond shoulder motifs. Rose-cut diamond winder. On onyx and pearl bracelet with *deployant* buckle. The watch made in Paris, the bracelet in New York. 1912. Sold to Princess Orlov

'Turtle' bracelet watch, the lobed case in *calibré*-cut onyx and diamonds. Onyx and diamond winder. On onyx bead and diamond rondelle bracelet with diamond clasp. 1927

Lady's bracelet watch, the gold and platinum case with border of cabochon sapphire, cabochon emerald, diamond and red enamel. *Calibré*-cut rubies and 2 engraved emerald leaves of 6.17 cts. On silk cord. 1925

Below: Lighter, striated in blue enamel on gold. Central carved jade plaque with coral and diamonds. Cartier's New York

8. Diamond necklace, of collet design with tied ribbon centre, and flexible navette and pear-shaped diamond tassels. 1911

9. Designs in the garland style (*top to bottom*): ear-of-wheat tiara, 1911; 3 diamond dog collars; laurel leaf tiara, *c.*1909; and stomacher, *c.*1909

10. *Left to right:* Pendant, the articulated diamond hexagonal mount with onyx and cabochon sapphire flower above *calibré*-cut sapphire border. Cabochon sapphire and diamond clip surmount. Cartier's New York

Star sapphire pendant necklace, the egg-shaped star sapphire of 311.33 cts below a cabochon sapphire of 35.13 cts. On diamond link chain. 1911. Sold to Grand Duchess Cyril (see p. 121)

Pendant, the onyx mount with diamond border and diamond tassels. Set with 5 cabochon sapphires. 1920. Cartier's New York

11. *Top:* Pendant, with twin birds at a fountain, in moonstone, *calibré*-cut sapphires and onyx. 1920. Cartier's London

Centre: Brooch, the frosted rock crystal panel with mother-of-pearl, diamonds and pearls. Central cabochon sapphire of 57.63 cts

Below left: 'Orange Tree' hat pin, in engraved rock crystal, onyx and diamonds. 1926. Sold to Jean-Philippe Worth

Below right: Belt-buckle, in engraved rock crystal, black enamel and diamonds. Gold and platinum mount. 1927

12. *Above:* The blue heart-shaped diamond of 30.82 cts, mounted as a ring. Sold in a diamond pendant in 1910 (see p. 288)

Below: The Hope diamond of 45.52 cts (see p. 283)

13. The Sarcophagus vanity case, the gold mount with curved ivory lid carved with a maiden amid flowers. Emerald, onyx, and diamond border with lotus column capitals. The sides with blue and green cloisonné enamel lotus flowers, alternating with granulated gold buds. The ends (*top*) with diamond and onyx sphinxes wearing the royal headdress (*nemes*), their faces carved in emerald (a reference to the green face of Osiris), the gold bottom (*centre left*) with female offering bearer with ibis carrying basket and lotus flowers (after an Old Kingdom stone relief in the Mastaba tomb). The interior with compartments. 1925. Sold to Mrs George Blumenthal (see p. 153)

14. Scarab necklace, the oval heart-scarab in glazed steatite within diamond and onyx lotus surround, suspended from a pearl ribbon band. Commissioned in 1932. The scarab formerly in the collection of the French Egyptologist Gaston Maspero (1846–1916)

Scarab brooch, the winged heart-scarab in engraved smoked quartz with cabochon emerald eyes, the outstretched wings in antique blue faïence with cabochon emeralds and striated with diamonds. 1924. Cartier's London

15. *Left:* 'Egyptian' cigarette case, the gold mount with lapis lazuli plaques framed by coral, diamond and enamel. Each side applied with a turquoise glazed faïence figure of Goddess Bastet seated on a papyrus column (late period, 4–3 BC). With mother-of-pearl background. The end pieces in black enamel. Commissioned in 1929 (see p. 153)

Centre and right: 'Egyptian' vanity case, the gold mount with mother-of-pearl plaques etched with hieroglyphs (name and titles of Pharaoh Tutmosis III) and framed by coral papyrus columns with cavetto cornice. The front mounted with an antique blue glaze faïence double-flute player (late period, 26th Dynasty, 630–525 BC) with lapis lazuli background and coral and onyx lotus. Onyx and diamond base. The case suspended from onyx finger-ring. Leather thongs with lotus attachments. The interior with compartments. 1924 (see p. 153)

1

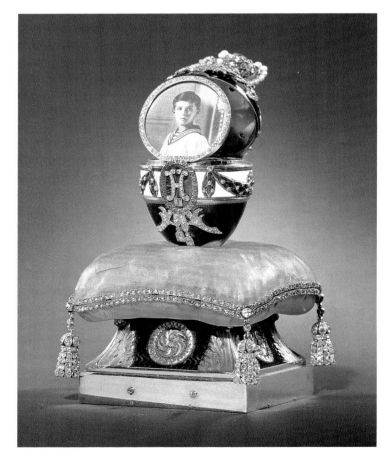

2

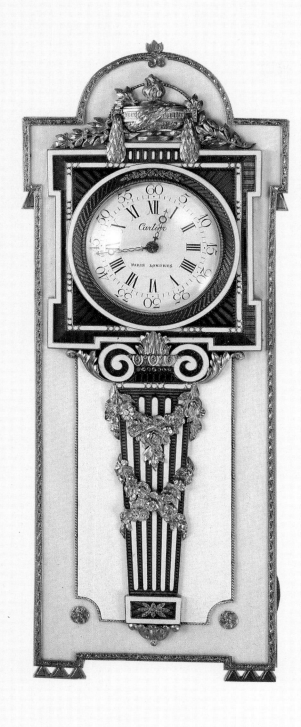

3

4

6

7

8

9

10

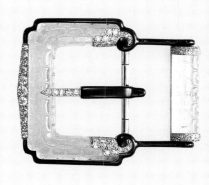

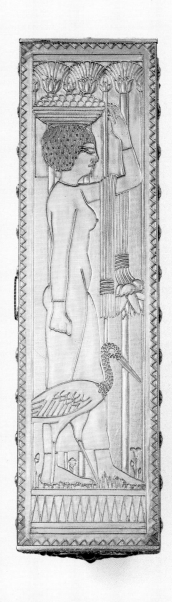
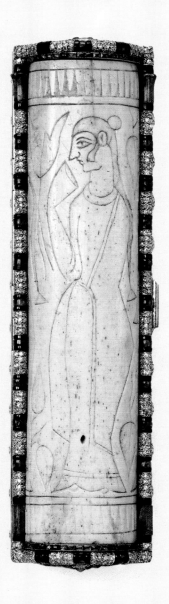

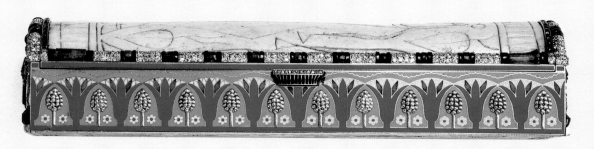

13

14

15

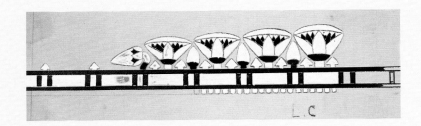

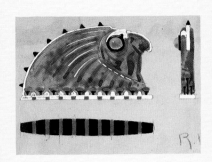

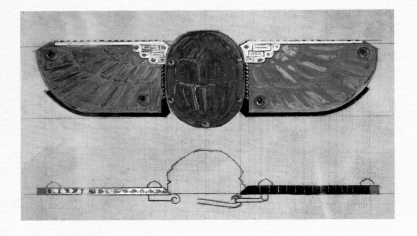

As a rule, the manufacturer's or master's stamp entered in the register of the state-controlled 'Garantie' was the only indication of who had produced a particular jewel. Cartier's had their first stamp in 1846: it showed an ace of hearts in the shape of a lozenge. The pieces of jewelry which the firm made in the nineteenth century are nowadays rarely identifiable, although they ought to show either Cartier's own stamp or that of the workshop from which they had been commissioned. On the whole, French jewels were only rarely signed in the nineteenth century. This practice was generally restricted to particularly impressive pieces of a three-dimensional character, such as those exhibited at world fairs. For purely technical reasons, the gold and silver alloy used in jewelry was based on 14-carat gold, which was in fact illegal. Because of this jewelers preferred neither to stamp nor to sign the orders which often passed straight from the workshop into the hands of the buyer, since in that way they were able to avoid state controls.

Cartier's had already begun to sign items of silver during the final years in the boulevard des Italiens, whereas jewelry was not signed until after the move to the rue de la Paix; specially trained engravers traced the signature by hand, without the aid of machinery, using italic script.

A further difficulty which besets attempts to recognize those items produced during the nineteenth century in their own workshop and elsewhere is that, unlike Boucheron or Chaumet, almost no drawings unequivocally identifiable as Cartier's have survived. At the same time we know that the then much-respected Eugène Julienne (1808–75), who had begun his career as a draughtsman in the Sèvres porcelain factory, and who later gave drawing lessons to Princess Mathilde, instructed Cartier, as well as various other jewelers, in ornamental drawing.[9] Another draughtsman who was well known at that time was Félix Duval, who published his lithographic jewelry designs in Paris around 1861, basing them on cubes, discs, cylinders and spheres. He, too, worked for Cartier as a graphic artist.

Although we know scarcely any of Cartier's original jewelry drawings from the second half of the nineteenth century, we have access to later copies which date from around 1900 and which may be in Alfred Cartier's hand.[10] They are to be found in Cartier's stock books, and provide information about the numerous forms of jewelry then being made.

The earliest articles of jewelry produced by the firm can be dated to the period between 1850 and 1855, when the business operated from the rue Neuve-des-Petits-Champs. The pieces in question are agate and obsidian cameos, together with articles of jasper, pearl, malachite and onyx. The workshop of Pierre Caillot in the rue de la Grande-Truanderie supplied similar items, as did Adolphe Picard, Louis-François Cartier's former master. The first workshop of general importance in Paris to act as supplier for Cartier's was that of the above-mentioned Jules Fossin the Younger in the rue de Richelieu, who continued the tradition started by the great Nitot. Especially famous were his naturalistic flower brooches, which prepared the way for those of the more important figure of Oscar

16. 'Egyptian' designs: *top*: headband with onyx lotus flowers, 1923; *left above*: antique faïence hawk's head brooch, 1925; *left below*: powder compact with Horus, 1927; *centre*: handbag with maidens amid papyrus, Cartier's London; *centre below*: belt-hook with winged heart-scarab, 1926; *right above*: brooch with Goddess Maât, 1927; *right below*: brooch with Goddess Sekhmet

Massin in the second half of the century. In 1853, for example, Fossin supplied Cartier with a 'Byzantine' bracelet.

Equally important as suppliers were the two firms of Daux and Delamare, both of which were located in the Palais-Royal, together with Guillaume Falize (1820–1906), brother of the even more famous Alexis Falize, Froment-Meurice (1802–55) and Jules Chaise, whose pupils were later to include Frédéric Boucheron. Another supplier, Alexandre Gueyton, has gone down in history as the inventor of a galvanoplastic process for refining jewelry which differed from that of Charles Christofle.[11] Christofle devoted himself from 1849 to an exclusive study of electrochemistry, although in later years his firm supplied Cartier's with silver tableware. In the nineteenth century this side of the Cartier business was almost as important quantitatively as the section devoted to jewelry. It was supplied principally by the Paris workshop of Queille; Wolfers in Brussels and, at a later date, Robert Linzeler of the rue d'Argenson were temporary suppliers.

The types of jewelry made by Cartier's in the 1860s which provide the most interesting clues to contemporary styles and fashions were bracelets, necklaces, earrings and brooches. The first three types were mainly designed in a very linear classical form, which testified to the influence of an important cultural event: the exhibition of the Campana Collection at the Louvre from 1861 onward. Napoleon III had bought up the collection, numbering over one thousand items and formerly owned by the Italian Marchese di Campana, who had run foul of the law. With its articles of Greek, Roman and Etruscan jewelry, its classical pottery, bronzes and glass, it offered a complete cross-section of the arts and crafts of the Mediterranean cultures in antiquity. The impression which the exhibition made upon Paris jewelers, and especially on Fontenay and Christofle, was immediate, whereas the Italian jeweler Fortunato Pio Castellani and his two sons (Alessandro was in Paris at the time of the Campana exhibition) had already been exposed for some time to the influence of classical goldsmithry.[12] Inspired by the Campana jewels, Eugène Fontenay (1823–87) created necklaces using amphora and cereal motifs. The items which he had begun to supply to Louis-François Cartier as early as 1850 show that even at that date his work embraced a style which was indebted to classical antiquity for its decorative meanders and palmettes, such as are to be seen in the paintings of Ingres or the German artist Anselm Feuerbach.

This classical style did not achieve its fullest expression in Cartier's work until the 1870s. Whereas it exercised a dominant influence on bracelets, necklaces and earrings, châtelaines remained in the eighteenth-century style; brooches, on the other hand, were unlimited in their choice of motifs. In necklaces and bracelets the neo-Graeco-Roman style replaced the naturalistic snakes, wood and fruit motifs in bright enamel colours of the 1850s and 1860s. Popular at a later date (around 1880) were golden chain bracelets (*gourmettes*) studded with diamond roses and turquoises. Three bracelets above all stand out from those which Cartier's produced during this later period – a silver bracelet made in 1887 with a representation of 'Dance' based on the sculpture by Jean-Baptiste Carpeaux,[13] a 'Celtic' bracelet made in 1893 with a horse medallion and mistletoe motifs,

and a steel bracelet dating from 1895 with Gothic arabesques in gold.

In the case of earrings, however, the classical influence led to pendant motifs of long matt gold drops,[14] or else to girandoles of lapis lazuli or coral drops.[15] These were followed after 1875/76 by round, concentric forms: simple pearls fastened by screws, diamond solitaires in silver mountings (*dormeuses*) or diamond-surrounded pearls. The mineral tiger's-eye was launched in Paris around 1882, and Cartier's made a pair of earrings with the new stone in 1883.

The greatest variety of style between the years 1850 and 1880 was to be found in brooches, which, together with bracelets, proved to be the most popular of all the various types of jewelry. From the time of Cartier's move to the rue Neuves-des-Petits-Champs in 1853 we find records of brooches consisting initially simply of gold or else decorated with mosaic work, cameos or Limoges enamel. From around 1870 the dominant motifs, not only in Cartier's work but throughout the whole of Paris, were animals and flowers. The fashion for animals led to depictions of horses' heads, horseshoes and stirrups in yellow gold and enamel, which are evidence of the popularity of horse-racing during the Second Empire (the racecourse at Longchamp was inaugurated in 1857) and which point to England as the country of origin. It was the so-called *genre anglais* which very much set the tone at that time in the manufacture of jewelry in France.[16]

A second type of animal, again influenced by Victorian England, included small reptiles, crabs, bees and dragonflies and led directly to the style of art nouveau.[17] Cartier's rival, Oscar Massin, had popularized these motifs as early as about 1863. Cartier himself introduced dragonfly, salamander and turtle brooches after 1870. Snake heads became popular as hatpins around 1890, carrying baroque pearls in their gaping jaws. The menagerie was completed by flies and butterflies made of translucent *plique-à-jour* enamel. Two butterfly brooches, for example, were made in 1880 for Princess Mathilde.

The third variant on the animal motif moved into the realm of pure fantasy and produced the macabre chimaeras and griffins which achieved popularity in Paris above all through the work of Alphonse Fouquet (1828–1911), who was located from 1879 in the avenue de l'Opéra and who at that date was undoubtedly the most interesting of Cartier's suppliers. He had exhibited his dragons, sphinxes and chimaera brooches at the World Fair in 1878. Similar designs first began to appear in Cartier's output in 1883, though produced by other workshops. The most original item which Fouquet supplied to Cartier's was a brooch with an interlaced anchor, dolphin and sword (1880). The dolphin in particular made frequent appearances in Fouquet's work.[18]

Bird brooches occupied a special position among the various animals. The fashion for birds, especially humming-birds, had been started by Cartier's rival, Rouvenat. Cartier's preference was for birds of paradise, storks, cockerels and owls. With the lovebird motif, two birds sitting together on a branch, the firm invented an image which retained its appeal until well into the twentieth century. To these may be added five bird brooches, forming a flight of swallows

51

made of diamond roses, which were supplied by René Lalique in 1887. They may well be identical with the model which Henri Vever describes as having been sold to Boucheron: 'In 1887 Lalique had the idea of a large set of jewelry *en joaillerie*, representing an entire flight of swallows; he hoped to give them a sense of perspective by means of the decreasing size of the birds.'[19]

Dove brooches, a further variant, appeared in 1893 to celebrate the Franco-Russian alliance of that year.

Flowers were as popular as animals. Whereas animal motifs ran the risk of becoming anecdotally sentimental (one thinks for example of the motif of 'Three Cats as Musicians'), flowers, which lent themselves to naturalistic representation in diamonds, could be turned into *haute joaillerie* whose fame spread far beyond the confines of France. The most famous floral brooches in the shape of three-dimensionally modelled wild roses were produced by the above-mentioned Oscar Massin. His forms are characterized by a greater sense of virtuosity than those of his rivals, and his products show a reworking of English influences, together with those of eighteenth-century France. Among the blossoms in Cartier's lavish displays were wild roses, narcissi, Parma violets, poppies and marguerites. After 1895 these floral motifs were to be eagerly taken up by art nouveau in miniature and using different techniques.

7. Crowds gather at 13 rue de la Paix to see King Alfonso XIII

Rue de la Paix

THE HISTORY OF CARTIER'S in the boulevard des Italiens shows clearly the irresistible rise of a family business in which father and son complemented each other in ideal fashion. Contacts with the court and with a bourgeoisie which owed its wealth to speculative dealings on the stock market ensured that even during the crisis-ridden 1880s the firm enjoyed ever-increasing support and patronage. An American customer was noted as early as 1854, but it was really only after the return from London in 1873 that Cartier's clientele assumed an international profile. It would be incorrect therefore to claim that only following the move to the rue de la Paix did Cartier's begin to attract the big spenders of the *belle époque*, such as J. P. Morgan, or those who formed the fun-loving entourage of the Prince of Wales. A letter which Alfred Cartier wrote from the boulevard des Italiens to Lady de Grey in 1898, when plans were temporarily being formulated for the marriage of Princess Victoria and Prince George of Greece, contains a request that the English lady might use her influence to recommend the firm of Cartier for the wedding presents.[1]

Nevertheless, there were differences in size and style between the items on display in the boulevard des Italiens and the later ones: the jewelry chosen by customers in the older shop was thoroughly bourgeois in both format and appearance, and the articles produced by Cartier's at that time were essentially the same as those being made by their rivals. It was only as a result of the discovery of the great diamond deposits in South Africa in the late 1860s and diamond sales made by the De Beers Mining Company that the French jewelry industry took on new dimensions. A young international clientele made up of bankers, industrialists and speculators now competed with the long-established aristocracy. They came for the most part from North and South America, England and Germany, and ordered jewelry worthy of a Napoleon, which would indeed have placed the jewels of the Empress Eugénie herself in the shade. One of the main reasons for Cartier's move to the rue de la Paix was to satisfy the pretensions of these inordinately wealthy customers. Here at No. 7 were the premises of the world's most famous couturiers, Jean-Philippe and Gaston Worth, patronized by this international set who were prepared to pay the same prices for clothes as for works of art and who wished to complement their wardrobes with matching jewelry. Friendship and marriage brought the two firms of Worth and Cartier into the closest contact, so that their policies and spheres of influence now became inextricably linked: Cartier profited from Worth's clientele and this liaison turned the rue de la Paix into the leading shopping street of the age.

Then as now, the rue de la Paix formed an indivisible whole with the adjacent Place Vendôme, whose central column provides its crowning monument. The square and the street, however, had come into being under different historical circumstances. The all-powerful minister Louvois had persuaded Louis XIV to lay out a square which would impress foreign ambassadors on their way to Saint-Germain and Versailles. The king accordingly acquired the

8. Photograph of J. P. Morgan (1837–1913), the American banker, in a blue and green enamel and gold frame which he commissioned in 1907

Hôtel Vendôme in 1685 and commissioned the architect Hardouin-Mansart to design a square which would be closed on three sides. By the time the square was completed in 1699 Louvois had died and the plans had been altered: the Place Louis-le-Grand was rectangular in shape with cut-off corners, and at its centre stood Girardon's equestrian statue of the king. Like Bouchardon's statue in the later Place de la Concorde, it was a victim of the French Revolution and on Napoleon's orders was replaced in 1810 by the Austerlitz column, the material for which was provided by the bronze of 1,200 cannon captured from the Austrians and Russians; its summit was crowned by a statue of the emperor. At the same time Napoleon ordered the demolition of the Capuchin monastery on the north side of the square, as well as the church in whose crypt the mortal remains of Henri III's wife and Madame de Pompadour had rested. In this way a new street was created, known initially as the rue Napoléon and, from 1814, as the rue de la Paix.

Whereas the Place Vendôme remained the preferred seat of the city authorities, the rue de la Paix came to commercial life with remarkable speed: by 1823 it already numbered six or seven hotels, two or three *limonadiers*, a couturier and a bootmaker. But it was only when Baron Haussmann, the prefect of Napoleon III, created broad new arterial roads and redesigned the capital that the rue de la Paix became strategically important. In 1833 Balzac may have preferred the rue Royale, but by 1856 the rue de la Paix was described as 'large, cold, correct, brought into alignment, level, bordered by superb houses; together with the rue Royale ... the finest specimen of a street which any capital city might pride itself on owning'.[2]

All the trades which embodied the contemporary taste for luxury were to become established in the rue de la Paix in the course of the following decades, and, just as in the old guild pageants the goldsmiths marched at the head of the procession in token of their superior rank, so the jewelers were among the first to settle in the rue de la Paix.

Even while the firm was still in the boulevard des Italiens, Cartier's had maintained regular contacts with those that had already established themselves in the rue de la Paix during the nineteenth century. These included the firm of François Mellerio (1772–1843), whose family had emigrated from Lombardy in the sixteenth century and who transferred the family business to No. 22 rue de la Paix at some date around 1815, and later to No. 5. When he finally moved to No. 9, he found himself next door to Cartier's. Another of the famous jewelers in the rue de la Paix was Jean-Benoît Martial Bernard (1784–1846), who had established himself at No. 1 in 1826 and had become jeweler to the Royal Court and to the Duc d'Orléans. His son, Charles Martial Bernard (1824–96), was a founder member of the jewelers' design classes in which Louis-François Cartier also took part. The firm transferred to 12 rue des Pyramides in 1890.

No. 19 had been occupied since 1834 by the firm of Charles Marret, who also kept a subsidiary branch in New York from 1848 to 1857. In Paris the Marret brothers worked in association with the far more important figure of Gustave Baugrand (1826–70), and the shop, established in 1861, was long regarded as the very height of fashion. Following Baugrand's death the firm was taken over by Ernest Vever (1823–84) and subsequently by the latter's sons Paul (1851–1915) and Henri (1854–1942). Henri Vever was the author of one of the standard works on the history of jewelry, *La Bijouterie française au 19ème siècle*, published in 1906. Vever moved to 14 rue de la Paix in 1904 and there is evidence of Cartier's links with him from as early as 1853.

One of the most famous of European gold- and silversmiths of the day was the firm of Aucoc at 6 rue de la Paix. Louis Aucoc the Elder took over the business in 1854, adding to it a further range of *bijouterie* and jewelry. André Aucoc (1884–1911) produced silver and silvergilt in the style of the eighteenth century, as well as dealing in antique silver. In 1912 Cartier's bought from the firm a silver tureen, made in Augsburg in the eighteenth century.

From 1848 Eugène Jacta (1815–93) carried on his business at 17 rue de la Paix. Like Louis-François Cartier, he too enjoyed the patronage of Princess Mathilde and the empress, in addition to that of the tsarist court. His firm was taken over in 1868 by Eugène Bassot and in 1886 by Edgar Morgan. In 1867 Cartier, at that date still in the boulevard des Italiens, received silver lighters from Jacta and, later on, golden *bonbonnières*, bottles, and silvergilt and gold snuffboxes in the Louis XVI style.

Jules Debut, who had previously worked with Boucheron, joined forces with Léon Coulon at 12 rue de la Paix prior to setting up in business on his own at No. 1 in 1890. At the house of Worth, the famous No. 7, was to be found the jeweler Fontana, who like so many others had left the Palais-Royal for the rue de la Paix.[3] An additional branch of the same family of jewelers was established in 1896 in the rue Royale, where it provided the same sort of attraction as that offered by the premises of Georges Fouquet.

These jewelers, to name only the most important, turned the rue de la Paix into the most expensive street in the world. It was not only their wares that were costly but also the ground rents, which turned the shop premises into valuable objects of speculation that were almost impossible to come by after 1890. In 1893, for example, Boucheron attempted to find suitable rooms for his business in the rue de la Paix, but had to settle in the end for the Place Vendôme. Much the same thing happened to René Lalique at a later date: he found it impossible to move from the cours de la Reine to the rue de la Paix, and so he, too, transferred his business to the Place Vendôme.[4]

All the same, the rue de la Paix was anything but a mere bastion of jewelers in the nineteenth century. Whereas the neighbouring Place Vendôme served as headquarters for the Commune following the collapse of the Second Empire (a circumstance which led to the destruction of the victory column), the rue de la Paix was spared such ideological disputations. True to its calling, it offered for sale in the smallest available space all that the *grande dame* of Paris or the most widely travelled globe-trotter might need by way of jewelry or finery. Visitors were accommodated at the Hôtel Mirabeau (No. 8), or the more pretentious Hôtel de Hollande (No. 20), and, at a somewhat later date, the Hôtel des Iles Britanniques (No. 22) and the

Hôtel Westminster, the last-named mentioned in Cartier's archives from 1860. At No. 17 was to be found Siraudin's coffee-shop, lit by modern gaslight, where in the late afternoon elegant barouches were to be seen drawing up and discharging their occupants. As from 1898, the focus of social attention shifted to the Place Vendôme, when César Ritz opened his hotel.

But what really turned the rue de la Paix into a latter-day Vanity Fair were the couturiers, shirtmakers, hat- and glovemakers and perfume manufacturers.[5] The empress herself bespoke a fashion founded upon personal taste, which was declared to be the style of the epoch and with which neither the court of St James nor those of Madrid or Rome were able to compete. She now found all the purveyors of fashion assembled together in the rue de la Paix, at their head the fashion house of Worth, her shoemaker Viault, her corsetière Mme Gringoire, and the perfume manufacturer Guerlain, who concocted his 'Bouquet de l'Impératrice' especially for her.

Close proximity to the international fashion houses had given Cartier a sense of creative incentive even while he was still in the boulevard des Italiens, with the result that jewelry became an integral part of the image of a person of fashion. The relationship between Cartier's and the various couture houses was that of professional colleagues, neighbours, suppliers and buyers. A good example of this was Alfred Cartier's dealings with the gentlemen's shirtmaker Charvet, who had initially been installed in the rue de Richelieu and later moved to the Place Vendôme, where he shared his first customers, including the Prince of Wales, with Cartier's. Around 1860 Charvet ordered buttons from Cartier's, which were used for shirts and as cuff-links and which included the more accurately described *boutons hongrois*. The Maison Doucet, at 21 rue de la Paix, which specialized in men's and women's fashions, also proved an influential neighbour.[6]

In 1898, when Alfred Cartier began to cast around for suitable new premises, the rue de la Paix was clearly the most desirable location. His shop in the boulevard des Italiens was no longer adequate. Additional pressure for a quick move came from the twenty-three-year-old Louis, who had become a partner in his father's firm that same year. In 1897 the Hôtel Westminster had been auctioned off to a joint-stock company for half-a-million francs. It occupied the site of Nos. 11 and 13, and Alfred Cartier expressed an interest in one of the arcades of No. 13, while the other half was rented by the lingerie business of Martial et Armand. At first, No. 11 was occupied by the handkerchief shop of Chapron and the porcelain business of Le Rosey.

The new Cartier premises were formally inaugurated in November 1899. The move happened to coincide with the introduction of a new kind of platinum jewelry in the then fashionable garland style, and the young Louis Cartier and his brother Pierre used this as a pretext for drawing the attention of the world's aristocracy to the firm's new premises. They sent charming, handwritten invitations to the Duchess of Sutherland, who was then staying at the Hôtel Bristol, to Countess Fels, Baron Hottinger and Baroness Edmond de Rothschild. The architect Gauthier was commissioned to redesign the interior of the shop, but no records have survived describing its appearance. We have, however, a good impression of the front of the building thanks to a photograph taken on the occasion of one of King Edward VII's frequent visits: the façade is already decorated with the first of the royal coats-of-arms which began arriving from the English court in 1904. The king is seen leaving the shop through the main entrance, which was then still at the left-hand side of the building. It was not until 1912 that Cartier's took over No. 11 and had the shopfront redesigned in a unified style, with four display windows flanking the main entrance and forming that magnificent frontage of dark green marble which continues to excite the world's admiration even today. Like Cartier's own creations in the eighteenth-century style this late-classical façade breathes the spirit of France's great château architecture.

At the time of the shop's expansion in 1912 Louis Cartier was in Russia. Even at a distance, however, he continued to take an interest in the smallest details and offered his father Alfred affectionate advice and precise instructions which were passed on to the interior designer Boulanger and to Houdot, who supplied the marble. What emerged was a room-plan which remained unaltered until 1927.

The main room was the *grande galerie* with its coffered ceiling, allegorical lunette painting, wall-decorations of arrows, lances and masks, and a new type of indirect lighting which was also to be found at the Hôtel Ritz. The customer was received in the entrance hall and then escorted, according to his particular wishes, to the Jewel Salon, or the White, Green or English Salon, all of which glittered in the light of Baguès' chandeliers. A separate room for pearls was set aside to the left of the entrance, since 60 per cent of the firm's turnover continued to come from the sale of pearls right up to the end of the 1920s. In addition, the ritual of trying on the pearls frequently involved the presence of Mme Visage, who was in charge of stringing the pearls, and the ceremony required its own setting. With the exception of the *grande galerie*, the oak walls were all carved with the vase and garland motifs which were a hallmark of Cartier's jewelry at that time.[7] Beyond the pearl room was the office of René Prieur, who was employed as Louis Cartier's secretary from 1901; he became one of the firm's leading salesmen in 1911 and spent the years of the First World War in New York. It was in this office that he negotiated in 1921 with Prince Stirbey the sale of the great sapphire necklace, on behalf of King Ferdinand of Romania (see p. 236).

Prieur was one of Cartier's star salesmen who had originally worked for Worth; another was Alfred Buisson. They refined and polished their style in their daily dealings with crowned heads of state and the international nouveaux riches, and themselves appeared in the role of *grands seigneurs*. Countless anecdotes circulated about Buisson who arrived at Cartier's every morning in his chauffeur-driven Delaunay-Belleville, the door of which was opened for him by a sales assistant wearing white gloves.

Beyond Prieur's office lay that of Louis Cartier, in whose hands all the threads of the firm were gathered. Here, in private conversation, he received the Grand Duchess Vladimir, the Aga Khan and the Queen of Spain. Since 1902, his father Alfred Cartier had had his own

9. Gladys, Lady de Grey (later Marchioness of Ripon), wearing her diamond dog collar. 1901. Photo dated 1915

10. Cartier's London, the New Bond Street premises (advertisement in *Country Life*'s 'Book of London', 1951)

office on the other side of the street at No. 4, and it was there that Alfred transacted the purchase of diamonds and coloured stones; until the time of the First World War the firm's draughtsmen were also housed there.

The earliest plans to expand the Paris business were the result of a suggestion made by the Prince of Wales: a branch in London had been a strong possibility ever since the English high nobility had begun crowding into the rooms in the rue de la Paix and, back in London, been forced to wait impatiently for their orders to be delivered from Paris. Cartier's in Paris were regularly visited by Lillie Langtry (1853–1929), the actress and later baroness, whom Millais had painted with a lily (an illusion to her name rather than her lifestyle); by Louise, Duchess of Manchester (popularly known as the 'double duchess' following her second marriage to the Duke of Devonshire), who in later years frequented the casinos of Monte Carlo under the close watch of distrustful private detectives; and above all there was Gladys, Lady de Grey, whom Sir Osbert Sitwell described, full of admiration, as 'the most striking individual to look at in any room she enters'.

Queen Victoria died on 22 January 1901. Following the obligatory period of mourning at court, England's leading families began their preparations for the ensuing coronation of Edward VII in 1902 and the attendant celebrations. Jewelry was feverishly reworked and Cartier's workshops were scarcely able to meet the demand for tiaras, necklaces and stomachers. Pierre Cartier and Alfred Buisson used the Hotel Cecil as their base of operations in London; they visited Buckingham Palace, where they received orders from Queen Alexandra, and they looked around the West End for a likely site for their new premises. They were helped in their search by the Hon. Mrs Alice Keppel, wife of the younger brother of the Duke of Albermarle, and the king's lifelong friend. She first drew their attention to Old Bond Street, but both Pierre Cartier and Gaston Worth finally chose 4 New Burlington Street, where a shop was opened in 1902. From 1906 the firm was managed by Jacques Cartier, the youngest scion of the family, and Arthur Fraser, who was the sales director. They moved to 175 New Bond Street in 1909, five years after having been appointed official purveyor to the court of King Edward VII.

Cartier's new jewelry from Paris created something of a sensation in England, which at that time was still relatively conservative. Admittedly, the Countess of Warwick wrote in a letter 'of all these silly women, including Gladys de Grey, all thinking life is bounded on one side by Worth and Cartier and on the other by King Edward VII's court and bridge';[8] but, for all her strictures, the astute countess, who invested her money in agricultural schools and who met with the socialist Jean Jaurès in Paris, was not averse to wearing a magnificent emerald tiara bought, naturally, from Cartier's.

The business in England had scarcely been established when America began to beckon. Reconnaissance trips were undertaken in 1903 and 1907, and not even the sixty-seven-year-old Alfred Cartier hesitated to cross the Atlantic. In financial terms, New York was the only possible choice for a branch which would be the culmination of

Cartier's empire. In 1901 the United States Steel Company had been sold to J. P. Morgan for a billion dollars and in the wake of this economic boom, more than one thousand Americans, of whom three hundred lived in New York, acquired vast fortunes in excess of one million dollars each. An outward sign of this affluence was the society balls held by Mrs August Belmont, Mrs Cornelius Vanderbilt, Mrs Herman Oelrich and Mrs Ogden Mills, who together had inherited the social sceptre from the retiring Mrs William Astor and who strove to outdo each other in almost vulgar displays of magnificence. Diamonds and emeralds were brought into action in the campaigns waged by the most ambitious hostesses of the day and used as coefficients to determine their individual standing in a constantly shifting social hierarchy. Gemstones glittered not only in the mansions along Fifth Avenue and (from July to September) in fashionable Newport, but also in the thirty-five boxes of the Metropolitan Opera House, which had been inaugurated in 1883 and where the same ostentation was flaunted before the public, causing the elegant interior to be named 'the Diamond Horseshoe'.

It was on 1 November 1909 that Pierre Cartier opened the firm's American branch on the fourth floor of 712 Fifth Avenue. The antique dealer Alavoine had supplied the wood panelling which in its main aspects reproduced the decor in the rue de la Paix. The firm's neighbours were the jewelers Schumann at No. 716 and Coty's perfume shop at No. 714, which had been furnished by René Lalique. At No. 560 was Dreicer, the most feared of Cartier's rivals, who did not shrink from copying models from the rue de la Paix and putting them on sale faster than Cartier's American branch could import them.[9] Just as the London branch was patronized by Mrs Keppel and Lady de Grey, and the St Petersburg branch by the Grand Duchess Vladimir, so Pierre Cartier enjoyed the custom of Mrs Clarence Mackay and Mrs Rita Lydig who, with Mrs Stuyvesant Fish, were accounted among the social avant-garde and who provided him with introductions to the houses of Mrs Blumenthal, Gould, Widener and Stotesbury.

Initially the New York establishment had all its jewels sent over from the rue de la Paix, but the firm's own workshop, which employed forty goldsmiths, including eleven stone-setters, was soon in a position to produce jewelry on American soil.[10] The business of manufacturing this jewelry, which never attempted to deny its Parisian origins, was in the hands of the two masters Maîtrejean and Bouquet, the latter having been trained in Charpentier's Paris workshop.[11] The draughtsmen, recruited in Paris, were Georges Genaille, the young Maurice Duvallet and, from 1912, Emile Faure.[12] Paul Muffat and, at a somewhat later date, Jules Glaenzer were in charge of the sales staff, who often spent the winter months in the American branch and the summer in France. It was not uncommon for them to find the same customers in Paris as in Fifth Avenue. Each time the great ocean liners crossed the Atlantic in May, telegrams prepared Louis Cartier for the arrival of Mrs George Gould on the *Lusitania*, Mrs Clarence Mackay on the *Kronprinzessin Cäcilie*, and Mrs Rita Lydig and Mrs Vincent Astor on the *Mauretania*.

In 1917 Cartier moved to 653 Fifth Avenue, the house of Morton

11. Cartier's New York, the Fifth Avenue building (drawing: A. Genaille, brother of the designer Georges Genaille), 1917

Plant, a transfer which was sealed with the symbolic exchange of a two-row pearl necklace (see p. 131). The Rockefeller family architect, Welles Bosworth, who was also responsible for the Massachusetts Institute of Technology in Cambridge, Mass., supervised the transformation of the interior of the former patrician residence into an international business establishment, although a touch of the private mansion remained. The Wedgwood Room displayed its priceless art deco clocks from Paris, gemstone snuffboxes, plants and miniature hardstone animals. The most expensive jewels were to be found glittering in the Blue Room where in 1931, for example, fifteen sales assistants were employed, as against eight in London at that time. The displays in the Pearl Room, where the pearl expert Etcheberry officiated, surpassed even those of the rue de la Paix. The Silver Room was dominated by a resplendent porcelain *gloriette* (arbour) and in the former family chapel, which was kept intact, religious jewelry and chalices awaited their prospective buyers.

As Pierre once remarked to Louis Cartier, the addition of the New York branch turned the firm into a worldwide institution; but what remained of paramount importance to the customers was the close connection between fashion and jewelry, a link which for them symbolized the rue de la Paix. The photograph which had the greatest impact upon the public of New York in 1914 was one of the rue de la Paix garlanded with flowers on the occasion of a state visit by the King and Queen of England.

Whenever visiting heads of state came to Paris and were officially received at Cartier's, crowds would gather on the pavement outside, jostling to see what was going on and withdrawing to a respectful distance as the royal visitors left the building. The state visit of King Haakon VII and Queen Maud of Norway took place in 1907. The Paris city council's official gift to the queen, a daughter of Edward VII, was a turquoise and diamond necklace bought from Cartier's. In 1909, the year in which Guerlain named a perfume 'Rue de la Paix', the city was presented with the spectacle of a visit from King Manuel of Portugal, and in 1910 the King and Queen of Spain passed through Paris on their way to England. Following a banquet in the château of Rambouillet, the Spanish queen drove to see her godmother, the Empress Eugénie, at the Hôtel Continental, and then had Cartier's show her their latest creations. The following year it was King George of Greece, and the list of visitors could easily be extended right down to the 1930s. The street and what it stood for were by then so famous that in 1912 a play entitled *Rue de la Paix* was staged with costumes by Paquin after designs by Paul Iribe.[13]

12. Adoring fans of 'Le Prince Charmant', the Prince of Wales, future Edward VIII

3

The garland style

THROUGHOUT THE NINETEENTH CENTURY a series of historical styles had put their stamp upon the various arts, beginning with the neo-Gothic revival of around 1820 and passing through neo-Renaissance and neo-Baroque influences before culminating in a resurgence of the Louis XVI style in the 1890s. This latter style was to retain its appeal until shortly before the First World War, and around 1900 was one of the starting-points for the vigorous counteroffensive of art nouveau, a style which was directed against the sterile resuscitation of a taste associated with an aristocratic and monied élite. Art nouveau artists such as Grasset and Lalique took their inspiration directly from nature, whereas the painter, architect or interior designer who was committed to the Louis XVI style remained bound within the framework of an eighteenth-century theatrical setting. The court of Versailles was the inspiration which motivated his customers, whose unique desire was for pomp and splendour. They were generally entrepreneurs who had grown rich through industry or financial speculation and who, behind the imposing façade of their private Trianons or Bagatelles, lived in a world of theatrical pretence. Those who moved within this realm of sophisticated illusion, whether Mrs Cornelius Vanderbilt, Mrs Nancy Leeds or Sir Ernest Cassel, were unwitting adherents of a *fin-de-siècle* aesthetic whose origins may be traced back to Ruskin, Oscar Wilde and D'Annunzio. Thus the English court, the French aristocracy and the monied classes of America indulged in the ceremonial of a past century which they used as a pretext for masquerades, hunting parties and balls in New York, Paris, St Petersburg, London or Venice. The hostess received her guests like some lady of the manor, a modern Mme de Pompadour or Mme Dubarry; and the portrait which she had painted of herself by one of the much sought-after artists of the day – Antonio de la Gandara, Philip Alexis László or Giovanni Boldini – showed her striking attitudes reminiscent of Velasquez, Largillière and Reynolds.

The interiors were traditionally eighteenth-century in form; dress and thus jewelry, too, were adapted to match them, and it was precisely such a range of jewelry that Cartier's used from 1895 onward to captivate the discriminating taste of contemporary high society. What came into existence in this way were those delicate garland-style jewels which Cartier's, though not the first to reintroduce them, handled with greater virtuosity and elegance than, say, Hamelin, Falize or Vever. The latter often added writhing art nouveau plant-forms which turned the jewels into strange hybrid shapes lacking the playful ease of Cartier's confections.

The new Louis XVI style had been apparent in the work of French jewelers for some time, since the 1850s to be exact, when Empress Eugénie had had her jewelry reset by Bapst and Lemonnier in the style of Marie Antoinette. The form of the queen's legendary necklace was the model for this work, and with the appearance of crinolines at the Tuileries court there came a revival of the unsurpassed elegance of the eighteenth century, recorded in the work of Winterhalter, the official court portrait painter.

This borrowing of motifs from earlier centuries was made easier for the jeweler by the existence of pictorial records and pattern books. Ever since the time of the young Albrecht Dürer, woodcuts and the, at that time, recent innovation of copperplate engravings had ensured the spread of motifs from Italian, French and German designers and goldsmiths across the whole of Europe. In the nineteenth century jewelers continued to use Renaissance sources until around 1870:[1] the work of a leading jeweler such as Froment-Meurice (1802–55) simply cannot be understood without some knowledge of the influence of Renaissance artists like Etienne Delaune, Théodore de Bry or René Boyvin. In England so-called Holbeinesque pendants, based on designs by Hans Holbein the Younger, were being made as late as 1870. It must be added that the jeweler used whatever motifs he thought necessary, including interlaces, sinuous plant-forms and grotesques, which he freely mingled with later ornaments, generally borrowing them not directly from pattern books of the Renaissance but from popular compendia of the nineteenth century. These provided a summary of fifteenth- and sixteenth-century sources for professional groups such as goldsmiths, interior designers, cabinet-makers and so on.[2]

Eighteenth-century pattern books, which are of especial interest in our own context, began to circulate in the 1850s. They reproduced eighteenth-century printed texts and received particular encouragement from the patronage of the French imperial court. Unlike the Renaissance designs, the pattern books of the eighteenth century (Louis XV and Louis XVI) dealt with flowers, wreaths, garlands and vases. The most important works of this type which Louis Cartier owned and which were at the disposal of his draughtsmen were:[3]

PÈQUÈGNOT   *Ornements, vases et décorations d'après les maîtres.* 1872. A compendium of every aspect of interior art, including vases, columns, bouquets and friezes.

THÉODORE BERTREN   *Ouvrages de bijouterie & gravure; médaillons, trophées, vases et autres sujets nouveaux.* A reprint of fourteen fascicles of copperplate engravings dating from 1771, from which Cartier took largely motifs for frames, pendulettes and floral garlands.

JEAN-FRANÇOIS FORTY   An engraved text from the age of Louis XVI, reprinted in Paris in 1896 and containing, in eight fascicles, motifs for goldsmiths including candelabra, latticework, chalices, clocks, barometers, figurative motifs, acanthus leaves and garlands. This volume provided Cartier with the inspiration for *objets d'art* and jewelry, as well as plaques for dog collars.

POUGET FILS   *Traité des pierres précieuses.* 1762. A work which provided models for bow-knots, clasps and flowers.

L. VANDER CRUYSEN   *Nouveau Livre de desseins.* 1770. Another work reprinted in Paris which provided models for bouquets, girandole earrings, aigrettes, stomachers and bow-knots.

13. Queen Alexandra wearing her diamond *résille* (see pp. 62, 63). From a painting by François Flameng (b.1856). Buckingham Palace. By gracious permission of Her Majesty the Queen

14. Mrs Cornelius Vanderbilt wearing her diamond necklace and a 19th-century rose brooch previously owned by Princess Mathilde and acquired from Cartier's in 1904 (see p. 51)

15. Princess Marie Bonaparte wearing her olive leaf diamond and emerald tiara (see p. 63)

Maria & Babel   A reprint of a copperplate engraved text from the age of Louis XVI which includes châtelaines, pommels for walking-sticks, girandole earrings, stomachers, boxes, fans and bow-knots.

J. H. von Hefner-Halteneck   *Eisenwerke oder Ornamentik der Schmiedekunst des Mittelalters und der Renaissance.* 1885. This work also included eighteenth-century grilles. Grille-enclosed tendril-like forms, which were important in Cartier's jewelry around 1900, were inspired partly by European wrought-ironwork and partly by Islamic lattice motifs.[4]

There were a number of specialist works devoted to flowers, especially the rose and lily which in the decorative art of the Louis XVI style had taken on an almost leitmotif character. The following were among those used by Cartier:

Eugène Grasset (ed.)   *La Plante et ses applications ornementales.* 1896–1900.

J. Foord   *Decorative Plant and Flower Studies.* 1906.

M. P. Verneuil   *Etude de la plante.* Undated. Containing motifs such as oak leaves and cereals, which were reproduced in tiaras particularly.

P. Plauszewski   *Encyclopédie florale.* Undated.

Pattern books, however, were not the only source of inspiration in this field. Louis Cartier constantly encouraged his draughtsmen to wander through Paris with their sketch-books and to note down details of seventeenth- and eighteenth-century architecture. In this way drawings were made of patrician houses in the Faubourg Saint-Germain; and the pediments above the doors at Fontainebleau and the garlands of fruit on the Petit Trianon also found their way into Cartier's sketch-books, where they were transformed by some process of alchemy to reappear in transmuted form on various articles of jewelry.

The ornamental motifs borrowed from the seventeenth and eighteenth centuries, and in rare instances from the Renaissance, produced a canonical style of jewelry around 1900 which was closely dependent upon the contemporary fashion in clothes. Its essential components were tiaras, dog collars and bodice jewelry. Other types, like bracelets, generally faded into the background as a result of the fashion for long sleeves, and this in spite of attempts to popularize them by such magazines as *Femina* and *Vogue.*

Dog collars were tight-fitting necklaces which first appeared in France around 1865 and in England around 1880; they remained popular until the outbreak of the First World War. Edgar Degas painted his ballet-dancers wearing black velvet ribbons, and similar textile models dating back to the eighteenth century may well have started a fashion which was by no means limited to aristocratic circles or to evening wear. Cartier's retained the black moiré or velvet base, which gave an extra dimension to the openwork diamond or pearl motifs. The stylized patterns of these plaques placed them among the earliest geometrical designs of the new century. Some of them were given fanciful names such as

16–20
Diamond and seed pearl dog collar, the centre of stylized sun design with four rubies. Commissioned by Princess de Ganay in 1908

Diamond *résille* dog collar in circular-cut diamonds. 1910

Diamond dog collar of scaly flowerhead design in circular-cut diamonds. 1909

Diamond dog collar of intertwined circle and laurel leaf design in circular-cut diamonds. 1906

Diamond dog collar of linked circular design with pear-shaped diamond centres. Commissioned in 1912

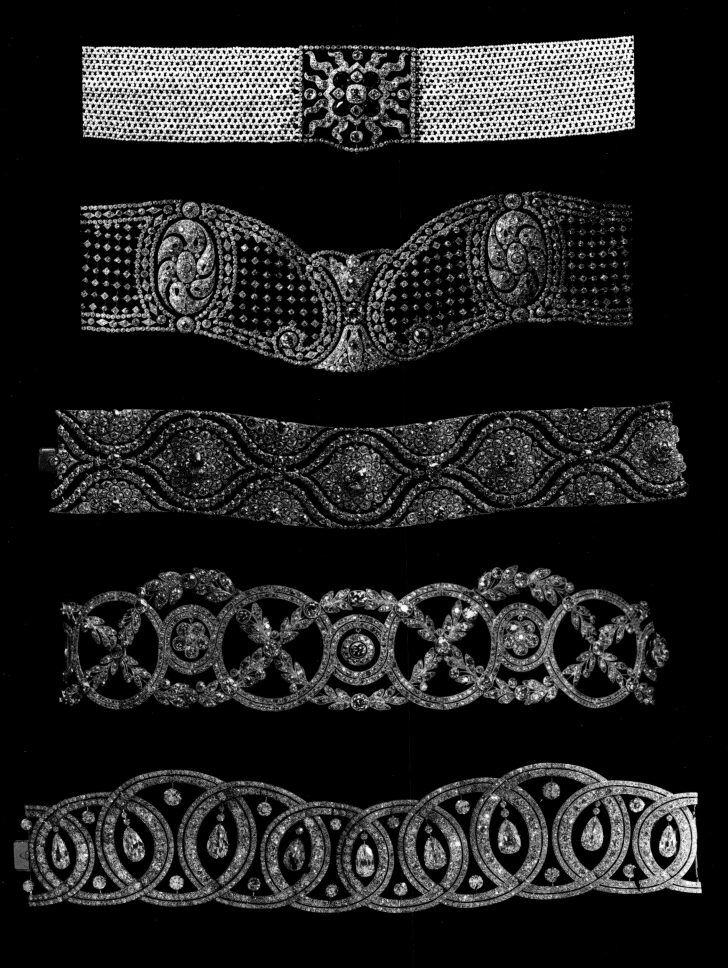

'Byzantine', others took up traditional floral motifs from the eighteenth century, including some found on snuffboxes.

The jeweler was naturally tempted to drop the traditional fabric ribbon and replace it entirely with gemstones, in which case the diamond plaques were held together with strings of pearls (as many as twenty strands being placed on top of each other), or else the pearl band was the result of laborious and detailed work which took weeks to complete and which produced a kind of beadwork based on old lace patterns.[5] The most important example of this first type was the Russian double-eagle pearl necklace made in 1900 for the Grand Duchess Vladimir. Before sending it to St Petersburg, Louis and Pierre Cartier invited friends and customers to view it in the rue de la Paix (see ill., p.70).

Occasionally pearls were dispensed with and the dog collars were made entirely of diamonds, refined wave-bands which reproduced the reflections of shot moiré silk and which may serve as early examples of a later stylization typical of art deco. In other cases the entire necklace was made in the shape of a continuous diamond garland, the centre of which was accentuated by an additional motif such as a pendant bow-knot. Entirely in keeping with the playful style of the eighteenth century was the *lacet de bergère* motif, whose laced design recalled the bodice ribbons of the earlier period and whose name revived memories of Marie Antoinette's rustic idylls in the park at Versailles.

Dog collars and stomachers together left very little space for large necklaces. For this reason only isolated examples of the last type are to be found at the beginning of the century, such as those ordered by the Grand Duchess Vladimir or the German banker Bleichroeder in the form of drop diamond cascades. Dog collars, on the other hand, were frequently worn with several ropes of pearls ending in geometrical pendants. A special form of necklace produced around 1900 was the *lavallière*, an imaginative allusion to a fashion named for the actress Eve Lavallière,[6] suspending two overlapping pendants, generally of different lengths. The necklace itself often consisted of a simple silk cord with diamond sliding motifs, in which the imaginative end motifs were often intertwined. Princess George of Greece (Marie Bonaparte) received a *lavallière* with two diamond fir cones, the Tsarina of Russia one with amethyst acorns.

21. *Lavallière* designed as 2 flexible circular-cut diamond and pearl pine-cones, on pearl and diamond chain. 1912. Sold to the Duke of Westminster.

One of the most original pendants was the motif of two doves beside a well. A single dove had been popular in Northern France and Flanders in the seventeenth and eighteenth centuries as a Saint-Esprit cross, while Marie Antoinette harboured a less exalted predilection for pairs of doves as attributes of Venus, which were found on snuffboxes, in painting and in décor, as well as in the pattern book of Théodore Bertren mentioned above. Cartier made a Louis XVI châtelaine in 1874 with the motif of two doves. The later motif of two doves moistening their beaks in a crystal fountain (with a moonstone inlay to reproduce the water) was fashionable as a charming transitional design leading the way to art deco. Lovebirds, two birds sitting on a branch, are still to be found on brooches right up to the present day.[7]

23. Choker necklace of lily and scroll design in circular-cut diamonds and 2 amethysts. Commissioned by Mrs H. Payne Whitney in 1907

22. *Lavallière* in navette-, circular- and triangular-cut diamonds, suspending a drop-shaped pearl of 102 grains and a faceted emerald drop of 31.8 cts. 1911

25. Diamond necklace suspending 3 hexagonal diamond pendants with circular and pear-shaped drop pendants. Commissioned by Mrs Cornelius Vanderbilt in 1908 (see p. 47)

24. Pearl and diamond chain with platinum bars suspending a rose- and circular-cut diamond sphere and spiralled drop-shaped pendant. 1907

26. Diamond flowerhead pendant of 'Persian' design in circular-cut diamonds, on seed pearl and diamond ribbon. 1909

27. Medusa-head pendant in pink coral within green enamel, with 3 pearls, a pink coral drop and rose-cut diamonds. 1906

28. Diamond pendant of openwork spiral design in circular- and rose-cut diamonds, on seed pearl ribbon. 1909

29. Diamond ribbon bow pendant brooch in circular and drop-shaped diamonds, with a square-cut diamond in the bow knot. 1911

30. 'Arabic' pendant in circular- and rose-cut diamonds. 1910

31. Edwardian pearl and diamond pendant, the plaited rose-cut diamond mount with 8 pearls

32. Diamond stomacher of hexagonal flower trellis design with two grey pearls of 57 and 45 grains. Commissioned by la Belle Otéro in 1909

33. Diamond ribbon bow stomacher in circular-, rose-cut and pear-shaped diamonds, with cushion-shaped diamond of 15.21 cts. 1905

35. Stomacher of stylized grape design in circular-cut diamonds. Commissioned in 1913

34. Diamond stomacher in circular- and square-cut diamonds suspending pear-shaped pearls of 285 grains and an egg-shaped pearl of 145 grains, and mounted with 3 button pearls of 247 grains. Commissioned by Countess Hohenfelsen

There is no doubt that, tiaras apart, the greatest variety of traditional motifs was to be found on the stomacher. No form of jewelry was as dependent upon costume as was this type of bodice ornament. It often reproduced the shape of the bodice, and when the bodice disappeared around 1910 it became unwearable and in most cases was broken up. No other form so obviously embodies the ostentation of the *belle époque*, a mode it recaptures far more effectively than the tiara, which was in keeping with the strict rules of court etiquette and thus survived the passing fashion in clothes. The new, freely articulated platinum settings produced stomachers which could be adapted to any change of fashion in clothes. The various types of material used provided Cartier's with a background onto which the ornaments were sewed directly by means of small eyes, in the eighteenth-century manner. Motifs found on stomachers include acanthus shoots, laurel wreaths, garlands of lilies and roses, as well as abstract lattices. They were all used unrestrictedly and are often built up around the axis of symmetry.

A painting dating from 1762 and produced in Allen Ramsay's studio shows Queen Charlotte of England wearing a stomacher similar to a later piece made in 1905 which reproduces the severe triangular lines of the bodice. One cannot fail to notice the latter's affinity with the eighteenth-century designs of Vander Cruysen and Lucotte. Of similar geometrical shape was a stomacher consisting of ten bow-knots tapering towards the lower end, as well as a model acquired by Mrs W. K. Vanderbilt with similarly designed rhomb motifs.

The luxuriantly expansive forms of bodice jewelry became a thing of the past when, thanks to the influence of Paul Poiret, the bodice disappeared around 1910 and was replaced by new fashions, emphasizing vertical lines. In 1907 Cartier's had begun creating new models with perpendicular strands of diamonds attached to two lateral points. Curving lines and sinuous plant-forms were relegated to the border areas, which led by a process of gradual assimilation to the oblong pendant of the 1920s.

Length came to dominate fashion, and it was this feature which was accentuated around 1910 by the new type of epaulette,[8] fastened at the shoulder and generally consisting of two parallel pendant diamond cascades. The epaulette often ended in motifs tapering towards the base and known as aiguillettes, a term used interchangeably with the epaulette itself. The latter might also assume the shape of a diamond band of up to 35 cm in length, similar to the *régente*, except that the latter also contained a pendant watch.

The most important type of epaulette, however, covered the breast rather like a diagonally draped sash made of several articulated strands of diamonds and pearls, fastened at one shoulder and often ending in aiguillettes. Symmetry was rigorously avoided here. Important examples include those made in 1909 for Mrs Frederick Vanderbilt, in 1910 for Mrs W. K. Vanderbilt, and the magnificent epaulette made in 1912 for Mrs Nancy Leeds, which culminated in a 70-carat emerald.[9]

Apart from the garland and laurel wreath, there were three motifs in the garland style which recurred with almost leitmotif

36. Diamond corsage ornament set with a pear-shaped diamond of 34.25 cts, two navette-cut diamonds of 23.54 and 6.50 cts, and a heart-shaped diamond of 3.53 cts. Commissioned in 1912 by S. B. Joël, owner of diamond mines in South Africa

37. Diamond corsage ornament of festoon design in circular-cut diamonds. Made to order in 1912

39. Diamond corsage ornament designed as 2 sprays of lilies in circular- and rose-cut diamonds. 1906

40. Diamond corsage ornament as 10 decreasing bow motifs in circular, rose-cut and pear-shaped diamonds. 1905

38. Diamond corsage ornament with aiguillettes. Centre diamond 7.30 cts. 1907

regularity, the bow-knot, tassel and lace motif. The tassel and bow-knot had been essential components of festive Baroque dress since the seventeenth century and, fashioned in velvet or silk, enlivened the surface of the object they adorned. The workshops of the leading jewelers of the time soon began to supply refined imitations in metal, enamel and gemstones. Bow-knot brooches had been popular since the seventeenth century as far afield as Spain. The most elegant models were designed around 1670 by the French jeweler Gilles Légaré.[10] They were the Baroque bodice ornament *par excellence*, and at a later date became known simply as *sévignés*,[11] after Mme de Sévigné (1626–96), the most famous correspondent of her time. During the age of Marie Antoinette, the fashion for bow-knots spread to England, and strictly symmetrical models henceforth maintained their place in the repertoire of the best of European jewelers. The Russian crown jewels[12] and the Green Vault in Dresden preserve important examples from the eighteenth century, and the auction of the French crown jewels in 1887 included not only a bow-knot with pendant tassels (No. 38) but, above all, two shoulder knots from Bapst's workshop (No. 2), used by Empress Eugénie to fasten the robe of state. Curiously enough, these two shoulder knots passed into Cartier's hands shortly before 1900, as attested by some undated photographs in the firm's archives. They inspired the creation of further bow-knot brooches around 1900. Cartier's earliest experiments with bow-knots date from 1895: 'Shoulder knot with tassel' runs an early entry, followed by another in 1897. The majority of the bow-knots were entrusted to Naudet's workshop,[13] a large and a small model being supplied. The first could measure up to 12 cm in width and was therefore a proper bodice ornament, unlike the simple brooch. An example of the large bow-knot brooch was acquired by the King of Spain in 1902; four more followed in 1904, while three small bow-knot brooches went to the Aga Khan.

Cartier's designers produced countless variations on the same motif: Empress Eugénie's brooch provided the inspiration for a brooch made for Lady de Grey, while eighteenth-century engravings by Maria & Babel inspired bow-knot brooches for Mrs Goelet and Mrs Lydig. This last item was made in Picq's workshop in 1909 and covered an area of 16 × 14 cm. The smaller of the two models was backed with velvet, Cartier's here recalling the textile origins of the motif. When velvet temporarily went out of fashion around 1910, the same colour contrast was achieved by means of black onyx.

The second motif, the tassel, generally appeared in conjunction with the bow-knot, or else as a separate pendant motif. French engravings, such as those of Vander Cruysen, influenced those models which have survived in the Russian crown jewels and which date from around 1780.[14] Initially they were only slightly curved in form. The tassel motif remained popular until around 1910 in Russia: at fancy dress and masked balls, fully curved three-dimensional tassels dangled from long strings of pearls, linking the traditional head ornaments with the costume. The ballet *Schéhérazade* brought the motif to European attention around 1910, reinforced by memories of the Indian turban tassel. This originated the art deco tassel of onyx, coral and pearls, a central motif of 1920s jewelry fashion.

41. Pearl and diamond bracelet designed as 2 circular-cut diamond snakes holding a pearl and diamond panel. Commissioned by Baroness Henri de Rothschild in 1912

42. Diamond 'écharpe' in circular and pear-shaped diamonds. Commissioned by Mrs W. K. Vanderbilt in 1910

43. 'Persian' diamond pendant in circular-cut diamonds. Commissioned in 1910

44. Diamond pendant of festoon design in circular-cut diamonds with framed cushion-shaped diamond centre. 1910

45. Ruby and diamond dog collar with 11 rubies of 14.55 cts. Commissioned by Queen Amelia of Portugal in 1913

The third motif, an openwork lace pattern, inspired the jeweler to a degree of illusionistic imitation comparable to the Baroque art of trompe-l'oeil.[15] Lace and embroidery (*passementerie*) were a feature of the annual Paris salons, and in 1909 the Musée des Arts Décoratifs organized a specialized exhibition which evoked widespread interest and which fascinated Louis Cartier. He incorporated the sinuous lines and symmetrical bird-and-plant motifs of lacework into the garland style, presenting his draughtsmen with pattern books which the firm's resident photographer copied for despatch to Cartier's London and New York designers.

The impression of lace, Islamic grilles and European wrought-ironwork produced the transparent, articulate, insubstantial background that was characteristic of items made in the garland style. This was one of the reasons why traditional gold and silver settings were slowly abandoned and platinum was favoured instead.[16] Silver, because of its softness, had the great disadvantage of requiring massive stone settings and dampening the fire of the diamond as a result of its oxidation.[17] In the eighteenth century, when large diamonds were still relatively rare and jewels worn on festive occasions at court shone merely in the glimmer of flickering candlelight, the illusion of flashing jewelry could still be preserved. But the time was not far off when the newly discovered electric light would expose those same jewels to a relentless glare.

Although platinum had been used in ancient Egypt, it had not been recognized as such, and it was really not until the sixteenth century that it began to be mined in Colombia.[18] As late as 1748 the Spanish mathematician Don Antonio de Ulloa (1716–95) reported from New Grenada (Colombia) that a new metal 'platina' (*lit.* small silver) had been found, which could be distinguished only with difficulty from gold. Although platinum was soon recognized as a separate chemical element, it was still being described in 1785 by the great French naturalist Buffon in his *Histoire naturelle des minéraux* as an alloy of gold and iron. At the same time, however, platinum was beginning to enjoy its earliest popularity in the Paris of Louis XVI: the German scholar F. C. Achard (1753–1821) had succeeded in alloying platinum and arsenic and thereby lowering the mineral's very high melting point of 1,769°.[19] Marc Etienne Jannetti began making platinum salt-shakers, boxes and candelabras in Paris in 1792; the standard metre and standard kilogram were similarly made of platinum. At the same time, new platinum deposits were discovered in the Urals, and the chemist Sobolevsky invented a new and efficient process for obtaining it. Kankrin, the Russian minister of finance (1775–1845), minted a limited series of platinum coins. The German scholar Alexander von Humboldt issued vain warnings about the dangers of such an experiment, and it proved indeed to be a lamentable failure. As a nonprecious metal which was valued for its softness and conductivity, platinum continued to be used on a regular basis in industry.[20] At the 1855 Paris exhibition, the jeweler Eugène Fontenay caused a sensation with a blackberry blossom tiara whose setting was partly made of platinum.

Cartier's records contain an entry for 1853, when the firm moved to the rue Neuve-des-Petits-Champs, which reads: 'Sale of platinum

142,50 francs'; and that same year Cartier ordered from Fossin's workshop a seal made of gold and platinum.[21] But what continued to stand in the way of unlimited use of the mineral were the technical difficulties of obtaining a pure enough form, difficulties which the German researcher Wilhelm Carl Heraeus (1827–1904) was finally to resolve in Hanau, shortly before 1900, with his invention of a new melting process. Platinum was first found in Cartier's work not on large surfaces but on small buttons, needles and rings, and it was only the technically unnecessary backing with gold that increased the value of platinum so that it came to be regarded as a precious metal. A partial summary of Cartier's archives shows platinum being used as follows:

From 1859   Shirt buttons in platinum (perhaps the model which Cartier supplied to the shirtmaker Charvet).

1874   Cuff-links edged in platinum.
Lead pencils of gold and platinum.

1886   Tie pins, buttons and earrings, in addition to a sapphire and diamond ring of gold and platinum. The same year also includes an entry for white gold.

1894   Diamond necklace with platinum setting, link bracelet in platinum.

1899   Butterfly brooch *en tremblant* (from Robin's workshop); also 'maternity' brooches (in the form of safety pins), rings and a heart-shaped watch.

This takes us up to the year in which the firm moved to the rue de la Paix, when its stock increased dramatically and platinum settings were very much a novelty. In the intervening years platinum had slowly come to be regarded as a precious metal, equal in value to gold. In 1903 world consumption reached 7,525 kilograms.[22] But it was not entirely the mounting price of platinum which persuaded Cartier to retain traditional gold and silver settings and to sell them alongside platinum jewelry: the large and small Louis XVI bow-knot brooches made in 1900 were of platinum, but those made in 1902 and 1904 were of silver. Since the purchasers in the last two instances were the King of Spain and Mrs W. K. Vanderbilt, the change is unlikely to have been the result of any price concession, but rather because individual craftsmen strove tenaciously to maintain traditional nineteenth-century techniques. The price may nevertheless have played a role in the case of certain commissions: in 1901 Pierre Cartier left the final decision between platinum and silver to Countess Killarney but drew her attention to the lower price of silver.[23]

Cartier's was said to use the best platinum in Paris. It was renowned for its white, shimmering surface, an alloy of which the Picq workshop was especially proud. The stone which was to be set was surrounded by a platinum girdle whose surface was knurled with a regular series of indentations known as 'millegrain' or 'serti perlé'. In this way the platinum was 'demetalized' and broken up into shimmering reflections of light. Later the stone was set from behind with a delicate platinum girdle or *chaton*, and held in place by four or six claws; the cold white shimmering surface of the *chaton* was intended to enhance the reflective properties of the diamond. The most delicate platinum setting in the garland style was the so-called 'lily-of-the valley setting' or 'serti muguet', which reproduced the outline of the flower's calyx.[24]

As a result of the new technical freedom of form created by the use of platinum, the garland style, in spite of its eighteenth-century origins, came to be seen as a 'new style' and as an alternative to art nouveau. And so, when the firm moved premises, customers such as Lady de Grey were shown 'nouveaux modèles' or 'bijoux entièrement nouveaux', whose much-lauded characteristics included mobility and transformability. Items of jewelry having a multiple purpose were less known in the nineteenth century but were now once more the current fashion, as is clear from a letter written by Louis Cartier to Countess Orlovska in Nice: 'The bodice ornament is articulated by removal of the lower part and in that way may be worn on the shoulder. On the other hand, it may be attached to a velvet ribbon and worn as a dog collar.'

Apart from the use of platinum, what was also of importance for the form of this new type of jewelry was the jeweler's intimate familiarity not only with textiles but with fashion as a whole. The move to the rue de la Paix had brought Alfred Cartier and his family into the closest contact with Worth's worldwide couture enterprise.

The second half of the nineteenth century has been described as the *époque Worth*. Charles Frederick Worth (1825–95) had left London for Paris at the age of twenty. Soon he was to revolutionize costume design just as Louis Cartier was to revolutionize the world of jewelry forty years later. Whether Worth was really the first to introduce the crinoline may be difficult to establish today; but the new fashion, which turned women into unattainable objects of luxury, was taken up and adapted by Worth in numerous commissions for Empress Eugénie and Princess Metternich, reaching its climax around 1865. He was certainly the first to propagate the *tournure*, a style of dress which was straight at the front but with a bustle at the back. The Franco-Prussian War was the great turning-point for Worth. Louis-François Cartier could not bear 'to watch the Prussians parading up and down the boulevard in front of my window' and went into self-imposed exile in San Sebastian from where he sympathized at a distance with his son Alfred, who, before emigrating to London, was living in Paris 'on horsemeat, dogs and rats'; Worth, on the other hand, closed his business and set up a field hospital in his premises in the rue de la Paix, reopening in 1871, this time without his former partner, Otto Bobergh of Sweden. When the war was over and Cartier complained from Etretat of the general absence of jewelry, the hour of the great couturier had finally come. 'Dress', wrote Cartier, 'is becoming more magnificent by the day; on the beach at Etretat at eight o'clock this morning, women from the *demi-monde* spread out more silk, satin and lace than a queen herself would need for her entire trousseau.' The successful Worth, who was half businessman and half Venetian doge, and whose style of dress, like Richard Wagner's, was inspired by Rembrandt, encouraged Louis-François Cartier in their joint mission 'to live through and for luxury'. It was Worth who drew Cartier's attention to American hostesses who, especially since the time of the 1876 Philadelphia Exhibition, had undertaken regular pilgrimages to Worth's establishment in the rue de la Paix, much to the annoyance of his long-standing French customers who henceforth avoided Worth's and gave credence to a mocking remark in *Harper's Bazaar* that 'not a word of French could be heard' at Worth's. Cartier used a display window at Worth's to attract the attention of the international élite from Russia,[25] Germany, England and America; and, following the death of Charles Frederick Worth in 1895, the friendly relations of his sons Gaston and Jean-Philippe were transferred to Alfred Cartier's sons, Louis and Pierre. Whereas Gaston was the more commercially minded of the two, Jean-Philippe, who had studied painting with Corot and who continued his father's creative tradition, was as great an aesthete as Louis Cartier. In addition, Louis Cartier married Jean-Philippe Worth's daughter, Andrée, in 1898, and Louis' sister, Suzanne, later became the wife of Gaston's son, Jacques.

By 1900 the Worth brothers were the uncrowned kings of Parisian *haute couture*. The silk factories at Lyon were ruled by their dictates, and every week the horse-races at Longchamp spurred both Worth and his rivals, Doeuillet, Redfern, Laferrière and Beer, to feats of *à la mode* achievement. From 1900 there were striking parallels in the ranges of the couturier on the one hand and the now related jeweler on the other: although formal dress had passed through a number of stylistic phases in its development between 1880 and 1900, and although by 1900 it was clearly being influenced by the sinuous curves of the art nouveau aesthetic (the Gibson Girl), the Louis XVI style of Marie Antoinette and the *directoire* style[26] of Joséphine de Beauharnais continued in turn to provide the inspiration for both costume and jewelry, the ideal silhouette of the period being topped off by a 'Récamier' hairstyle.[27] Fashionable materials – heavy velvet from Genoa, lightweight satins, mousseline-de-soie and crêpe de chine – were embroidered with the familiar roses and lilies of the garland style, each dress being turned into a precious gem with the addition of silver and gold trimmings. Cartier bought velvet and moiré silk from the couturier to be used as a black, grey or white background for jewelry, and the articles made in this way were placed on display at Worth's. In 1899, for example, two months before the shop moved to the rue de la Paix, there were eighteen items, including belt buckles, buttons, combs and clasps. The coronation fever accompanying the accession of Edward VII in 1902 saw Cartier busily producing tiaras while Worth was kept fully occupied for three months making coronation trains. Influenced by Whistler, the fashionable pastel shades around 1900 were *cuisse de nymphe*, lilac, mauve, straw, hydrangea blue and maize; and so Cartier produced monochromatic jewelry to match, in diamonds and pearls discreetly relieved by amethysts and turquoises.[28] When the fashion for strongly contrasting colours returned under the influence of Worth's pupil Paul Poiret, the jeweler was ready with a corresponding colour palette. The affinities between the two arts were so close that a Worth dress made in 1900 for the soprano Lillian Nordica included shoulder motifs in the form of Cartier 'cravats',[29] and on another occasion Boucheron designed diamond sleeves. The most

46. Edwardian diamond *résille* necklace set with circular-cut diamonds, rose-cut diamond and diamond tassel border

48. Diamond *résille* necklace of laurel-leaf and garland design in circular- and pear-shaped diamonds weighing 141.4/64 cts. Commissioned by Queen Alexandra in 1904

47. Diamond *résille* with bow tassel stomacher in circular- and rose-cut diamonds. Commissioned in 1903 by la Belle Otéro and mounted with the stones of her famous boléro after the design of the 'Necklace of the Queen' (i.e. Marie Antoinette)

successful blurring of the distinction between jeweler and couturier was achieved in 1901 with the creation of the 'boléro' for the beautiful Caroline Otéro. This was a sleeveless jacket of diamonds and coloured cabochons by the jeweler Paul Hamelin with an openwork lattice design or *résille*. A *résille* literally means 'hairnet', and Cartier used this same netlike technique to produce a series of approximately ten necklaces which fitted snugly round the neck like a second skin, banishing all thought of rigid metal. Was it surprising that Mlle Otéro quickly tired of Hamelin's boléro, which contained a whole series of false stones, and commissioned Cartier to rework it as a *résille* necklace? The model on this occasion was Marie Antoinette's famous necklace with its tasselled ribbons crossing over the breast. The most magnificent of *résilles*, however, was the one ordered by Buckingham Palace from Pierre Cartier in 1904: an ethereal web of superimposed diamond drops and bow-knots, it adorns Queen Alexandra in the portrait of her by the French painter François Flameng.

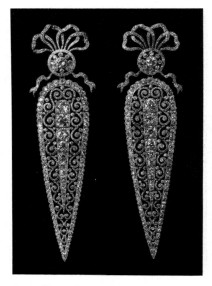

49. Pair of circular- and rose-cut diamond aiguillettes. 1907. Sold separately to A. Vanderbilt and Vincenzo Florio

When Princess Marie Bonaparte, the illustrious descendant of Lucien Bonaparte and heiress of the wealthy Blanc family of Monte Carlo, married Prince George of Greece in 1907,[30] Cartier held a special exhibition to show off the wedding gifts, jewels in the garland style which had been produced for the occasion; and the sumptuous trousseau was the subject of a similar exhibition at the 'Hôtel des Modes'. The American *Vogue* observed that, just as the actress Cécile Sorel embodied the style of Louis XV, so Louis XVI and the Empire were the style of Marie Bonaparte, an analogy confirmed by Cartier's stomacher, epaulette and olive tiara in the austere style of her Napoleonic ancestor (see ill., p. 47).

Motif analogies between the two arts are also revealed by a branch of jewelry which it is impossible to appreciate nowadays, namely mourning jewelry. Instructions for bereavements were based upon a form of strict ritual until the 1920s, rules which in the nineteenth century had been lived to the letter by Queen Victoria and Empress Eugénie. The materials, colour and cut of the clothes which were worn in mourning and half-mourning were all clearly prescribed. Not only the clothes, but also the shoes, umbrella and purse, whose clasp had to be made of browned steel or more precious materials, were subject to the protocol of mourning, and it was only to be expected that jewelry should conform to the same rules: black pearls and jet had been the official expressions of mourning since the nineteenth century. When, around 1910, the fashionable use of black and white as a colour contrast led to the creation of onyx and diamond jewelry, the latter immediately became a legitimate form of mourning jewelry and as such was often newly set.[31] The new models were launched by *Vogue* as 'new models for smart mourning' — an echo of 'Black Ascot' following the death of Edward VII. When the *Titanic* sank in 1912,[32] models such as these inspired Cartier's New York with the idea of discreetly advertising onyx and diamond jewelry.

As was to be expected, the customers for Cartier's garland-style jewelry were among the most famous society names of the day: royal houses, the international aristocracy, trade, commerce and the

50. Diamond shrimp brooch in circular- and rose-cut diamonds. Cabochon ruby eye. Made to order in 1913

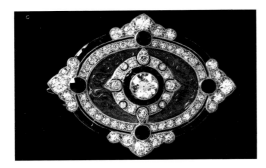

51. Oval diamond, onyx and engraved rock crystal brooch. Commissioned in 1913

52. Onyx and diamond pendant of Egyptian 'pylon' design suspended from a pearl ribbon necklace with circular-cut diamond centre motif. 1920

world of the theatre. According to the taste of the individual buyer, traditional forms alternated with more fashionable designs borrowed from the Orient: a traditional stomacher in the shape of a curtain pelmet was produced in close association with a Persian-inspired piece of twenty-nine emerald cabochons, following the outline of the Persian carpet medallion. Mrs Walter Burns, née Evelyn Cavendish-Bentinck, who was a cousin of the Duke of Portland and daughter-in-law of J. P. Morgan, wore this particular jewel on a number of occasions including the coronation celebrations of George V in London.

The *demi-monde* of the courtesans was every bit as fond of jewelry and ostentation as the very best of society circles. Caroline Otéro bought from Cartier's not only the *résille* necklace already mentioned but a stomacher in the form of a six-sided floral grille with pendant drop pearls. As one of the most famous representatives of the new genre of 'vamp' which had begun with Sarah Bernhardt, she continued to be seen at Cartier's as late as 1919 when, at the age of fifty-one, she ordered a ten-strand pearl sash made of 1,015 pearls and diamonds.[33]

From a somewhat more dubious sphere came Adolph and Olga de Meyer, enthusiastic adepts in Cartier's new aesthetic (stomacher and bow-knot tiara in 1901,[34] laural tiara in 1905, and a vanity case in 1925). Olga Caracciolo, godchild and possibly also the illegitimate offspring of the Prince of Wales, was painted by Whistler and Boldini as a somewhat lesser Misia Sert. As Mrs Adolph de Meyer she was accounted among the social élite, both after 1900 (the couple were raised to the peerage to enable them to attend the coronation of Edward VII) and during the postwar café-society years of Elsie de Wolfe, Elsa Maxwell and Cole Porter. Adolph de Meyer's work as a photographer was influenced by the aesthetic of Ruskin and Whistler. As a supporter of the Ballets Russes (his work on *L'Après-Midi d'un faune*[35] was published by Iribe in 1914), as a contributor to *Vogue*, *Vanity Fair* and, from 1923, *Harper's Bazaar*, de Meyer became the leading pictorial chronicler of the war years and of an aesthetic which Cartier had helped to mould. His technique of using diffused lighting and immobile groupings reminiscent of still-life paintings remained influential until the late 1920s. Not until the 1930s was de Meyer's work made to appear anachronistic by the later photographic techniques of Hoyningen-Huene, Horst and Beaton, who celebrated sport and movement with a new sense of colour.

The tiaras and stomachers Cartier's made not to order but for stock frequently contained a lavish variety of large stones and represented a considerable capital investment which was tied up for months. What frequently happened, therefore, was that the most expensive stones were removed from their setting and used in another context as a new jewel, not uncommonly as the result of some unexpected order from New York or London. The following diagram traces the odyssey of one series of large diamond drops between 1904 and 1905:

1904 Tiara with three diamond drops and four pearls:

39 15/64 cts
17 53/64
15 3/

Tiara with 7 drops

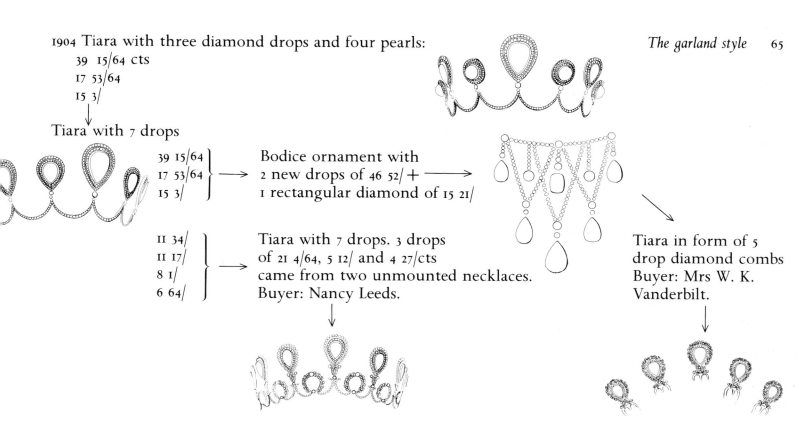

39 15/64
17 53/64 } → Bodice ornament with
15 3/ 2 new drops of 46 52/ + → 1 rectangular diamond of 15 21/

11 34/
11 17/ } → Tiara with 7 drops. 3 drops
8 1/ of 21 4/64, 5 12/ and 4 27/cts
6 64/ came from two unmounted necklaces. Buyer: Nancy Leeds.

Tiara in form of 5 drop diamond combs Buyer: Mrs W. K. Vanderbilt.

As a result of these various reworkings, the original diamond tiara of 1904 produced two new pieces, both of which went to American buyers, Nancy Leeds and Mrs W. K. Vanderbilt. Increasing numbers of items in the garland style found a market in America as a consequence. Around 1917, when the First World War discouraged the production of large jewels in Europe, *Vogue* sent out a patriotic appeal to all American women, asking them to contribute to national morale by means of beauty and elegance. ('The American woman realizes that she can do this by looking her loveliest. She is a true patriot.') The de Meyer photographs accompanying the article extol the garland-style tiara and stomacher such as had been fashionable ten years previously in Europe ('the American woman is really just beginning to realize the possibilities of the diamond tiara').[36]

An 1863 photograph shows women alpinists dressed in crinolines for their ascent of a Swiss glacier. However, by the end of the nineteenth century, women's clothes had begun to be adapted to the practical needs of female labour and sport. In 1880 Viscountess Harberton founded her Rational Dress Society which, encouraged by similar movements in Germany, attempted to simplify fashion in favour of comfort and hygiene. Women were taught how to mount a bicycle decently; they began to play hockey around 1900, and they were advised by their couturier to protect themselves from dust while driving by using a *voilette d'automobile*. In 1907 Mlle Bayeux climbed the Matterhorn and two years later the Comtesse de Lambert clambered aboard Wilbur Wright's aeroplane. In the meantime, Paul Poiret had left the couturier Doucet in order to work for Worth, for whom he designed simple dresses for buses and walking. The reform of day- and evening-wear had begun, and with it the heyday of garland-style jewelry was to draw gently to a close.

Tiaras

THOUSANDS OF CURIOUS VISITORS flocked to London's Bond Street during the first week of April 1911 to witness a spectacular exhibition at Cartier's. There, in return for a guinea's admission – the proceeds of which went to the Prince Francis von Teck Foundation (named after Queen Mary's brother who had died the previous year) – they were able to admire at close quarters nineteen tiaras which two months later would be visible to them only at a distance during the coronation celebrations of King George V. The Duchess of Marlborough, Princess Alexander von Teck, Lady Desborough, the Marchioness of Cholmondeley, the Duchesses of Norfolk and Beaufort were all brought together in this display of their jewelry. Not only did the exhibition present a cross-section of Cartier's products, but it provided a foretaste of the coronation balls and of performances at Covent Garden with Caruso, Nijinsky and Melba.

In the typology of jewelry, the tiara occupied a special place right up to the end of the First World War, inasmuch as it was reserved for an hereditary and monied élite who wore it at ceremonies and on festive occasions as an outward sign of their privileged status. The woman who wears a tiara towers above all around her; she is identifiable from afar and the glittering aureole around her head turns her into the Queen of the Night herself. At the same time, the tiara can convey every mood from the sublime to the merely theatrical – theatrical as in the case of the Vicomtesse de Janzé, a pillar of Parisian society around 1910, who seemed to brush the crystal chandeliers with her pagoda-like headdress of flashing diamonds; or sublime like the Comtesse de Haussonville who, even when not wearing a head ornament, always appeared to be 'crowned by an invisible tiara'.[1] Like the eighteenth-century minuet, the traditional tiara symbolized the prerogatives of a society which in Paris and London had essentially outlived itself by the late 1920s. The economic conflicts of the time led to the disappearance of the tiara as the leading type of jewelry, a development which became evident earlier in Paris than in London. Tiaras, for which Worth and Paquin created their magnificent gowns and which were the subject of glittering parades every Monday and Friday at the Paris Opéra, had in fact already gone out of fashion by 1910. 'Soirées de diadèmes' had been the name given to those astonishing processions of jewels which, at the end of each performance, had wended their way to Durand's, the fashionable restaurant in the Place de la Madeleine. There are reports of a 'surging sea of tiaras' at official receptions held in the Russian Embassy in Paris, when orchids were shipped in specially from the distant Crimea and the Grand Duchess Vladimir showed off her latest masterpiece from Cartier's. But even before the outbreak of the First World War, the pseudo-Oriental aigrette and then the simple bandeau supplanted the classical tiara and came to be numbered among the favourite items which Poiret and Vionnet established as part of the prevailing image of what women should wear.

In Paris great aigrette balls were organized by aristocratic families

54. Invitation card to Cartier's tiara exhibition in London, 1911

53. Princess Paley (Countess Hohenfelsen) wearing her diamond and pearl stomacher as a hat brooch and her tiara of pear-shaped diamonds (1911) as a corsage ornament. Dress by Worth (photo: Boissonas & Taponier, 1912)

who were proud of their name and their past, such as the Duchesse de Gramont with her 'Crinoline Ball' and Princesse Jacques de Broglie with her 'Gemstone Ball' of 1914. In distant New York, Philadelphia and Newport, on the other hand, Mrs William Astor, Mrs George Gould, Mrs W. K. Vanderbilt and Mrs Eva Stotesbury entertained with a degree of magnificence which made European balls appear almost insignificant. The monied classes of the United States, who had originally raised themselves above their bourgeois origins through their own hard work, set out to rival the historically evolved aristocracy of Europe. In friendly competition with her fellow rivals, the well-to-do American woman refused to forego any of the attributes sanctioned by society. These accessories included country houses imported from Europe, complete with ancestral portraits and furnishing, as well as tiaras ordered from Cartier's branches in Paris and later New York. Like the grandiose palaces modelled on Blois and Versailles, tiaras revealed the financial power which made luxury possible and could therefore never be too expensive. The emerald tiara that Cartier's made for Eva Stotesbury was so heavy that she not only got a stiff neck wearing it but was advised 'either to attach a few helium balloons to it or wear it without complaining'.[2] Although the First World War did not have the same socially disruptive influence in America as it did in Europe, it seemed like the swan song of an era when, at an advanced age, Caroline Astor stood at the entrance to her ballroom, wearing a tiara and stomacher and 'greeting imaginary guests long dead, exchanging pleasantries with ghosts of the utmost social distinction'.[3]

Even after they had gone out of fashion in Paris and New York, tiaras continued to set the tone in London. The fact that in 1923, on the occasion of a reception at Bath House, Lady Lucknow 'wore her enormous Cartier tiara which, with its flashing diamonds, made one think of a halo', was something that struck only the fashion reporter as being in any way excessive. Private detectives kept an eye on the bejewelled guests in the dining room of the Savoy Hotel, and the court of St James even included the wearing of tiaras in its rules of protocol. Edward VII made his displeasure felt when guests arrived without a tiara. In later years, Consuelo Duchess of Marlborough recalled

a dinner in honour of the Prince and Princess of Wales to which I wore a diamond crescent instead of the prescribed tiara. The Prince with a severe glance at my crescent observed 'The Princess has taken the trouble to wear a tiara, why have you not done so?' Luckily I could truthfully answer that I had been delayed by some charitable function in the country and that I had found the bank in which I kept my tiara closed on my arrival in London.[4]

As late as 1953 Queen Elizabeth the Queen Mother received a tiara from Cartier's: the strict rules of court etiquette remained unaltered, although many members of the nobility, including Princess Marina, the Duchess of Kent, regarded the tiara as a nuisance and out of keeping with the times: 'Soon after the Queen left, the Duchess of Kent [Marina] removed her tiara and handed it to the bandleader, Tommy Kinsman, complaining that it was far too

55. A Cartier diamond aigrette as a bridal ornament (photo: Baron de Meyer, American *Vogue*, May 1918)

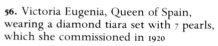

56. Victoria Eugenia, Queen of Spain, wearing a diamond tiara set with 7 pearls, which she commissioned in 1920

57. Her Majesty the Queen Mother wearing her diamond tiara. 1953

58. Mrs Nancy Leeds (Princess Anastasia of Greece) wearing her emerald and diamond necklace (1921) and her emerald and diamond tiara (painting: Philip de László)

heavy. Kinsman placed the tiara on the piano while the Royal Duchess danced with her old friend Chips Channon.'[5]

Since tiaras were specially made in Paris, London and New York for important occasions and in association with expensive dresses, not only do Cartier's photographic records help us to identify specific fashions, but their chronology reveals a most fascinating chapter in the social history of the twentieth century.

The word 'diadem' (tiara) comes from the Greek 'diadeo', literally 'I bind together'. Originally it meant a helmet band worn by a military commander; but then it became any secular or sacred head ornament denoting high office.[6] It was the Renaissance painters who finally became the chroniclers of its modern meaning – one thinks, for example, of Titian's *Girl with the fruit peel*, in which the tiara appears as the crowning attribute of a magnificent evening gown. Cartier's tiaras, which belong to the final stage of this change in functional transformation, may be divided into various groups according to their form and style:

The kokoshnik *or* tiare russe

The term is derived from the Russian word *kokosh* meaning 'cock's-comb' and initially described a head ornament based in design on a cock's-comb and worn in ritual Russian folk-dances. Originally made of material in the form of a pelta and fastened at the side with ribbons, it was taken up by the Russian court during the sixteenth/seventeenth centuries and reproduced in expensive materials. The *kokoshnik* was accentuated at its central point by a slight swelling in shape and was placed around the head like the disc-shaped aureole of a Byzantine madonna. A portrait of Catherine the Great dating from about 1775 shows her wearing a crescent-shaped *kokoshnik* studded with precious stones. In a portrait of Tsarina Maria Feodorovna of around 1830, however, it has grown into a huge fan-shaped halo. After 1800 the *kokoshnik* became fashionable in Western Europe, too. When Cartier's took up the motif around 1900, memories of its Russian origins were still so vivid that the archival records of the rue de la Paix consistently used the terms 'kokoshnik', 'tiare russe' or 'in the Russian style'.

In order to relieve the static impression produced by its solidity of form, Cartier's returned to one of the purest inspirations of the First Empire and created a group of *kokoshniks* with diamond drops freely suspended from a gallery within the openwork mount. Every movement on the part of the wearer was gently transmitted to the stones, which increased in size towards the centre. This group was followed by other models with a lozenge-shaped grille pattern, each opening of which was ornamented with a pendant diamond.

An additional series of *kokoshniks*, designed in the Louis XV style, was reminiscent of tiaras among the French crown jewels made by Bapst around 1820. They included a tiara for Queen Elisabeth of Belgium in 1912, by the Cartier designer Henri Chenaud, and one made for the opera-singer Lina Cavalieri, who first appeared with Caruso in Paris in 1905 and who was celebrated as the most beautiful woman of her day.

In 1912 Charles Jacqueau designed a flat *kokoshnik* with crystal

59. Grand Duchess Vladimir in traditional Russian costume. Her briolette diamond tiara (1908) appears through the opening of her Russian headdress which is mounted at its base with her 19th-century Russian emerald necklace. Her 107-ct emerald brooch suspends a cabochon emerald drop

60. Diamond and pearl tiara suspending alternate pear-shaped diamonds and pearls within interlinked diamond and pearl hoops. Weights of diamonds: 21.60, 15.35, 11.82, 11.54, 9.85 cts. Weights of pearls: 64.60, 62.72, 49.60, 45.04, 35.76, 35 grains. Commissioned by Mrs Nancy Leeds in 1913

61. Diamond tiara mounted with 7 pear-shaped diamonds within interlinked circular-cut diamond hoops. Weight of centre diamond: 27 cts; total weight of 7 stones: 121.42 cts. Transformed in 1911 from an earlier tiara dated 1908 by order of Princess Paley (Countess Hohenfelsen)

62. Rock crystal tiara, the scroll engraved rock crystal band with rose-cut diamond base, navette-cut diamond centre, circular-cut diamond gallery. Commissioned by Baron de Gunzburg in 1912

63. Sapphire and diamond *kokoshnik* set with a cushion-shaped sapphire of 137.20 cts flanked by 6 cabochon sapphires weighing 102.16 cts, on circular-cut diamond mount. Commissioned by Grand Duchess Vladimir in 1909

64. Tiara mounted with engraved rock crystal bars below a circular-cut diamond gallery. Central diamond of 3.66 cts. 1911. Sold to Princess Youssoupov (see p. 72)

trimmings and diamonds. The sinuous plant-forms engraved on the rock crystal owed their inspiration to Renaissance pattern books, although the geometrical diamond motifs proved the piece to be an early example of revolutionary art deco stylization. The wedding tiara of Princess Youssoupov was made in a similar style in 1911 and its fame soon spread far beyond Russia's borders. It was seized by the Soviets in 1925 and has not been heard of since. We should also include in this group a small series of *kokoshniks* of much less expensive design: their background of blackened metal or grey and green copper was decorated with star diamonds and sinuous vine-shoots. The boldest item in the series showed a symmetrically stylized art deco tree with black onyx leaves on a diamond background. Pearls set at rhythmic intervals enlivened the unbroken contour of the tiara.

Although *Vogue* predicted a revival of the 'tiara russe' in 1923, very few women in Parisian society seemed inclined to wear huge tiaras with the latest creations of Lanvin and Vionnet; they regarded the bandeau as more in keeping with the time and easier to wear. In London, on the other hand, Cartier's workshops designed a special *kokoshnik* as late as 1928: rounded towards the bottom edge, it covered the back of the head and at the front ended in a delicate ribbon; but the model found no imitators. The last great buyer of *kokoshniks* in London was the American Lady Granard, *née* Ogden Mills. In 1922 she ordered a delicately worked model made of 435 seed pearls with diamond embroidery in the centre; and a year later another which, with its sixteen aquamarine beads, sapphires and pearls, achieved what for the time was a novel effect of colour. One wonders whether it was the very last of Lady Granard's *kokoshniks*, with its priceless diamond drops and heavy helmet-like form, which Chips Channon had in mind when, in 1937 (the year it was ordered), he confided in his diary that 'Lady Granard could scarcely walk for jewels'. The Granard *kokoshniks* signify the end of a tradition which was fatally checked by the Second World War.

The bandeau

The expression refers to a ribbon-shaped tiara whose centre is not accentuated, as was that of the *kokoshnik*. Basically, the bandeau represents the most timeless form of head ornament and gives us a clear idea of what the tiara must have looked like in early civilizations, when it was still worn as a hairband.

Cartier's records include an entry dated 1854 describing a hair ornament of two blue enamel flowers and pearls, but the firm's first verifiable tiara is a silvergilt bandeau recorded in 1859. Plain narrow hairbands or *ferronnières* had been popular during the reign of Charles X and were typical of the age of Biedermeier, that late bourgeois phase of nineteenth-century classicism.[7]

The bandeaux which Cartier recreated in the garland style around 1900 were capable of meeting the requirements of court protocol in spite of their simple appearance. The Australian soprano Nellie Melba (1861–1931), who was one of Cartier's regular clients, ordered a 'Greek' bandeau in 1908, presumably with a meander design.

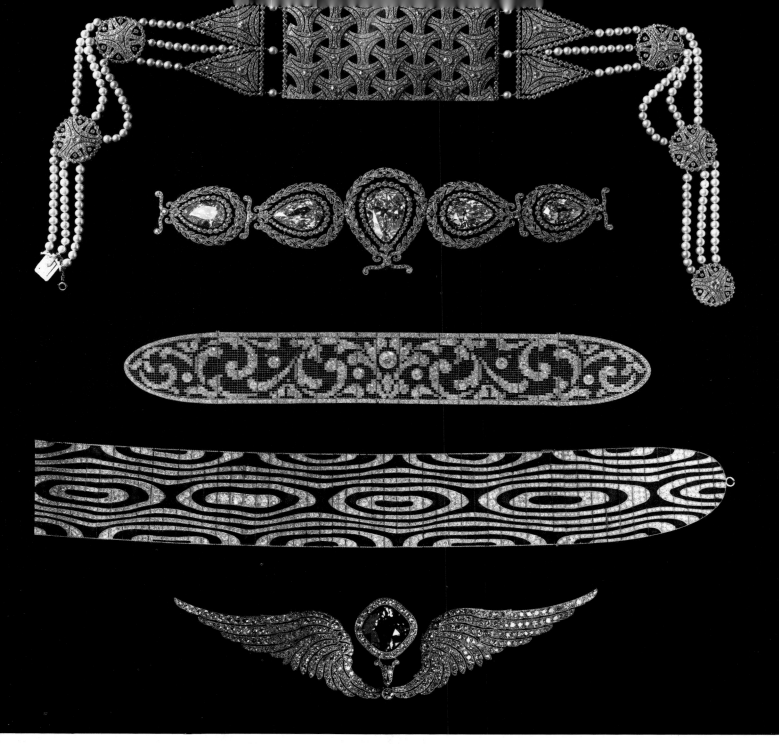

65. Diamond bandeau designed as an intertwined 'Byzantine' circular- and rose-cut diamond plaque with triangular ends, on pearl and diamond band. Commissioned by Mrs W. K. Vanderbilt in 1909

66. Diamond bandeau mounted with 5 pear-shaped diamonds weighing 39.60/64, 24.44/, 22.8/64, 15.3/64, 17.53/ cts within laurel leaf surrounds. Transformed in 1909 from 5 hair combs dated 1905 by order of Mrs W. K. Vanderbilt

67. Stomacher/bandeau designed as a platinum canvas studded with circular-cut diamonds. 1912. Sold to Mrs Leeds

68. Moiré bandeau with concentric diamond 'silk reflections'. 1912. Exhibited at the 1912 Canadian Exhibition as the most precious item ($10,080). Sold to Princess A. Bibesco

69. Diamond wing tiara set with circular-cut diamonds, central cushion-shaped fancy-brown diamond of 33.48/ cts. 1909

Two of the most original bandeaux from the period before the First World War are evidence of Cartier's intimate knowledge of Worth's fashions and of textiles, fabrics and embroidery in general. Mrs Leeds bought the first of these two bandeaux, in the form of a 28-cm-long embroidered tapestry. Platinum threads formed a transparent base, the 'web' onto which the diamond plant-tendrils were embroidered. It is interesting to note that two years later, in 1914, Fabergé used a similar type of 'platinum embroidery' on his 'mosaic egg', and Cartier's original idea was taken up again by LaCloche in 1925. The second tiara used black moiré silk as a background on which elongated concentric diamond ellipses reproduced the shimmering surface structure of silk. This fabric *trompe-l'oeil* bandeau found its way into the collection of Princess Bibesco. At the same time bandeaux were beginning to be worn with aigrettes, a fashion which was launched by Paul Poiret. In New York Cartier sold Mrs Stotesbury a bandeau with a 23.40-carat drop diamond projecting upwards as its central peak. He also attached the historic Star of the East diamond to a similar mounting for Mrs Mclean, and in 1914 he designed a simpler model for Mrs Leeds, surmounted by a single drop pearl.

The bandeaux of the 1920s showed the geometric wealth of invention which characterized art deco forms: openwork honeycomb patterns, star shapes of Islamic origin and lozenges which were fully developed in Cartier's work from 1913/14 and which recurred in identical form on bracelets and necklaces. In keeping with the fashion for multipurpose jewelry, these bandeaux could easily be dismantled and turned into bracelets, brooches and earclips. As late as 1938 a multipurpose bandeau was made for Barbara Hutton (then Countess Haugwitz-Reventlow); its diamond drops were removable, so that it could be worn as a bracelet, while its star and half-moon motifs could be used as brooches.

Occasional excursions into exotic regions enlivened the simple silhouette of the bandeau. From 1923 dates an onyx and diamond bandeau of Egyptian character surmounted by stylized lotus blossoms inspired by tomb frescoes at Deir el Bersha. Another model was based on a simple diamond bandeau which was bought back from a customer in London in 1929 and felicitously enhanced by the addition of engraved turquoise palmettes, a Greek design from the third century BC.

In 1931 Viscountess Astor ordered a diamond Peacock Bandeau: its openwork band was made up of lozenge-shaped designs and its central pearl was flanked by two peacocks made of diamond drops, while a stylized peacock fan crowned the motif like a canopy.

The linear form of the bandeau matched the geometrical style of art deco, and was also an ideal complement for bobbed hair, the *garçonne* hairstyle which had begun to catch on around 1917. Colette and Polaire had worn a similar shock of hair as early as 1903, when it was considered a revolutionary thing to do, and at a somewhat later date the revue dancer Caryathis launched the alternative Joan-of-Arc cut. Worn low on the forehead below a bobbed hairstyle, the bandeau, like the long cigarette-holder and hip-length pearl sautoir, embodied the chic and eroticism of the 1920s vamp.

In 1925 Cartier's London workshops produced a bandeau which the designer Charles Jacqueau had worked on previously in Paris: crossed by a single arch, it was indebted in form to the barred crown of the Middle Ages and enclosed the bobbed hair like a helmet. It must also have been influenced by the hair ornament worn by Lina Cavalieri in the Massenet opera *Thaïs*, set in early-Christian Alexandria. Jacqueau took over its lateral ear motif which, in a bandeau made for Queen Marie of Romania, gave the embarrassing impression of earflaps.

Meander tiaras

The name Meander is derived from the small river Maiandros in Phrygia. In ancient Greece the river's serpentine curves inspired the design for an ornamental band of regular lines set at right-angles to each other. It was a popular design in both architecture and vase-painting. When Cartier's workshops began using the meander in 1902 on tiaras and stomachers, there were no doubt people who could still remember the most famous of all nineteenth-century meander tiaras, that of Empress Eugénie. She had ordered it from Bapst in 1867 and for two years wore the Regent diamond as part of it. It was during this same period that Princess Mathilde was often to be seen wearing two meander bracelets.

In the classical phase which preceded art deco and which produced a profusion of new ideas in Cartier's designs, the adoption of the meander was almost *de rigueur*, and it may be seen on a number of tiaras, especially those in the form of a *kokoshnik*. One such meander tiara was made in 1907 for Baroness Henri de Rothschild, with a circular floral motif at its centre; and the following year a meander *kokoshnik* was sent to Princess Shakovskoy in Russia. In 1912 Countess von Fels and Mme Larivière of Argentina both chose almost identical meander tiaras from Cartier's.

Sun tiaras

Like the meander tiara, the sun tiara was based on the form of the *kokoshnik*. 'Sunbeams' made of diamond radiate from a central point close to the hairline, most of them circumscribed within a flat ellipse called a 'sun'. Several of these ellipses may be placed on top of each other, in which case one speaks of several 'suns'.

The sun tiara may well have originated in the mythological tradition of the Baroque theatre, where goddesses and demons would appear wearing a radial glittering head ornament. The Queen of the Night in Mozart's *Magic Flute* was one of the last representatives of this pagan spirit-world to be seen on a stage in the Enlightenment era.

Sun tiaras are recorded from the beginning of the nineteenth century. At the 1889 World Fair the jeweler Vever exhibited a model containing a 54-carat diamond. A Russian photograph taken in 1914 of the wedding presents of Princess Youssoupov clearly shows the family's sun tiara.

Cartier's first sun tiaras date from 1904 and were delivered to J. P. Morgan in New York and Countess Suffolk in London. In London Cartier's were still designing sun tiaras in the 1920s, some of which

were set with a large sapphire or emerald cabochon at the centre. The last sun tiara was ordered in 1926 by the daughter of Mrs Cavendish-Bentinck.

Winged tiaras

In Greek mythology, Hermes, the messenger of the gods, was depicted wearing a winged helmet and shoes. He remained a popular figure in pictorial representations right down to the nineteenth century, including, for example, the statue by Bertel Thorwaldsen in Copenhagen (1818). In the second half of the nineteenth century the winged motif made its appearance on Richard Wagner's operatic stage. Germanic winged helmets were worn by such acclaimed singers as the Croatian soprano Milka Ternina as Brünnhilde or much later the Danish *Heldentenor* Lauritz Melchior as Siegfried. Cartier's Valkyrie aigrette of 1899 is evidence of the Wagner mania which gripped Paris when the soprano Lucienne Bréval performed. The winged motif passed quickly from the theatre to fancy-dress balls and thereafter became fashionable in the form of a winged tiara.

The jeweler Alphonse Fouquet had designed a winged tiara in 1883 and six years later the firm of Boucheron's former colleague Debut (Debut & Coulon) exhibited a tiara in the form of doves' wings.

At Cartier's it was once again J. P. Morgan who sparked off the new fashion. In 1901 Cartier produced a winged tiara which was made in Charpentier's workshop. It had ten wings arranged to create a lively interplay of lines, and the American banker liked it. In 1909 Cartier had an expensive model manufactured for him in Lavabre's workshop with a fancy-brown 33-carat diamond at its centre; this, too, found its way to America. In contrast to the earlier models, the winged tiara made for Lady Ross of England was a naturalistic imitation of elongated birds' wings. Years later, in 1935, Cartier's in London were to receive a final order for a winged tiara, this time from the Duchess of Roxburghe.

Plant tiaras

Like the headband, the chaplet of classical antiquity is regarded as the forebear of the tiara. It was originally worn in the service of fertility rites and subsequently awarded as a distinction on the occasion of victory celebrations and other cultic festivals. In Rome an oak wreath was the reward for Augustus's service to the state, whereas a golden laurel wreath honoured the victorious general. At the time of the Renaissance, great poets were crowned with a laurel wreath to signify them as princes among poets, and in 1804 Napoleon crowned himself emperor in much the same way.

Cartier's began producing plant and floral tiaras shortly after 1900. The majority were laurel or olive tiaras in the form of a wreath; an example of the latter was to be seen in 1907 in the wedding jewelry made for Marie Bonaparte. Laurel motifs continued to appear in garland-style wreaths, independently of tiaras, and it would certainly not be wide of the mark to claim that Cartier's garlands were based in general on the laurel leaf and acanthus shoots.

Mrs Keppel ordered a laurel tiara in Paris in 1903, to be followed in

1904 by Boni de Castellane, husband of Anna Gould, and by Countess Greffulhe. Laurel tiaras enjoyed great popularity in America, as is shown by the models ordered by the two banking families of Drexel and Stotesbury, as well as that of the American Lady Astor. As late as 1927 Queen Victoria Eugenia of Spain ordered a tiara with arching laurel wreaths intertwined around two horizontal garlands of leaves, a thematic invention which, considering the predominant style of art deco at this time, can be explained only by reference to the requirements of traditional court etiquette.

In 1902 and 1903 the Paris branch of Cartier's created two fern tiaras, one of which was bought by Sir Ernest Cassel, the private financial adviser and friend of Edward VII. The banker, who had entered the London establishment of Bischoffsheim & Goldschmidt in 1873, later went on to mine ore in Sweden, had an interest in the American railways as well as Egyptian irrigation schemes, and became a regular visitor to the rue de la Paix.

The tiara exhibition organized by Cartier's in London in 1911 included the oak-leaf tiara of the Duchess of Norfolk. Lady Granard, too, frequently wore an oak-leaf tiara that was much admired.

Naturalistic flowers, such as the jeweler Oscar Massin had produced in the nineteenth century, were seldom found in Cartier's range; thus floral tiaras were comparatively rare, although two were to be seen at the 1911 exhibition. Cartier's only other botanically authentic plants were in fact part of the series of gemstone potted plants influenced by Carl Fabergé. In 1911 Countess von Bredow ordered a trefoil tiara to be sent to her in Germany; it was based on a model of uncertain origin which the German empress frequently wore in Berlin.

Genuine floral tiaras were, however, produced in the London workshops at this time, although they gave the impression of an anachronistic revival of Massin's rose motifs. Individual rose blooms could be detached from the tiara and worn separately as brooches. As late as 1947, the Nizam of Hyderabad chose a diamond necklace and a rose-blossom tiara from Cartier's in London as wedding presents for Princess Elizabeth.

Wheat-ear tiaras

Demeter was the Greek goddess of agriculture and fertility, and her priestesses wore sacred wheat-ears in their hair. It is doubtful whether complete wheat-ear tiaras were ever produced by Greek and Etruscan goldsmiths, although pieces which have survived include the remarkable wheat-ear necklace now in the Hermitage in Leningrad, together with Etruscan hairpins and pendant brooches.

After a brief vogue at the time of the First Empire, the wheat-ear motif returned in the second half of the nineteenth century, when jewelers such as Castellani and Fontenay were influenced by the techniques of Etruscan goldsmithry. The 'Ceres' tiara of Oscar Massin (1861) is one early example of this neo-Etrusco-Roman fashion.

Cartier's first wheat-ear ornament was in the form of an aigrette and dates from 1901. Wheat-ear tiaras consisted either of ears of wheat tied in bundles at their centre, or else of husks of wheat which followed the rhythmic movement of the tiara band. A particularly delicate example consisted of two bundles of wheat with freely moving husks, which produced the illusion of a breath of wind passing through a field of wheat. Cartier's wheat-ear tiaras were available in any combination of stones: one bought by the Ottoman Riffat Pasha combined ears of wheat with diamond drops; and the wheat-ear tiara chosen by the banker Maurice Ephrussi was studded with rare pink pearls.

Tiaras with vertical ornaments

Even in Byzantium the circlet or *stemma*, which had originally developed out of the diadem, had included ornaments projecting vertically upwards from a narrow band. These projections, which were in the form of geometrical motifs, were found only on women's crowns. Not until the Middle Ages were similar ornaments placed on men's crowns, as on the Crown of St Stephen in the Hungarian crown jewels. The motifs varied according to the social rank of the wearer and hence the function of the crown, and they ranged from heraldic lilies to rhythmic dentate motifs.

In Cartier's case, the preferred ornaments consisted of drop diamonds or pearls set, pointing downwards, on a *kokoshnik* or Louis XVI-style garland. A tiara made in 1905 for Mrs Leeds consisted of a continuous series of Louis XVI garlands, surmounted by seven diamond drops. Others of similar inspiration had marquise or brilliant diamonds as their vertical ornaments. In 1906 the Charpentier workshop produced the 'Renaissance' tiara of curving tendril-like motifs, surmounted by five rectangular emeralds. Another group dispensed with any structural base and set seven drop diamonds on top of a delicate garland. The first such tiara was made in 1904, with a central stone of 39 carats. It could also be worn as a necklace or, alternatively, with round pearls. In 1906 a tiara was sold to the Berlin banker Bleichroeder with a central stone of 13.50 carats and two years later one with a central stone of 27 carats was chosen by Grand Duke Paul of Russia for his wife the Countess of Hohenfelsen.

Tiaras with pendant drops

When the Russian tiara of Grand Duchess Vladimir (now in the possession of Queen Elizabeth II) was temporarily deposited with Cartier's in Paris, the firm used it as the basis for three new tiaras of similar design, all having interlinking circles of diamonds at whose centres hung a pendant pearl. The first of these was made in Picq's workshop in 1911 and consisted of eleven diamonds increasing in size towards the centre. The second and more important one was a reworking of the 1908 tiara owned by the Countess of Hohenfelsen. Those of Cartier's free-moving tiaras which were worked in platinum could generally only be worn on the head with the aid of additional metal fittings. When these metal supports were removed, the tiaras were turned into necklaces or even stomachers. A photograph taken on the occasion of one of Mme de Yturbe's receptions shows the countess wearing the drop tiara as a stomacher, while the stomacher of 1908 has become a hat ornament. The

third piece in this group was made for Mrs Leeds in 1913 and consisted of alternate drop diamonds and pearls.

Between 1906 and 1908 a further series of tiaras was produced at Cartier's with openwork heart motifs, in the centre of each a pendant diamond. Made in the workshops of Harnichard and Bellemans, one of them found its way to Argentina and another came to England, though not until 1919. Perhaps the most stunningly simple tiara of pendant drop diamonds consisted of a pointed arch to which were attached twenty-one briolette diamonds. It was made in 1905 for the soprano Lillian Nordica from Maine, whose brilliant career took her to Paris, London, St Petersburg and New York before she was killed in a shipwreck off New Guinea in 1914. Lillian Nordica was one of the great operatic prima donnas of her day, together with Nellie Melba, Lina Cavalieri and Mary Garden, all of whom wore their Cartier jewels as much on the stage as in private life. Thus Victor Dautremont, Pierre Cartier's young London assistant, was regularly sent down to Covent Garden with extravagant jewelry for Nellie Melba, which had to be warmed before it could touch the sensitive skin of the artist. These tragediennes of the operatic stage enjoyed the ecstatic idolization of a public which was to turn its attention, after 1925, to the more remote idols of Hollywood.

Aigrettes

Ever since aigrettes became important in the seventeenth century as vertically projecting head ornaments, they appeared as subject to cross-fertilization between Eastern and Western cultural influences: the Victoria and Albert Museum in London preserves sketches of aigrettes by the Danish designer Arnold Lulls, dating from around 1610, which invite comparison with an aigrette worn by the Mogul emperor Shah Jahan in a miniature dated 1616/17. Whether we are dealing here with a piece made in Lulls' workshop or with a Mogul work of the same period may be a matter for conjecture, but it is clear that the East as well as Europe had an interest in the aigrette.

Aigrettes were also popular in the eighteenth century and are preserved in the set of cornelian ornaments which form part of the Saxon crown jewels (pre-1719), as well as in sketches by Augustin Duflos, who made Louis XV's crown. In the reign of Louis XVI, as fashions took on an Oriental look and inspiration was no longer sought in distant India but in Constantinople, the aigrette was the crowning jewel on exotic sultans' turbans. An aigrette of a heron's feather and drop pearls in the Russian crown jewels was in fact called the 'Sultane', and Marie Antoinette had herself painted by Vigée-Lebrun with an Oriental hairstyle crowned by an aigrette. Madame Mère, Napoleon's mother, similarly wore an aigrette on the occasion of her son's coronation in Notre-Dame.

Aigrettes again became fashionable around 1860. Oscar Massin launched them in the form of small posies worn with or without bird-of-paradise feathers. His most famous aigrette was a model of five burgeoning diamond posies for the Duchess of Medina Coeli. Tiffany designed a peacock-feather aigrette, set with the 'Brunswick' Diamond, which was admired at the Philadelphia Centennial Exhibition of 1876.

70. Emerald and diamond aigrette mounted
with 2 pear-shaped cabochon emeralds on a
19th-century diamond leaf motif.
Commissioned in 1913 by Grand Duchess
Vladimir

71. Aigrette bandeau designed as a pierced
circular-cut diamond band with lancet
centre. 1913

During the 1890s aigrettes became the most popular of all forms of head ornament. They complemented Oriental turbans and historical costumes, and at masked balls they became an indispensable accessory. At the great fancy-dress ball held in the Winter Palace in St Petersburg in 1903, Grand Duke Michael and Prince Youssoupov appeared dressed as boyars, with aigrettes in their fur hats. In Paris, fancy-dress balls became illustrated broadsheets of history and mythology, in which illusion and reality were mingled in some ingenious game.

Cartier's aigrettes were an essential part of Worth's evening wear. The requisite feathers came from specialist establishments, the most famous of which were Lurot in the rue des Petits-Champs and Judith Barbier in the rue Daunou, who employed 450 women assistants. The most popular feathers were those of the Egyptian white egret (from which the hair ornament took its name), the bird-of-paradise from New Guinea, the Cape ostrich, the Egyptian ibis and the Central American green-shimmering quetzal. Black feathers, which in Cartier's jewels provided the desired pitch-black contrast with diamonds, were initially dyed. Especially rare feathers were sold individually and by weight.

Not only Worth obtained his feathers from Judith Barbier; so, too, did Worth's former colleague, Paul Poiret, who was shortly to undermine his master's supremacy and appropriate the aigrette as his own symbol. Poiret had opened his own business in the rue Pasquier in 1903, and, together with Raoul Dufy, who continued to design fabrics for him until 1912, he, like Louis Cartier, contributed to shaping the rising art deco style. He designed corsetless dresses, the tunic dress and minaret dress and also, in 1910, the narrow skirt or hobble skirt, against which the Pope inveighed. What was important, in the immediate context of tiaras, was Poiret's Oriental style with its turbans and striking aigrettes, a fashion influenced by the Ballets Russes and Persian miniatures. In 1911 Poiret held a magnificent party on the theme of the Thousand and One Nights, at which three hundred invited guests paid court to their host, who received them dressed as a sultan on a golden throne. Poiret's ball was followed in 1912 by the 'Persian Balls' of the Marquise de Chabrillan and the Comtesse de Clermont-Tonnerre, at which frescoes by Bakst provided a background for Oriental tableaux of Hindu slaves, Shiraz dancers, elephants, tigers and peacocks. The heyday of the Cartier aigrette coincided with those years preceding the First World War when Oriental influences were most clearly felt.

In 1899 the stock book lists a 'Persian' aigrette, and in 1901 a wheat-ear aigrette, together with a lily-of-the-valley aigrette made of eight diamond drops suspended from a platinum thread. This first period, which was dominated by floral motifs, came to a climax in 1908 with the magnificent aigrette tiara of Grand Duchess Vladimir: whenever they moved, its three curving aigrette bundles, set with Indian-cut briolettes like cascades of blossom, evoked the illusion of dewdrops shaken from a stem. And yet the symmetrically arranged shoots made no attempt to disguise their stylistic origins in the freer wheat-ear tiara of the nineteenth century and in Massin's aigrette for the Duchess of Medina Coeli. From 1910, when Cartier began making

72. 'Chinese gong' aigrette, the circular-cut diamond mount with *calibré*-cut ruby border. Weight of centre diamond: 3.37 cts. Sold to Countess Ouvarov in 1912

74. 'Pine-cone' aigrette in circular- and rose-cut diamonds. 1913

73. Diamond aigrette mounted with 3 pear-shaped and a cushion-shaped diamond in diamond surround. Commissioned in 1912

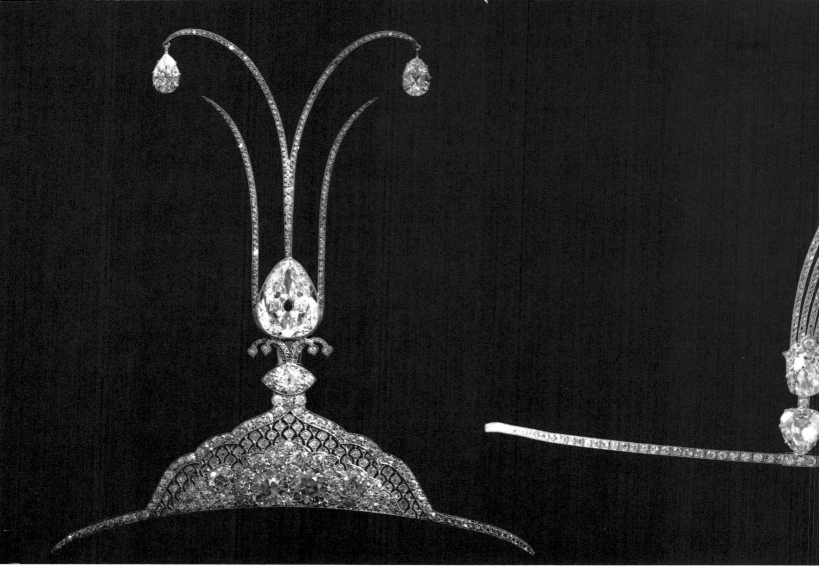

75. Diamond aigrette designed as a lobed diamond base with navette-cut diamond tip and pear-shaped diamond of 19.42 cts from which rise 2 scrolled diamond lines with pear-shaped diamonds weighing 4.55 cts. Commissioned by Prince Gortchakov in 1912

76. Diamond aigrette designed as a scrolled diamond plume in rose-cut diamonds and suspending a briolette-cut diamond. Weights of 2 diamonds at the base: 8.12 and 16.60 cts. Commissioned in 1913

77. Diamond aigrette designed as a stylized rose-cut diamond plume. 1913. Sold to Lord Derby

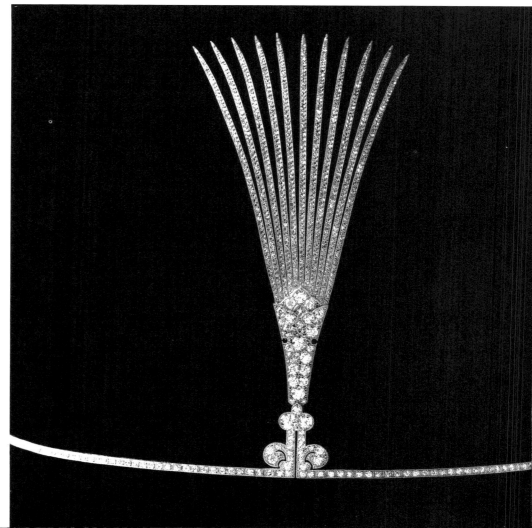

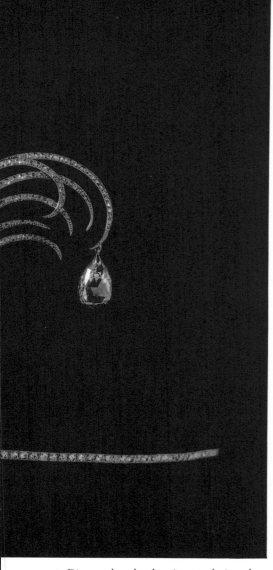

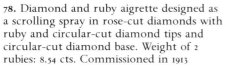

78. Diamond and ruby aigrette designed as a scrolling spray in rose-cut diamonds with ruby and circular-cut diamond tips and circular-cut diamond base. Weight of 2 rubies: 8.54 cts. Commissioned in 1913

79. Briolette diamond aigrette designed as 3 floral sprays with circular-cut diamond base, the tips suspending briolette-cut diamonds. Commissioned by Grand Duchess Vladimir in 1908

aigrettes in the Oriental style of the Ballets Russes and Poiret, he reproduced Arabian grille motifs and Persian carpet medallions. Two years later, a Chinese gong motif first appeared in the design of an aigrette. Two calyx-shaped radial aigrettes of 1911 and 1912 were based upon an eighteenth-century model in the Green Vault in Dresden.

Also dating from 1912 is the first aigrette with an Indian *sarpech* motif. The *sarpech* was a golden feather ornament studded with gemstones and generally consisting of a disc with a stalk growing out of it, from the end of which dangled a pendant stone. Cartier's *sarpech* aigrettes were not only admired at Oriental balls in Paris and London but were even bought by the Indian potentates with whom Jacques Cartier did business in London. As late as 1937 the Maharajah of Nawanagar commissioned a *sarpech* from Cartier's which was set with the Tiger's-Eye diamond weighing 61.55 carats. Apart from Oriental aigrettes, Cartier also launched a number of particularly lavish examples which were set with only a single gemstone. Thus the heron aigrette ordered by Paul-Louis Weiller consisted of a single 69-carat drop diamond. In general, however, the most popular aigrette, even as late as the 1920s, was one consisting of bundled rays. The designer Paul Iribe and his group influenced Cartier's aigrettes with fanciful arabesques; and the motif of a fountain, which became a *leitmotif* of art deco, also found favour as a head ornament: the vertically rising aigrette needed only to be bent back on itself, like a jet of water, to create the impression of a spray.

Hair combs

Hair combs, with their twofold function of holding the hair in place and decorating it, were popular throughout the whole of the nineteenth century. But it was only during the art nouveau period that they became the leading fashion accessory, whether made of horn or tortoise shell, or decorated with osiers and creepers made of enamel and pearls. Cartier had begun producing combs around 1850. An invoice dating from 1859 shows the case-maker Trepat charging Fr18 for a large comb-case, and Fr30 for two small ones. Combs and tiaras were often sold together, just as they were often worn together.

Although art nouveau was of only marginal importance in Cartier's work, Charpentier's workshop in the rue de Richelieu produced a comb with an art nouveau snake motif in 1888. The most expensive combs were a series of five, dating from 1905 and sold to W. K. Vanderbilt in New York. The combs could be assembled to form a bandeau and were set with five garland-framed diamond drops, the largest of which weighed 39.60 carats (see ill., p. 73).

Combs once again became sought after in the rue de la Paix during the art deco period, when couturiers such as Callot launched their Spanish fashions. Made of coral, onyx and diamonds, they were no longer overshadowed by the larger tiara, but often formed the only head ornament, on which designers lavished the whole of their imagination.

Art nouveau – Religious jewelry – The war years

$\mathcal{A}$T THE TURN OF THE CENTURY there were two opposing forces in jewelry design. On the one side were the entrenched supporters of the elegant garland style, led by Louis Cartier; on the other, the supporters of art nouveau, such as René Lalique and Georges Fouquet, who declared war on a style that was lacking in emblems and figurative elements.[1] As devotees of the cult of a new symbolism derived from nature, they propagated the idea of asymmetrical, sinuous lines in ornamentation, seeing them as part of a dynamic field of force charged with life. Goldsmiths and *orfèvre-bijoutiers* already subscribed to the art nouveau aesthetic,[2] whereas the jewelers who worked chiefly with gemstones continued to embrace the garland style. On the whole, the latter were not interested in the great variety of new art nouveau materials such as enamel, horn and ivory and the celluloid synthetics. 'We use very little material and a great deal of stones,' Pierre Cartier remarked to one of his customers.

The art nouveau artist aimed at reform, and this aesthetic stance, together with his unusual materials, was bound to ensure him public interest and, unlike the commercial jeweler, might even entitle him to limited state support. Under its president Louis Aucoc, the 'Chambre Syndicale de la Bijouterie, Joaillerie et Orfèvrerie', founded in 1864, and the 'Union Centrale des Arts Décoratifs', which was reorganized in 1872, arranged an active programme of competitions, courses and schools. In addition, there were annual exhibitions, or salons, held in the Grand Palais; all of them, practically without exception, propagated the art nouveau style. There were some jewelers prepared to entertain a compromise between art nouveau and the garland style: Vever, Aucoc and above all Boucheron attempted to combine the garland with the writhing plant forms of art nouveau, but they were never able to resolve the conflict between symmetry and asymmetry. Louis Cartier, on the contrary, was decidedly cool to art nouveau, which may help to explain why a few years later, between 1906 and 1908, the linear style of art deco was able to develop much more naturally and purely out of the geometrical patterns of his own garland style than it could out of the style of those artists who had been exclusively committed to art nouveau.

In spite of Cartier's negative attitude, a number of unequivocal examples of art nouveau jewelry may be attributed to him in the period shortly before 1900 when there were certainly some fruitful contacts with art nouveau artists, including the Belgian jeweler Philippe Wolfers (1858–1929), who supplied Cartier with small snake brooches, and Georges Le Turcq who, on the occasion of the one-thousandth performance of Gounod's *Faust* at the Paris Opéra, produced a silvergilt bracelet depicting scenes from the opera.[3] Le Turcq was also responsible for a number of floral enamel brooches, including a Japanese azalea, an orchid and a red enamel convolvulus. Cartier's records for 1887 include an entry for a brooch by Violard depicting the most popular of all art nouveau insects, the dragonfly, and another entry dated 1900 mentions a pearl-studded brooch by the little-known Zorra, with a gold enamel girl's head in the 'nouveau style'.[4] The description 'nouveau style' and 'art moderne' alternate with each other in Cartier's books, in an attempt to distinguish these few items from others in the radically different garland style. The majority of the art nouveau pieces taken up by Cartier were from Charpentier's workshop, which supplied a number of floral brooches in *plique-à-jour*, or translucent enamel, between 1899 and 1901 – vine leaves and ivy, thistles and cornflowers were among Charpentier's favourite plant motifs, and were popular for their lively contours. Although the customers who bought these art nouveau brooches were largely recruited from bourgeois circles or from the artistically avant-garde, Cartier's was able to interest the fashion-conscious Duchess of Devonshire in one of Charpentier's floral brooches, and Louis Cartier even recommended a set of enamelled art nouveau buttons to Prince Lieven of Russia while he was staying at the Hotel Continental.

Another type of jewelry suited to art nouveau forms was the hatpin, some of which were set with pearls of up to 100 grains in weight. During the Renaissance the strangely distorted shapes of baroque pearls had given rise to amusing dwarfs, sea monsters and other mythical animals. In Cartier's jewels they became spherical landscapes crawling with frogs and snakes.

Among the most important of Cartier's art nouveau products were two necklaces. One of them, from Louis Aucoc's workshop, depicted a row of daisies from which was suspended a blue peacock pendant. The peacock motif had been popular during the reign of Napoleon III, although the earliest example in Cartier's jewels is dated 1883. After 1905 it gave its name to the colour contrast of blue and green. The second necklace, which was sold to Hungary, was made of *plique-à-jour* enamel[5] with a design of turquoise-studded fuchsias.

The quintessential art nouveau gemstone, the opal, which recurred time and again in the work of such artists as Gaillard and Lalique, was never of much interest to Louis Cartier. Admittedly, a delightful heart-shaped opal pendant was made for Nellie Melba in 1903, but it sounds almost like an excuse when, in a reply to a supplier in Antwerp, Louis justified his reluctance to work with opals by appealing to the superstition concerning them which, he claimed, was particularly pronounced in France.[6]

Restrained echoes of the art nouveau style appear in association with neo-Gothic motifs in the numerous religious pendants which were stocked by Louis Cartier's father, Alfred, who was a devout Catholic. In France the years between 1901 and 1906 were marked by a series of power struggles between Church and State, which led to a strict division of their respective spheres of influence. Emile Combes, the socialist minister of the interior and minister of culture, threatened congregations and closed down parochial schools. The ecclesiastical opposition, however, succeeded in organizing a patriotically inspired protest campaign called 'La Ligue de la Patrie française' which met on the steps of barricaded churches and used popular art on religious themes for propaganda purposes. Joseph Chaumet had already caused a stir at the 1900 World Fair with his allegorical 'Christus Vincit', and four years later, at the international exhibition held in St Louis, Missouri, he exhibited his monumental sculpture 'Via Vitae' or 'Way of Life', the symbolism of which embraced all the world's major religions. Cartier's range included not only patriotic themes such as 'Joan of Arc at the stake' (1905), but silver statues of St Anthony of Padua, which numbered Jean-Philippe Worth and King Edward VII of England among their varied purchasers. The most popular line, however, was in medallions on religious themes, based on the work of the French medallion-maker Frédéric Charles Victor de Vernon, who had won the Prix de Rome in 1887. Cartier ordered them from Duval's workshop in the rue de Louvre. If we are to believe the magazine *Femina*, Vernon's medallions addressed themselves 'to the sensitivities of young daughters for whose profound edification they were intended'; they included themes such as Christ and John the Baptist (obtainable at Cartier's from 1885), the Immaculate Conception, the Virgin among virgins, the *virgo purissima*, as well as St Cecilia.

80. Diamond skull and cross-bones pendant. Commissioned by Baroness Henri de Rothschild in 1913

From the Baroque Age onward, poets, painters and sculptors had used the death's-head motif as a reminder of earthly transience, the *vanitas vanitatis*. Cartier's shelves contained death's-heads made of coral, and in 1913 Baroness Henri de Rothschild ordered one in diamond to add to her already exemplary collection.[7]

Religious miniature art like Vernon's medallions was generally made of *plique-à-jour* enamel, which ultimately derived its mystic appeal from Gothic church windows. When in the course of the First World War the cathedral of Rheims — which Jean Cocteau had dismissed as 'a mountain of old lace' — went up in flames, Jacques Cartier suggested buying up fragments of the cathedral's stained glass windows and resetting the angels and saints in articles of jewelry.[8]

During these same years (1914–18), a new form of patriotic jewelry came to the fore, based on martial motifs. The firm's leading employees, including the three Cartier brothers — Louis, Pierre and Jacques — were all at the front, so that the workshops shrank and limited themselves to producing small-scale works using gemstones of no great size.[9] Just as during the Franco-Prussian War of 1870 there had been a market for items of jewelry made of shrapnel and military emblems, what was now produced, against the background of the Battles of the Marne and of Verdun, were pendants and pins from which were suspended aeroplanes, the Red Cross or the Cross of Lorraine, and miniature replicas of the 75-bore cannon, 'notre glorieux 75'. While the pendants with fragments of glass from Rheims Cathedral conveyed the impression of priceless reliquaries, the brass rings which were made from grenades fired by the 75-bore cannon and which Cartier's sold as armlets, as their contribution to the war effort, became actual trophies of war.[10] The iron jewelry made in Berlin at the time of Prussia's resistance against Napoleon had aroused similar feelings of patriotism. Other traditional ornamental motifs which had previously been free of any martial symbolism were technically reinterpreted: a minor modification turned the black-and-white onyx bow-knot into an aircraft propeller, an item which remained one of Cartier's most popular lines

81. Pendant mounted with a fragment of stained glass from a broken window in Rheims Cathedral, within rose-cut diamonds and topazes. On silk cord. 1920

throughout the war years. The illusion of a martial trophy jewel was perfected by Cartier's *étuis* in the form of military peaked caps, French naval berets and English soldiers' caps. Among these picturesque examples of international rig-out, the 'machine-gun' brooch was admired even by the British Prime Minister Lloyd George, while the 'Lebel Bayonet' brooch was purchased by Lord Lonsdale. The somewhat eccentric Princess Murat decided in favour of a brooch depicting a Red Cross ambulance, perhaps to remind her of the widely admired Misia Sert, who with Paul Iribe at the wheel had turned delivery vans from the Paris fashion-houses into ambulances.

Of all the workshops which supplied Cartier's with such intriguing examples of trophy jewelry between 1915 and 1918, the most important was that of Paul Templier (1866–1944), who at that time was President of the Chamber of Commerce. His work, which was based on drawings by Théodore Lambert, had already attracted attention at the 1901 salon by virtue of its simple linear style. His son, Raymond, was later to transfer his father's business from the Place des Victoires to the rue du Quatre Septembre.

The commision which brought Cartier the greatest honour during the First World War related to General Foch (1851–1929). Shortly after the offensive of the 'Battle of France' in July 1918, Foch was appointed commander of the combined allied forces, and on 6 August the title of field marshal was formally conferred on him by the President of the Republic Raymond Poincaré and his Prime Minister Georges Clemenceau. The ceremony was held in the château at Bompon.[11] The marshal's baton, that symbol of authority, was the work of Cartier's. From the sixteenth century onward, it had been made of blue velvet (over wood or silver) and was originally adorned with gold fleurs-de-lys. During the time of the First Empire, its decoration was changed to imperial bees, which under Louis-Philippe became stars and under Napoleon III eagles. With its gold and silvergilt ornamentation, the marshal's baton presented to Foch marked a return to the star pattern of the nineteenth century; it was surmounted by the motto *Terror Belli — Decus Pacis* ('Terror of War — Adornment of Peace'). The same design was used in November of the same year, when a second marshal's baton, again by Cartier's, was presented to Marshal Pétain in Metz. (Both batons are now in the Musée de l'Armée in Paris.)

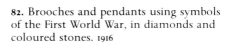

82. Brooches and pendants using symbols of the First World War, in diamonds and coloured stones. 1916

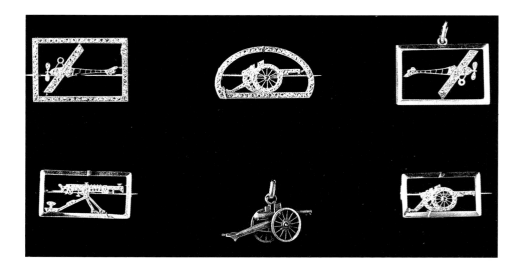

Under the spell of Fabergé

AT THE TURN OF THE CENTURY European interior design was a pale relic of its former self: gone was the linear order of the eighteenth century, the spare, elegant, expensive furniture carefully accenting classical proportions. Its place had been taken by a dark, inchoate decor; heavy curtains kept out the daylight, and dark furniture heightened the impression of artificial gloom. But this twilit world of shadows was brought to life and illuminated by every kind of object of virtu. Photograph frames, plants and animals carved in gemstones, table ornaments and small clocks shone out like brightly coloured points of light. From priceless treasures to the most garish kitsch, such objects were the latest fad in the homes of the aristocracy, the upper classes and the stars of the theatre in London, Paris and New York. The representatives of this society, be they Lady de Grey, Mrs Keppel or Leopold de Rothschild, had discovered the bibelots of Carl Fabergé and his rivals, popularized them as ideal gifts from St Petersburg, and raised them to the height of chic, acceptable to any member of their own circle, up to and including the court itself.

Around 1900 Fabergé was producing what was indisputably the most refined enamel of the day, using a process which remained a closely guarded secret within the confines of his predominantly Scandinavian workforce. Most of his enamel ornaments were made using the *guilloché* technique and designed in the Louis XVI style of the late 1780s. Those which found their way to Europe as gifts gave Parisian craftsmen the idea of reviving their own local eighteenth-century style transmitted through a Russian intermediary.

Fabergé's great skill lay in applying five or six layers of enamel chosen from 144 different shades of colour to a metallic base of silver or 14-carat gold. The firing took place at a temperature of 700–800° C, the metal first having been engraved with lines and dots to produce a geometric pattern which remained visible through the transparent enamel, often creating the impression of shot silk.

Cartier's Russian-inspired range contained a similar technical variety of *guilloché* work: frames and small clocks have the sunray pattern engraved in straight lines radiating from a central point, while other items include a moiré silk or scale motif, or else the Russian undulating *guilloché* design was evolved into zigzags.

In 1904 Cartier's wrote to Yahr's workshop in Moscow, which produced items for the goldsmith Ovchinnikov among others, requesting Yahr to send two complete palettes of his enamel colours to the rue de la Paix. As a result of this request Yahr began to manufacture and enamel items for Cartier's, including cigarette cases, frames, table bells, clocks and belt buckles.[1] Although Cartier's were unable in their Paris workshops to match the variety of enamel colours of their Russian models, they succeeded instead in creating a number of new colour combinations, such as the blue-green or violet-green match which Louis Cartier himself liked. A white enamel border sometimes framed the *en plein* enamelled surface of an object. In a few instances the technique of opalescent enamelling was used for the face of small clocks, a technique which involved variegating some of the layers as they were being successively fired, until the famous iridescent surface effect of the opal was produced. The most precious product of Cartier's experimentation with the technique of *guilloché* enamelling was undoubtedly the Easter egg made in 1906 and later presented to Tsar Nicholas II (see p. 122), which was followed in 1907 by the production of a second egg, this time in the form of a small clock with a star diamond which showed the hour.

A second aspect of Fabergé's work to find an echo in Cartier's jewels was one which reveals the entire wealth of the Siberian mineral deposits — gold-mounted, enamelled objects of virtu were produced in nephrite, lapis lazuli, agate and serpentine, and there was not one which could not have stood comparison with the most fabulous treasures of the Renaissance curiosity cabinets. The fact that these gemstone bibelots were admired in Paris and London may be explained not only by reference to the fascination which the remote Russian lands exercised on cosmopolitan Europeans, but also because, quite apart from their aesthetic perfection, Fabergé's products were intended to be functionally useful: a jade apple might turn out to be a glue-pot, and the garlanded Louis-XVI column would conceal a barometer.

Pierre Cartier visited Russia in both 1904 and 1905, and in the course of his travels familiarized himself with the leading workshops in St Petersburg and Moscow. The lapidary Svietchnikov was among those who, as a result, began supplying Cartier's with animals made according to either his own designs or those of Cartier's.[2] If, however, the article contained gold and enamel, Svietchnikov had it completed by the above-mentioned Yahr, before it was sent on to the rue de la Paix. In 1904 there were no fewer than 160 commissions which the by now overworked Yahr was expected to send to Paris. His best craftsmen having enlisted in the war against Japan, he requested reinforcements from Cartier's Paris workshops, but the desired help never arrived.

Cartier considered Svietchnikov's animals expensive, and it is certainly true that they cost more than the models of Karl Woerffel on the Obvodny Canal in St Petersburg, who was Fabergé's supplier.[3] From Woerffel's shop Pierre Cartier ordered an alabaster hen, gemstone fruit, ashtrays, jade bottles and objects of virtu made in purpurine.[4] This latter substance was a synthetic dye, crimson in colour, generally thought to have been invented by the Italian Alessio Mattioli around 1750; it was taken up again by Petouchov in the nineteenth century for use in the imperial glassworks, and by 1900 had come to be regarded as one of Fabergé's specialities.

A purpurine toad was also supplied by Ovchinnikov, whose firm had been founded in Moscow in 1853. A branch was opened in St Petersburg twenty years later, but the firm really became known in the West only when it exhibited at the 1900 World Fair. As a rival of Fabergé's, Ovchinnikov's business specialized in *cloisonné* enamelling in the Byzanto-Russian style. Cartier's first orders also included an obsidian elephant and a dog's-head umbrella handle made of jade. The prices of Ovchinnikov's menagerie varied from Fr45 ($11) for the elephant to Fr265 ($66) for the purpurine toad. Size, type of engraving and stone quality were the decisive factors, though purpurine was treated as substantially more expensive than the different types of natural stone.

Not in every case, however, did the taste of Russian suppliers meet with approval in the rue de la Paix: when a rhodonite desk set arrived from the firm of Denissov-Ouralski, which had already supplied Cartier with miniature animals and other objects of virtu, exception was taken to the hideous silver mounting. Sarda, Cartier's contact in St Petersburg, approached Denissov on the matter and reported back to Cartier that 'only with difficulty had Denissov allowed himself to be talked into removing the "ironwork", which he considered elegant and necessary'. Only the inkwell survived the operation, which Denissov himself described as a 'massacre'.

In 1910 Cartier bought two animals direct from Fabergé, a little pig made of pink jade and a cornelian fox. But it is safe to assume that many of the animals nowadays attributed to Fabergé were produced in one or other of the French or Russian workshops which supplied Cartier's needs. In view of their stylistic similarity and the absence of any signature, it is often only the signed and individually lined cases which give any information about the firm which sold them. At all events, a number of animals are found only in Cartier's range, including an ostrich emerging from an egg, and a group of three chickens.

French workshops in the meantime had familiarized themselves remarkably quickly with the popular Russian style. Workshops such as those of Varangoz, Fréville and Césard, together with the Taillerie de Royat, were soon providing the greater part of Cartier's stock. Their suppliers further included the Japanese dealer Yamanaka, who specialized in ivories and bronze animals in the style of *netsukes*, similar to ones which had already served as models in Russia.[5]

The most popular miniature animals in Cartier's menagerie were the ibis, owl, stork, elephant and piglet. Not until 1907, the year in which Fabergé made models of all the animal species at Sandringham as a present for Edward VII, did Louis Cartier begin to fear that the market was being flooded and turn his attention to launching different types of gemstone fruit.[6] Animals had been of little practical use, except as umbrella handles or hand bells, whereas fruit could serve as desk fittings, inkwells or water jugs.

One of Fabergé's specialities which fell on fertile ground and remained popular for many years in Paris, surviving even the passing mania for all things Russian aroused by the Ballets Russes, was his flower vases. As late as 1916 *Vogue* wrote of 'Cartier's dainty hothouses in which fairy-tale trees with gold and silver trunks sprout leaves of jade. On a coral branch a bird begins to sing, just like something out of *Schéhérazade*.'[7] Unlike Fabergé's flowers, those which Cartier sold were in fact all housed within glass cases with an ivory base, the edges of the glass being both protected and decorated by golden stepped motifs. These architectonic shrines allowed the flowers to be arranged inside in stylized groupings. One cannot fail to notice here the influence of the traditional Japanese art of flower arrangement, ikebana, which inspired the design of a number of Cartier's arrangements of individual sprays of cherry blossom and lilies. Also indebted to Japanese models was the picturesque association of plants and birds, together with the motifs of individual calyxes detached from the plant and lying on the ground. This last motif underlined the melancholy charm of transitoriness, just as moonstone cabochons on jade leaves could give the illusion of fresh dew. The propinquity of plant and insect – a grasshopper, for example, or sometimes even a pygmy tortoise – widened the visual range of the floral image, turning it into a still-life.

Cartier's floral vases surpassed those of Fabergé in the number of materials used: carved in agate, lapis lazuli or crystal and decorated with coloured cabochons, their colour was chosen to match the individual flower. New models included flowerpots of jasper or rose quartz for geraniums and cyclamens, some of the pots growing almost to the size of handled buckets which thus framed the flowers in a geometrical design. A particularly elaborate hollyhock raised its powerful stalks out of two pots, its delicate rhodonite blooms intertwined above them like an arbour. Vases and urns made of gemstones alone, and copied by the firm's resident designers from eighteenth- and nineteenth-century models in the Louvre, antedate the floral vases in Cartier's output.

Cartier's flowers differed substantially from Fabergé's and included the magnolia, iris, hyacinth, hydrangea, tulip and lily. They could be monumentally large in size and were unlike Fabergé's more delicate, naturalistic flora.[8] Cartier's basic type remained stylistically unchanged over the years, except that during the 1920s the principles of art deco required a stylized treatment of leaves and calyxes. In 1907 the firm's archives recorded thirty-seven plants which soon found admirers throughout the world, including J. P. Morgan in New York, Lady de Grey in England and King Alfonso XIII of Spain. Among the most expensive plants were the Japanese magnolia, which then cost Fr1,500 ($300) and orchids which sold at up to Fr2,000 ($400) each. The prices charged during the same period by Fabergé in London ranged from 10 guineas ($50) for pansies to 117 guineas ($585) for a chrysanthemum.

The workshop to which Alfred Cartier entrusted the task of producing these flowers and other gemstone objects was that of Berquin-Varangoz's widow at Saint-Siméon in the *département* of Seine-et-Marne. The firm had been awarded a gold medallion in 1904 at the St Louis exhibition. It was taken over in 1918 by Aristide Fourrier (1875–1941) and subsequently bore his name. Except for a period during the war, Fourrier employed between twenty-five and thirty craftsmen, who were joined in 1922 by his son Roland (1906–83). Although no Russian craftsmen were employed, the firm remained conscious that it was producing a Russian speciality, and to the end of his life Fourrier continued to refer to Fabergé as his mentor.[9] From time to time he undertook journeys to Idar-Oberstein in Germany and to London in order to buy minerals and ivory, as well as the specifically 'Russian materials': lapis lazuli, jade and rhodonite. From these were made not only plants but, in far greater numbers, animals, ashtrays, frames and bowls, in addition to the complicated casings of *pendules mystérieuses*. One of the most highly respected of Fourrier's craftsmen was the engraver Hubert who brought to life the birds and flowers which he embellished.

On one occasion a cornflower with a wheat-ear motif, bought direct from Fabergé's, served as a model for Fourrier, but as a general rule the latter would make a copper model using a preliminary sketch provided by Cartier's, who would then forward their approval of the model from the rue de la Paix.[10] The enamel in every available colour was fired on to the metal base, which in the final product was made of silver. Transparent or opaque glass (opaline) produced umbels and blossoms of shimmering translucency. Snow-drops were made of chalcedony, chrysanthemums of jade and later of enamel. Leaves were carved from jade or aventurine quartz, the latter to imitate the rough surface of a geranium leaf.

Whenever enamelled gemstone objects needed additional work, Cartier turned to the workshop of Henri Lavabre in the rue Tiquetonne, where between fifteen and twenty expert craftsmen were employed for up to twelve hours a day. Detailed commissions were carried out in smaller workshops in the Marais, tiny concerns which generally passed from father to son. Lavabre's workshop, like Picq's in the rue du Quatre Septembre, was Cartier's preferred supplier, although internal problems meant that Lavabre's collaboration with Cartier's failed to survive the crisis of the 1930s.[11]

Berquin-Varangoz and, at a later date, Fourrier also experimented with carved figural pieces. Although the realism of Fabergé's gemstone figurines of peasants, coachmen and sweeps found no imitators in France,[12] Fourrier manufactured agate portrait busts of Roman emperors, including Caesar, Vitellius and Vespasian, based on originals in the Louvre. Buddhas were made of jade, rose quartz and turquoise, and remained popular until the late 1920s. Buddha-like was the comical Billiken, the Anglo-Saxon god of the under-world and of plenty. The figure was made of chalcedony, nephrite or agate and, looking like some Disney creation *avant la lettre*, it sat enthroned on ashtrays, table bells or *pendules mystérieuses*.[13] Queen Alexandra was pleased with her Cartier Billiken, and Maxim Gorki presented one to H. G. Wells on the occasion of the latter's visit to Russia.

It was at first by no means certain that all these articles in the Russian style would find favour in Paris and London. At the 1900 World Fair, for example, Fabergé's basket of lilies-of-the-valley, made in 1896, had been criticized for being 'a colour photograph taken from nature'. But the Russian millionaires who had settled in Menton, Nice and Paris and who patronized Cartier's, including Grand Duchess Xenia, Grand Duke Paul and Princess Lobanov-Dolgorouky, expected to find the same items on sale in the rue de la Paix as in their native St Petersburg. They repeatedly suggested to Louis Cartier that he should settle in St Petersburg. For a time he considered taking over in Paris as European representative of the imperial stone-grinding factories in Ekaterinburg (modern Sverd-lovsk), as well as the grinding shops in Peterhof (modern Petrod-vorets), but the project never materialized, any more than did plans for a Cartier agency in Berlin. But a year before taking the plunge in America in 1909, Cartier finally gave in to the insistent pleas of Grand Duchess Vladimir and established himself, after all, in St Petersburg.

Colour plates 17 — 31

17. Art deco designs: *left above:* onyx and pearl tassel, 1922; *left below:* strawberry pendant in onyx, coral and diamonds, 1913; *centre above:* Indian turban ornament in emeralds and diamonds by Charles Jacqueau; *centre:* belt hook with satyrs' heads, 1923, not executed; *centre below:* sapphire and emerald necklace with engraved sapphire beads and engraved sapphire and emerald tablets, 1924; *right above:* epaulette in emeralds, diamonds, onyx and rubies, 1922; *right below:* panther châtelaine in onyx and diamonds by Charles Jacqueau, c.1915

18. Early leather cases in pink and green Indian moroccan leather with eighteenth-century floral festoon repeating the outlines of the jewelry inside: *left:* red leather case containing a pink enamel, rose-cut diamond and gold hatpin, 1908; *above right:* green leather ring case, its base following the contour of the ring; *below right:* green leather case recalling an eighteenth-century sedan-chair and containing a travel clock. All pre-1910

19. *Woman with Black Panther*, watercolour commissioned from George Barbier by Cartier in 1914 as an advertisement for the firm (see p. 188)

Black panther brooch, carved in black jasper with fancy-yellow navette diamond eyes. Commissioned in 1962

20. The Polar Star diamond of 41.28 cts (see p. 286)

The Star of South Africa diamond of 47.75 cts (see p. 288)

Diamond necklace, the 33 diamond collets suspending a cushion-shaped fancy-blue diamond of 26.26 cts, a cushion-shaped pink diamond of 22.97 cts, and the Polar Star diamond (see p. 243)

21. *Above left:* Panther brooch, in diamonds and onyx, on coral and onyx base. Commissioned in 1928

Above right: Vanity case, enamelled black on gold. The lid applied with 3 diamond greyhounds between emerald cypresses. Emerald ground. Cabochon ruby and emerald hinges and clasp. The interior with compartments. 1920. Offered to Mrs Pierre Cartier

Below left: Vanity case, enamelled black on gold, with rose-cut diamond borders. The lid applied with a miniature diamond and onyx panther between emerald cypresses. Calibré-cut ruby and diamond ground. The interior with compartments (see p. 230)

Below centre: Panther châtelaine watch, in circular-cut diamonds and onyx, with 3 pear-shaped diamond tassels. The watch on reverse. 1915. Offered to Mrs Pierre Cartier (see p. 229)

22. Emerald tiara-necklace, mounted with 19 pear-shaped engraved emeralds (230.95 cts) and 2 emerald beads. Pearl and diamond base. 1923. First sold to Sir Thomas Beecham, subsequently to the Aga Khan

Emerald fibula, set with 2 engraved emeralds, calibré-cut emeralds and circular-cut diamonds. 1924. Cartier's London

23. Necklace, alternately mounted with sapphire and emerald beads. Diamond rondelles. The centre with an engraved emerald of 24.62 cts below a cabochon sapphire vase of 25.60 cts. Commissioned by the Aga Khan in 1927, enlarged 1928 (see p. 177)

Bracelet, the central emerald of 76 cts engraved with a verse from the Koran, the band set with engraved sapphire and emerald leaves and onyx. Mounted for the Aga Khan in 1930.

The verse translates: *'Say: God the Almighty gives prosperity to whom He wishes; dispossesses whom He wishes; honours whom He wishes and disgraces whom He wishes; He, the Almighty./He watches over the succession of day and night; out of life he makes death; and out of death, life; He bestows power without reckoning'*

Emerald pendant, the cushion-shaped emerald tablet of 142.20 cts engraved with an Islamic prayer. Onyx and diamond mount. Mounted for the Aga Khan in 1930

24. Necklace, in triangular-cut onyx and circular-cut diamonds, with 'Chinese' button clasp. 1919

Pendant brooch, the articulate mount in *calibré-*cut onyx. Circular- and rectangular-cut diamonds. 1921

Bracelet, mounted in *calibré-*cut onyx and circular-cut diamonds. 1922

(The set sold to Mr W. Fox, founder of Twentieth-Century Fox)

25. Onyx tree tiara, the circular-cut diamond mount with stylized onyx tree. Pearl crest border. 1914

'Egyptian' pendant, of lotus vase design in *calibré-*cut onyx, circular, triangular and pear-shaped diamonds. 1913

Pendant, the engraved frosted rock crystal mount with circular-cut diamond border and centre. Pear-shaped diamond tassel. On silk cord with sliding motif. 1912

26. Emerald necklace, alternately mounted with 50 engraved emerald beads and pearls. The diamond-set centre suspending an engraved emerald of 85.60 cts. Emerald tassels. 1925. Cartier's New York

Emerald ring, the engraved cabochon emerald of 31.33 cts on black enamel base, flanked by 2 cabochon rubies of 4.35 cts, 2 sapphires and diamonds. 1927

27. *Left:* Lapel 'seal' watch, suspending a carved jade buddhist lion (Chinese, nineteenth century), with ruby, diamond and onyx mount concealing the watch, from a ruby bead, jade, onyx and diamond suspension. 1929

Centre: Jade pendant, suspending flexible pear-shaped jade tassels with cabochon sapphire, ruby, and pearl intersections from an onyx, pearl, cabochon sapphire and ruby dome. 1921

Right: Pendant, the waved articulate diamond and onyx mount with engraved ruby and onyx top suspending a pear-shaped pearl of 89.09 grains and a pear-shaped red tourmaline of 18.45 grams. 1914, subsequently lengthened

28. Emerald necklace, the chain with flexible circular-cut diamond rondelles suspending 29 graduated cabochon emeralds with diamond tips. Cartier's London. Commissioned in 1938 by Merle Oberon

29. Emerald pendant, of 'Persian' design, set with 21 cabochon emeralds, smaller emerald intersections, circular-cut diamond borders. 1910, subsequently shortened to its present shape

The Kapurthala headdress, mounted with 19 emeralds of various shapes, circular- and rose-cut diamonds, and pearls. Weight of central hexagonal emerald: 177.40 cts, weight of remaining 18 emeralds: 254.84 cts. Commissioned in 1926 by Maharajah Jagatjit Singh of Kapurthala (see p. 179)

30. Pendant necklace, the pearl necklace with engraved emerald leaf clasp suspending a Mogul engraved hexagonal emerald of 86.71 cts above a pearl and emerald bead tassel with central cabochon emerald drop of 27.50 cts. 1925. Cartier's New York

Emerald brooch, mounted with a cushion-shaped engraved emerald of 154.50 cts, circular-cut diamonds, *calibré-*cut sapphires, and emeralds. 1927. Sold to Mrs Cole Porter

31. *Left:* Jade pendant, the articulate jade mount with turquoise, diamonds and cabochon sapphires. Sapphire tassel. Sapphire, turquoise and diamond surmount. 1913. Sold to Lord Derby

Centre: Jade ear-pendants, the Chinese engraved jade pendants with onyx, coral and diamond motifs. 1923

Above right: Jabot pin, the large engraved jade palm within black enamel, with pear-shaped ruby finial; the smaller leaf in jade, ruby and diamond. 1925

Below right: 'Buddha' ear-pendants, the Chinese engraved jade Buddhas as 'Gods of Happiness' on onyx and diamond mounts. Cartier's New York

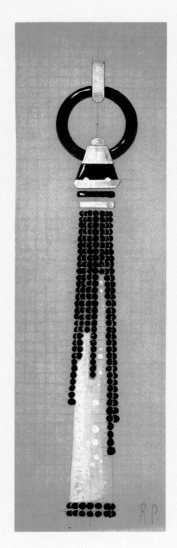

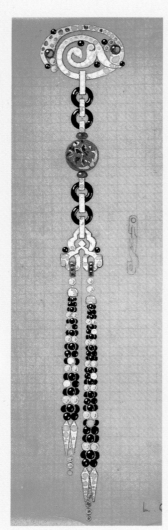

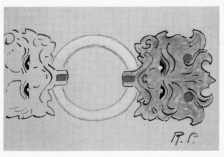

17

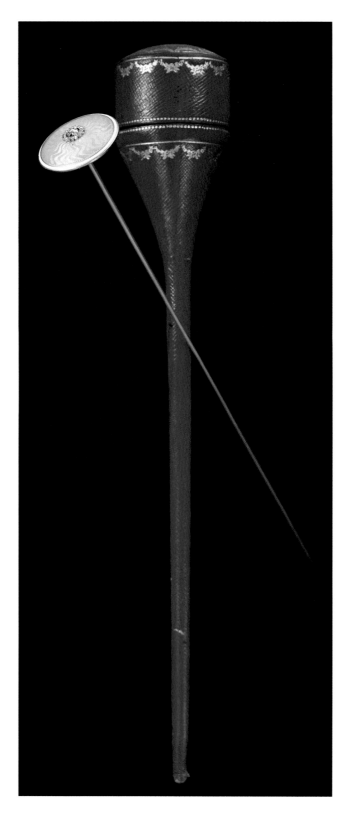

1914 GEORGE BARBIER

19

20

22

23

24

25

26

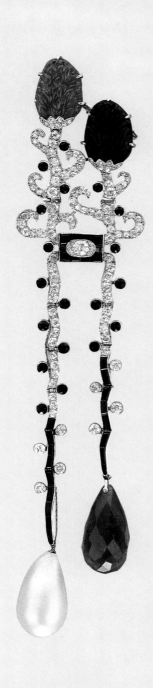

28

30

32

In St Petersburg

T WAS ON 2 DECEMBER 1908 that Louis Cartier's assistant, Paul Cheyrouze, together with his aide Desbaines, climbed aboard the Express du Nord in Paris for the start of a three-day journey that was to take them via Berlin to the imperial city of St Petersburg. Their fellow travellers included Prince Orlov, Count Benckendorff and — a portentous confrontation — Peter Carl Fabergé. We no longer know what brought Fabergé to Paris, but since his triumps at the World Fair eight years previously, he had not allowed the French capital to slip far from his mind. On that occasion the brothers Louis and Pierre Cartier had been confronted in the Esplanade des Invalides by the fairy-tale spectacle of fifteen imperial Easter eggs, dating from 1884 onwards and devised as presents from Alexander III and Nicholas II to the tsarina and the Dowager Empress Marie Feodorovna. It was the first time these had been exhibited in the West, and alongside them could be seen reduced replicas of the Russian coronation insignia. Admittedly, a French critic had reproached Fabergé's eggs for their lack of 'any clearly defined practical utility'; yet they were clear proof of the debt that Russian goldsmiths owed their eighteenth-century French counterparts. After all, Fabergé's ancestors themselves had been driven from France following the revocation of the Edict of Nantes.

Russia in fact had never ceased to be fundamentally indebted to French artistic influences, influences that in the mid-nineteenth century ran parallel to efforts aimed at revitalizing Russian art from the well-spring of its Byzantine origins. By the same token — and not only for political reasons — France was making every effort to show the greatest possible appreciation of all things Russian, especially art. On the occasion of the 1867 World Fair, Napoleon III had offered a particularly ceremonial welcome to Alexander II and his two sons, Grand Duke Alexander and Grand Duke Vladimir, and at the 1878 Exhibition the Russian exhibitors had been singled out for special honours: the goldsmiths Ovchinnikov and Sazikov were each awarded a gold medal, and Khlebnikov a silver one. In addition, after the assassination of Alexander II in Moscow in 1881, many rich Russian émigrés had settled in France, making it their second home.

Cartier's earliest dealings with a Russian customer date back to 1860, when Prince Saltikov visited the boulevard des Italiens and chose an emerald bracelet in a black enamelled gold setting. Cartier's jewels soon found their way to Russia, where they were much admired, and the firm's reputation for excellence spread quickly to the Russian imperial court. According to the accounts of Grand Duchess Olga, daughter of Alexander II, the fairy-tale atmosphere which descended upon the palace at Gatchina before each Christmas owed its special charm to the jewels that Cartier used to send. In 1888, when Olga was a mere six years old, 'Grand Duchess Xenia, a great favourite with her mother, happened to be in the empress's rooms when two ladies-in-waiting were unpacking cases of jewelry and bibelots sent by Cartier from Paris. Xenia, aged thirteen, had not yet decided what she would give her mother. But suddenly she saw a filigree scent bottle, its stopper studded with

32. *Left:* Vanity case, the gold cylinder with cream enamel chequer pattern, the sides in black enamel with rose-cut diamond borders. Onyx finger-ring. Onyx and diamond attachments. Interior with compartments. 1914

Right: Vanity case, the flattened gold cylinder overlaid with a trellis of cream enamel, the sides of lapis lazuli. Rose-cut diamond border. Central lapis lazuli and diamond initials 'M C' for Marion Cartier (daughter of Pierre). Rose-cut diamond push-piece. 1926. Presented to Marion Cartier by Jacques Cartier in 1927

Below: Powder compact, in cream enamel over gold with swastika pattern. Blue enamel border. Central jade, cabochon sapphire and diamond bonsai tree. 1928

sapphires. She snatched at it and begged Countess Stroganov not to give her secret away. That scent bottle must have cost a small fortune and Xenia duly presented it to her mother on Christmas Day. A little later the empress made it known that boxes arriving from Cartier and other jewelers could be admired by the children and no more.'[1]

At a later date Russian aristocrats regularly sought out Cartier's salons each time they were in Paris, spreading the fashion for 'Russian' bibelots from their native St Petersburg and, in return, taking back to Russia jewels from Cartier's which were more elegantly worked than anything they could have obtained at home from Fabergé or Bolin.

In 1899 it was Grand Duke Alexis, First Lord Admiral of the Russian fleet, who came from St Petersburg to buy jewels from Cartier's. He was followed in 1900 by Grand Duchess Vladimir and in 1901 by Countess Scherbatov and Grand Duke Paul, who ordered first a pair of opera-glasses with a Wedgwood design and then a necklace with nine drop diamonds and a meander tiara.[2] Louis Cartier later recalled an episode in connection with the Grand Duke which offers a delightfully atmospheric picture of the salons in the rue de la Paix: 'The Grand Duke and his wife, the Countess of Hohenfelsen, were sitting in my office, having ordered a magnificent sapphire tiara for their daughter, the Grand Duchess Marie. To my amazement, the Grand Duke, who was sitting close to the half-open glass door, suddenly called out the name "Arthur" to somebody. A dignified-looking Englishman turned round in surprise at hearing his name called. It was the Duke of Connaught, brother of Edward VII. The two princes shook hands, delighted at their unexpected meeting.'

Another welcome visitor to the rue de la Paix was Princess Vera Lobanov-Dolgorouky. Her first, somewhat hesitant, purchase was a delightful pansy brooch in amethyst and diamonds, followed by three pin brooches for a boa. She had married Prince Jacques Lobanov of Rostov when she was sixteen, but early widowhood had persuaded her to exchange Moscow's 'Small Hermitage' for the Hôtel du Ranelagh in Paris, where her circle of intimate friends included Princess Yourievsky, the widow of Alexander II, and her sister, Countess Georges Berg. Every spring, this miniature princely household would leave Paris and take up residence in a villa in Menton, or else in the Villa Zina at Vevey.

In 1906 Grand Duchess Xenia made her first visit to Cartier's.[3] She had received a number of magnificent jewels in 1894 on the occasion of her marriage to Alexander Mikhailovich, and her black pearls, which she was later able to rescue from Russia in the wake of the Revolution, caused a not inconsiderable stir in the rue de la Paix. In France, both she and her mother, the Empress Marie, stayed in the Villa Espoir in what since Empress Eugénie's days had been the fashionable resort of Biarritz; from Cartier's she bought a nephrite frame and a *boîte de jeux*. It was on 22 April 1907 that the Empress Marie Feodorovna finally entered Cartier's establishment in the rue de la Paix. Together with her ladies-in-waiting, she had travelled to Paris from Biarritz where she was spending the spring.[4] Admittedly, she bought only small presents – two tie pins and two hardstone rabbits;

but Louis Cartier, who had heard of the empress's passion for jewelry and of her legendary pearls which, with their ten strands, reached down to her waist, placed before her one case after another containing the most luxurious and costly jewels the firm could produce.

As the empress expressed a wish to be able to buy such jewels in St Petersburg, she was delighted to discover from Louis Cartier that a first exhibition was already being planned for that same year in the Grand Hôtel d'Europe. Cartier's interests in Russia at that time were represented, with justifiable pride, by Désiré Sarda who, though not a jeweler, was a very shrewd businessman. Sarda knew that a single expedition would not be sufficient for Cartier's to gain a foothold in St Petersburg: 'The Russians do not like changing their supplier.' It was this insight which persuaded Cartier's to send out 562 individual letters of introduction and invitations. On hearing of these, the firm's Russian rivals did not remain idle for long, and set about spreading rumours of Cartier's fabulous prices.

Sarda travelled to Paris in March 1908 to discuss the forthcoming Christmas season, and it was to prepare for this that first Pierre Cartier and then the above-mentioned Paul Cheyrouze travelled to St Petersburg in December. Upon their arrival, Cheyrouze and his assistant put up at the Grand Hôtel d'Europe, with its famous view of the Neva, and then turned their attention to arranging suitable premises at 28 Quai de la Cour. The astute Grand Duchess Vladimir had first suggested that they should rent premises in another of her buildings, but Sarda preferred the building in the Quai de la Cour, which the Grand Duchess leased to him at 900 roubles for a two-month period. The building was fitted up with feverish haste; throughout the conversion, the Cartier staff led a spartan life, after the example of Alexander II, sleeping on campbeds and wrapped in travelling rugs. The work was completed on 9 December and the name of Cartier was emblazoned in elegant black letters on the front of the building, whose five windows overlooked the quayside.

'I received your letter just as I was on the point of going to Fabergé's. For the time being I'll buy only a trifle [Fr400], but I'll recommend you to my friends and I'll certainly be back.' These were the words spoken by Cartier's first customer, the director of the Northern Bank, Westrach. The delivery by hand of 562 brochures had borne its first fruit! Their method of delivery, which Cartier's archives have recorded, is worth quoting:

'Cartier's card, with its polite invitation, to be handed in at the house by a clean and intelligent boy. He shall hand it to the doorman and at the same time conceal all his other cards, so as to give the impression that he has come for that purpose alone.' Then, as an entertaining postscript, 'Doormen are very naive. They never fail to pass on the invitation to the maid.'

'I was just on the point of going to Fabergé's . . .': Cartier's could have had no greater satisfaction during these first few days than to be compared to their great rival. The elimination of their competitors became the guiding motive behind all their activities in St Petersburg, so that by the time they left in 1914 they could proudly observe: 'As is fitting, we are now the leading firm in St Petersburg.' Of course, St Petersburg was bound to strike its foreign visitors as provincial, and competition in such a town was not particularly strong, with the exception of Bolin and, naturally, Carl Fabergé. From his magnificent granite-columned premises on the Morskaya, Fabergé had for years concentrated on *objets d'art* rather than jewelry and, besides, made few changes to his models, all of which adhered to a traditional style. Although his enamel colours revealed the most subtle variations in all Russia, the forms he preferred remained restricted to the same basic types, so that a not entirely implausible story began to circulate, to the effect that five regimental officers were dismayed to discover that they were all wearing the same Fabergé buttons!

In the selection of items which Cartier put on display in St Petersburg he took into account both the experience he had gained during a previous year's journey and the most recent Paris fashions: diamond-studded platinum brooches so delicately worked as to imitate lace; necklaces on black velvet backing; stomachers in Renaissance designs; a meander tiara, and a tiara of five interlaced loops; a ruby necklace with diamonds from the former French crown jewels;[5] and thirty-five watches and clocks in platinum, enamel and precious stones. One of these clocks was designed in the shape of an Easter egg, as a concession to Russian taste; and fifteen fobs in the shape of eggs were similarly designed with Russian customers in mind.

News of the opening of a branch of Cartier's spread with great speed: among those who appeared in person were Countess Sergei Zoubov, Countess Bobrinsky, Princess Shakovskoy and Grand Duke Michail Michailovich.[6] In December Cheyrouze travelled to Gatchina, where the widowed Empress Marie Feodorovna had lived since the death of her husband Alexander III.[7] She bought a pair of cuff-links and a belt buckle in *guilloché* enamel similar to those which Fabergé had brought into fashion. In addition, she had recently received two jewel-filled caskets from Cartier's in Paris, one of which contained purchases made by her daughter, Grand Duchess Xenia. The empress was clearly impressed by Cartier's range, for, on her recommendation, an audience with the tsar followed at Tsarskoe Selo. On the frosty winter morning of 21 December, Paul Cheyrouze was greeted at the station by Prince Putyatin and accompanied to the Alexander Palace, where the imperial family had resided since 1895. He was given no time to admire the palace, but taken at once to the billiard room, where he laid out his jewels for the tsar and tsarina to examine. They were engrossed in grave discourse, and it must initially have appeared that Cheyrouze's visit had come at a particularly inopportune moment; but the imperial couple chose a brooch, excusing themselves from further purchases by pointing out that they must first consider their own local jewelers. It was no secret that Alexandra Feodorovna had less time for jewelry than her mother-in-law, the Empress Marie Feodorovna.[8] Admittedly, she wore her pearls most gracefully, and was fond of light-blue sapphires and turquoises, but opulent jewelry did not suit her reserved character, a fact not well understood in Russia. Yet even so trifling a transaction as this, which was of little more than symbolic value, was a significant event for Cartier's. The news was immediately reported back to Paris, as was the conjecture that it would not be long before Cartier's was appointed official purveyor to the imperial court.

On the banks of the Neva, meanwhile, the approach of Christmas could be keenly felt. Paul Muffat, one of Cartier's assistants from Paris, had arrived, and the three employees often worked until two in the morning, while a young Russian kept guard over the safe. Shortly before the holiday period began, Countess Cheremetiev ordered for her niece a pearl choker, each pearl weighing $13\frac{1}{2}$ grains; and for herself a crescent-shaped hair ornament costing 2,000 roubles (1 rouble = Fr2.64). Count Moy ordered a diamond tiara of heart-shaped openwork scrolls, for which he supplied his own gemstones. All the orders were sent off to Paris by letter, for there were as yet no telephone links between Russia and France. The items which were ordered from the Paris workshops for a specific date were often awaited with considerable anxiety. Parcels were initially sent by diplomatic courier, and later carried by express train, a journey which took six days. Among the items which made this journey was the tiara for Countess Stolypin, wife of the Prime Minister. The Louis-XVI style tiara with its intertwining garlands of blossom had been ordered for the New Year's Day reception, which was due to take place in the Winter Palace two weeks later. But the keenly awaited jewel did not arrive in time and Cheyrouze was forced to come to the rescue of the irate countess by lending her an item from his stock, which proved no less delightful to look at than the one of her choice.

In spite of their industry, the firm ended the Christmas season with a deficit: total takings had amounted to 29,534 roubles (Fr77,970), with expenses of Fr94,871. Many deals could not be properly completed during the brief period when the shop was open, so Sarda once again recommended that Alfred Cartier and his three sons establish themselves on a permanent footing in the city, citing as an example the way in which Georges Delavigne acted as Boucheron's representative in Moscow.[9] Alfred Cartier, however, refused to give in even to the entreaties of his sons Louis and Pierre. He was in the process of opening the New York headquarters, and there was not enough staff for yet another branch. He suggested instead that in future there should be two Russian expeditions each year, and during the rest of the year Sarda should be on the spot to maintain the firm's interests.

Soon Cartier's were to attract one of their most important customers: the Grand Duchess Vladimir. She had been born in 1854 as Princess Marie von Mecklenburg-Schwerin and had married Grand Duke Vladimir, one of Alexander II's sons. On the death of her husband in 1908, she had found herself in possession of an annual pension of one million francs, plus all the allowances to which the Grand Duke had been entitled as commander-in-chief of the army. It was a sum which allowed the self-important Grand Duchess to run a truly regal household and to complete a casket of unique jewels.[10] Her decisions, however, often sprang from a momentary whim, and in her patron of the arts role Marie Pavlovna was feared by many, including Diaghilev who, following the Grand Duke's death, found himself abruptly deprived of the support previously granted him. The summer's days spent on her Orientally magnificent estates at Ropsha near Peterhof passed more cheerfully than did those spent at the imperial palace at Gatchina, for which the Grand Duchess rarely had a good word. And on long winter's evenings, the rooms of her brown palace in St Petersburg were lit by the glow of thousands of candles, and the most sophisticated members of St Petersburg society amused themselves dancing a quadrille or polonaise. The Christmas bazaar, which she used to organize with great acumen, formed the official start of the St Petersburg winter season.

In the year of her husband's death, the items that the Grand Duchess ordered from Cartier's included a briolette aigrette tiara (see p. 85) and a tiara made of rubies, which included the Beauharnais ruby (see p.297); in 1909 Cartier's made her a sapphire *kokoshnik* with a 137-carat sapphire at its centre. Sapphires, though cut *en cabochon*, had recently been a source of some distress to her: when her brother-in-law, the Grand Duke Alexis, died in 1908, the sapphire cabochon tiara which she coveted had gone instead to the wife of Grand Duke Paul. Her annoyance had been great; but a similar tiara from Cartier's was soon to help her over her loss. Quite by chance, Cartier's had a similar piece in stock in the rue de la Paix, and its five large diamonds were easily replaced by five sapphire cabochons. There were reservations about sending such an expensive item on the long journey to Russia, so photographs and a copper model were sent on ahead. But then, in spring 1909, Louis Cartier himself travelled to St Petersburg, and at ten o'clock on the evening of 17 March he received a visit from the Grand Duchess, accompanied by three of her children, Helen, Boris and André. Marie Pavlovna was enchanted with her sapphire cabochon tiara. Not only the Grand Duchess herself but the whole of her family delighted in Louis Cartier's company, for he knew how to charm and entertain them with reports of the cosmopolitan life of distant Paris, a city of which the Grand Duchess's children had only dreamt. An invitation followed, to the home of Grand Duke André, who was on intimate terms with the dancer Matilda Khessinska and whose friendship with Louis Cartier was to last for many years.

Grand Duke Michail died shortly before Christmas 1909. The whole of St Petersburg was plunged into mourning and, in accordance with court protocol, the Christmas balls were called off, a great loss to all the luxury trades, including Cartier's. Notwithstanding, the Grand Duchess Vladimir could be relied upon to complement her sapphire tiara with a sizable stomacher sporting a 162-carat sapphire at its centre.

Among the highlights of the curtailed winter season was a visit from twenty-five débutantes, who called on Cartier at the suggestion of the tsarina. Accompanied by maids of honour, they marvelled demurely at the glittering displays of jewels, prevailing upon Cheyrouze to explain to them the unique qualities of each individual piece.

The spring season of 1910 brought few surprises. Grand Duchess

Vladimir continued to remain loyal to Cartier's, and in the presence of her sister, the Duchess of Sachsen-Coburg, went into raptures over a four-leaf clover brooch which Louis Cartier had had made for her. He was increasingly conscious of the influence which his powerful patron exercised on St Petersburg society. Countess Cheremetiev, for example, specifically mentioned the Grand Duchess's sapphire tiara when ordering a diamond tiara for herself shortly before the following Christmas, though she asked that it should not be in the same rigid *kokoshnik* form.

Louis Cartier at that time was having to contend with severe difficulties which threatened to endanger the whole of the 1910 Christmas season: his rivals in St Petersburg, jealous at the growing influence of the French firm,[11] had prevailed upon the customs authorities to impound the goods that Cartier was importing; in that way they hoped to be able to prevent any further sales exhibitions.[12] Forty-four watches and important items of jewelry, without which the exhibition could not open, lay in a bonded warehouse, while Louis Cartier wrote desperate letters to the Ministry of the Interior, requesting an audience. What was the crime of which he stood accused? Gold imported into Russia was taxed at Fr343 a kilo, whereas platinum was duty-free, not yet having been recognized as a precious metal. An insignificantly small quantity of the items that Louis Cartier had brought with him were made of yellow gold and had inadvertently not been declared as such. Thanks to the help of a certain Raffalovich at the Ministry of the Interior and also to the fact that Cartier's had in the meantime been appointed official purveyor to the imperial court, the jewels were released in time to be exhibited at the Grand Duchess's Christmas bazaar, which soon had the whole of St Petersburg talking.

In 1908 Cartier had regarded this occasion as a serious disruption to business, whereas the opportunity to participate himself was now most welcome. The chance had arisen as a result of an invitation to tea with Count Mita von Benckendorff. Dressed in a silk jacket and Russian orders, Cartier had been driven by sleigh to the Benckendorff Palace, where Grand Duchess Vladimir and twenty ladies-in-waiting were gathered. 'The Grand Duchess', Cartier later recalled,

escorted me into the vast salon where I remained alone with her, feeling somewhat intimidated, while her attendants waited respectfully in the antechamber. I asked her if I might be allowed to take part in a charity sale at the bazaar organized by the Society of Nobles, of which she was president. With her usual generosity she at once agreed and allocated to me two sales assistants from the court, Princess Demidov and Princess Belosselski. In addition, I was encouraged to seek out Mlle Lalive, one of her ladies-in-waiting, and secure for myself the best sales pitch.

The next morning I met Mlle Lalive in the palace where the bazaar was to take place. From the stairs I gazed down into the cathedral-like interior and at the vast horseshoe-shaped sales counter over which presided the Grand Duchess together with the flower of St Petersburg's aristocracy. To the right of Marie Pavlovna sat the Duchess of Leuchtenberg. 'Guess whose necklace she's wearing,' the Grand Duchess asked me. It was, would you believe it, the one which Napoleon had given the Empress Josephine. I sat down at a table with

Princess Demidov and Princess Belosselski, where we received a visit from the Empress Marie Feodorovna, Grand Duke Michail Michailovich and many other Grand Dukes whom I never saw in Paris. In particular I recall Prince Gabriel. Throughout the proceedings the guards' band played plaintive music which filled the vast halls and seemed to rise up out of the depths of history. An old peasant-woman wearing a *kokoshnik* descended the flight of stairs slowly and solemnly before approaching the Grand Duchess's table, bowing low and kissing her hand. The crowd of onlookers surged everywhere: freedom and order prevailed. At the end we were able to present the Grand Duchess with a sum of between 23,000 and 26,000 roubles, which was distributed among the poor people of St Petersburg.[13]

Although Louis Cartier omits to mention them, the Grand Dukes Cyril, André, Boris and Dimitri, Counts Fersen, Orlov and Baryatinski, Countess Schouvalov and Kleinmichel, Dr Emanuel Nobel[14] and Teliakovsky, the director of the Imperial Theatre, were also present, crowding the stage of a spectacular show which the Grand Duchess had mounted with theatrical brilliance. Reflecting the social importance of the event, Cartier's range contained his choicest items, comprising ninety brooches, nineteen necklaces, including one in the Arabian style, thirteen tiaras including a *kokoshnik* with seven drop diamonds, a winged tiara, and sixty-nine timepieces of varying sizes, of which twenty-seven were wrist-watches.

The turnover since December had amounted to Fr1.5 million, an astonishing sum in view of the fact that, in Cartier's experience, the Russians were far more inclined to spend their money abroad, where they could make a great show of it, than at home. 'Outside his own country, the Russian is indecisive and shy. Within three months he may easily spend seven-eighths of his wealth. In Russia, on the other hand, he is distrustful, and only on his third visit does he buy anything' – so runs one of the business reports sent back to the rue de la Paix.

Scarcely had the bazaar closed when Louis Cartier set off for Kiev and Moscow, in the company of his designer Charles Jacqueau and sales assistant Farinès. They received prospective customers in Moscow's Hotel National and visited the great art-collector Ivan Morozov. This was the first contact Louis Cartier had had with a collector and patron of the arts who was not a member of St Petersburg's old and long-established aristocracy. Morozov had acquired his wealth through industry, and, through his informed purchasing of works by Bonnard, Vuillard, Matisse and Gauguin, he had a noticeable influence on Russian art in the years leading up to the First World War.

Charles Jacqueau, whose talent for drawing had been recognized at an early age by Louis Cartier, was sent to Russia not only to set down on paper the orders placed by important customers, but to take back to Paris fresh creative impulses absorbed from the Orientalism of the imperial capital, from its theatres and from Fabergé's displays. Cartier and Jacqueau visited the Hermitage together countless times, marvelling at harnesses of emeralds and diamonds, priceless enamel clocks from the eighteenth century, and, of course, at Fabergé's eggs, photographs of which Cartier was to take back with him to Paris.

He also returned home with the memory of an historic collector's piece which Count von Benckendorff had shown him in St Petersburg.

Following tea with the Grand Duchess, he insisted on showing me a curiosity of great interest, and so we betook ourselves to the home of Prince Lvov, who was later to play an important role in the Kerenski administration. The prince opened a locked casket and removed from it a large cuirassier's helmet made entirely of gold. It had belonged to King Murat, who had worn it in all his battles, in Smolensk as well as on the Moskova; it is mentioned by General Marbot in his memoirs.

Cartier was soon able to report a new victory over Fabergé: Mme Andreiev ordered a tiara from him, leaving behind a sketch which Fabergé had already produced and which Louis Cartier took back with him to Paris for costing. In spite of his pressing commitments, he found time to congratulate his brother Pierre on the sale of the Hope diamond and — his sense of the need for publicity already being fully developed — to place an announcement of the sale in the international press. 'It is a marvellous advertisement for Cartier's,' he said.

It was during the busy Easter exhibition of 1911 that Cartier's received the dreadful news that Boucheron's Moscow representative Georges Delavigne and his son Henri had been murdered as they were returning to Moscow from the Caucasian resort of Baku. They had been carrying diamonds to the value of 600,000 roubles. Five months later came the death of Prime Minister Stolypin, one of Cartier's faithful customers, who was gunned down by an assassin following a performance in the Kiev Theatre, at which Tsar Nicholas II had also been present. A prerevolutionary, panicstricken mood gripped the country.

In St Petersburg the approaching Christmas season brought with it the first requests for jewelry made of diamonds and onyx. Grand Duke André bought an onyx bow-knot brooch, as did Grand Duchess Vladimir. She gave it as a present to the tsarina, and for herself chose simply a lorgnon.[15] On Christmas Day her eldest son, Grand Duke Cyril, bought for his wife Victoria-Melita a sapphire necklace from which was suspended an oval star sapphire weighing 311 carats; in its severity of line it reflected craftsmanship at its best in the Empire style.[16]

For Easter 1912 Cartier's produced brooches with arrowhead motifs in onyx, emerald, sapphire and amethyst, one of which was chosen by Princess Zenaïde Youssoupov. While tortoise-shell combs inlaid with diamonds proved very popular as presents, aigrettes now made their first appearance alongside tiaras, though they had been a traditional element in Russian dress for several decades. Countess Ouvarov bought an aigrette in the form of a Chinese gong with diamonds and a *calibré* ruby rim. The most remarkable gem in stock was a blue diamond weighing 11.59 carats and set as a pendant, while one of the rarest was the 'Reine des perles', a jewel which was presented at court. The most significant order, however, and the one which brought Cartier into closer contact with the imperial court at this time, was the Easter egg for Tsar Nicholas II. On this occasion, the order was placed not by a private individual but by the city of Paris. The present was intended to have symbolic value and lend emphasis to the diplomatic activities between the two countries which were unusually lively on the eve of the Great War. Attempts had been made over a number of years to further both countries' interests by means of exhibitions and reciprocal official visits at the highest governmental level. When celebrations were held in 1903 to mark the two hundredth anniversary of the foundation of St Petersburg, the members of the Paris City Council travelled to Russia for the occasion, bringing with them the good wishes of the people of Paris. In 1911 it was the turn of Russia, and the mayor of St Petersburg, Goutchkov, and Alderman Poutchkov were given a jubilant reception in Paris, where a gala performance of Wagner's *The Valkyrie* was held at the Opéra, specially decorated for the event. The Paris City Council was officially invited to pay a return visit, and the President of the City Council, Félix Roussel, duly arrived in Moscow on 9 February 1912. Before leaving Paris, the City Council had turned to Cartier's in their search for a suitable gift. In 1906 the craftsmen of the rue de la Paix had been sufficiently impressed by Fabergé's Easter eggs to produce a similar egg, which Louis Cartier had taken with him as a showpiece to Russia in 1910. The City Council was attracted by the idea of honouring the tsar with a present which, uniquely, symbolized not France but the host country. The presentation took place at Tsarskoe Selo, where the tsar admired the purple and white enamelled egg which bore both his monogram and a mitre crown of pearls and diamonds, and which opened up to reveal a circular photograph of the tsarevich.[17]

At least as far as foreign visitors were concerned, the pomp and ceremony of the events which were held in 1913 to mark the three hundredth anniversary of the Romanovs' rule seemed calculated to drive away the dark stormclouds of destruction which were already gathering on the horizon. In spite of the political uncertainty of the times, Cartier's traditional customers remained loyal: Princess Youssoupov still preferred to buy her presents at Cartier's, and was particularly taken by some charms bearing a lucky star and the inscription in English, 'I love you'. Another member of her family, Count Elston, bought an emerald and diamond aigrette tiara, a pearl necklace and a billiken (see p. 95).[18] Only Grand Duchess Vladimir remained undecided, in spite of her initial interest in three large diamond drops of 21.06, 15.46 and 15.15 carats. She was unable to make up her mind, despite the favourable conditions which Cartier offered her of deferred payment over a period of three years; and in the end she chose only one of them. All the rage during the 1913 season in St Petersburg were Cartier's platinum evening bags, for which the demand was so great that Paris had to insist on twenty-eight days' delivery. Count Alexis Orlov paid Fr5,100 for an evening bag made of green gold with a diamond clasp.

Thus began the year 1914, and with it Cartier's final season in Russia. Once again it was the Grand Duchess Vladimir who risked a major order, in spite of the adverse conditions which now prevailed, paying 45,600 roubles (Fr121,000) for a 39.25-carat drop diamond. Was it through lack of political foresight, or simply through fear of offending so important a customer, that Cartier agreed to her repaying the sum in instalments spread over three years? Mme de Balashev chose some miniature hardstone animals in the style of Fabergé, including a piglet and an elephant, as well as two Easter eggs.

The wedding of the year took place in February between Prince Felix Youssoupov and Princess Irina, the daughter of Grand Duchess Xenia and niece of Tsar Nicholas II. The family's wealth was immeasurable – greater even than that of the tsar himself, and the family palace at Archangelskoe outside Moscow housed a collection of paintings surpassed only by that of the Hermitage.

For Princess Irina, Cartier provided a wedding tiara of rock crystal, a piece of which the Paris workshops were particularly proud. A photograph of the princess wearing her diamond-studded wedding regalia was so coveted in St Petersburg that Sarda was unable to acquire one for his head office in Paris. Further celebrations followed a few months later, this time for the grand wedding of Prince Scherbatov, grandson of the fabulously wealthy Count Stroganov, and the daughter of the late Prime Minister Stolypin. In the face of competition from both Bolin and Fabergé, it was Cartier who was commissioned to design the wedding ring.

Although the outbreak of war brought a premature end to Cartier's activities in St Petersburg, there was to be an epilogue only a few years later on French soil. Following the murder of the tsar and his family, the Russian aristocracy and members of the imperial household fled to Monte Carlo, Paris, Cannes, Lausanne and London, quickly establishing themselves in what they soon came to regard as their second homeland. Empress Marie Feodorovna returned to her native Denmark, where she died in 1928. Her jewels remained with her till the end, and were then divided up in England. Grand Duchess Vladimir, Cartier's loyal patron, fled from Russia by crossing the Caucasus in her own private railway. She reached Switzerland in 1920, remaining in Zurich until her death that same year in Contrexéville. She had entrusted her jewels to an English friend, Albert Stopford, who got them safely out of the country. Following her death, they were shared among her four children: Grand Duke André, who henceforth divided his time between Paris and Cannes, received the rubies; Grand Duchess Helen, the mother of Princess Marina of Kent, the diamonds; Grand Duke Cyril the pearls; and Boris the emeralds (see p. 301). The diamond bow-knot tiara with its drop pearls, which the Grand Duchess had treasured more than any other item, went to Queen Mary of England, and the sapphire tiara to Queen Marie of Romania.

The dramatic nature of the exodus of many Russians from their homeland, and their struggles for existence abroad, are the subject of an account by the Paris dealer Léon Rosenthal who witnessed many of the forced sales which circumstances made necessary:

How many of them risked their lives to escape across the frontier with their jewels, the only thing they still possessed. Only under cover of darkness did they dare advance along the Finnish border, sliding in the snow and clutching desperately to the small sacks which contained an entire fortune. How the bullets whistled through the air whenever the Red Guards caught sight of their fleeing countrymen! What tricks they used to protect their precious jewels from the snares of Bolshevik agents! A luxuriant head of hair might serve to conceal jewels worth millions. Others who feared the rigours of persecution swallowed their diamonds, pearls, emeralds and rubies, leaving nature to return them to them. All the great jewelers and dealers in gemstones knew the Russian aristocrats and bourgeois who, before their eyes, threw open cases filled with magnificent jewels, saying, 'Buy these, they're all that stands between me and starvation.'[19]

It was not only the Russian refugees who sold their jewels on the European markets; the Bolsheviks did so too, though in their case the jewels had been robbed from banks, private houses and hiding places. Such was later the fate of the Youssoupov treasure. These jewels came via Reval on to the London market between 1918 and 1921 and then, following the French government's agreement to such purchases, on to the Paris market, too. Rosenthal calculated that the total value of all the jewels sold by the Soviets amounted to Fr300–400 million. An equally large amount accrued from sales that took place privately and which, in the early 1920s, plunged the European jewel market into a crisis that threatened its very survival.

83. Pierre Cartier in a horse-drawn sleigh on his first visit to Russia in 1904

Pearls

WHEN THE MAGAZINE *Femina* held a competition in 1906 and the lucky winner was offered a choice of prizes between an automobile and a pearl necklace, 4,582 readers opted for the former, while only 1,776 — a clear minority — decided in favour of the necklace. Was their decision a symptom of the fascination exercised at that time by the novelty and speed of the automobile? Or did it merely reflect the fact that by the turn of the century a pearl necklace was an obligatory item of jewelry in every privileged household? Two years later there was no mistaking the note of social criticism in the same magazine's condemnation of a pearl-embroidered dress belonging to Mrs George J. Gould, which was valued at one million dollars: the extravagance of the garment 'in no way increased its attractiveness', the writer commented; and 'it tied up vast sums of money which could have been spent in much more useful ways'.

In the ten years leading up to the First World War, Europe rather than the United States witnessed a visible shift in standards of 'morality' as they related to jewels and to lifestyle in general. It was American customers above all who were now buying the largest parures, which was one of the main reasons why the Cartier brothers opened up their New York branch in 1909. There and in Philadelphia, Chicago and Washington were to be found vast fortunes that had been accumulated since the time of the Civil War. Marriage ties with the old aristocratic families of Europe,[2] Fifth Avenue palaces modelled on the *châteaux* of the Loire, and the purchase of foreign family jewels whose age and provenance gave their new owners a spurious pedigree as flattering as the ancestral portraits which the art-dealer Duveen provided for their drawing rooms — all these were intended to legitimize their vast wealth in the eyes of the world and to establish them firmly within the desired cultural context.

At no other time was the demand for historical jewelry as great as it was in the United States at the beginning of the twentieth century. And the greatest demand of all was for pearl necklaces which, despite their often nebulous origins, were invariably attributed to Catherine the Great, Marie Antoinette or Empress Eugénie. Mrs Belmont wore Marie Antoinette's pearls; Consuelo Vanderbilt, or, as she then was, the Duchess of Marlborough, wore a strand that had belonged to Catherine the Great and the Empress Eugénie; Mrs Eleanor Whitney, aptly bearing 'Pearle' as a middle name, also wore the French empress's pearls; and Barbara Hutton later acquired those of Marie Antoinette. The following anecdote of the sale of the spectacular Dodge pearl necklace takes us right to the heart of a society whose characters, motivated by temptation and envy, appear to have stepped straight out of Vanity Fair:[3]

Not long before the wedding Mr. Dodge took his future son-in-law aside. 'Jim,' he said, 'I'm worried about Mother.' 'What about her?' Cromwell wanted to know. 'Well, Mother doesn't have the kind of pearls your mother has. In the church, people are going to notice that sort of thing. Where does your mother buy 'em?' Cromwell mentioned Cartier. 'Never heard of him,' Dodge said. 'But get me an appointment with this fella.' And so Cromwell arranged a meeting between Pierre Cartier, Horace Dodge, and himself.

At the meeting, Cartier – whom Mr. Dodge persistently called 'Mr. Car-*teer*' – produced several trays of pearl necklaces. 'No, no, Mr. Car-*teer*,' said Mr. Dodge. 'I want something bigger than that for Mother. Something to match Mrs. Stotesbury's pearls.'[4] Finally Cartier said, 'Monsieur Dodge, I do have one very fine set. They belonged to the Empress Catherine.' 'Never heard of her,' said Mr. Dodge, 'but let's see 'em.' Cartier then brought out a magnificent strand of pearls the size of robins' eggs. 'That's more like it,' said Mr. Dodge. 'How much?' 'Ah, Monsieur Dodge,' said M. Cartier, 'that necklace is one million dollars.' 'I'll take it,' said Dodge, pulling out his checkbook and writing a check for $1,000,000.[5]

The pearl necklaces mentioned above were of somewhat dubious pedigree, but there were others that appeared on the European market, especially in London and Paris, in the years leading up to the First World War, whose credentials are impeccable:

1872   Sale by auction of the private jewels of Empress Eugénie: 1 pearl necklace consisting of 41 pearls (Christie's, London)[6]

1887   Sale by auction of the French Crown Jewels: 6 pearl necklaces, 1 pearl tiara by Bapst, the Régente pearl, and 4 pearl brooches

1901   The 5-strand pearl necklace of Countess Castiglione, the famous *intrigante* at the court of Napoleon III (auctioned in Paris)

1902   The sale of the famous Dudley pearls in London (auctioned by Christie's, London)

1903   The dispersal of the stock owned by the jeweler Paul Hamelin, including 'magnificent' pearls weighing $415\frac{1}{4}$ grains (auctioned in Paris)

1904   The 3-strand pearl necklace of Princess Januaria de Bragance (auctioned in Paris)

1904   The pearls of the late Princess Mathilde, including a 7-strand pearl necklace originally owned by the Queen of Westphalia, and a single-string pearl necklace from Queen Sophie of Holland (auctioned in Paris)

1911   The pearls of Sultan Abdul Hamid, including a 3-strand necklace of 154 pearls (auctioned in Paris)

1915–18 Four auctions of pearls held by the Red Cross in London, one of which included an enormous sautoir of 4,000 pearls assembled by a commission headed by the Princess Royal. The original plan to hold a lottery was called off following objections by the Archbishop of Canterbury. The sautoir was divided up into separate necklaces and auctioned by Christie's, London

1919   The pearls of the Austrian imperial family were acquired by Cartier's of Paris as the result of a private transaction.[7] Louis Cartier travelled to Prangins in Switzerland for a private audience with the last Austrian emperor, who was living in exile there

1920   The pearls belonging to the revue star Gaby Deslys: 4 pearl necklaces and a tight-fitting band of alternate black and white pearls, said to be presents from King Manuel of Portugal (auctioned in Paris)

1923 Sale of the pearls which had been part of the Prussian crown jewels; they were bought in Doorn, Holland, by the dealer A. de Sondheimer, and included 6 pearl necklaces and 13 pearls

1924 The sale of the pearls of Mme Thiers, an event which the international press (including the *Gazette de Constantinople*) treated as having political significance. Under the terms of her will, Mme Thiers, wife of the first president of the French Republic (1871–77), left her husband's art collection to the Louvre in 1880. Comprising 1,470 separate items, it was an anomalous collection which the Goncourt brothers ridiculed as a 'frightful hotchpotch of bourgeois art' and which the Louvre accepted only reluctantly.[8] It included, however, Mme Thiers' famous pearl necklace which she had bought, pearl by pearl, from Germain Bapst. The items were put on display, together with the French Crown Jewels, in the Galerie d'Apollon, but since, as far as the Louvre was concerned, they had neither 'artistic character' nor any 'educative function', a draft bill of 1922 finally allowed the museum to auction them off. The sale took place in the Salle Denon in the Louvre on 16 June 1924 in the presence of more than one thousand spectators. The three strands of pearls, together with their clasp, were first called out separately and knocked down for Fr3,220,000, Fr2,680,000 and Fr5,030,000, the first two strands being bought by the dealers L. Hemsy and Baron Lopez de Tarragoya, and the third by Oscar Kahn. The clasp went to Paul Esmerian.[9] Immediately afterwards, the necklace was called out as a single piece, and it immediately passed into Cartier's hands for Fr11,280,000 ($2,256,000), since it was none other than Cartier who had given the buying order to Hemsy and Lopez. The necklace was exhibited both in the rue de la Paix and in New York, an entire room being set aside as 'a suitable shrine for the fabulous jewel, which the public came to view as though to a temple'.

Since the time of Louis XIV it had been diamonds which commanded the highest prices among precious stones, but around 1900 pearls began to enjoy a privileged position in the European and American markets, with prices being paid which seemed almost in the realm of fantasy. In 1908 G. F. Kunz wrote in his *Book of Pearls*,

Pearls of 100 grains are even more rare at the present time than are diamonds of 100 carats. Until the middle of the 19th century the diamonds of the world weighing 100 carats or over could be counted on the fingers, but since the opening of the African mines in 1870 the number of large diamonds has increased at a much greater ratio than have the pearls of one quarter of their weight. It would thus seem that pearls of great size are worth four times as much as diamonds of equal weight.

After 1900, whenever a perfect pearl was found in the Persian Gulf the whole of the European pearl trade was put on a state of alert. In this context, Paul Claudel observed that 'their appearance on the market depresses all other values. It alters their rates of exchange and causes the banks considerable alarm, since the latter feel that their operational stability is under threat, once a new and unquantifiable element has been introduced.'[10]

Auctioneers and retailers watched in amazement as prices rose above a million francs, and in one case even went beyond the million-dollar barrier. Trade journals were eager to report the spectacular prices being paid, which included:

1891	The pearls of the actress Léonide Leblanc, 4 strands with 212 pearls weighing 3,300 grains (auctioned in Paris)	Fr181,000 ($36,000)
1895	The pearls of the late Caroline Duchess of Montrose, 7 strands with 362 pearls (auctioned by Christie's)	11,500 gns ($57,500)
1900	At the World Fair, a single pearl weighing 128 grains and sold by the Russian jeweler Koechli	Fr150,000 ($30,000)
1901	The pearls of Countess Castiglione (auctioned in Paris)	Fr463,500 ($92,600)
1901	Mme Humbert's pearls, 6 strands with 424 pearls (auctioned by Christie's)	20,000 gns ($100,000)
1902	Count Dudley's rose-coloured drop pearl weighing 209 grains (auctioned by Christie's)	13,500 gns ($67,500)
	The Dudley pearl necklace, 47 pearls weighing 1,090 grains	22,200 gns ($111,000)
1904	The pearls of Princess Mathilde (auctioned in Paris)	Fr445,000 ($89,000)
1906	A 5-strand pearl necklace of 285 pearls (auctioned in London)	10,000 gns ($50,000)
1907	Mrs Lewis-Hill's pearls: 1 strand of 229 pearls (auctioned by Christie's, London)	16,700 gns ($83,500)
1907	Mrs Gordon-Lennox's pearls: 5 strands of 287 pearls (auctioned by Christie's)	25,500 gns ($127,500)
1909	Mme Polovtov's pearls: 4 strands weighing 3,852 grains (auctioned in Paris)	Fr1,003,000 ($200,600)
1910	Sale of pearls to Eva Stotesbury: 49 pearls weighing 656 grains (Cartier's, New York)	Fr810,000 ($162,000)
1910	Proposed sale of a pearl necklace to Mrs George D. Widener (Cartier's, New York)	$750,000
1910	Sale to Nancy Leeds of 39 pearls	

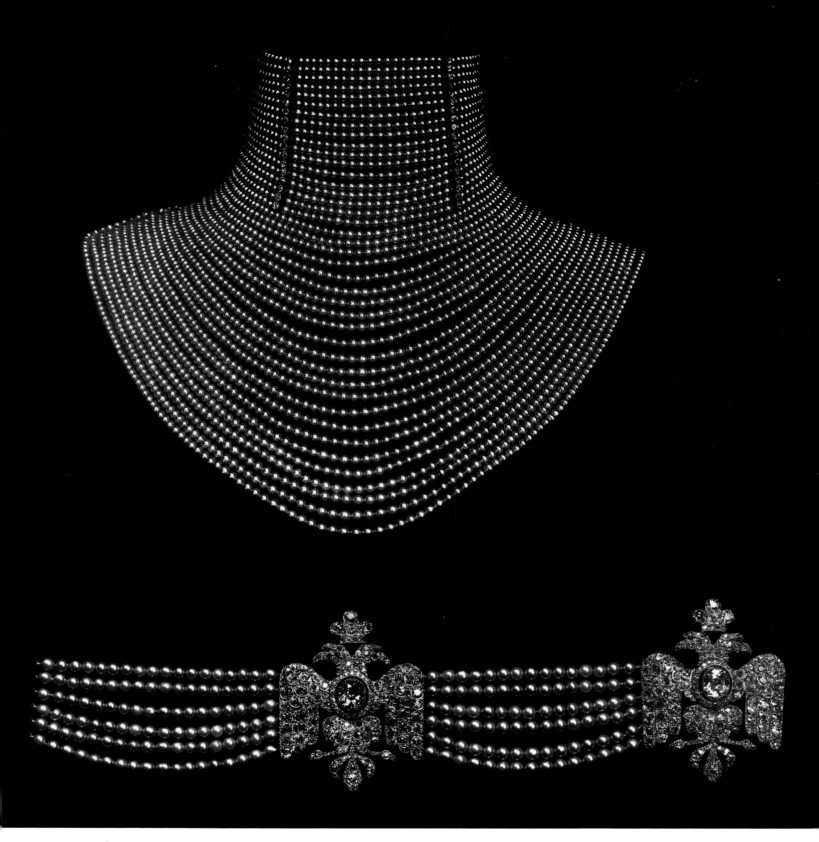

84. Edwardian 'draperie de décolleté'
mounted with 41 strings of pearls and rose-
cut diamond bars

85. Six-string pearl choker with 2 diamond
imperial eagles. Commissioned by Grand
Duchess Vladimir in 1900

	with diamond rondelles weighing 1,122¾ grains (Cartier's, New York)	Fr2,850,000 ($570,000)
1911	The pearls of Sultan Abdul Hamid (auctioned in Paris)	Fr920,000 ($184,000)
1913	Sale of 1 strand of 59 pearls weighing 1,199.34 grains (Cartier's, New York)	Fr859,117 ($171,822)
1918	The pearl auctions held by the Red Cross: total raised at the four auctions since 1916 (Christie's)	300,000 gns ($1,500,000)
1918	Mme de Falbe's pearl necklace (auctioned by Christie's)	47,000 gns
1919	Purchase of the Austrian imperial pearls (Cartier's, Paris)	Fr1,000,000
1920	A pearl necklace of Russian provenance made up of 188 pearls (auctioned by Christie's)	54,000 gns
1920	Purchase of a 3-strand pearl necklace of 171 pearls formerly owned by Tsar Nicholas I (bought by Cartier at the Lobanov Auction in Lausanne)	Fr553,000

This list, which is necessarily incomplete, can give us no idea of the relationship between price and quality. In the absence of reliable information about the quality of the pearls in question, it is impossible to say anything about the shape, colour and lustre of the individual pearls, or, in the case of the necklaces, about the graduation of the pearls. An indication of weight in grains (1 carat = 4 grains) simply makes it easier for us to imagine their approximate size. But what the list does show is the enormous value potential which pearls represented within the jewel market up to the 1920s, an impression confirmed by a comparison with the prices then being paid at art auctions:

1910	J. M. W. Turner's *Rockets and the Light* (auctioned in New York and bought by Duveen)	$129,000
	Frans Hals' *Portrait of a Woman* (auctioned in New York and bought by Knoedler)	$137,000
1911	A Gutenberg Bible (auctioned in New York and bought by Huntingdon, who also bought Gainsborough's *Blue Boy* from Duveen for $620,000)	$50,000
1927	Rembrandt's *Titus* (auctioned by Parke Bernet, New York)	$270,000
1928	Rembrandt's *Young Man with a Harelip* (auctioned by Christie's, London and bought by Knoedler)	44,000 gns
	Rembrandt's *Man with Torah* (auctioned by Christie's, London and bought by Knoedler)	48,000 gns

These few examples show that during the 1910s and 1920s pearl necklaces commanded the same prices as the most expensive Rembrandts and similar works by Old Masters. That there was also a connection between these prices and those being paid at the same time in the fluctuating and imponderable property market emerges from the now legendary events surrounding Cartier's purchase of the premises at 653 Fifth Avenue in New York. Pierre Cartier had long been searching for an ideal site in New York to replace the arrangement by which he occupied only a single storey of 712 Fifth Avenue (now the home of Rizzoli International). His eye was caught by the splendid six-storey Renaissance palace of the banker Morton F. Plant,[11] which Robert W. Gibson had built on the southeast corner of 52nd Street between 1903 and 1905.[12] With the sure instinct of a sales psychologist and market tactician, Cartier proposed a deal in 1917 to buy the building in exchange for his most valuable two-strand pearl necklace, which he had been assembling over the years and which Mrs Plant was keen to possess. Like the pearl parure previously bought from Tiffany's by Mrs George Gould, the two strands of fifty-five and seventy-three pearls were valued at one million dollars. The transaction was accepted without hesitation by the shrewd banker.[13]

Cartier's, Tiffany's, and Chaumet were the leading firms in the international pearl market. Cartier's made headline news in 1910 when they sold a necklace worth Fr2.85 million ($570,000) and consisting of thirty-nine pearls alternating with diamond rondelles. The buyer was Nancy Leeds, widow of the American tin magnate William B. Leeds and one of Cartier's most regular customers up to the First World War. In 1910, however, she was involved in a long-drawn-out court case with the American government about another necklace, which she had bought from Bernard Citroen in Paris in 1906 and which was valued at $220,000.[14] The pearls, which Mrs Leeds had imported loose into the country, were initially taxed at 60 per cent of the purchase price. The case dragged on for years, during which time Mrs Leeds lost her husband, and it was not until 1911 that the customs authorities declared themselves satisfied with a 10 per cent duty, and paid back the disputed sum of $110,335. The newspaper reports provoked by the affair took up almost as many columns as the sale of the Hope diamond which Cartier was then transacting.

The affair came to the ears of King Edward VII, who was passing through Paris on his way to Biarritz when Cartier showed him a perfect black pearl.[15] The king hesitated over buying it, and only later learned from Pierre Cartier that it had been sold in the meantime to Mrs Leeds. When, shortly afterwards, King Edward discovered that both he and Mrs Leeds were staying together at the Hôtel Bristol in Paris, he sent word via Cartier that he would be flattered by the favour of seeing her pearls. Clearly, Mrs Leeds' own charms were as seductive as those of her jewel casket, for Pierre Cartier was asked to present the sophisticated American woman with the king's dog 'Caesar', whose silver collar bore the inscription, 'I belong to the king.' The sequel to all this is not recorded, but Mrs Leeds did subsequently become a frequent visitor to the English court.[16]

In 1922 Prince Felix Youssoupov made his first contact with Pierre Cartier in New York. Once the owner of Russia's largest private fortune, he had engaged, since fleeing the Revolution, in reckless speculations which were to trouble him for the remainder of his life and which were often to try Cartier's patience throughout the twelve years of their relationship. Youssoupov, too, had had problems with the American customs: on entering the country, he had been carrying with him the items of jewelry that he had managed to salvage from Russia and which the authorities immediately seized. There was also litigation with the Widener family over two paintings by Rembrandt, and then an unsuccessful attempt to sell parts of his collection of snuffboxes to Elsie de Wolfe for her New York gallery. Before the Revolution, Felix's mother, Princess Zenaïde, had so frequently paraded her historic jewels in Paris and Rome, that no one could say that there was not tangible proof that they actually existed (see p. 121). In 1887, for example, on the occasion of the sale by auction of the French crown jewels, Fabergé had successfully bid for the 'Régente' pearl on behalf of the Youssoupovs, and it was later worn by the princess as a hair ornament.[17] Her jewel casket also contained the black drop pearl 'Azra',[18] the pearl known as 'La Pelegrina', and a black pearl necklace. Her daughter-in-law, Irina, wife of Prince Felix, was given on the occasion of her marriage in 1914 a pair of pearl ear pendants, together with a two-strand pearl necklace presented to her by the tsar and a diamond necklace with a pink pearl drop, given her by Grand Duke Nicholas.

When Prince Youssoupov turned to Pierre Cartier for financial help, the first pledge he laid before the astonished jeweler was his mother's black pearl necklace, once owned by Catherine the Great.[19] Black pearls — those 'drops of liquid rose-beetle-coloured darkness' — had always had a sinister significance to superstitious minds,[20] more so, certainly, than white pearls — a fact which Empress Eugénie discovered on her wedding day, when she was advised against wearing the black pearls that she owned. It was therefore not until 1924 that Cartier succeeded in selling Prince Youssoupov's black pearls when Mrs Peter Goelet Gerry of Washington acquired them for $400,000. In the meantime, the prince had received an advance from Cartier of $75,000, and, as an additional pledge, deposited with the jeweler a second necklace of thirty-one pearls.

Further negotiations involving the Youssoupovs' jewels began in London in 1927, when the participants included Jacques Cartier, and Felix and Irina Youssoupov. The princess, whose 'severe beauty would have suited an icon, while her classically perfect profile recalled a cameo',[21] was still in mourning for her relatives who had been killed in Russia, and she attended the negotiations dressed in black. The couple offered Cartier button pearl earstuds weighing 130 grains; two drop pearls weighing 184 grains; the 'La Pelegrina', weighing 133.20 grains; a pearl necklace of 151 pearls, weighing 1,380.80 grains; a pearl necklace of 35 pearls, weighing 911 grains; a pearl necklace of 3 strands made up of 276 pearls, and 7 pendants comprising 83 pearls, together with a clasp of red stone and diamond (formerly owned by Count Branicki of Poland).

The collection was repeatedly mortgaged by the prince between 1927 and 1929, Cartier's and the firm of T. M. Sutton operating jointly and advancing the by no means inconsiderable sum of £37,807. Not until 1934 did Cartier buy the pearls, long after the family's diamonds had found new owners. But the crisis which by then gripped the world's economies had so weakened the market that the proceeds from their subsequent sale were considerably less than the original advance of 1927. 'La Pelegrina' was the only jewel Prince Youssoupov seemed reluctant to part with, and not until 1953 did he finally sell the jewel whose history has always been mysterious.[22] The buyer was the jeweler Jean Lombard of Geneva.

A single perfect pearl may inspire awe and amazement, as is clear from the hymn of praise written by Paul Claudel following a visit to Cartier's: 'I turned it between my fingers with the aid of a needle, and observed how it shone from every angle. But not like the diamond, that geometric pentacle with its hard, penetrating fire; no, the pearl is something attractive, charming, delicate, one might almost say − human.'[23] In describing the kingdom of Heaven, the Bible tells of a merchant who sold all he had in exchange for a 'goodly pearl'; and it can hardly surprise us to hear it said, in a far more prosaic context, of the American silver millionaire Clarence Mackay, that one of Cartier's pearls weighing 130 grains was 'the only thing in the world that had ever impressed him in his life'.[24]

In 1933 the 'wedding of the year' took place in Paris, when the heiress Barbara Hutton and Prince Mdivani were married in the city's Russian Church. The witnesses included the artist José-Maria Sert;[25] the Maharajah of Mysore appeared wearing a picturesque turban, Ganna Walska wore her sapphire and emerald jewels bought at Cartier's, and the Hon. Mrs Daisy Fellowes her two Indian-inspired Cartier cuffs. The bride's engagement ring was also from Cartier's and consisted of a single black pearl weighing 105 grains. She had recently returned from Bali, where she had admired the natives' traditional wooden headdresses, and prevailed on Louis Cartier to design a Balinese wedding tiara made of tortoise shell, with a diamond pattern identical to the blossoms of her wedding veil. But Cartier's most substantial commission came from the bride's father − a necklace of fifty-three pearls that had formerly been worn by Marie Antoinette. It was described by the press as 'one of the rarest strands of pearls ever sold by Cartier'. But even the most awe-inspiring piece of jewelry was not spared unorthodox treatment by Barbara Hutton, as Elsa Maxwell discovered one day when she asked after it: ' "Where are your wonderful pearls, Barbara?" Barbara was suddenly glad to smile. "The goose has them," she said. "The goose?" questioned Elsa astonished. "Mr. Cartier told me," explained Barbara, "that if the goose swallowed my pearls they would come out with a brighter luster." '[26]

Pearl necklaces such as Barbara Hutton's and the one her aunt, Mrs J. P. Donahue, bought from LaCloche, were well-known in the trade, and often remained in the possession of one or more dealers, who consigned them to individual jewelers until they were definitively sold. Pearl experts, such as Suzanne Ricaud, who later married Cartier's designer Charles Jacqueau, assembled the best pearls owned by various dealers, turning them into exquisite necklaces, with different coloured threads distinguishing pearls from different sources.

Among the leading pearl dealers in New York at that time were Joseph Frankel (who, as a dealer in diamonds, had acquired the Hope diamond in 1901), and the firms of Adler, Bass and Eisenmann (the last-mentioned an associate of the Paris firm of Munroe), while the leading dealers in Paris were Jacques Bienenfeld (who maintained his own flotilla of ships off the coast of Venezuela),[27] Baron Lopez and Bernard Citroen. Paris was the world's leading market in pearls between 1910 and 1930, employing around four hundred specialists. London, in comparison, represented only about 30 per cent of European trade until after the Second World War, when it became Europe's busiest centre.

The undisputed head of the pearl trade, however, was the firm of Rosenthal, owned by a family from the Caucasus, where they had originally acted as representatives for Baccarat, the crystal firm. A triumvirate of brothers — Leonard, Victor and Adolphe — brought the business worldwide recognition. For Louis and Jacques Cartier they had nothing but the highest regard, though on a purely professional level, while important trading partners, they were also bitter rivals. The eldest of the Rosenthals, Leonard (b.1875), settled in the rue Lafayette and later wrote two standard works, *Au royaume des perles* and *Au jardin des gemmes*. His brother Victor (1880–1961) moved to the Persian Gulf around 1895 and then to Bombay where, like Jacques Cartier, he counted local dealers and maharajahs among his friends. In the case of the Maharajah of Kashmir, the ties were not merely personal but extended to their mutual interest in the country's world-famous sapphire mines.

Around 1910 the rarest white pearls came to Europe from the Persian Gulf, Ceylon (modern Sri Lanka) and Australia, whereas black pearls generally came from Tahiti and Panama. American freshwater pearls from Ohio and Wisconsin were normally confined to the American market. The Persian Gulf had been famous since Biblical times for its pearls: Bahrain, with its vast oyster beds, was the Greek Tylos. After its colonization by the Portuguese in the sixteenth century, the Gulf was then administered by Arab sheikhs. Bahrain pearls were sent to Bombay, which was the chief trading centre[28] and where, around the year 1910, the lion's share of the market was held by two Arab dealers, Abdul Rahman and Sheikh Jassim, who in consequence of their status were regularly heaped with attention by Cartier and Rosenthal. The Bombay market reacted with seismographic sensitivity to disruptive influences in the Gulf and in Europe. If the Gulf's pearl harvest was small, few items of any interest found their way to Bombay. If, on the other hand, it exceeded expectations, there was the danger that the Arab traders would bypass Bombay and deal directly with Paris. But if the European market was endangered, as it was, for example, at the time of the Balkans War of 1912, business in Bombay came to a standstill. At the beginning of the First World War in 1914, Bombay lost 30–35 per cent of its share of the world market, and Abdul Rahman, the 'Prince of Pearl Traders', went bankrupt, as did nine banks scattered across the Indian subcontinent. In 1917 the Indian market was down a further 30–40 per cent on its previous year's turnover, and only when Rosenthal (together with the bank Bloch Dreyfuss) unexpectedly bought himself a huge share of the market at between 5 and 7.5 million francs was the situation saved. In 1918 the Indian government placed a temporary ban on the export of pearls.

Cartier's maintained a permanent representative in Bombay, the Parsi Sethna, who sent weekly reports on the state of the market to Paris and London, and frequently arranged for pearls to be forwarded to Europe. Like his father Alfred, Jacques Cartier was the firm's special expert on pearls, and it was he who accompanied the sales assistant Maurice Richard on various journeys to the Persian Gulf and to India. In accordance with Oriental custom he would sit cross-legged in his negotiations with local traders, and he learned the customs, languages and habits of the various nations which he visited. Two of his journeys were recorded in the form of a diary and various other reports. Parts of one of them are worth quoting from.

His ship the *Tynesider* left the port of Karachi on 3 March 1911. On board were twenty Arabs, including the influential dealer Alibin Ahmed Chiravi from the island of Moharek, Jacques Cartier, his cook, Maurice Richard, the ship's first engineer and the captain. Jacques spent the time practising his Hindustani and considering the idea of a permanent office in Bombay. He frequently fled from the noisy Arabs, seeking refuge in the quiet of the captain's private chapel. On 9 March they arrived at Muskat. The island seemed to the visitors to resemble a pirates' den. The sultan received Cartier in his residence surrounded by a 'confused mass of French furniture resembling the junk room of a middle-class Frenchman'. An unexpected caller was the Sheikh of Dubai, accompanied by his servants, 'handsome Arabs with proud expressions, and armed to the teeth'. Was the secret meeting between the two princes an indication that some major sale of pearls was in the offing? The travellers returned to their ship, where all at once 'The sea was lit with a phosphorescent glow. The bow of the ship ploughed a furrow through the deep-blue waves, which seemed to be shimmering from below. The ship appeared to be surrounded by a girdle of light; fish darted past in dazzling zigzag patterns; a veritable firework display rose up out of the sea.' They sailed past Musandorn, which 'enjoys the reputation of being the hottest place on earth; neither birds nor insects can remain there in summer, and even the fish leave the waters'; and on to Bunder Abbas. From the distant island of Hormuz, the 'Pearl of the Orient', beckoned the ruined Portuguese fort. On 12 March they reached the port of Lingah: 'One would find it difficult to justify the existence of this town: it has neither a proper harbour nor a river, neither woods nor mountains, and not a trace of culture. A few hundred houses, a labyrinth in which a guide is indispensable.' The pearl traders of Lingah received their merchandise from Dubai, reselling the pearls to Bahrain or dispatching agents direct to Bombay.

Dubai itself, where the *Tynesider* arrived on 12 March, resembled some 'cannibals' beach in a popular novel. The inhabitants do not spare the lives of those they rob, for the Koran forbids them from robbing the living but not from emptying the pockets of the dead.' It was 285 miles from Dubai to Bahrain, where they dropped anchor on 14 March in the port of Manassa.

86. Pearl and diamond pendant necklace suspending a pink pearl of 83.36 grains from a baton diamond of 2.17 cts and rose-cut diamond links. 1912

Jacques Cartier was welcomed by his host, Sheikh Mujbal, 'a tall, stout man with a beard and the profile of a goat'. The guests were shown to a small house where they spent the night, the servants sleeping on stone benches while raucous birds built their nests in the rafters above them. 'We're never alone for a moment,' Cartier confided feelingly in his diary. Sheikh Mujbal placed at Cartier's disposal an old motor car of which he was particularly proud, for there were only two cars on the entire island, everything being transported on the backs of white donkeys, which were as strong as horses. And the women? They wore black veils, which hid them from prying glances and to Jacques they seemed simply 'walking sacks'. The greatest effort at self-control required of the Europeans was during their communal meals with the sheikh, when ginger syrup was drunk and enough food consumed 'to keep the shipwrecked sailors on the raft of the *Medusa* alive for a month'.

The sheikh suggested a visit to one of the oyster beds and its fisheries, but although the divers opened as many as two hundred oysters, they failed to find a single pearl. Jacques took the opportunity to observe the divers at work. Each diver earned between two hundred and four hundred rupees in the course of the season; he was paid not in money but in essential items, including a sum of money which allowed him to pay back what he had been advanced at the beginning of the season. His equipment was simple: nose clip, leather finger protectors and ear wax for great depths. In addition, a basket was fastened to a rope with which the diver was pulled back up to the boat again. The diver would stand with one foot in a stirrup, beneath which a stone was attached; he would press the stone with one foot and glide down, with his basket, into the ocean depths. The stone and rope were then immediately pulled back up again, leaving the diver free to collect the oysters with both hands, while the basket remained round his neck and his legs were stuck up in the air. As a rule, he would stay down for a minute, after which time he would give the 'puller' a sign by means of the rope, and be pulled up again. The divers were paid so little that they inevitably became enslaved to their masters. At the bazaar, Cartier paid 500 rupees for a pearl weighing 16 grains, intending to have it bleached in Bombay.[29]

Cartier then visited Sheikh Isa on the neighbouring island of Moharek, where his party were shown the hot-water springs, Phoenician tumuli and a German trade settlement which imported rice, coffee and cotton, and in return sent mother-of-pearl to Europe for the manufacture of buttons. Sheikh Isa was 'a handsome old man: I showered him with compliments, for I was slowly coming to understand the Oriental way of expressing oneself. The conversation was very slow: I spoke in English, Sethna translated what I said into Hindustani, and then Sheikh Yusuf Kanon translated it into Arabic for the benefit of Sheikh Isa, so that a sentence of fifty words turned into a conversation lasting half an hour.'

Soon, however, the party had to take its leave of Bahrain. It was a solemn occasion: Sheikh Mujbal read from the Koran, while a slave handed round coffee and rosewater. Jacques presented his host with his watch and chain, together with a gold pencil, and to the women

87. Jacques Cartier with two sheikhs on his pearl trip to Bahrain in 1911

of the house he gave costly fabrics. Mujbal returned the compliment with a gift of baroque pearls.

Journeys to India and the Persian Gulf in the footsteps of Tavernier brought Jacques Cartier and his companions into direct contact with the cultures and customs of the Orient. They could judge for themselves, on the spot, what imagination went into the reworking and wearing of pearls. On their return to Paris they presented the designers with suggestions and brief sketches. And, just as at the time of the Renaissance strands of pearls had been used as imaginative dress ornaments, in the 1920s fashion designers and jewelers, tired of the traditional pearl necklace, attempted to use pearls in new and unfamiliar ways, in order to incorporate them into the latest fashions. Around 1900, for example, the height of fashion had been the *bayadère*, composed of several strands of seed pearls plaited together and generally decorated with a pendant or tassel.[30] From around 1910 their place was taken by long sautoirs, which during the 1920s measured up to anything between twenty-five and twenty-eight inches; their famous models were the string of pearls owned by Princess Pless of Germany, which was over seven metres long, and the pearls of the French actress Cécile Sorel, which reached down to below her waist. At the Manhattan Opera in New York, on the other hand, Mary Garden caused a furore in the opera *Thaïs* when she appeared wearing a costume embroidered with long pearl sautoirs.

The tendency at this time to exaggerate vertical length was echoed by ear ornaments in the form of large drop pearls, which were all the rage at the time of the *garçonne* style of the 1920s. There were varied ways in which ear pendants reproduced the form of the eighteenth-century girandole, as one can see from a model ordered from Cartier's in London by the Rani of Pudukota. But it was New York which at that time already had the greatest turnover in the sale of pearls. 'The salesmen are asking for nothing but pearls, and then more pearls,' we read in a report sent to Pierre Cartier at that time. In 1920 Cartier's of New York launched a novel article of jewelry, which was 'neither an ear pendant nor a necklace', but a strand of pearls attached to the ears, with a single drop pearl dangling beneath the wearer's chin. Ideally, it would be complemented by the chic of a bandeau worn low on the forehead and a strand of pearls wound several times around one wrist.[31]

It was in the 1920s that Japanese cultured pearls, full of the charm of novelty, began their successful assault on the markets of Europe and America.[32] Firms such as Cartier's and Chaumet steadfastly ignored the new product: the term 'boules blanches' ('white beads') which was frequently found in insurance valuations treated the new and unpleasant process with the requisite scorn. But it would be wrong to assume that it was the appearance of cultured pearls which precipitated a crisis in the pearl industry. The crisis which really affected the market and which brought about its radical restructuring was the Wall Street Crash. During the 1930s, prices fell to a tenth of those that had been paid up to 1928, remaining at that low level until around 1942, when they climbed back to 15–20 per cent of their former values. But Bahrain, which remained the most sought-after supplier of pearls, had in the meantime lost most of its divers to the new oil refineries, which paid higher wages, offered less unhealthy work conditions, and promised year-round work rather than a mere four months. As a result, numbers fell from 60,000 to under 6,000. The second industry which was involved – the mother-of-pearl market, which was important for the manufacture of buttons – was severely weakened by the spread of synthetic materials. The supplies which reached Bombay from Bahrain became so scarce that after 1942 prices on the Indian market rose to three times their previous level, becoming prohibitively expensive for buyers from Paris and London, and indirectly from America, too. Between 1920 and 1930 America's annual pearl imports had amounted to around $10 million, but by 1942 this figure had fallen to $200,000, and in the following year it shrank still further. Cultured pearls profited from this weakening of the market. They were already the subject of scientific study and as a result their yields increased. Japan was to produce cultured pearls up to 9.5 mm in diameter, and in the 1950s Burma responded with the world's finest and largest specimens, measuring on average 16–18 mm. Oyster beds continued to be set up in Australia, Tahiti and the Philippines until the 1960s, and since 1968 the descendants of Leonard and Victor Rosenthal have had a leading share in this market. Tahiti is additionally important as one of the few places where black cultured pearls are produced.

88. The Rani of Pudukota wearing her Cartier pearl and diamond girandole ear-pendants. 1929 (photo: Cecil Beaton)

89. Model wearing Cartier's pearl and diamond ear-pendants-cum-necklace (photo: American *Vogue*, December 1920)

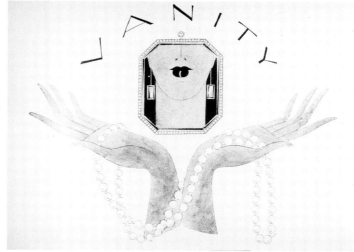

90. Contents page of *Vogue*, 1 November 1926

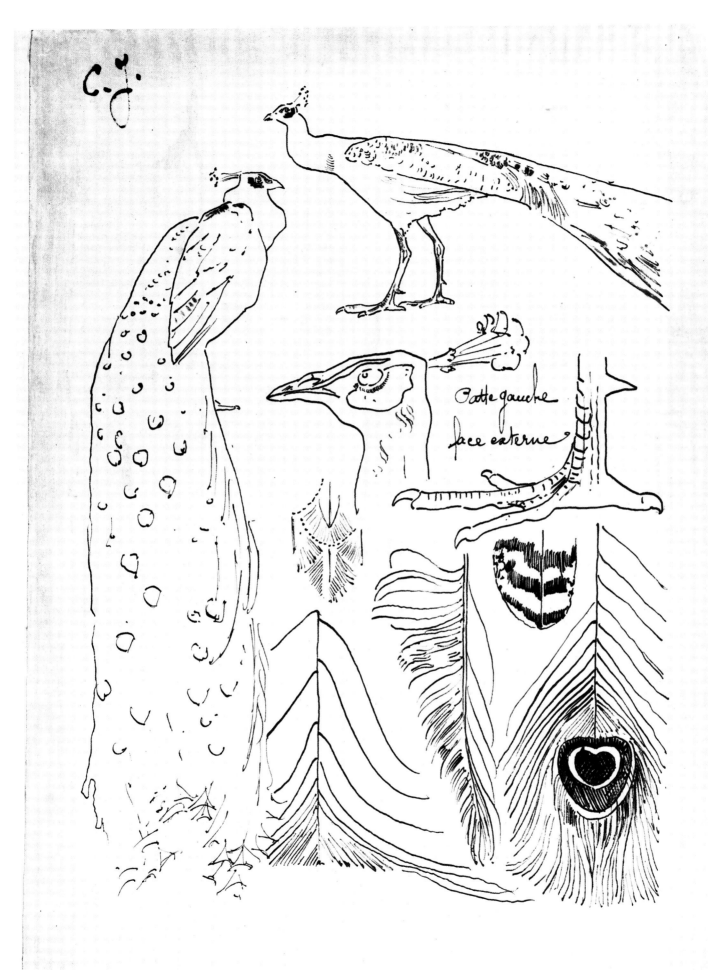

Patte gauche
face externe

Charles Jacqueau and the Ballets Russes

9

WRITING IN 1934, in a retrospective account of the 1925 Exposition Internationale des Arts Décoratifs et Industriels Modernes, Emile Sedeyn expressed his regret that Louis Cartier had not published the names of the resident designers who had been responsible for the firm's magnificent exhibition in the Pavillon de l'Elégance.[1] But Cartier's policy was aimed at propagating the firm's name alone as the epitome of exemplary achievement. The contributions of individual designers were consequently viewed as the work of an anonymous collective – an attitude which has important repercussions for the historian, for it has proved extremely difficult to ascribe the surviving sketches and designs to any one designer simply on the basis of stylistic characteristics. As a rule, sketches of ideas and designs left the studios unsigned, the only mark on them being the abbreviation 'A Ex.' (*à exécuter*, to be implemented), added by whoever may have been responsible for the idea in the first place, whether Louis Cartier, Jeanne Toussaint or René Revillon. The chosen design was then forwarded for costing and finally passed on to the workshops.

Because of Cartier's insistence on anonymity, the name of his most brilliant employee, Charles Jacqueau, remained largely unknown outside the firm. But in retrospect Jacqueau appears, alongside Paul Follot, or Georges Verger, as one of the pioneers of the art deco style.

Jacqueau was born in Paris in 1885, the son of a master butcher from the Morvan. He won first prize for drawing at the Ecole de Neuilly, and in consequence was offered a scholarship to the Ecole des Francs-Bourgeois in Paris. This Jacqueau instinctively turned down, enrolling instead at the Ecole Bernard Palissy, where he studied drawing, pottery and porcelain painting, before transferring in 1902/3 to the Ecole des Arts Décoratifs. To gain further practical experience he then took a job with Raingo Frères, a firm dealing in bronze sculptures, and it was here, in 1909, that the Cartier designer Georges Genaille, shortly before moving to New York, noticed Jacqueau almost by chance; and Louis Cartier, sensing the young student's talent, took him on virtually without conditions.[2] Cartier's had recently lost Maurice Rauline – one of their most important figures and a leading exponent of the garland style – whose quarrelsome temperament had forced him to resign. His place had been taken by Henri Chenaud, who had joined the previous year and whose work was similarly influenced by the style of the eighteenth century. It was he whom Cartier's entrusted with designing the majority of the tiaras. Emile Thomas (b.1869), who had entered the studio in 1907, bringing with him a training in architectural design, took over its management on Rauline's departure. His designs were of clear mathematical structure, making up in precision what they lacked in spontaneity of inspiration. Another identifiable designer, Olivier Baloche (1878–1943), had been in tapestry design and worked at Cartier's Paris from 1902, then in their London workshop from 1909 to 1911. Also deserving of mention are Gaston Vignal, who was both a designer and an enameller;

91. Page of peacock designs from Charles Jacqueau's sketchbooks

Edmond Forêt; Finsterwald and Massabieaux, both of whom followed Cartier's to London; and Maurice Duvallet, whose future lay with Cartier's New York.

The Paris studio, which in the early years of the century already employed eight designers, was housed along with Alfred Cartier's offices at 4 rue de la Paix, where it remained until the First World War. The designers' work was divided into items which went into stock and those ordered specially by customers; the majority were naturally intended as stock, but whenever there was an increase in customers' orders, the designers responsible would be assisted by the other department. Initially Jacqueau was placed in the department producing items for stock, but he soon made himself indispensable designing customers' orders, too.

The garland style which was fashionable at Cartier's in Jacqueau's time was, as we saw, based on a revival of the Louis XVI style being taught at the Ecole des Arts Décoratifs. As an alternative to the revolutionary mode of art nouveau, it was an elegant idiom which Jacqueau continued to use occasionally up to the beginning of the First World War. His sketches include examples of all the items produced in this style: tiaras, stomachers, necklaces, belt buckles, umbrella handles and boxes. Jacqueau handled the garland style with impressive virtuosity, in command of its every nuance and often inventing new formal combinations. Basically, though, he was too brilliant an innovator ever to feel completely at home in the style's confining world. The greatest service he rendered Cartier's and contemporary design in general was to abandon the garland style, espouse bold colours and design, and become the champion of a new aesthetic which, following the First World War, was given official but belated recognition at the 1925 Exposition Internationale des Arts Décoratifs et Industriels Modernes and which later gave its name to an entire period of early twentieth-century art. Thanks to Jacqueau, it was Cartier's which produced the most convincing examples of the art deco style well before the outbreak of the war, giving the firm that artistic advantage which distinguished it from its rivals.

By 1900 it was no longer thought necessary for an artist's training to include the classical tour of Italy; knowledge of the different historical styles was transmitted by the art academies. Jacqueau's work lies at the intersection of all these styles. There is evidence of a very early visit to Florence, Rome and Venice (a journey repeated many years later in 1937) and of course of that trip to Russia, accompanying Louis Cartier, in 1911. But the experiences gained in the course of these travels were not such as to affect Jacqueau's style. Also, his later visits to Morocco in 1928 and subsequent years were motivated simply by the desire to see his brother who was living there, and were not responsible for the Islamic element in his style, which had been present from as early as 1910. The same is true of his visit to Spain in 1951.

The close cooperation between Louis Cartier and Charles Jacqueau lasted for twenty years, ensuring the highest level of inspiration in all the designs that the firm produced during that period. The first sketches suggesting new motifs were generally the work of Louis Cartier, who would often jot down his ideas, with unpractised hand, on menus from the Ritz or loose scraps of paper. Before Jacqueau's arrival, it had always been Louis' influence which had prevailed in his work with the designer Maurice Rauline. At that time the credit for inventing many new motifs in the garland style was quite clearly Cartier's (for example, his rhomb with its fluttering ribbons). But from the time of the First World War, when Jacqueau first began to adapt the ideas of the Ballets Russes and of the *Gazette du bon ton* for jewelry designs, Louis Cartier's direct influence on the design studios started to wane, a fact which may also have been due to the demands then being made on his time by the firm's international expansion.

In the designs he produced, Jacqueau showed himself to be both a visionary and a realist. His Egyptian, Greek and Chinese fantasies, which were the basis of many of his standard designs beginning in 1910, show his wide-ranging imagination. In the majority of cases it was the Louvre which provided him with his first crucial impression; he visited the museum on countless occasions to sketch objects on the spot. His interests were eclectic: an Assyrian temple relief, an Egyptian stela, a Celtic trumpet-pattern ornament, and a Chinese *famille noire* vase were all recorded in his notebook with precise technical details, to appear at some later date, utterly transformed, in Cartier's products. It is amusing to observe the way in which stylistically unequivocal motifs, noted down in the Louvre, re-emerge in a new and often functional context – an Islamic architectural arch appears as part of an art deco comb, and an Egyptian mosque lamp as a stylized pendant, while a Greek column with an Ionic capital turns into a pendant or a letter opener. Conversely, the simple geometric form of an inkwell might be transformed into a pure architectural fantasy in which the sketch was so far removed from reality as to be impractical to execute.

The civilizations which provided Jacqueau with the greatest stimuli were those of Egypt, Islam, India, China and Japan. He borrowed from them all. What most interested him in Egyptian art was the stylization of masklike faces, the flat outline of the lotus, and simple architectural cubes. From Indian and Persian miniatures he took stylized plant motifs, and from Persian carpets came the central medallion which reminds the devout Muslim of the garden beyond the grave. His reworking of Chinese motifs is somewhat more superficial. He was fascinated by the writhing forms of the Chinese fire-breathing dragon, as well as by the curving silhouette of Chinese and Japanese temples and the flat outline of the peony, which he adapted in innumerable studies. But as during the 1920s the main emphasis in Cartier's chinoiseries lay in the adoption of original Chinese and Japanese lacquerwork and since such pieces were already perfect, self-contained works of art, the copyist was frequently left merely with the task of designing border ornaments to match the lacquerwork in colour and form.

Among the profusion of designs included in Jacqueau's sketch-books, or *cahiers d'idées*, are a handful of African motifs inspired by both the 1925 Exposition and the Colonial Exhibition of 1931. One thinks, for example, of his design for a Sudanese necklace and

92. Charles Jacqueau (1885–1968), Cartier's most brilliant designer, drawn by his colleague Auguste Lenglen

bracelet, or the sketch for a necklace with tiger's paw motifs. Greek art, on the other hand, was a relatively minor influence on his work. Admittedly, he used meanders and Vitruvian scrolls as border motifs, and the palmette was incorporated into a Greek tiara, but the canon of Greek forms belonged to that very historicism from which he was striving to liberate himself.

Apart from the Louvre, the other source of his inspiration was the Jardin des Plantes. Here he observed animals fighting, birds in flight and plants, and once again he captured every detail with his pen. The series of gemstone plants which Jacqueau inspired Cartier's to produce bears witness to his deep affinity with organic nature which resulted in his fellow designers goodnaturedly nicknaming him 'Jacqueau la Fleur'.

Yet all the impressions garnered in museums, churches and in nature itself pale before the shock (no other word can describe it) which the Ballets Russes induced in him overnight.[3] Jacqueau's wife Suzanne recalls him following the Ballets Russes with bated breath, a sketchbook in one hand. His obsession with ballet in general was so great that in 1913 his colleagues in the design studio drew playful caricatures of him looking like Isadora Duncan in billowing veils. Diaghilev's dancers – Nijinsky, Karsavina, Ida Rubinstein, Anna Pavlova (who was soon to leave the company) – provoked veritable storms of enthusiasm in the Châtelet Theatre where they first appeared in 1909, pushing the opera performances, which had been intended as the more important part of the programme, very much into the background.[4] In 1910 it was the ballet *Schéhérazade* which fired the imagination of critics, artists and audiences, all of whom reacted as though in a daze to the colour of the costumes and the swirling movement of the production.[5] The colours included an emerald-green curtain which opened to reveal the harem of Shahryar, King of India and China. In the background were orange-coloured pillars and three blue doors, a gold-blue coverlet and cushions in garishly colourful designs, piled up in indiscriminate profusion. And the sense of movement! Nijinsky, the gold-clad Moor, shot on to the stage, where he joined Zobeida, the favourite wife of Shahryar, at which the frenzied movements turned into a veritable bacchanal, to the accompaniment of Rimsky-Korsakov's music. The choreographer, Michael Fokine,[6] had been inspired by Persian miniatures, while Leon Bakst had designed sets evoking the world of a sultan's harem, flashing with colourful costumes of geometrical design. Overnight Paris fashion designers were persuaded to turn to the Orient in their search for inspiration. The couturier Paul Poiret who, thanks to Ida Rubinstein, had direct access to Diaghilev's world, created turbans topped with aigrettes, and a harem dress with Turkish trousers lifted straight out of *Schéhérazade.*[7]

The impact of the Ballets Russes enabled Louis Cartier and Jacqueau to break free from the confining influence of the somewhat schematic Louis XVI garland style. Although Jacqueau, as already noted, was to continue to exploit it, the way was now officially open for a much wider choice of unrefracted colours. There could, however, be no clearer proof of Louis Cartier's superb awareness of colour than the fact that, even before the Ballets

Russes, the colours used by his designers covered the entire spectrum of complementary combinations.[8] As early as 1903 pendants described as 'Chinese' or 'Japanese' were designed and set either with sapphires and amethysts or with emeralds and sapphires. An entry for 1906 lists tie pins described as 'rainbows' and made up of *calibré* sapphires, emeralds and amethysts.[9] Green was paired with blue, red with black, and purple with bright green, producing brilliant phosphorescent shades which replaced the subtle pastel shades of the fashionable Marie Antoinette style.

A similar revolution had been brought about by the fauvist painters, especially Matisse and Derain, who at the Paris Autumn Exhibition of 1905 had first declared their commitment to the use of unrefracted colour. Applied to the manufacture of jewelry, this resulted in contrasting combinations of sapphires and emeralds, amethysts and sapphires, jade and amethysts, with rock crystal being used as the neutral background in a new contrapuntal handling of colour. Colour contrasts were accentuated on enamel surfaces by means of cabochons, while coloured *calibré* gemstones produced linear border designs which, during the earlier period, had been achieved by means of enamel lines. These bold experiments in the handling of colour were Cartier's unchallenged prerogative, and amounted to nothing less than a revolution in the jewelry trade. Particularly the blue-green match, which Louis Cartier called his 'peacock pattern', was an innovation which, in the light of traditional attitudes towards colour, was bound to be seen at least as risky, if not as simply tasteless. Isolated examples of such a colour contrast may be noted in earlier periods, as in the coronation sword of Gustav III of Sweden (1780), where amethysts and emeralds were paired together; and in France around the year 1860 one finds a predilection for green and blue enamelling.[10] Also worth mentioning here are a number of peacock feather brooches which were shown at exhibitions and which employed *calibré* gemstones in a blue and green pattern; they included Mellerio's peacock feather brooch of 1867 and Coulon's necklace of 1900.[11] The jeweler Robin produced brooches based on Persian designs, pairing together sapphires and emeralds, or rubies and emeralds. But the most direct — and in view of Louis Cartier's known predilections — the most likely influence determining his choice of blue and green as a colour combination is probably to be found in enamelled Mogul jewelry of the seventeenth and eighteenth centuries.

The Ballets Russes' use of flat geometrical designs also became generally fashionable around 1910 but found no immediate response in Cartier's designs. If it were a question of structuring the surface of vanity cases with the so-called *jeux-de-fond* design, then the immediate inspiration was Islamic trelliswork and star motifs, which in the 1920s gave way to Chinese patterns, and only toward 1930 to cubist forms.

Another important collaboration between Louis Cartier and Jacqueau was the setting up of 'Department S' (S for silver), which sold both elegant gifts and everyday consumer goods (see p. 197). Even a most cursory glance at Jacqueau's sketchbooks reveals the way in which aesthetic invention and functional design were for him parts of the same creative process. The ornaments which he included in his work were always to be found in their proper place, but were only justified by the functional context of the whole, from which they could not conceivably be divorced. Unlike the earlier garland style, in which ornaments were simply added to each other, though in relation to some central point or axis of symmetry, the mature Jacqueau now designed 'structural' ornaments, logical beyond the purely decorative level.

The idea of a functional aesthetic, which tolerated ornamentation only within a meaningful context, had been advocated in England around 1860 by William Morris and his circle, and had had a determinative influence on the arts and crafts movement shortly before 1900. In turn this had left its mark on Jacqueau's generation of the 1890s. Throughout his life, the French designer continued to work on these problems, and developed into a notable innovator. Just as Nijinsky invented a windscreen wiper and a ball-point pen, so Jacqueau, adhering strictly to the aesthetic rules of art deco, invented a pocket chess set in a gold-embossed leather case, a night lamp, a folding tape measure, a portable toothbrush, and an expensive onyx container for dental floss. He liked to design objects with a twofold function, such as a magnifying glass with a letter opener attached, which was both practical and elegant. There was a direct link between this emphasis upon practicality and the thousand-and-one luxury items which made up the greater part of Cartier's art deco range – articles such as vanity cases, cigarette cases and desk sets, which threatened to relegate items of pure jewelry to a subordinate position. Among the designs for Department S, which Jacqueau provided with his usual extremely precise technical instructions, are sketches for handbags, one with a chequered pattern which anticipates the op art designs of Victor Vasarely.

In Jacqueau's choice of materials for his designs, we find an echo of the theory that all materials are equally valid, a belief that artists such as Lalique and Fouquet had propounded around 1900 as a reaction to the overblown, grand style of the Third Republic. Gérard Sandoz had advanced this thesis in 1902: 'Assuming its technique and manufacture to be flawless, a well-designed item of jewelry costing Fr200 is just as attractive as one similarly designed and costing Fr2 million.' Jacqueau's designs confirm this fundamental tenet: agate, lapis lazuli and coral were used alongside the most expensive gemstones, and priceless diamonds weighing 15 and 20 carats were attached, with great effect, to a simple black silken cord.

What distinguished Jacqueau's geometric art deco forms from those of his rivals was the impression they gave of floating on air. Whereas the massive, constructivist forms of Sandoz and Fouquet were often difficult to reconcile with the essential character of jewelry, Jacqueau's geometric forms remained within a framework of dainty lightness. He never tired in later years of encouraging the workshops to produce delicate, lightweight pieces. His instructions repeatedly advised, 'surtout très léger' ('above all very light').

In 1947 Jacqueau signed a contract enabling him to spend the following year producing designs for Cartier's London. At the same time he introduced Jacques Cartier's son, Jean Jacques, to the world of jewelry design.

Whereas Jacqueau's artistic vocabulary helped to form the aesthetic language of the 1910s and 1920s, he was deeply uninterested in the aesthetic outlook of the 1940s, which no longer stretched his imagination, but rather allowed his inventiveness to atrophy. Moreover, his mentor, Louis Cartier, had died in 1942, leaving a gap similar to that suffered by the Ballets Russes following Diaghilev's death in 1929. In view of this, it is not surprising that Jacqueau's style during the late 1930s and 1940s was virtually indistinguishable from the style found in every studio in Paris at the time. What was needed was the artistic enthusiasm of a new generation of designers, which at Cartier's found its ideal expression in Peter Lemarchand, who was to evolve new ideas of jewelry design from the spirit of the postwar years.

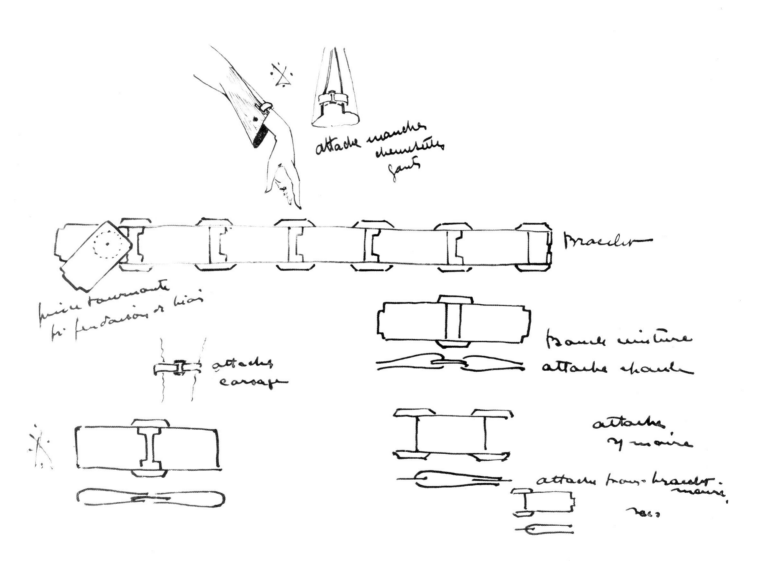

93. Sketches for designs of bracelets by Charles Jacqueau

'THE DAY OF DAYS, the most wonderful of my life,' exulted Howard Carter the archaeologist,[1] and on 30 November 1922 *The Times* published its matter-of-fact report of the discovery and official opening of the tomb of Tutankhamun, in the remote Valley of the Kings in Egypt. It was the most sensational archaeological find of the twentieth century – comparable with Heinrich Schliemann's excavations at Troy in 1871 – and thanks to astute manipulation of the media it awoke considerable interest outside the academic world. The discovery released a wave of excitement which, overnight, swept the fine arts, literature, fashion and film. An ancient myth had been reborn.

Carter's excavations, undertaken in the service of Lord Carnarvon,[2] are commonly dated to the year 1922, but in fact they were a complicated and drawn-out process which took ten years to complete. For eighteen years before the discovery, Carnarvon had poured a fortune into the search for the tomb of Tutankhamun, the pharaoh who married a daughter of Akhenaten and died, aged eighteen, in the year 1352 BC. It was not until 4 November 1922 that Carter came upon a first, sealed wooden door, and on 26 November, with the discovery of a second entry bearing the seal of Tutankhamun, he knew that at last he had reached his goal. The antechamber, containing the throne and two life-size statues of the pharaoh, was the first to be inspected. After that came the actual burial chamber: four gold-plated shrines concealed the quartz sarcophagus, with its one-and-a-half-ton lid. It was not until two years later that the lid was raised; then, to the horror of the academic world, a dispute caused it to be left suspended for a further eleven months. The contents of the coffins within the sarcophagus – the golden mask of the pharaoh, the diadem embellished with cobra and vulture, the sixteen-row cloisonné pectoral, armlets, rings and much more – were deposited in the Cairo Museum while Carter continued to investigate further treasure chambers until 1932.

Against Carter's wishes, the tomb became a spectacle in which the whole world participated. While Egypt debated bitterly whether or not the treasure should be used to settle the national debt, commerce, industry and public imagination began the systematic exploitation of the find.

Yet there would have been an Egyptian craze during the 1920s even without Tutankhamun. European interest in the ancient Nile civilization dated from at least the eighteenth century: at that time, the newly discovered frescoes at Herculaneum and Pompeii were seen to have reference to the cult of Isis which had reached Italy via Alexandria during the Roman period.[3] From the Renaissance onward, the canons of classical Greek and Roman art were taught in every academy, whereas Egyptian art, with its reference to the world of the sacred and mysterious beliefs concerning the afterlife, was considered esoteric and was more sparingly studied. It was not until 1798 that Egypt became the focus of European attention; in that year, aiming to weaken England's colonial position decisively, General Bonaparte launched his Egyptian campaign. It was to end in

10

Pharaohs, sphinxes and pyramids

94. 'Egyptian' temple gate clock in blue engraved mother-of-pearl, the base and top in lapis lazuli, the mother-of-pearl face framed by coral batons, with lateral coral handles. 1927

catastrophe for France, yet it had been planned with considerable foresight as more than a merely military expedition. The leading scientific names of the period — Berthollet, Monge, Denon and Geoffrey Saint-Hilaire — were associated with the undertaking and brought to an astonished Europe the first topography of Egypt to be based on exact observations, in *Description de l'Egypte*. This was followed in 1802 by Vivant Denon's *Voyage en Haute et Basse Egypte*, which was to inspire every field of art in the opening years of the new century. By Napoleon's command, Egyptian décor made its appearance in the design of furniture and the art of bronze and porcelain. The Sèvres factory produced Egyptian dinner services and table ornaments in the forms of Egyptian statues, temples and obelisks; the emblem of the goddess Isis was incorporated in the Paris coat of arms. The groundwork done under Napoleon eventually enabled Jean-François Champollion to decipher the Egyptian hieroglyphs in 1822 and thus to gain a systematic understanding of Egyptian culture and its connections.[4] At the same time, and of much greater interest to Champollion's contemporaries, Mehemet Ali, vice-regent of Egypt, promised Louis XVIII an obelisk from Alexandria. In 1831 an obelisk, though not the promised one, was shipped to France aboard the *Luxor* and erected in the Place de la Concorde. Its influence on decorative arts and jewelry was immediate. From then on it would be impossible to imagine the repertoire of French and English jewelry without exotic Egyptian motifs alongside the themes of romantic glorification of the Middle Ages.

A second factor in promoting the Egyptian fashion was the long-drawn-out building of the Suez Canal (1859–69), the brilliant accomplishment of the Frenchman Ferdinand de Lesseps. Impressed by such pioneering achievement, the jewelers Mellerio, Boucheron and Baugrand created Egyptian pieces, while Baugrand also decorated his showcase at the Paris Exhibition of 1867 with an Egyptian statue and chariot. Two years later, the Empress Eugénie attended the celebrations of the official opening of the Canal by the Khedive Ismail; among the spectators were Théophile Gautier, Henrik Ibsen and Eugène Fromentin. The delayed culmination of the festivities came in 1871 with the first performance of Verdi's *Aida* at the inauguration of the Cairo opera-house. In the year of the empress's Egyptian journey Lemonnier, Eugénie's court jeweler, created his aigrette with lotus flower and birds' wings, and in 1873 the Egyptian pieces of the jeweler Emile Philippe, pupil of Jules Wièse *père*, made their appearance. By this time, the Egyptian fashion was no longer confined to France. In London, the Italian jeweler Carlo Giuliano created his important brooch with two horse's heads, lotus flower and mask.

While Castellani and Fontenay were experimenting with jewelry in the Etruscan style, based on exact and analytical observation, workers in the Egyptian style contented themselves with a formal repertoire which lacked archaeological authenticity and concentrated on the exotic in pharaonic Egypt. One example is the ancient Egyptian technique of cloisonné-enamelling which was used only sparingly in ancient times, the desired colour contrasts usually being achieved with inlays of stone or glass. In the nineteenth century, however, cloisonné enamel was lavished on jewelry which was called 'Egyptian' but which nevertheless remained faithful to the Second Empire style of Napoleon III. In its most popular form it was handled as souvenirs, in which sphinxes, lotus flowers and scarabs in embossed gold predominated, while the favourite intarsia stones were turquoise, cabochon garnets and lapis lazuli.

At first, the Egyptian collection of Louis-François Cartier, the firm's founder, was much the same as his competitors'. An early entry for an Egyptian piece in Cartier's stock book for 1852 concerns a scarab bracelet of pearls and enamel; it is followed in 1854 by a scarab brooch and in 1860 by a scarab ring. In Egyptian mythology, the scarab beetle, sacred to the god of the morning sun, was a symbol of resurrection and, though deprived of its protective character as an amulet, the scarab, in lapis lazuli or garnet, remained a favourite Egyptian theme in the nineteenth century.[5] In 1856 Cartier even sold a scarab brooch in turquoise and diamonds to Princess Mathilde, who also received a pair of Egyptian earrings of unspecified design in 1861.

Cartier's most sophisticated Egyptian piece dates from 1873, when the fashion peaked: it is a châtelaine in the form of an Egyptian head in gold, rose diamonds, rubies and a cameo. From this hangs a watch, its back decorated with an Egyptian figure in traditional headdress, the mount of which stands as an early example of the use of *calibré*-cut rubies. The next notable Egyptian pieces come in 1893: a brooch with an Egyptian head and lotus blooms of matt yellow gold and a lotus brooch with five navette diamonds, a pearl and coloured stones.[6]

It is not surprising that art nouveau, supreme in Paris by about 1895, included Egyptian motifs: one example is René Lalique's tiara of 1899 with Isis and lotus motifs. It is, however, somewhat remarkable to find examples of Egyptian ornament in Cartier's contemporary garland style, essentially eighteenth-century in inspiration. The explanation lies in a stylistic adaptation based on vague formal associations. In 1908, Cartier produced a dog collar with diamond drops and lotus motifs, and in 1911 a necklace of diamond bars adapted from the ancient Egyptian type known as the 'broad bead-collar'.[7] These pieces were as far removed from true Egyptian forms as the 1906–07 series of obelisk and pyramid clocks in fluorspar, diorite, thulite and porphyry in which Cartier followed late eighteenth-century fashions in interior decoration.

That enthusiasm for Egyptian archaeology remained high during the early twentieth century is clear from a sequence of sensational discoveries which widened historical knowledge of Egypt and considerably swelled the academic literature. After 1850, the French archaeologist Auguste Mariette[8] laid the foundations of the Bulaq Museum in Cairo with a number of important finds, and after Mariette's death in 1881 the French Egyptologist Gaston Maspero continued the work,[9] dividing his time between excavations in Egypt and a professorship in Paris. It was he who opened up the temples at Karnak. In 1908, Edward Ayrton discovered a royal tomb at Thebes and four years later the German Borchardt came upon the head of Nefertiti. In 1914 Flinders Petrie laid bare the Pyramid of Sesostris II in

Lahun. At the same time, large collections of Egyptian art were being assembled, of which the most important in private hands was that of Lord Carnarvon (now in the Metropolitan Museum, New York).

In the wake of these great discoveries, a number of important art dealers specializing in treasures of the ancient Mediterranean world opened businesses in Paris. Among them were the brothers Kalebdjian of Cairo and Dikran Kelekian, who was also represented in Cairo and New York. Young Louis Cartier became a regular visitor to both establishments: neighbourly relations were soon established with Kalebdjian at 12 rue de la Paix, and Kelekian, at 2 Place Vendôme, was not far away. Louis bought rare pieces of antique art from both, which he displayed at his house in the rue Saint-Guillaume: we know of an Egyptian cat in faience from Kelekian, as well as a bas-relief portraying the Pharaoh Rameses. That Louis took his business with the two dealers very seriously is indicated by the technical discussion concerning an Egyptian wooden mask; both he and Kalebdjian consulted the curator of the Egyptian department in the Louvre as to its precise identification.

Arising from his study of the art of the Mediterranean peoples, Louis Cartier came up with the idea of a new synthesis in jewelry design which was to enrich the wide-ranging selection at the rue de la Paix with a novel Cartier speciality: fragments of ancient jewelry and *objets d'art*, complemented with contemporary settings and presented in fresh contexts. The idea was both daring and up to the minute, yet there were interesting precedents in earlier centuries.[10] An exhibition was planned in which jewelry of different periods and cultures would demonstrate the richness of colour and variety of theme of the new design programme. The show opened at rue de la Paix on 2 June 1913 and later at the Copley Plaza Hotel in Boston. The catalogue, embellished with Louis Cartier's favourite motif of a Persian carpet medallion, promised 'a selection of Persian, Indian and Tibetan jewelry to suit the latest fashion'. Although Egyptian jewelry was not mentioned on the title page, an Egyptian lotus pendant and a turquoise amulet featured among the exhibits.

Some of the exhibits were from Kalebdjian's collection; some from the London dealer Imre Schwaiger, a specialist in Indian art. The following year Kalebdjian was to deliver a whole series of Egyptian pieces to Cartier, among them a head from the Said period in turquoise-blue enamel; a Greek Alexandrian sphinx in gold; two Egyptian capitals with seated cats; a turquoise-blue falcon pendant; a Uraeus snake in cornelian; and a lotus collar in faience and gold. However, Kalebdjian did more than merely supply Cartier. Six months after the latter's exhibition Kalebdjian staged a Christmas show of his own, consisting of a selection of 147 pieces of ancient jewelry. The catalogue observed laconically: 'Today fashion decrees that the elegant Parisienne should wear ancient jewelry; and not merely stale imitations, but the very jewels themselves that once adorned the bosom of an Egyptian queen or a Greek empress.'

The inventive concept of combining ancient and non-European art of earlier epochs in modern settings led Cartier to astonishing syntheses in the fields of Egyptian, Indian and Chinese/Japanese art, which were unique in the art deco of the 1920s. In his Egyptian pieces

Louis Cartier preferred to employ ancient faience motifs, either figurative or embellished with hieroglyphs, as in the pendants, brooches and buckles produced from 1920.[11] The scarab remained popular: as early as 1904 Cartier had given his first wife a scarab ring, and as late as 1932 he received a commission for a necklace composed 14 of a faience scarab from the former Maspero collection, framed in ornamental diamond lotus blooms. Among the brooches inspired by representations of the Egyptian pantheon we find the goddess Isis, the falcon god Horus, the god Nefertum born from a lotus blossom, and the lion goddess Sekhmet.[12] The last-named is found in two sketches from the London workshop, produced for a customer with different border designs. Cartier's of Paris found Sekhmet very popular, and even used her as a motif on hatpins.

In 1920 Louis Cartier and Charles Jacqueau had created a vanity case in mediaeval style with an ivory plaque from Louis Cartier's collection inlaid on the lid. Later they produced four cases which represent the most significant examples of inlay work with Egyptian 15 elements. The first was a vanity case with the turquoise-blue faience figure of an Egyptian flute-player which dates from the months in 1924 when Howard Carter raised the lid of the sarcophagus in Tutankhamun's tomb. A large lotus plant in coral and onyx fanned out over the background of lapis lazuli and mother-of-pearl. The 13 following year saw the appearance of perhaps the greatest of these Egyptian-style cases, in the form of a sarcophagus: the arched cover consisted of an engraved ivory panel depicting a maiden among lotus flowers, framed in archaic Greek and lotus motifs in cloisonné enamel. At head and foot, the sarcophagus was embellished with figures of engraved emerald and *calibré*-cut sapphires, which recalled the recently excavated mummy of Tutankhamun and the enigmatic Sphinx. On the underside was a gold plaque adorned with a female offering-bearer surrounded by ibises and lotus stems. This case was acquired in the year it was made by Mrs George Blumenthal, wife of the American collector and banker. From 1927 comes a powder compact adorned with two bands of lapis lazuli and inlaid with an Egyptian stone relief depicting the god Ched.[13] The last in the series was a 1929 vanity case of lapis lazuli and coral, decorated on the narrow sides with two antique faience representations of the goddess Bastet as a cat on a pillar.

The Egyptian pieces produced by Cartier before 1920 bear out the supposition that the postwar years would have witnessed an Egyptian fashion even without the discovery of Tutankhamun's tomb. It was also predictable that the fashion would verge on hysteria — exploited as 'Tutmania' by the film industry and the luxury trade in both Europe and America — from the moment that Queen Elisabeth of the Belgians, Lloyd George, Cécile Sorel the French actress, and the Maharajah of Poona made pilgrimages to the site of the pharaoh's tomb, pursued by the press.[14] To accommodate the streams of tourists from America and Japan, Egyptian railways inaugurated the 'Tutankhamun special' between Cairo and Luxor. Would not the pharaoh, some asked, punish the desecration of his tomb? According to ancient Egyptian belief, the sun descended to the King of the Dead every evening, where it overcame the powers of Darkness, permitting the Dead to share in the radiance of eternity during the night, and then returned the next morning, rejuvenated, to climb the heavens once more. In fact, it did seem that Tutankhamun was taking his revenge when in 1923 Lord Carnarvon died of an insect bite. The legend of the curse of the pharaohs was thus born, and fear of an impending tragedy clouded the Egyptian expedition. Collectors disembarrassed themselves of their treasures and rushed to commit them to the security of the British Museum. The fashion industry, however, had no such qualms. Tutankhamun umbrellas and cigarettes, Leon Bakst's 'Isis' collection and Madeleine Vionnet's Egyptian models . . . the curse of the pharaohs became an overnight money-spinner. While Ramses, the Paris cosmetic firm, promoted their 'Ambre de Nubie' and 'Poudre de Riz au Secret de Sphynx' with sphinxes, pyramids and palms, René Boivin the jeweler, working until 1931 in the rue des Pyramides, decorated his firm's letterhead with appropriate Egyptian symbols.

The outlines of sphinxes, obelisks and pyramids came to evoke an entire culture. The fact that imitation hieroglyphs often introduced into art deco designs were quite meaningless is hardly to be wondered at. After all, in ancient Rome, the incomprehensible hieroglyphs on late Egyptian monuments had provided decorative models. It is interesting to note, however, that on Cartier's flute-player case, the hieroglyphs were in fact real. During this period Van Cleef & Arpels executed an exquisite series of brooches and bracelets, which conjured up anecdotal Egyptian scenes of pharaohs and priests, lotus plants and soul-birds in designs of coloured tesserae. In 1928 Boucheron, who did not rate the Egyptian style among his design priorities, created his cloisonné-enamel tiara with the sun falcon for King Fuad, who had opened the 1911 Franco-Egyptian Exhibition at the Louvre and who made a further visit to Paris in 1927.

Through Louis Cartier's personal preference for Egyptian art, his designers became more familiar with Egyptian materials and techniques and this led to a new synthesis of colour and form. From then on, the cool Egyptian combinations of cornelian and lapis lazuli; cornelian and turquoise; and turquoise, lapis-lazuli and gold enriched the art deco palette. Amethyst alone, which had also been known to the Egyptians, was put aside, having played out its dominant role in another fashion context after the year 1910. Gold, the preferred precious metal in the Nile civilization where it was much used for cloisons, was, however, less favoured than platinum by Cartier's designers. In the common art deco combination of black and white – onyx and diamond – platinum had the advantage that it did not create colour conflicts.[15] By contrast, the low-relief style and hieratic figures of Egyptian sculpture suited the two-dimensional orientation of art deco and were transferred without difficulty to the aesthetic of the 1920s. Cartier's designers, above all Jacqueau, despite his unconvincing assertion that the Egyptian style was alien to him, found inspiration in the Louvre, which, since the days of Mariette, could boast the largest Egyptian collection in continental Europe. Moreover, they could encounter remarkable traces of earlier Egyptomania on their sorties into the streets of Paris: for example, on the Egyptian house in the Place du Caire or the palm-bedecked fountain in the Place du Châtelet of 1858. Further inspiration was to be found in the study of the technical literature provided by Louis Cartier. Thus the 'torpedo' pendant launched by Cartier's in about 1912 derives from an animal-tail motif on a loincloth of the early XIIth Dynasty,[16] while Jacqueau's lotus blossom tiara of 1923 (later to be broken up) owed its inspiration to the headdress of the daughters of Djehuti-hotpe (d. *c*.1850 BC) in the Cairo Museum.

25   Next to the pyramid, the most favoured Egyptian architectural form in Cartier's jewelry was the pylon, a cone-shaped temple porch structure for a pyramidal base. It was first employed in 1913 as a frame ornament on a lotus vase and for the base of a sphinx. Above all, however, the pylon provided the outline for the most splendid of all Cartier's works in the Egyptian style: the temple gate clock of 1927. The cube-shaped carcase was freely modelled on the Khonsou Temple at Karnack and inlaid with mother-of-pearl with blue hieroglyphs. The plinth is adorned with a pharaoh and plants and a Nile river god making an offering, while on top a goddess spreads her wings wide. The coral mount of the clock face is complemented on plinth and upperwork with a counterpoint of lapis lazuli.

Louis Cartier provided the continuing stimulus for jewelry in the Egyptian style, but it was Jacques Cartier of London who organized the various exhibitions that were held in Cairo. After his death in 1942 this responsibility passed to Marcel Marson (b.1900), who had been a sales representative of the firm since 1928. In 1937 he went to Egypt on the occasion of the engagement of King Farouk, and the following year was sent to Albania for the wedding of King Zog I. Although Cartier's Egyptian style enjoyed a certain vogue up to the outbreak of the Second World War, the symbolic climax of its creative phase had been reached in 1929, the year of the Cairo Exhibition. On that occasion, Jacques Cartier played host to King Fuad, and the company received the royal warrant as suppliers to the Egyptian court.

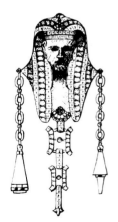

95. The Maharajah of Dhranghadra wearing his emerald, pearl and diamond turban ornament (1935) set with a cushion-shaped emerald of 160 cts and a drop-shaped emerald of 7 cts

96. Jean-Philippe Worth (1856–1926), father-in-law of Louis Cartier, dressed as an Indian potentate for a masked ball (photo: Nadar)

N THE SUMMER OF 1901, during the year of mourning for Queen Victoria, Pierre Cartier was called to Buckingham Palace. He was commissioned to create an Indian necklace from various pieces of the queen's jewelry, to be worn with three Indian gowns sent by Mary Curzon, wife of the Viceroy of India. Pierre Cartier was familiar with the Indian jewelry of the English royal house, which had accumulated as costly presents since the eighteenth century and become the greatest collection in Europe. However, the jewelry which Queen Alexandra wanted to wear had been mainly designed for men and was therefore too stiff and heavy to harmonize with the fashions of 1900. For this first commission from the palace, the Paris designers created a light and elegant Indian-style necklace, comprising seventy-one pearls, twelve cabochon rubies and ninety-four cabochon emeralds. Alexandra was pleased with the piece and wore it frequently.

For Cartier the commission meant not only the start of a long and profitable period of royal patronage, but also his first contact with the exotic world of the Orient. Thanks to the British imperial experience, Indian influence was much more marked in England than in Paris. It is hardly surprising, therefore, that from 1909 the Paris house assigned all aspects of its Indian business – the purchase of stones in Delhi, customer contacts in Bombay, and contacts with the maharajahs during their frequent visits to England – to Jacques Cartier and the London house.

While Europeans fostered grotesque ideas about India – 'India the great unknown – most people have a better idea of the moon' – Lady Curzon is said to have exclaimed, it became fashionable for the maharajahs to make extended tours of the European capitals, frequently undertaken on the pretext of engaging in political discussions in Whitehall or of escorting their sons to Eton or Harrow. The British authorities did not approve of the princes' long absences from their territories; indeed, Lord Curzon twice refused permission for the Gaekwar of Baroda to travel. But the princes relished the freedom and comforts of the great European cities and indulged themselves in luxuries and hotel life. While Curzon thundered against 'this class of uncultured, sporty, womanizing young princes', the Maharajah of Kapurthala dined unconcernedly with Queen Victoria at Balmoral and, later, Ranjit Singh of Nawanagar diverted himself with cricket at Cambridge.

The highpoints in the display of European–Indian magnificence were Edward VII's coronation in London and its celebration a little later at the Delhi durbar, where the king-emperor was represented by his brother the Duke of Connaught. The Delhi celebrations were opened by the Nizam of Hyderabad and the Maharajah of Mysore, India's two most powerful princes, and featured the ceremonial elephants of the Maharajah of Benares. At the ball which followed, Lady Curzon created a sensation with the later famous emerald-adorned peacock robe by Worth of Paris.[1] Edward VII, while still Prince of Wales, had visited India and Nepal in 1867 but his royal progress of 1906 is more famous. Pictures of Queen Alexandra riding in her howdah, accompanied by the Nawab of Bhopol and Lord Kitchener, stimulated throughout Europe an interest in all things Indian. In the following year Princess Lucien Murat described the gardens of Golconda and the lake palace of Udaipur, the 'Venice of India', in *My Journey to India*. Up to the 1920s, India, together with Persia and Egypt, was to provide exotic backdrops for European society life and inspiration to literature, fashion and interior décor. Poiret sketched the Indian turbans in the Victoria and Albert Museum; Diaghilev created his Hindu ballet *Le Dieu bleu*; Hindu-brown became the fashionable colour; and Mrs Payne Whitney decorated her house in Westbury, Connecticut, with Indo-Persian frescoes.

The first points of contact with the forms of Indian jewelry and ornament came in the nineteenth century with the world exhibitions.[2] Shortly before the Great Exhibition of 1851 the East India Company presented Queen Victoria with examples of Indian jewelry together with the legendary Koh-i-noor diamond.[3] Further pieces reached Europe following the looting of Delhi after 1857–58. By the 1860s Mogul jades decorated with flowers and birds had become known in England. Liberty's began to adapt Indian designs and jewelry, alongside its Japanese pattern range, which were eagerly taken up by the avant-garde, such as the Pre-Raphaelite artist Rossetti. In 1876 Victoria was proclaimed Empress of India, and from 1880 Indian jewelry enjoyed a vogue in both England and France. Hamilton the British jeweler set up in Calcutta, while in London the Italian Giuliano enjoyed success with his Indian-inspired enamelled jewelry. In France, Oscar Massin executed a commission for a belt for a maharajah and his competitor Rouvenat hit upon the idea of the long pin, which he called the 'Kashmirienne', to be worn with the then popular Kashmir shawl. The (Paris) Exhibition of 1867 included engraved and pierced Indian diamonds.[4]

At about this time we find the first mention of jewelry of Indian provenance in the Cartier archives: 1872, Indian earrings of gold and turquoise; 1879, a five-strand pearl necklace with six small enamelled Indian plaques; 1884, two three-rope necklaces with Indian gold coins and Indian enamelled buttons.

It was not until 1900, prompted perhaps by the World's Fair of that year, that the firm itself created an 'Indian' ring of two cabochon emeralds. Like the earliest pieces described as 'Egyptian', this ring was formally inspired by the Orient, but the platinum setting was undoubtedly determined by contemporary Parisian trends. Shortly after this Queen Alexandra placed her first order with the firm. But it was not until about 1910 when, under Poiret's influence, fashion began to dictate Persian-Indian aigrettes and pendant motifs, that Indian creations became of any significance. Interestingly, *The Grammar of Ornament* by Owen Jones, a popular pattern book with numerous Indian designs, was frequently used by Cartier's in both Paris and London. In 1910, we find an entry for a pendant in the Persian manner at Cartier's New York and in the same year the *Herald Tribune* was praising the 'Persian and Indian designs of Cartier'.

The first important contacts with maharajahs were consolidated during the celebrations of George V's coronation at the durbar in

Delhi in 1911, and in the same year Jacques Cartier embarked in the *Polynesia* at Marseilles for his first journey to India. The voyage to Bombay, via Malta, Port Said and Aden, took sixteen days. To his surprise he found that the maharajahs, who welcomed him into their palaces, were chiefly interested in pocket-watches, which were then high fashion in Paris and London.

Thanks to the merchants of the East India Company, European watches, clocks and automata had been known in India since the eighteenth century, being among the European wares on sale at their Lall Bazaar in Calcutta. Tipu Sahib, the feared Sultan of Mysore from 1782 to 1799, was said to have commissioned a life-size automaton of a tiger which, to musical accompaniment, savaged a European, from a French clockmaker. Jacques Cartier had no man-eating predators on offer, but he did sell a number of harmless watches. The Maharajah of Kapurthala purchased one in blue enamel; the Nizam of Hyderabad one in gold; the Maharajah of Nawanagar one in platinum; and the Aga Khan one ornamented with pavé diamonds. The Nawab of Rampur was enticed by four chiming carriage clocks, which were to sound the 'charming peal of European cathedral bells'.

Sayaji Rao III, the Gaekwar of Baroda, whom Cartier visited in his five-hundred-room palace of Lakshmi Vilas, proved more fastidious. The founder of India's most modern state, he had proscribed the caste system and introduced free education, and his popularity was demonstrated later at his golden jubilee by the presentation of a cannon made of pure gold, which fired a twenty-one gun salute. But his great passion was jewelry and he commissioned Jacques Cartier to reset his entire collection in platinum, then more prized than either gold or Indian enamel work in the westernized courts of India. Shrewdly, Jacques had included some 133 pieces of platinum jewelry in his sample cases for the Indian trip – among them combs, brooches, stomachers, an 'Egyptian' necklace and, of course, numerous watches. The Gaekwar was so taken with the young Cartier that he immediately wanted to entrust him with the maintenance of all his jewelry. However, disturbed by Cartier's growing influence in Baroda, envious Indian jewelers stirred up suspicion among the rival factions at court. After a few days, therefore, Jacques took honoured leave of the 'court circus' to embark again in the *Tynesider*.

Jacques Cartier's important Indian journey demonstrated something that was to hold true for the next quarter of a century: Indian rulers were exclusively interested in Parisian jewelry and had no hesitation in handing over their family treasures for reworking in fashionable European styles. Conversely, India's traditional enamel jewelry with its engraved gemstones became something of a craze in Europe, and inspired in the designers of Cartier's art deco style a special feeling for the Orient.

It was the colourful quality of Indian enamel work that made the first impression. In contrast to European enamel, which mostly adhered to the cloisonné technique, Indian champlevé enamel preserved some centuries-old colour patterns.[5] From Benares came the exquisite rose-coloured enamel, with lotus, leaf and bird

Colour plates 33 — 44

33. *Above left:* 'Chinese' vanity case, the gold mount enamelled in red, with black enamel and gold dragon amid 'Chinese' clouds and cabochon emeralds. The sides in fluted onyx and rose-cut diamonds. Interior with compartments. 1927

Above right: 'Chinese' compact, the circular gold powder compact enamelled in red and black. Rose-cut diamond motifs. Applied with a European chinoiserie of a mother-of-pearl dragon on waves. The chinoiserie possibly by Vladimir Makovsky (1884–1966). 1927

Below: 'Chinese' powder box, the circular white agate cover applied with an ivory chinoiserie of a dragon amid waves, inlaid in mother-of-pearl and gold. The base with coral and gold bead border. Ebonite mount. The chinoiserie possibly by Vladimir Makovsky. 1924

34. *Left and centre:* 'Chinese' vanity case, in gold with coral and turquoise, applied with 2 wood and hardstone plaques, one with fanciful depiction of two of the three Han heroes accompanied by the stork of long life and sheep, the other with a Taoist immortal and animals (Chinese, nineteenth century). Black enamel pagoda scroll border with diamond dragon surmount. 'Shou' emblem of long life at top and bottom. Onyx finger-ring and engraved Persian turquoise amulet. Interior with compartments. 1924

Above: 'Persian' vanity case, the gold mount with lobed mother-of-pearl medallion with engraved emerald leaf on turquoise. Rose-cut diamond, black enamel, cabochon emerald and pearl border. The interior with compartments. 1924

35. *Above left:* Chimaera bangle, in gold, green, red and blue enamel and cabochon emeralds, applied with 2 coral, diamond and cabochon sapphire chimaera heads holding 2 engraved emerald beads of 48.43 cts with onyx tips. 1928. Sold to Ganna Walska

Below left: Designs for the above bangle

Above right: Chimaera bangle, the articulated sprung mount in coral with onyx intersections. Circular-cut diamond crest and eyes. Commissioned by Louis Cartier in 1924

36. 'Chinese' repeater clock, the gold mount applied with 3 lacquered mother-of-pearl plaques depicting garden scenes (Chinese, nineteenth century). Mother-of-pearl numerals. Rose-cut diamond hands. Jade and red enamel borders. Onyx base. Jade buddhist lion push-piece. Two similar clocks are dated 1927 and 1930

'Chinese' cigar box, the gold mounted nephrite case with applied lacquered mother-of-pearl plaque showing a Chinese pavilion scene (nineteenth century). With rose-cut diamond and cabochon ruby additions. Coral border and thumbpiece. 1925

37. *Above left:* 'Chinese' vanity case, the gold mount applied with two jade plaques carved with animals amid foliage (Chinese, nineteenth century), the sides in marquetry of mother-of-pearl with coral, onyx and rose-cut diamond borders. Interior with compartments. 1929

Above right: 'Buddha' brooch, the god carved in chrysoprase and seated on a gold, diamond, onyx and rose-cut diamond throne. Similar Buddhas are dated between 1927 and 1928

Below: 'Chinese' vanity case, the gold mount enamelled red and overlaid with 2 pierced jade plaques carved with birds among foliage. Cabochon sapphire and rose-cut diamond motif. The sides enamelled green and blue. Sapphire and emerald clasp. The interior with compartments. 1928

38. *Above left:* 'Chinese' vanity case, the gold case with reeded coral borders. Diamond and black enamel surround applied with 2 lacquered mother-of-pearl plaques depicting nocturnal scenes (Chinese, nineteenth century), mounted with 2 sapphires, a ruby, an emerald, and a rose-cut diamond. Interior with compartments. 1926. Sold to Mrs Joseph Pulitzer

Above right: 'Chinese' vanity case, the gold case with black enamel, carved jade and diamond corners, applied with 2 lacquered mother-of-pearl plaques depicting a sage with disciple in contemplation (Chinese, nineteenth century), framed in coral, with cabochon ruby and rose-cut diamond. Interior with compartments. 1927

Below: Snuff bottle, in coral carved with lotus flowers (Chinese, nineteenth century). The stopper with pearl, diamonds and black enamel. On black wooden stand. Mounted to order in 1926

39. *Left:* 'Chinese' vanity case, the lid depicting a lady with fan on a terrace, on mother-of-pearl plaque set with aventurine, jade, coral, sapphires, emeralds and turquoise, on gold. 1928

Right: Vanity case, the gold mount applied with two European chinoiserie plaques in mother-of-pearl and hardstones depicting land- and seascapes with cabochon ruby sun and sapphire moon, framed by cornelian batons, jade, black enamel and rose-cut diamonds. The plaques possibly by Vladimir Makovsky. 1927

40. Invitation card, in Indo-Persian style, to an exhibition of Oriental jewels at Cartier's London in 1912

Nephrite cigar box, carved in nephrite, on lapis lazuli feet, the front inset with a gold clock with rose-cut diamond hands, within coral surround. Lateral gold and black enamel Persian motif, similar hinges and clasp. Inside the lid a gold plaque reads 'King George's Six Maxims'. A similar box is dated 1928

41. *Left:* Vanity case, applied with black enamel over gold. Central pierced carved jade (Chinese, nineteenth century) and diamond medallion. Borders with black enamel dragons on gold. Cabochon emeralds. Onyx finger-ring with rose-cut diamond attachment. Interior with compartments. 1924

Centre: Pen, enamelled black and red over gold, with rose-cut diamond band and coral tip. Cartier's New York

Above right: Brooch, enamelled black on gold in geometric zig-zag pattern. Rose-cut diamond centre line with bullet-cut diamond. The brooch opens to reveal interior compartments. Cartier's London. 1930

Right: Pocket watch, the square gold case enamelled black, the reverse with gold Persian pattern. Cabochon sapphire winder. 1924. Sold to Mrs James Corrigan

42. 'Chinese' vanity case: the gold case enamelled black and applied with 'Chinese' cabochon sapphire and coral peonies derived from *Famille Verte* designs, cabochon emeralds, topazes and moonstones. The sides with similar floral pattern. Interior with compartments. 1927

Art Deco handbags, one with diamond and black onyx frame with barrel-shaped engraved emerald clasp, the other with a frame in circular-cut diamonds and black and red enamel, with coral, diamond and onyx handle, and pearl, onyx and coral tassel. Sold to Mrs Harrison Williams

43. *Above left:* 'Egyptian' vanity case, the gold mount enamelled black, the lid with Goddess Maât in circular- and baguette-cut diamonds. Rose and baguette-cut diamond border and push-piece. 1930. Sold to Princess Amaryt of Kapurthala

Above right: Vanity case, the gold mount enamelled black. Rose-cut diamond borders with onyx bead corners. The lid with applied diamond flower. Suspended from diamond and onyx button. Cartier's New York

Below left: Belt-buckle, mounted with 2 onyx hoops with turquoise matrix, and onyx and diamond centre. 1922

Below right: Powder compact, the gold mount enamelled black with applied grapes of engraved and cabochon rubies. Circular- and baguette-cut diamond borders. With matching lipstick. Commissioned in 1931 and 1933

44. *Above:* Double clip, set with ruby and emerald leaves and berries with diamond scroll centres. 1929. Cartier's New York

Centre: Bracelet, designed as a band of engraved ruby and emerald leaves and onyx berries, with ruby, diamond and black enamel clasp. Cartier's New York

Below: Bracelet, designed as a band of engraved ruby leaves with emerald and sapphire berries, mounted on a diamond branch. Cartier's New York

33

34

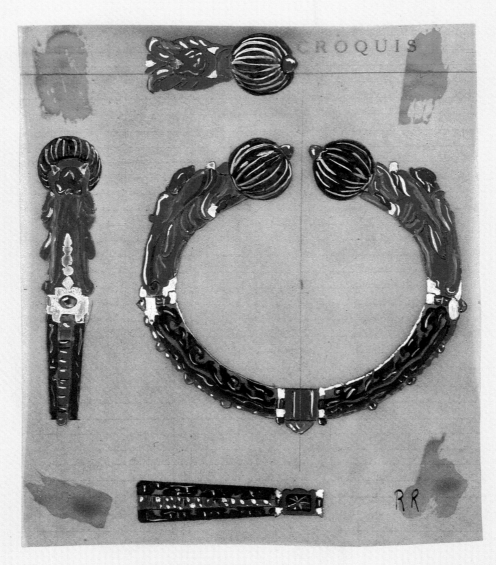

CROQUIS

RR

35

36

40

41

43

44

48

patterns which in the eighteenth century were influenced by Isfahan. The decorative motifs of Jaipur were still older – birds, elephants and wild boar gambol across a red, green or white ground. Centuries of consistent manufacture made Jaipur enamel a synonym for enamel itself. Miniature plaques from Jaipur became popular lid medallions for Cartier's vanity cases. However, the enamel which had most powerfully fired the imagination of Cartier's designers, even before Jacques' Indian journey, came from Lucknow, the capital of Oudh. Since the eighteenth century this enamel had been fused on silver, with blue and green the dominant colours. Next to the black and pink blend of onyx and coral, it became the colour combination most favoured by Cartier's art deco. Taking his cue from this enamel Cartier boldly juxtaposed sapphire and Indian engraved emerald with nothing to soften the startling colour contrast. Even before the Ballets Russes championed this same colour combination, Cartier's produced a necklace with an engraved emerald of 105 carats and a sapphire of 70 carats for J. P. Morgan, which was followed by similar items for Mrs Burns, Eugène de Rothschild and the Aga Khan.

Just as Indian enamel influenced Cartier's colour sense, so did the towering *sarpech* (*jiqka*) and the drooping *turah*, Indian turban ornaments, influence the designers in Paris, London and New York, in their choice of motifs. The principal component of the *sarpech* is the Kashmir palm or mango, a cone shape bent over at the point, found on Persian Mir and Serabend carpets, Mogul drawings of the seventeenth century and Kashmir shawls of the eighteenth.[6] From 1912 the Kashmir palm inspired the basic shape of the Cartier version of the fashionable aigrette. In the 1920s, however, it was adapted with a drop stone dangling from its tip to lapel and hat brooches. The *turah*, on the other hand, was a turban tassel of several strings of pearls fitted to a curved enamel bar; a specially valuable Indian example was the black pearl tassel worn by the Maharajah of Kutch-Behar. Cartier derived the rounded tassel indirectly from India – directly via the Ballets Russes and Russian costume – and transformed it into by far the most popular pendant motif of the art deco period. The Cartier tassel, often made up of hundreds of small pearls or coral or onyx beads, was generally attached, as pendant, to a necklace, to an onyx hoop brooch, or to an embellished jade stirrup bow. When worn as a shoulder ornament, the tassel might be as long as 25 cm.

The Indian *bazu* upper armlet, with its carpet-like central section framed in gold thread, inspired a Cartier bracelet in which a textile-patterned central section of diamonds was secured by a black silk cord. Other designs were derived from the Indian talismanic pendants of crystal or jade[7] with the planetary stones prescribed by Indian astrology. They inspired art deco pendants in a variety of colours: jade, amethyst or onyx were inlaid with cabochon gemstone or diamond floral patterns which recalled the marble friezes of Mogul architecture or the border decorations of Indo-Persian miniatures.

Diamond had many associations with the Hindu pantheon and was often given a gold-framed setting in the form of a lotus – an

23
31
27

Colour plates 45 — 48

45. Necklace, mounted with a fringe of emerald berries, sapphire and emerald beads, engraved sapphire and ruby leaves and suspending 13 briolette-shaped sapphires. Weight of sapphire clasp: 93.25 cts

Earrings, mounted with an engraved emerald with diamond calyx motif below an emerald bead and diamond flower head. Commissioned by the Hon. Mrs Daisy Fellowes in 1936

46. *Above:* Double clip, set with engraved rubies, sapphires and emeralds within circular- and baguette-cut diamond borders. Commissioned by Mrs Cole Porter in 1935

Centre: Bracelet, designed as a band of engraved sapphire and ruby leaves and emerald and onyx berries on a diamond branch. 1925. Sold to Mrs Cole Porter

Below: Bracelet, designed as a band of engraved emerald, sapphire and ruby leaves and berries, studded with circular-cut diamonds. 1929. Sold to Mrs Cole Porter

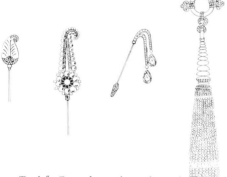

47. *Top left:* Crystal vase brooch, with diamond handles, ruby and sapphire berries, engraved emerald leaves and ruby and diamond base. Cartier's New York

Top right: Onyx vase brooch, mounted with jade, cabochon ruby and onyx flowers and diamond leaves. 1929. Cartier's New York

Centre: Lapis lazuli vase brooch, with coral lining and diamond base, displaying carved coral and diamond roses with emerald leaves and black enamel stalks. 1928

Below left: Lapis lazuli basket brooch, with diamond handle, displaying engraved ruby and diamond leaves with onyx berries. 1927. Cartier's New York

Below right: Onyx bowl brooch, set with circular- and baguette-cut diamonds, 2 cabochon rubies, and a cabochon emerald of 8.15 cts. 1925. Sold to Mrs W. K. Vanderbilt

48. A page from Charles Jacqueau's sketchbooks with designs for pendants and brooches reflecting Mogul India and the palette of the Ballets Russes

allusion to the ancient legend according to which Brahma, the World Principle, had emerged from a lotus blossom. Cartier's designers adapted the idea, assimilating it into the already existing lily-of-the-valley mount. The various forms of Indian necklaces, such as the *gulu*, a choker-style wedding ornament, were also influential while, in the 1930s, the stiff hoop collar known as *hasli* inspired necklaces and bracelets of massive design.

In India, Jacques Cartier learned to distinguish the age, origin and function of the local jewelry under the guidance of Imre Schwaiger, the Hungarian art expert. Schwaiger, who looked after Cartier's interests in Delhi and negotiated the purchase of Indian *objets d'art* and jewelry, divided his time between Delhi and London — his son later worked for Cartier's in London. It was from Schwaiger that Cartier bought a number of Mogul boxes, an enamelled *turah* and gold-painted green glass miniatures as ornaments for vanity cases, as well as turquoise and crystal figures of the elephant-god Ganesha, Krishna the flute player, or Buddha. In addition, precious stones were bought from Hindu, Jain or Parsi merchants. During the period of Jacques Cartier's Oriental journeys, a number of stones from the princely collections came under the hammer. In 1912 and 1913 the Nizam of Hyderabad had both gemstones and antique weapons auctioned while the Gaekwar of Baroda disposed of pearls and jewels. At these great auctions the Delhi jewelers were principally interested in emeralds while those from Gujarat concentrated on pearls — and each time emerald prices were high while there was hardly any demand for pearls.

The emerald was the stone most closely associated with India, even though, paradoxically, the subcontinent had no significant emerald deposits. By contrast, Ceylon was rich in sapphires and rubies and in 1881 unexpected finds had revealed the world's most valuable sapphires in Kashmir. Up to the sixteenth century, the only noteworthy emeralds known in India came from Egypt.[8] From then on Colombian emeralds began to reach India by adventurous routes,[9] through Spain's colonies in the Philippines and the Far East, as the great traveller Jean-Baptiste Tavernier was one of the first to suspect.[10] With these great velvet-green Colombian crystals[11] the emerald came to be reckoned with the ruby and the pearl among the most valued of stones. This was especially the case in India where the prismatic form of the beryl crystal, hexagonal in outline, was preserved in the outline of the cut stone.

In the early 1910s Cartier's spared no effort in a systematic search for rare Indian stones. In addition to Schwaiger in Delhi they had buying agents, like the Parsi pearl specialist Sethna, in Calcutta and Bombay, and the Bombay Trading Company, an autonomous Cartier subsidiary, developed the export–import trade between India, Europe and America, rather like Cartier's later European Watch and Clock Company. In 1912, it is true, the antique Roods red diamond escaped the net, but the wholesale purchase of engraved gemstones and gemstone beads broke all records. Cut and naturalistically engraved in leaf, blossom and berry shapes, they recalled the Islamic flower cult of the Mogul emperors and gave rise to some of the airiest creations of Jacqueau in Paris and Genaille in New York —

44 flower and fruit bracelets, and brooches in the shape of fruit bowls or flower baskets. The themes were often repeated but never became stereotyped. Of specially inspired design were a fruit bowl for W. K. Vanderbilt; a little Persian tree for Mrs Blumenthal; and two
46 bracelets and a clip for Mrs Cole Porter. In 1923 an elegant pendant was created from a 136-carat emerald sphere together with an emerald of 42 carats cut to the shape of a bunch of grapes.

Although the terms 'Persian' and 'Indian' were both used in these categories, the reference was always to the art of the Mogul empire which fused Hindu and Persian elements. The nomenclature employed in the special exhibition mounted by Cartier in 1913 (see p. 152) was equally variable. In the Indian context the catalogue made special mention of 'a bracelet with eighteen large diamonds, similar to that of the Maharanee of Gwalior; a necklace of a cushion-cut and two drop-shaped engraved emeralds, nine large pearls and a ruby bead; an Indian aigrette, in Indian princely style, with cabochon sapphires and diamonds; a white jade rose, set with pearls and rubies; a necklace of five emerald flowers on two ropes of pearls; and a turban ornament of white agate with rubies and pearls.' In addition, there were a number of necklaces of sapphire, ruby and emerald beads, from which it appears, interestingly enough, that emerald beads cost more than ruby beads of the same quality.

The multistranded necklaces of the Indian maharajahs, which covered the whole breast, started the fashion for casually draped coloured-bead sautoirs which, with hip-length ropes of pearls, dominated the 1920s style in necklaces. Cartier's bead style was plainly Indian though the colour combinations were often outside the Indian colour range – New York, for example, combined rose tourmaline beads with little onyx tubes, amber with engraved sapphire, rose coral with engraved turquoise and Lalique crystal beads. From AD 500 to 1500, India had been the world's principal supplier of beads with exports to Arabia, Egypt, Persia and Europe; her monopoly was broken only with the advent of the agate industry of Idar-Oberstein in Germany and the glass-bead industry of Venice.[12]

The engraved emerald-bead necklaces, often months, if not years, in the making, were naturally valued more highly than the various types of hardstone bead necklaces in Cartier's range of fantasy jewelry. Thus the London firm was especially proud of an example whose central stone weighed 136 carats, yet necklaces made for Mrs J. D. Biddle and Mrs J. P. Donahue were surely its equals.

One jewel, destined for an Indian collection, stands out among all these Indian-inspired art deco pieces. This was the turban
29 ornament designed for the Maharajah Jagatjit Singh of Kapurthala (1872–1949), which breathes the spirit of pure Oriental tradition and seems to owe nothing to European influences. The maharajah, friend of Theodore Roosevelt and Clemenceau, was a man of sophistication who toured Europe annually from 1900 and whose love of France led him in 1909 to build a palace on the model of Versailles. When Jacques Cartier visited Kapurthala, he found himself waited on by servants in Louis XV-style perukes. In 1926, the year before his golden jubilee, the maharajah commissioned this

pagoda-style tiara from Louis Cartier and an entry in the maharajah's diary, dated 27 September 1926, reads: 'Lunch at the Ritz, where I was presented to the King of Yugoslavia. Afterwards to the painter Marcel Baschet in full regalia and the finished emerald tiara from Cartier. A piece truly unique of its kind.'

While work was progressing at Cartier's of Paris on this most elegant piece, the house was also busy with what, in purely quantitative terms, must be the biggest commission of all time: the remodelling of the crown jewels of the Maharajah of Patiala. In 1925, the coronation year of his neighbour the Maharajah of Kashmir, Dhiraj Singh Maharajadhirajah, Great King of Kings, the ruler of Patiala (the largest Sikh state in India), opened his treasury and handed over his most valuable pieces to Cartier. The fabulous collection of stones included the Victoria or De Beers diamond of 234.69 carats, which became the centrepiece of the great ceremonial necklace.[13]

After years of work, Cartier's had filled casket after casket of jewels for Patiala. The designers had taken the traditional forms of Indian jewelry into account in the resettings, but the new pieces represented elegant reworkings inspired by contemporary art deco trends. It was surely the first time that the Paris house had produced an example of the *nath*, a nose ring in diamond, ruby, emerald and sapphire, typical of south India. In addition there was ankle jewelry, armlets, a bracelet of the nine planetary stones, and the exotic *hathpul*, a traditional piece of Rajasthan wedding jewelry worn on the back of the hand, linking bracelet and finger rings. No fewer than 223 pearls were drilled to create a single bracelet. The photographic inventory constituted a 36-page album. In 1928, Cartier exhibited the principal pieces at the rue de la Paix before their delivery to the Moti Bash palace in Patiala. The show attracted society personalities like J. P. Morgan and his sister Anne, the Duchess of Alba and Mrs Laura Corrigan, and created a sensation in Europe and the United States.

From then on, perhaps influenced by this widely publicized event, the maharajahs sent increasing numbers of jewels to Cartier's for remodelling. In Paris and London the designers became accustomed to assimilating the mango leaf or the engraved emeralds of Indian jewelry into art deco style. The maharajahs in return proudly showed off their latest art deco acquisitions – labelled as the *dernier cri* at the 1925 Exposition in Paris – once they were back in India. The ruler of Mandi, married to Princess Amrit, daughter of the Maharajah of Kapurthala, had his emeralds, among them an engraved one of 68.81 carats, set into a tiara by Cartier's, while the Maharajah of Patna had his state necklace, with its three antique rose diamonds, remodelled in Paris in 1935.

The commission that stretched the Cartier expertise to its fullest was the resetting and enlargement of the exceptional jewelry collection of the Maharajah of Nawanagar. A regular visitor to London during the thirties, the maharajah ruled a small principality with its own pearl fishery on the Katiawar peninsula, though the pearls produced were of only modest value and mostly used in traditional Hindu medicine. The ruler commissioned from Cartier's a necklace of six ropes of pearls, embellished with an engraved emerald of 62.93 carats, for alternate use as a turban ornament. The maharajah's daughter was to recall that a black servant was employed at the palace at Jamnagar to wear the pearls on his velvety skin and so preserve their natural lustre. In Jacques Cartier's opinion, the prince's emerald collection was 'unequalled in the world, if not in quantity then certainly in quality'. It was further enriched by a state necklace, designed by Cartier's, of seventeen rectangular emeralds, including a stone of 70 carats which came from the Turkish sultan. In addition there was a close-fitting collar of thirteen emeralds with two absolutely identical stones at the centre; two turban ornaments, one with a 56- the other with a 39-carat emerald; and also a two-string bead necklace of rich velvety green. The settings of these pieces were characterized by the somewhat monotonous, geometrical style of the London work-shops of the 1930s which, in the case of a diamond *sarpech*, struck up a strange liaison with traditional Indian forms.

In 1932, Clifford North was sent as Jacques Cartier's representative to the King of Nepal; when he finally reached Kathmandu he found that the European crisis of the 1930s had reverberated even in the distant Himalayas. Leaving Delhi, the ten-man party passed through Patna, aiming to cross the Ganges by ferry; from the outset they encountered a number of amusing obstacles. Their Hindu servants resisted setting out at all without favourable omens from the astrologers, while the twenty-one coolies refused to carry European or Moslem baggage through the Nepalese jungle. In Kathmandu, where a cannon sounded the curfew at ten every night, North waited for days for a carriage to take him to the Singha Durbar palace. In the palace itself, a bard recited the praises of the ruler as North spread out his wares in the wavering torchlight. They were valued at a third their true worth by the envious Nepalese jewelers and, in addition, the ruler had read reports of the threatening world crisis in the *Calcutta Statesman*. Business was clearly out of the question and instead, swaying uncomfortably upon the back of an elephant, North attended the wedding of the ruler's grandson. On the last morning, North was awakened by cackling hens and the bleating of sheep: he was expected to accept a farewell present of livestock, corn, potatoes and oil. He left Kathmandu with an ivory box and signed photographs as gifts from the unpredictable ruler to his employer, and with the conviction that 'modern European jewelry with its valuable diamonds and costly settings would appear to be unsuited to Nepal'.

During the 1930s, European interest in India and its culture grew. At the Paris Colonial Exhibition of 1931, Cartier's display with an Indian emerald bead tiara won a prize. The exhibition provided a cross-section of the diverse cultures of France's colonies, but once again jewelers and decorators exploited the material shown indis-criminately, combining traditional forms and colours at will. Only this can explain why Cartier's made a hair ornament in the same year for the Maharanee of Nawanagar in a traditional Javanese bow shape.

Also by this time travelling conditions and communications had improved enough to encourage visits to India by wealthy if superficial tourists from the United States and Europe. In the opinion of American *Vogue* they were principally intrigued by the bejewelled elephants of Jaipur and the tiger hunts 'set up like a Broadway show', organized by the Maharajah of Kutch-Behar and reached by the Darjeeling Express. Though India declined to reveal her secrets to these comfortable 'gentry', they often returned to Paris with 'barbaric' Indian jewelry, as the expensive souvenirs of their trip. Remade and remounted by Cartier's, *Vogue* and *Harper's Bazaar* considered these the very height of fashion. Elsie de Wolfe's Indian necklace required an almost alchemical transformation by Cartier, and Misia Sert, the recently divorced wife of the painter, wore an eight-strand ruby necklace by Cartier's with a red silk cord hanging down her back, a motif sacred to Maya, the Indian Goddess of Earthly Illusions. Trendsetters like the Hon. Mrs Fellowes, Mrs Drexel Biddle, Ganna Walska and Mrs Harrison Williams spread the Indian fashion, which soon even the Duchess of Windsor was to take up.

Spoilt favourite of the 1920s Paris cocktail parties, the Persian Prince Firouz, was supplanted in the next decade by Princess Karam, wife of the fourth son of the Maharajah of Kapurthala, who wore the sari with as much inimitable chic as Cartier's 'Oriental' jewelry. Who today remembers the *diamants mystérieux* which she inspired at Cartier's? Apparently applied directly to the skin, they were just as 'mysterious' as the 'invisible setting' which Cartier and Van Cleef patented at about the same time.

The woman on Cartier's staff who proved herself mistress of the entire Indian range was Jeanne Toussaint. She had, in fact, been wearing Indian jewelry since the 1910s when, as an elegant young woman, she entered the firm. Elsie de Wolfe, holding her soirée complete with real elephants at her villa in Versailles, might be feted as an Indian expert, but only Jeanne Toussaint truly understood how a woman of fashion should wear Indian jewelry.[14] Overnight she brought yellow gold, in India sacred to the gods, back into vogue. 'Jewels start a new gold rush,' *Vogue* proclaimed in 1933, and the prophecy proved true. For thirty years platinum had determined the style and setting of the best European jewelry. Now these pieces were broken up and remade into exotic, massive gold jewelry, a trend which was undoubtedly in line with the crisis-laden prewar years.

97. Cabochon emerald necklace, the
diamond link chain flanked by pierced
cabochon emeralds, the pendant mounted
with a fancy-shaped cabochon emerald and
3 cabochon tassels. Cartier's London. 1927

98. Cabochon emerald tiara, the bandeau
mounted with a fringe of cabochon
emeralds with diamond tips, the centre of
lyre design set with an engraved emerald of
47.20 cts. Cartier's London. 1930

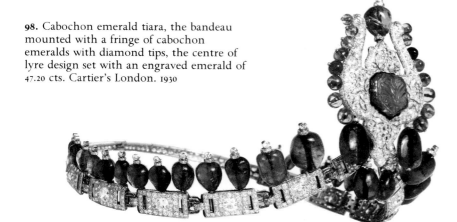

99. Cabochon emerald necklace, the
diamond chain mounted with 24 cabochon
emerald drops and similar beads, the
reverse of tapered bead cluster design. The
pendant suspending a pentagonal and oval
engraved emerald and 5 partly fluted
emerald drops from a diamond buckle
motif. Jointly made by Cartier's London
and New York in 1928 and 1929. Sold to Mrs
Edward F. Hutton (formerly Marjorie
Merryweather Post). Necklace: Smithsonian
Institution

101. Model displaying Cartier's new Trinity ring and bracelet (triple band ring and bracelet) in three-coloured gold. Also onyx calyx ear-pendants and a crystal, onyx and diamond ring brooch. (photo: Steichen, American *Vogue*, 1925)

100. Cartier showcase at the 1925 Exposition in Paris. The mannequin wears the epaulette with 3 engraved emeralds, the emerald, pearl and diamond tiara 'Bérénice' and a brooch in spiral design of emeralds, pearls and diamonds

102. Cartier showcase at the 1925 Exposition in Paris. The mannequin wears the onyx and diamond orchid hair ornament (1923) and a rock crystal and diamond belt with twin onyx tassels

N ABOUT 1906, encouraged by Louis Cartier, the main designers of the Paris house – Rauline, Baloche and Thomas – made their earliest ventures into an abstract, geometric style. Simple cubes, polygons and rhombs in *calibré*-cut coloured stones appeared as the logical reaction against the playful forms of the garland style:

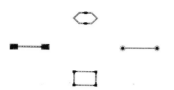

The virtuoso application of the new shapes and cuts of the period gave rise to charming samples of unlimited combinations of forms which first made their appearance on tie-pins:

These were soon followed by geometric diamond pendants:[1]

The new forms did not occur on large pieces such as stomachers and tiaras, which were still the preserve of the traditional Louis XVI forms. The revolution which was unfolding was a revolution in little, restricted, for the time being, to hatpins, pendants and brooches.

It has always been tempting to attribute the invention of this repertoire of geometric forms to the influence of the contemporary cubist painters but in fact their experiments concerned only a small intellectual and artistic elite and had no influence on the decorative arts. Only when in later years certain decorative and reproducible motifs had been detached from their painterly context was the way clear in design, in fashion and finally in industry.

In fact, the roots of art deco can be seen to lie more obviously within the circle of the Vienna Secession. Founded in 1897 by Klimt, Hoffmann and Olbrich, it led to the evolution of a style for architecture, painting and interior decoration based on squares and circles. It is also entirely conceivable that in an over-enthusiastic adoption of rigorously geometric forms, Cartier's might eventually have assimilated the aspirations of the later Bauhaus and thus the style of such artist-jewelers as Fouquet and Sandoz. Fortunately, Cartier's geometric idiom was turned in a new direction because towards the end of the first decade of this century the strongest and most up-to-date influences in style were flowing from the Orient.

The influence of Islamic forms on late nineteenth-century decorative arts had proved especially fruitful in France: as early as the Paris Exhibition of 1878 European manufacturers had shown vases with Arabic decoration. The mosque-style Trocadero was built during this period, and the copy of the palace of the Bey of Tunis still stands with its cupolas and horseshoe arches in the Park Montsouris (1867).

Obliged to renounce anthropomorphic representations, the Islamic decorative styles evolved linear-geometric forms which were reflected in architecture and the applied arts. This applies principally to the lattice work and star patterns in rhythmically broken forms of various coloured woods, ivory and faience as they appear together in the mosque.

Louis Cartier's interest in the Islamic style was furthered by the Exposition des Arts Musulmans held in the Musée des Arts Décoratifs in Paris in 1903 and was later to be deepened by a visit to the Alhambra, the Moorish citadel in Granada.[2]

Indian, Chinese and Japanese motifs also found their place in Cartier's work, enriching the geometric designs with new variations which used the circle and ellipse to conceal the purely constructional elements in the jewelry and make possible fluent ornamental forms.

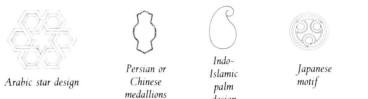

Arabic star design · Persian or Chinese medallions · Indo-Islamic palm design · Japanese motif · Far-Eastern motif

Parallel to these new forms were unfamiliar colour combinations, red-lilac for example, or blue-green, 'this mirror of sleeping water, which reflects the heavens and the woods together' (Henri Clouzot). As shown in Chapter 9, Cartier's use of the new colour range was partly stimulated by the Ballets Russes – which fused an Oriental fairy-tale world with the style of the theatre and the masquerade of the European eighteenth century: an achievement paralleled in jewelry by Louis Cartier at the same time. The curtain for *Schéhérazade* and Cartier's Persian jewelry derived, ultimately, from the same source!

The designers for the Ballets Russes, above all Benois, integrated French eighteenth-century floral elements into their theatre designs, and Cartier transformed similar patterns into his new style. This was especially true of the garland, whose curvilinear forms were never wholly renounced by the firm's designers.

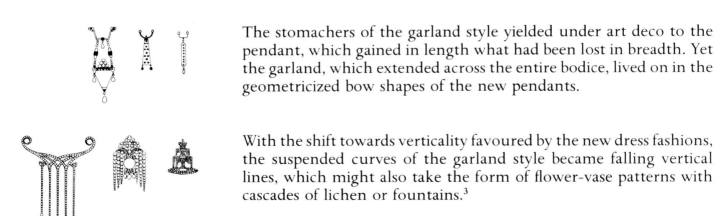

The stomachers of the garland style yielded under art deco to the pendant, which gained in length what had been lost in breadth. Yet the garland, which extended across the entire bodice, lived on in the geometricized bow shapes of the new pendants.

With the shift towards verticality favoured by the new dress fashions, the suspended curves of the garland style became falling vertical lines, which might also take the form of flower-vase patterns with cascades of lichen or fountains.[3]

Even the bar brooch, one of the most popular garland types, was given falling motifs or a floral aspect as a flower bowl.

while the circle, which with the ellipse represented one of Cartier's principal art deco forms, was varied and transformed with lateral motifs derived from nature:

Most of Cartier's art deco motifs derived from the stylization of forms from the vegetable kingdom, individual plants or fruits giving place to generalized types:

Unlike Boucheron, Cartier's rarely created naturalistic flower pieces, complete with petals and calyx. It was only in the 1940s that designers like Peter Lemarchand in Paris and Frederick A. Mew in London began to favour realistic representations of roses, orchids and dahlias.

But throughout the 1920s flower ornament was exclusively two-dimensional. The linear treatment of a leaf or a stylized orange tree was fundamentally more interesting to the designer than the three-dimensional reality of nature.

It is charming to find, in this world of organically derived, semisurrealist forms, which were to remain atypical of the Cartier oeuvre, such pieces as a mask pendant on a rope of woven hair, or a winged hour glass.

At this period we should not forget that the contacts between the arts and crafts, theatre, literature and soon film, were manifold, vigorous and taken for granted and that they yielded undreamed-of possibilities of inspiration. Louis Cartier, for example, cultivated his connections with Diaghilev, Sert, Foujita and Christian Bérard; he knew the most talented innovators in fashion and décor – Jacques Doucet, Jeanne Lanvin and Coco Chanel; he admired Paul Valéry and Jean Cocteau and had social contact with the brilliant Elsie de Wolfe, Misia Sert and Louise de Vilmorin.[4]

At this time a leading figure on the Paris art scene was Paul Iribe (1883–1935). At home in theatre, fashion, poster art and the film, the range of his friends and collaborators indicates the extent of his influence: Jean Cocteau represented the world of literature,[5] Misia Sert the Diaghilev circle, and Poiret the most obvious tie with the world of fashion.[6] Iribe used his personal symbol of a golden rose in his work for advertising, the theatre and fashion and also to stamp the most individual of his work – the eleven jewelry designs done at the prompting of José Maria Sert and executed by the jeweler Linzeler of the rue d'Argenson.[7] The fact that these pieces were presented on silk cushions and turbans was, of course, a tribute to the Ballets Russes. Two years later, *Vogue* carried a report on Mme Poiret's amethyst and emerald pendant, also designed by Iribe and worn by Gloria Swanson in Iribe's first film, *The Affairs of Anatole*. Iribe's most important jewel, an emerald aigrette with characteristic sunburst effect, was acquired by Cartier and was still in the vaults of the London branch in 1931.[8]

'The influence of Paul Iribe on contemporary decorative arts, and

103. Greek pillar pendant, the pillar in onyx, diamonds and *calibré*-cut opals representing an altar with Mexican opal flame. On silk cord with tubular onyx and diamond sliding motif. 1913. Sold to Mrs Nancy Leeds

104. Rock crystal and emerald pendant, the 99-ct emerald tablet engraved with Indian floral design and set in engraved rock crystal and diamond mount. Black silk cord with crystal sliding motifs. 1912. Sold to Lady Sackville

especially jewelry, is certainly not emphasized as it should be,' commented the designer George Barbier on the occasion of the 1925 Exposition.[9] Iribe was one of the first to propose large cabochons mounted as rings and his jewelry was among the earliest made in platinum and iridium. But above all, he influenced contemporary artists in their choice of motifs: a bowl filled with fruit or flowers – a memory of the ballet *Spectre de la rose* – was one of his preoccupations as well as Jacqueau's.[10] The Iribe rose inspired carpet designs by André Mare and textiles by André Groult and Bianchini-Férier.[11] It appeared on advertisements for the perfume manufacturer Lubin,[12] and also in jewelry with black enamel contours by Boucheron and LaCloche.

Just as in Russia Diaghilev's friends, such as Benois and Bakst and Nouvel, had joined in the *World of Art* (*Mir Izkusstva*) movement to promote exhibitions and ballets, in the same way Bernard Boutet de Monvel, Leon Bakst, Georges Lepape, A. E. Marty, Paul Iribe, George Barbier and others formed a group in Paris in the years before the First World War. Their spokesman was Lucien Vogel and his *Gazette du bon ton* their platform.[13] The group was in direct contact with the world of theatre and fashion; the rose garland and the Orientalism of the Ballets Russes became their artistic credo.

George Barbier appears today to have been the most prolific of their members.[14] Born in Nantes in 1882 he settled in the Latin Quarter of Paris in 1908 and held his first exhibition in 1911 in the Galerie Boutet de Monvel. His imaginative world was a compound of the carnival and masquerade of eighteenth-century Venice and the bucolic landscapes of ancient Greece, populated by Adonis, Psyche, Bilitis and Ganymede.[15] As a young dandy, Barbier took an interest in jewelry and was deeply impressed by Iribe's designs. He presented himself before Louis Cartier, bearing a portfolio of designs and, as a sequel, came to know Charles Jacqueau. Louis acquired his watercolour *Nijinsky and Ida Rubinstein in 'Schéhérazade'*[16] and placed a commission for another watercolour, *Woman with Panther*, to be used [19] in the firm's publicity. Barbier's vases, garlands and phosphorescent clusters of fruit were not directly copied but influenced Jacqueau's design of a strawberry pendant, the network of hanging branches of an onyx tiara and the design of an Ionic pillar. It was Iribe who influenced Barbier in the design of an aigrette of plaited spirals which, in turn, had its effect on a Cartier aigrette of 1913 which looks like a firework showering sparks.[17]

Although Cartier's received stimulus from men of the theatre or journalistic worlds, the firm's full-time designers – mostly trained at the Ecoles Boulle, Germain Pilon or Bernard Palissy – came from the neighbouring areas of the decorative arts, though rarely from the immediate competition:

HENRI CHENAUD (b.1876), trained with the decorator Rémond and worked in embroidery and tapestry before joining Cartier's in 1908.

OLIVIER BALOCHE (b.1878), tapestry maker. Joined 1902.

FREDERIC BESEME (b.1879), with Lalique from 1919 to 1925 when he joined Cartier's.

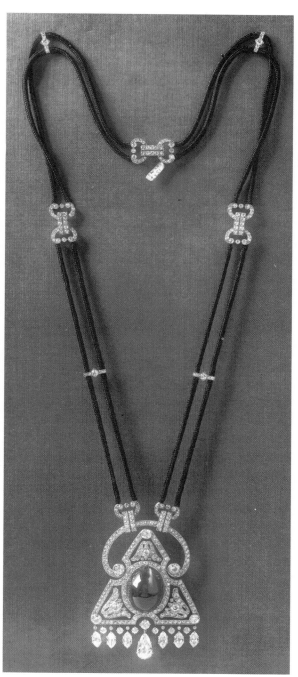

105. Pearl and amethyst sautoir, suspending a pear-shaped cabochon amethyst with amethyst and diamond calyx from a seed pearl and amethyst bead rope. 1912. Sold to Princess Shakovskoy

106. Pendant necklace with triangular diamond pendant and drop-shaped diamond fringe, centring on oval chrysoberyl cat's-eye of 90 cts. Black silk cord with diamond shoulder motifs. 1909

107. Emerald and onyx necklace mounted with 23 emerald beads of 252.48 cts, flanked by onyx beads. On diamond chain mount. Vase-shaped pendant tassel. 1913

108. Diamond dog collar, with 3 rows of circular and baton diamonds mounted as lilies-of-the-valley with off-centred rectangular-cut diamond of 23.92 cts. Commissioned by Mrs George Blumenthal in 1912

109. Orange-tree brooch, designed as a miniature orange tree in its pot flanked by two birds, in circular and pear-shaped diamonds and onyx. 1913

110. Crystal vase pendant, the carved rock crystal vase with circular-cut diamond handles and central diamond collet. Diamond flower head and onyx bead garland. Pear-shaped diamond tassel. 1914

111. Rock crystal pendant, the tapered carved rock crystal mount with cabochon rubies, with 2 pear-shaped emerald drops. The bow surmount with rubies and emeralds. 1913. Sold to the Aga Khan

CHARLES JACQUEAU (b.1885), in the workshop of Raingo, the bronze sculptor. Joined 1909.

JEAN PUCHMAGRE (b.1890), from 1909 to 1911 with Linzeler, at the period when Linzeler was executing Iribe's designs. With Cartier 1913–20.

HENRI-LOUIS LESUEUR (b.1891), from 1909 to 1925 with Keller's, 48 rue Matignon, a gift shop specializing in elegant silver, enamel and leather items. Joined 1926.

YVONNE CLUZEL (b.1895), designed silks for the Maison George. Joined 1921.

PIERRE LARDIN (b.1902), the first designer for Edgar Brandt, the wrought-iron artist, up to 1925, involved with the creation of the atelier La Maitrîse for Galeries Lafayette. With Cartier's 1925–26.

ANDRÉ COURTILLAT (b.1905), in 1920 he received the first prize for watercolour and ornamentation in a competition of the Ecoles de la Ville de Paris. In 1924 he attended the Ecole des Arts Décoratifs. With Cartier's 1927–31.

PETER LEMARCHAND (b.1906), from 1924 to 1926 with the jeweler Roger Sandoz on the rue Royale. Joined 1927.

JAMES GARDNER (b.1907), trained at the Chiswick and Westminster School of Arts and afterwards with E. McKnight Kauffer (1890–1954), the American-born graphic and poster artist who lived most of his life in England. Gardner worked with Cartier's of London from 1924 to 1931, at a time when most of the designs were still originated in Paris. He knew G. B. Shaw and was an enthusiast for the Ballets Russes.

With its team of employees experienced in wrought-iron work, tapestry, textile printing and graphics, the participation of Cartier's in the great exhibitions of the postwar years presented a creative challenge. In 1921 Cartier exhibited, together with Janesich, Van Cleef and Feuillâtre at the Salon du Goût français in the Palais de Glace on the Champs-Elysées; in 1924 at the French Exhibition in Grand Central Palace, New York, along with Boucheron, Mauboussin, Van Cleef and Sandoz. In 1925, the Paris Exposition Internationale des Arts Décoratifs et Industriels Modernes, in which industrial design ranked equal with the decorative arts, offered a synthesis of all the preceding exhibitions.[18] The idea had originated as far back as 1912; following the great success of the German stand at the Paris Salon d'Automne of 1910, the competitiveness of the French decorative arts had to be reestablished. But an exhibition planned for 1916 was tragically overtaken by the outbreak of war; scheduled for 1922, it was postponed to 1924 and finally to 1925.

The exhibition finally opened its doors on 16 May 1925. It covered an area of twenty-three hectares, stretching across the Seine from the Champs Elysées to the Hôtel des Invalides. Every night, the Eiffel Tower gleamed with a Citroën sign of 200,000 coloured electric lights and the statue of Bourdelle, 'the salute of France to the nations', received visitors behind the ceremonial gate on avenue Nicholas II. In fact the 'nations' were virtually confined to the wartime allies: though Austria participated, neither Germany, whose invitation was issued too late, nor the United States took part.

The show was organized on the same progressive principles that had governed the World Exposition of 1900. No exhibit was accepted which imitated earlier styles or which lacked either stylistic or functional novelty or originality.[19] However, there was a provision which amounted to a charter of privilege for the jewelers: 'The fact that a piece derives its inspiration from work in related fields, or from motifs of other times and places, shall not be sufficient grounds for exclusion, on condition that the model has been interpreted, reworked and transposed in a manner which suits the theme.'[20]

The exhibits were grouped in five categories:

I. Architecture
II. Furniture
III. Parure: Class 19 Clothing
              Class 20 Fashion and fashion accessories
              Class 21 Flowers
              Class 22 Gems and Jewelry
IV. Art of the theatre, the street and landscape architecture
V. Education

Of a total of some four hundred jewelry firms which took part, thirty displayed exhibits with a total value of Fr500 million, an impressive figure when compared with the jewelry exports of France for the previous years, which were valued at Fr20 million. The jewelry section in the Grand Palais had an exhibition area of five hundred square metres, designed by architect and jewelry designer Eric Bagge.

Louis Cartier was appointed vice-president of the organization committee for the 'Parure' (Jewelry) category.[21] With twenty-five years' experience of jewelry in the twin contexts of fashion and society, the Exhibition's belief in the unity of the decorative arts was his own personal credo. His firm's products were to be presented in the fashion context of hats, hairstyles, belts, materials and shoes. 'Modern decorative art in all its forms is to be understood as a living reality. A ceramic tile or a wallpaper can only properly be judged in situ — a desk lamp only when actually alight on the table.'[22]

Was it Jeanne Lanvin or Louis Cartier himself who had the brilliant idea of being the only jewelers exhibiting not in the Grand Palais but along with the fashion houses in the Pavillon de l'Elégance?[23] Jeanne Lanvin was president of the 'Fashion and fashion accessories' category and like Louis Cartier was interested in the major trends of art history:[24] her 'Décolleté à la Vierge' was inspired by the Madonnas of Raphael; 'Lanvin blue' owed its mystic colour quality to Fra Angelico; and she dreamed of antique jewelry 'on mandarin gowns, on Persian silks'. The décor of her private residence had been done by Rateau, the interior decorator who also designed the furnishings for the Cartier exhibit in his workshop at Levallois.[25]

'Fashion, the mirror of our time, is essentially an art,' claimed the official report[26] and in this survey of fashion and style, sixty-eight years after Baudelaire's *Les fleurs du mal*, the fragrance of a perfume was considered comparable to music and the plastic arts. The exhibitors included the couturiers Jenny and Callot; Hermès, which had

112. Rock crystal pendant, the rock crystal panel with floral engraving with diamond cluster and border, drop-shaped pearl tassel, plaited silk cord. 1912

113. Briolette diamond pendant suspending 6 briolette-cut diamonds of 42.67 cts and a pear-shaped diamond of 4.15 cts from circular-cut diamond arcades. Commissioned in 1913 by Grand Duchess Vladimir

graduated from saddlers to the leading fine leather workers; and Cartier's close friend and neighbour, Jean-Philippe Worth.

But how was the specific Cartier jewel to be presented as 'living reality'? The exhibition management advised against the 'paradox of a cathedral nave providing the setting for jewelers' diamonds of just a few cubic centimeters'.[27] Like the four couturiers,[28] Cartier presented his models on the 'Siégel' mannequins, made by the Canadian Siégel in a style reminiscent of Brancusi and Modigliani, after designs by Vigneau in Saint-Ouen. The 'Parure' group was promoted with a gala event in which Mistinguett appeared as 'Diamond Solitaire' and the girls from the Casino de Paris as gemstones and velvet ribbons, while Ida Rubinstein in the *Martyrdom of St. Sebastian*, with costumes designed by Bakst, drove her admirers into a frenzy.

In the exhibition, the abstract geometric tendencies of modernism, which were to dominate the 1931 Colonial Exhibition, were already asserting themselves alongside the stylized flowers of art deco. Georges Fouquet, for example, exhibited a black enamelled mask, and rings of crystal and ivory; Raymond Templier a tiara of amber and diamonds; and Boucheron a tiara of onyx blossoms as well as a necklace with two great diamond drops. The LaCloche showcase was the one most closely related to Cartier's, with its Chinese forms and unbroken colours, and with motifs from the fables of La Fontaine which revealed an anecdotal-narrative style. The most valuable piece in the entire exhibition was the 136-carat 'Queen of Holland' diamond, which sparkled in the display of the jeweler Friedmann.

Cartier's art deco programme, already fully developed by 1920, was represented at the exhibition by 150 pieces, produced in the workshops in the three years since 1922. Some had been created expressly for the exhibition and these were among the jewels, at least thirty-two in number, that were broken up when it was over. Among the specially created jewels was a 38 cm-long décolleté brooch designed to be viewed from a distance, an emerald shoulder ornament and the tiara, 'Bérénice'.[29] The fashion context of the display more or less forbade the inclusion of clocks or bibelots,[30] but the show presented an exemplary cross-section of Cartier's work in those categories that were exhibited:

Earrings: Pride of place went to the long earrings (up to 8 cm), comprising cascades of blossom shapes with pendant cabochons, mostly of emerald, lapis lazuli or onyx. In 1908 *Vogue* had already commented on long earrings and in 1921 it confirmed that 'one out of every three women seen in the Parc or the Bois, lunching at the Ritz or dancing at the Ambassador wore earrings an inch or two in length'. Another pattern was based on calyx or bell motifs, Oriental in inspiration, and with hanging cabochon grapes. By contrast a 'Creole hoop earring' with onyx and diamond beads, recalled a seventh-century Merovingian piece consisting of a 14-faceted polyhedron.[31] The elegant design derived from the seventeenth-century girandole, which remained popular from 1906 into the 1930s, was not displayed.

Bracelets: most of the exhibits were geometric link bracelets, of the type that remained popular up to the Second World War and were internationally produced. Their predecessors are to be found in the nineteenth century, or even the Renaissance. The Empress Eugénie, for example, wore a chain of geometric links.[32] The prevailing colour combination at Cartier's was the black-white contrast of diamond and onyx, while the open-work patterns derived from Persian work.

The collection contained only a single bracelet of coloured gemstone leaves, but surprisingly neither a chimaera nor an Egyptian lotus bangle. In their place was a spiral snake bangle of coral and emerald. However, the related chimaera motif did appear on a cigarette holder.

Tiaras: the Persian style still dominated the world of fashion. At the Paris Opéra Ball of 1922, Persian 'harem pants' were worn and Princess Karam of Kapurthala was escorted by a troop of Persian slaves. But aigrettes and tiaras were show-items rather than fashion accessories. The exhibition included a traditional bandeau with two black heron aigrettes; a comb embellished with onyx and diamond orchids; and the 'Bérénice' tiara by the designer Henri Chenaud.

Rings: Cabochon gemstones predominated, for example a 35-carat sapphire and a 13-carat emerald. The vogue for emerald-cut diamond solitaires, initiated around 1925, was represented by a 17-carat example. Interestingly, 1924 had seen the birth of the triple gold wedding-band (*bague trois anneaux*) and the 'trinity bracelet' that went with it. This ring was immediately shown to *Vogue* readers in a photograph by Steichen, and Elsie de Wolfe was one of the first to make it popular.

Necklaces: Here the emphasis was on colour-contrasting pendants — coral beads, emerald grapes and pearl tassels — on black silk cords or necklaces of onyx cylinders. Large diamond necklaces were not included, being thought out of tune with the artistic trends of 1925. The 'Fuchsia' necklace of carved coral revealed a charmingly playful side to Cartier's programme.

Brooches: Here the astonishing fertility of Cartier's imaginative invention appeared at its most convincing, not only in the variety of motifs, but also in the endlessly creative adaptation of the brooch as hat, belt or shoulder ornament. 'The shoe has become a work of art', ran the slogan, and the brooch now adapted equally as a shoe buckle![33] From about 1915, the airy and transparent mousseline-de-soie and crêpe de chine had been favoured as dress fabrics. These were clearly not suitable for brooch pins. But with the advent of O'Rossen's grey-flannel *tailleur* in 1921 and the immense popularity of aniline-dyed furs — karakul for the day and ermine for evening wear — the brooch pin could once more find purchase on clothes. The diktat of the great fashion houses such as Chanel still banished the brooch to the fringes of the wardrobe: Caroline Reboux and Suzanne, the finest milliners in Paris, eagerly took it up. The Parisian hat of the Charles Frederick Worth epoch, bedecked with flowers and fruits, had given way by 1913 to a small unornamented model that snuggled nicely down on the modish Eton crop hairstyles. From 1927 a host of new hat styles — béret, toque, Phrygian cap — provided the justification for an even wider range of hat ornaments.

The brooch as belt buckle often took symmetrical forms derived

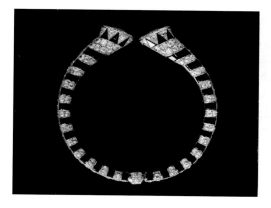

114. 'Egyptian' bangle, the mount striated in *calibré*-cut onyx and circular-cut diamonds. Commissioned by Pierre Cartier in 1919

115. Diamond pendant on chain, suspending 3 pear-shaped diamonds of 39.25, 36.11, and 31.51 cts. 1913. The necklace was subsequently transformed and the largest diamond sold to Grand Duchess Vladimir

116. Emerald and diamond necklace, the centre suspending 7 drop-shaped emeralds of 167.54 cts on half-moon and pear-shaped diamond mount, the neckchain in sections of emerald beads and cabochons, with lozenge-, triangular-, half-moon- and baguette-cut diamond links. 1923. Sold to Mrs Harold McCormick

117. Sapphire and emerald necklace, the sapphire bead mount with smaller emerald intersections suspending a 39.14-ct engraved sapphire cabochon and a 256.60-ct Indian engraved emerald cabochon drop with diamond tip. 1923. Sold to Mrs Harold McCormick

from bronze Chinese buckles of the nineteenth century. The 'belt-buckle' type provided one of the basic forms of the art deco brooch – in the shape of the double clip. In 1927, Cartier's patented a model with a spring system (*système à ressort*). The central motif of the belt buckle, a hoop of coral, onyx or crystal, proved from 1919–20 on to be the most widespread brooch pattern, which was embellished with stylized floral elements. One in four of all the brooches exhibited in 1925 were in this hooped style, to which were added rectangular and polygonal forms. On the other hand, floral brooches in the tradition of the Ballets Russes were in the minority.

The case of the brooch demonstrates the survival of nineteenth-century historicism into the 1920s. In addition to Persian, Chinese and Egyptian influences, the Cartier brooch during the art deco period, in the form of the fibula, was also to be enriched by seventh-century Merovingian forms.

The fibula as dress clasp was in fact the earliest form of brooch. The motif, which Cartier's designers were able to study in the Museum at the Château of Saint-Germain-en-Laye in examples of Merovingian art, was to pervade the entire art deco programme. As early as 1907 it had become fashionable to secure a kimono or kaftan with a fibula or clasp: a fibula, indeed, had featured as one of the wedding presents of the Queen of Spain.

A simple variety in the form of a safety-pin[34] (the *broche nourrice*) had featured in the Cartier programme since 1895, first in white gold, later in platinum.

But even the crossbow-fibula (Saint-Germain-en-Laye) was sketched:

A further type, the jabot-pin (*système cliquet* or *à double baïonette*), valued as a lapel or hat ornament, often had chimaera or serpent head terminals, which were equally indebted to Merovingian models and recalled Celtic scroll work from Ireland.[35]

Another type of fibula, comprising an open ring, with a sliding pin and a bayonet clasp was based on Irish or Scottish models of the eighth century.[36] The first Cartier examples are in linear enamel with cabochon gemstones, later in coral and onyx.

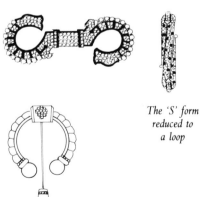

The 'S' form reduced to a loop

Even the above-mentioned hoop brooch in onyx or coral was decorated in its centre with chimaera motifs, which are reminiscent of the Merovingian 'rouelle' worn as a belt ornament:[37]

118. Turquoise vase pendant, the bell-shaped turquoise with fancy engraving studded with diamonds. Black enamel lining. Onyx and tapered baguette-cut diamond base. Connected by 2 onyx and diamond rings to a black silk cord. 1920 (Actual size)

From 1917, the important Le Secq des Tournelles collection of ironwork was moved to Rouen and opened to the public as a museum. Before this, parts of the collection had been exhibited in the Musée des Arts Décoratifs and recorded in four volumes of *Le Métal*.[38] Louis Cartier did a number of sketches from the work and handed them over to his design studio. The garland style had derived inspiration from ironwork, principally of the eighteenth century; now the designers were stimulated to evolve forms based upon the hinges and locks designed by Gothic and Renaissance craftsmen. The motif of the doorknocker and the mountings of the iron-bound chest occur again and again:

Another important design element, the stalactite, was derived from Islamic architecture. In the architecture of the mosque the stalactite was to be found wherever support encountered load – as in the transition from the round base of a dome to the square walls of the supporting space. Louis Cartier was fascinated by the stalactite form during his 1922 visit to Granada. As a result we find the stalactite pendant watch making its appearance, coincidentally, just at the time when George Barbier was creating his stalactite grotto set for the Folies-Bergère.

The various brooches of the 1925 Exposition summed up the endless possibilities of the combination of diamond and coloured-stone cuts: baguette, hexagons and half moons were the ideal 'building stones' with which to construct the tiny triumphal arches, pagodas, Taj Mahals, Vendôme columns and skyscrapers in the form of the brooch. Once again, it was Elsie de Wolfe who, with her *Temple d'Amour,* contributed to the wider application of this delightful miniature art.

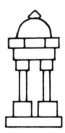

13

Vanity Fair

*O*NCE, CARTIER WAS MASTER of the exquisite *objet d'art*: his miniature plants, destined for the princely boudoir in their delicate glasshouses, reminded us of the Japanese and Chinese art of the *Belle Epoque*, with their jade leaves and quartz blossoms. But today he restricts himself to practical matters — the cigarette case and the vanity case, the familiar necessities of modern life.'[1] Thus wrote a critic in the *Gazette du bon ton* in 1925, alluding to precisely those items which had necessarily been omitted from that year's Exhibition.

In fact, what the critic saw as a chronological sequence was actually parallel production in Cartier's oeuvre. The Cartier plants, representing 'art for art's sake' at its most extreme, may have been somewhat out of place in the postwar period, but the cosmetic articles and desk and smokers' requisites ideally matched the postwar requirements of an aesthetic determined by function. As it happened, these practical articles had been well in the Cartier range since 1900, long before Louis Cartier's directive: 'We must make it our business to build up an inventory that responds to the moral mood of the public by producing articles which have a useful function but which are also decorated in the Cartier style.'

From the beginning such items had formed a part of the firm's repertoire: toiletries such as silver shaving brushes (1860), silver mirrors, moustache combs, beard brushes and powder compacts (1890). Desk accessories included pencil cases in jasper (1860) and platinum (from 1874) and gold pen-holders (from 1881). Calendar stands of jasper and agate (1905) were followed by stamp moisteners, paperweights, inkstands and barometers. Even earlier, Cartier's had been producing smokers' requisites, silver lighters (from 1867), matchboxes and cigarette-holders (1874). A smoker's lamp with ashtray was created in 1906 and bought by the Duke of Alba. But the most varied category was that of men's cigarette cases. From 1900 onwards these were in the Russian style in reeded gold or Russian birch and amaranth, and from 1910 in crystal, agate and jade. Their manufacture was put out to the workshops of Allard et Meyer (Place des Vosges), Kuppenheim (rue Volney), Lavabre, Chailloux (rue Turbigo) and Louis Bock in Colombes as well as to Russian makers such as Ovchinnikov and Yahr. The cases had to be flat, easily slipped into the pocket, scratch-resistant and, since they were designed for men, restrained in ornamentation. They were therefore less diverse in style than that most astonishing of postwar accessories — the *nécessaire de dame* or, to use the American term current in France by 1925, the 'vanity'.[2]

The actual necessities carried by a lady when travelling or at social events changed during various periods, but how she carried them depended on the extent to which pockets could be accommodated within the silhouette ordained by fashion. Neither the clinging Empire style nor the billowing crinoline of about 1850, which in fact also clung to a steel underframe, allowed pockets. Instead, reticules of various materials such as wool, taffeta or velvet were used, to be superseded for a time in the early 1870s by châtelaine purses, secured by a chain or cord. This period also saw the evolution of the graceful money purse of silver, enamel, mother-of-pearl or leather, generally carried on a chain attached to a finger ring or châtelaine girdle. Shortly after 1900 a man's model even came into fashion; compartments for coins, stamps and banknotes were contained in a silver case secured with a metal ring to the watchchain.[3]

The vanity case of the twentieth century combined the form and functions of these bags and purses and took over from them the chain and finger ring. The name, however, indicated the contents: powder compact, lipstick, tortoise-shell comb, mirror and an ivory dance card reminiscent of the former *carnet de bal.*

The ancestor of the vanity case was the *boîte-à-rouge-et-à-mouches* of the age of Louis XV, with mirror, two compartments and a little brush;[4] but its place was the dressing table and it would simply not have been fitting to use it in public at the theatre or a ball. The first mention of a fabric bag for portable cosmetic articles appears to have been in the English *Lady's Magazine* for 1820. But make-up was frowned upon throughout the nineteenth century — which accounts for the fact that Cartier's toiletries at this period were exclusively for men. *Vogue* does not mention lipstick and eyebrow pencils until 1902–03, and its first references to nail varnish and a vanity with a powder compartment are in 1907 and 1909 respectively.

Cartier's first simple vanities were in yellow gold and often embellished with a monogram. These were followed by models in Fabergé style of *émail pékin* striped in blue or rose and white. Now flat, now cylindrical, they might be up to 12.5 cm (5 in) in length. They might even contain that 'volupté nouvelle', hymned by the writer Pierre Louÿs — the cigarette. Already in 1893, Eulalia, the Spanish Infanta, had shocked opinion by smoking in public at the Chicago Columbian Exhibition; Baron de Meyer made a portrait photograph of Marquise Casati smoking a cigarette; and when, in 1916, the new fashion was permitted at the New York Ritz-Carlton Hotel, the taboo was finally broken. The vanity case, however, became increasingly sophisticated, having up to four compartments and sometimes even adorned with a watch. The eccentric Mrs Evalyn Walsh McLean also commissioned a miniature vanity to be worn with a leather strap on the wrist like a watch.

After the war cosmetics became big business. As early as 1914, the singer Lina Cavalieri had had a great success with her book *My Secrets of Beauty*, and in 1921 Helena Rubinstein opened her Paris salons. It was estimated that fifty million American women were using lipstick and, in 1928, Kleenex was invented. Appropriately, after 1930 the vanity adopted the form of a box, for which Van Cleef & Arpels patented the name 'minaudière'. Enamel, being easily scratched, was impractical on the large gold and silver surfaces and was replaced by more resistant lacquer. A resplendent, detachable diamond or gemstone clip provided the clasp, while Mme Larivière went so far as to have the ruby flowers on her Cartier vanity matched to her bracelet. Later, after the Second World War, the severe rectangular contours softened and the vanity was made in the form of a pouch (*pochette*) of gold. A total of eight hundred man-hours might be required to make such a piece, divided among a goldsmith, *guillocheur,* engraver and setter, the engraver working manually, the *guillocheur* with a machine.

During the heyday of vanities, the art deco period of the 1920s, their exterior decoration demonstrated the designers' fertile imagination: as well as the owner's monogram, Indian Jaipur-enamel tiles or jade medallions, they were often covered with geometrical *jeux de fond*. These small-unit Arab-style patterns later gave way to Chinese motifs or designs of boldly simplified cubes and bars. If the cubism of 1910 is to be found in any part of Cartier's programme, then it is certainly on these cases. Their manufacture was divided between the Renaud workshop on the rue Reaumur and the Bachaumont workshop – both of which were taken over by Cartier – and Boulon et Taragnat.

38

Less abstract patterns left room for figurative ornament, as in the vanity cases with gazelles in which can be traced the revived influence of George Barbier, or the vanity case with a stalking panther under a ruby sun.

The greatest diversity of representation came in 1924, the year of the Egyptian flute-player case. Its most profound enrichment, however, occurred in the late 1920s with the mounting of ancient Chinese lacquer plaques which, up to 1929, resulted in a unique series of 'Western-Oriental' vanity cases.

Beginning in the early seventeenth century, Europe's dialogue with the art of the Far East is one of the most fascinating chapters in the history of culture. It began with a passion for Chinese silk which later shifted to porcelain and lacquer, products which were virtually under the monopoly of the Dutch and British East India Companies. The precious cargoes, generally shipped via Dutch Batavia, along the Indian Coromandel coast or from the port of Canton, were marketed in Europe as 'Indian', 'Chinese' or 'Japanese'. By the middle of the eighteenth century, almost every European palace had its 'Chinese' lacquer cabinet – even if the majority were manufactured in European workshops – to the delight of all those 'tired of the elegance and symmetry of the Greeks'.[5] Basically, the eighteenth-century interest in Chinese art was a dilettante fascination with the exotic: the English architect Sir William Chambers characterized Chinese houses as 'toys in architecture'.[6] By contrast, the nineteenth-century attitude was grounded in the contacts of a pragmatic colonial and commercial policy: France acquired a privileged position through her bases in Indo-China[7] while Commodore Matthew Perry's expedition to Japan in 1853–54 opened up the undeveloped empire to enquiring travellers. In England and France the terms *japonisme* and *japonaiserie* were coined for the dominating Japanese modes in architecture, graphics and the decorative arts.[8] Whistler's décor for the dining room in the London house of the

Liverpool shipping magnate F. R. Leyland is representative of the many instances of eastern influence: the artist's painting of the kimono-clad *Princesse du pays de porcelaine* (1876) hung on a wall painted with Japanese golden peacocks. Literary Orientalism enjoyed a special vogue in France, represented for example by Judith Gautier's *Le Livre de jade* or Pierre Loti's *Madame Chrysanthème* (1887). After Edmond de Goncourt had completed his studies of Japanese art in the 1890s, it continued into the somewhat precious literary *fin de siècle* genre of Robert de Montesquiou.[9]

The new stimulus from China and Japan also spurred the imagination of contemporary jewelry designers. Shortly after the sack of the Summer Palace near Peking, Eugène Fontenay (1823–87) was using Chinese jades. Lucien Falize (1839–87), on the other hand, was absorbed by *japonaiserie* and, like Emile Gallé in Nancy a few years later, wished to take on Japanese craftsmen. In 1881 Lucien Gaillard (b.1861) began his researches into the Japanese techniques in lacquer and cloisonné-enamel; these found their echo in Cartier's 1885 collection, which included motifs derived from Japanese bronze and lacquer work.

After 1900, the terms 'Chinese' and 'Japanese' are frequently found in the Cartier archives but they are little more than vague formal allusions. Like the terms 'Arabic' or 'Byzantine' they serve only to show the astonishing diversity of the firm's output up to the First World War, which drew upon images and forms indiscriminately. The following examples are enough to indicate the Oriental contribution: in 1898 the firm produced Japanese and Chinese buckles, some with griffin motifs; in 1900, a Chinese nape brooch and a silver belt buckle 'Dragon and Chimaera fighting'; in 1903, jade pendants engraved with Chinese dragons,[10] and Chinese pendants which were bought by the Duchess of Devonshire and the Duc de Richelieu; in 1906, Japanese brooches and Chinese pendants, and a jade necklace sold to Lady de Grey; in 1907, Chinese gong pendants and Japanese lace pins; in 1912, a lacquered bamboo vase with bronze fittings and openwork jade pendants.

In 1919 Cartier's produced an elegant pendant on a chain in the form of the Chinese Taoist *tai-chi*, symbol of the universal *yin-yang*, within two onyx beads and gemstones. This was a concept ideally suited to the black and white colour scheme of art deco.

Apart from these pieces, Chinese and Japanese influence was to be restricted to *objets d'art* – vanity cases, clocks and scent bottles – whereas jewelry design as such inclined increasingly towards Indian models. In the context of the vanity case, the above-mentioned lacquer-work of the eighteenth and nineteenth centuries was to have outstanding significance and to achieve, like the Egyptian range, complete integration with the taste of art deco.[11]

In fact, Cartier's had handled Chinese lacquer-work as early as 1888 when a Chinese lacquer cabinet in the possession of the Vicomtesse de Bonnemain had been sent to them for reconstruction as a jewel case. In 1903, Louis Cartier acquired a Chinese lacquer snuffbox, probably in the French eighteenth-century style, from the antique dealers Au Vieux Paris.[12] It was another ten years before the first cigarette cases based on Chinese nineteenth-century work were produced in Chinese mother-of-pearl mosaic. From 1924 Cartier's used true mother-of-pearl lacquer which Louis collected systematically from the leading antique dealers of the time:[13] C. T. Loo in the rue de Courcelles,[14] Michon in the boulevard Haussmann, 'La Pagode', the Compagnie de Chine et des Indes on the rue de Londres, and also Yamanaka, the Japanese dealer in New York. For his own personal collection, Louis Cartier bought a Ming dynasty painting from Kalebdjian, better known as a Middle East specialist.

From ancient times Chinese mother-of-pearl was valued for the rose, lavender-blue and shimmering greens of the thin, innermost layers of sea and freshwater mussels (*Heliotis*). Early mother-of-pearl inlays from the Tang dynasty were too thick to permit the iridescence of the full colour range, but the craftsmen of the later Ming and Ching periods used tissue-thin slivers to produce delicately scintillating effects which they heightened still further by the application of artificial colourings.

Mother-of-pearl had a magical authority within the Taoist scheme. Moonbeams and the dust of powdered mother-of-pearl were the food of the immortal He Xiangu,[15] and its insubstantial shimmering colours were, for the Taoists, a token of eternity. Mother-of-pearl was a favourite material in depictions of the Taoist Paradise of the West, which showed the caves of the Eight Immortals, the goddess Djivangmu riding on her phoenix and the Peaches of Immortality which ripened every three thousand years.

The lacquers used by Cartier's in the 1920s were mostly taken from Chinese bowls, trays or tables; the relation to the original decorative context was necessarily sacrificed as a result. Because of their small format the motifs that came to hand were not concerned with the great themes of Taoist mythology. Even so, they conjure up the poetic and allegorical feeling for nature at the heart of Taoism. On one of these Cartier lacquers two of the Immortals are strolling beneath the summer moon, deep in conversation; on another a maid lights her mistress's way with a lantern; on another we observe a sage with his disciple in a pine grove. These little panels, which sit well with the art deco ensemble of coral, lapis lazuli and onyx, are often further embellished with cabochon gemstones: rubies may serve to pick out cherry blossoms or trace the line of a bridge, a sapphire lights up a distant boat, the moon shimmers through the facets of a rose-cut diamond.

Their preoccupation with China led designers to find ideas in various branches of the Chinese decorative arts. A plate in Louis Cartier's own collection provided the model for the court lady who graces a mother-of-pearl box of 1928; an eighteenth-century fluorite seal in the Musée Guimet suggested the outline for a vanity case, while the trellis-work patterns of Chinese furniture inspired brooches and also an important tiara. In his delightful reminiscences, *Elephants in the Attic*, James Gardner, the designer with the London firm from 1924, describes an instructive lesson he learned as a young man from Jacques Cartier: 'He would often open the bookcase, take out a leather-bound volume on Chinese furniture and turn to the illustration of a black lacquered table. I was to observe how the legs terminated.'[16]

One motif which the designs drew on time and again was that of the seated Buddha, and the Japanese *Hotei*, the bellied God of Happiness. From 1901 onward he appears on ashtrays and table bells, sometimes in jade, sometimes in rose quartz or turquoise, alternating as ornament with the related billiken (see p. 95). Fabergé had delivered two jadeite Buddhas to King Chulalongkorn Rama VI of Siam which are recalled by Cartier's large model in rose quartz and lapis lazuli executed by Fourrier's workshops in 1928. Small jade Buddhas provided brooch ornaments, and Mrs Harrison Williams 37 wore a hand of the Buddha in jade on her Cartier flower bracelet made of engraved gemstones.

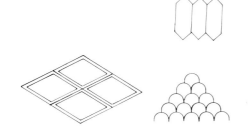

In addition to using Chinese lacquer, Cartier's designers covered the surface of their boxes with Chinese geometrical patterns. After all, even the mother-of-pearl inlays of Chinese lacquers were built up from standardized geometric tesserae. By the early seventeenth century more than fifty-five basic forms had been in use, which might serve, for example, to represent the foliage of a tree or the outline of a temple, while crushed fragments of mother-of-pearl provided the earth. The artists of the Ch'ing period (1644–1911), who created the lacquers used by Cartier, had, like their contemporaries working in porcelain, bronze or carpets, a deep *horror vacui* and therefore covered every available surface in repeating patterns built up of rhombs, hexagons, scales or circles. Landscape features were indicated by standardized decorative symbols and these were transmuted by Cartier in the *jeux de fonds* for his vanity cases.

	the Chinese 'air pattern' for heaven:	becomes	
	the 'water ground' for sea:	becomes	
	the 'earth pattern' for earth:	becomes	

These and other Chinese signs were taken over in Cartier's art deco, either directly or in adaptation. Various Chinese signs, for example, depict the clouds as 'cloud eddies', 'turbulent clouds', 'cloud ribbons' or as 'cloud peaks' – the last-mentioned taken over by Cartier as a pendant motif in 1907. Found already on Sassanian silver, though without its cloud connotation, the ornament further appears in the Indo-Islamic cultural area and, travelling backwards and forwards along the Silk Route, was adopted in China also with the meaning of 'sceptre' or 'sword pommel'. In Japan, on the other hand, it signified 'temple gong' and was adapted as such by Cartier.

The swastika was another motif frequently encountered in the decoration of Cartier's 1920s vanity cases. In origin an ancient Aryan or Vedic symbol associated with the cult of the sun, it has been traced as far afield as Scandinavia and Peru. In China, where it was regarded either as one of the sixty-five auspicious footprints of the

Buddha or as the seal of his heart, it was much prized as 'the good luck symbol of thousand-fold efficacy'.

Adaptation of the meander was a simple matter; in many cases it was evolved from the swastika, occurred already on archaic bronzes, and was frequently given a dragon's head termination. In the garland style of the prewar years, Cartier had made frequent use of the Greek meander; by contrast the Chinese variant made an ideal border pattern for vanity cases, and appeared once more in 1934 as a dragon-head brooch.

Compared with that of China, Japanese art played a comparatively unimportant role in Cartier's output; whereas Boucheron, for example, integrated Japanese lacquer work in both the *hiramakie* and *takamakie* techniques of raised gold straw work, Cartier's ignored it almost entirely. However, the Japanese *inro* did exert an influence on the form of Cartier's finger-ring vanity. A little drug and medicine case comprising a number of horizontal compartments fitting one above the other and held together by a silk cord, the *inro* was worn by Japanese gentlemen at the waist under the the kimono sash (*obi*). The cord was tightened by a sliding toggle (*ojime*) of, for instance, coral or metal, and buttoned in a carved *netsuke* of wood, ivory or lacquer which was tucked under the sash. Cartier's ring vanities originally made use of a Japanese-style silk cord, but this gave way to the more practical enamel chain, ending in an onyx finger ring or a lipstick.

Chinese lacquers and mother-of-pearl inlays were not only formally taken over from miniature artworks of previous centuries but recreated in Europe in the 1920s from Oriental models. An artist who specialized in the re-creation of Chinese lacquer and gemstone work was the Paris-based Russian, Vladimir Makovsky (1884–1966). A coastal scene by him uses traditional Chinese vertical perspective in which a ruby as the setting sun creates the illusion of a distant horizon along the join of the little panels. Sometimes, engraved mother-of-pearl rhombs of European workmanship were even used to frame genuine Chinese lacquers.[17]

Enamel plays a comparatively subordinate role in the chinoiserie vanities of the period – in its place we find monochrome lacquers, similar in colour to tortoise shell in its natural state. Chinese lacquer of the Ming period was built up from as many as two hundred separately dried layers: the French art deco lacquer artists contented themselves with about twenty layers.

During the First World War, aircraft manufacturers had employed Indochinese and Annamite workers for the lacquering of airscrews as their skin was apparently less affected by the fumes than a European's.[18] A number of workshops were established in the Boulogne-sur-Seine region and after the war they were able to take on commissions from Paris jewelers. The firm of Phung Dinh Van, which did work for Cartier's, had a workforce of fifteen Indochinese and had been established around 1915. From the salon of couturier Madeleine Vionnet to the work on the liners *Atlantique* and *Normandie*, lacquer was all the rage in interior decoration during the 1920s and 1930s.[19]

Cartier's used lacquer on scent bottles and table clocks of rose-coloured mirror panels which, with their strictly cubic structure, represent the firm's purest contribution to 1930s modernism. Ever since Mrs Harrison Williams had decorated her Paris residence with mirrors painted by Drian, the mirror had enjoyed a considerable vogue. In addition to large-size bottles in mirror glass, there were dainty snuff bottles of agate or quartz, presented as sets of two on elegant lacquer stands. A piece made for Mrs Blumenthal integrated the design of the stand and bottles into a stylish unity, whose step-wise contours echoed contemporary skyscraper architecture. But the impact of chinoiserie was also felt in the field of toiletries. The Maharanee of Nawanagar acquired a complete set, comprising brushes, mirror, boxes, scent bottles, glove stretchers and mantel clock, done in Chinese lacquer with obsidian settings. The Paris perfume houses were no more inclined than Cartier's to shut out the Chinese influence. Poiret had introduced his little 'Nuit de Chine' bottle in the prewar years, in 1925 came Elizabeth Arden's perfume, 'Ming', in its lacquer bottle, and in 1929 *Vogue* wrote of Guerlain's 'Liu', 'the bottle sits in its package like a Buddha in its shrine'. Perfumers and couturiers often pursued common ends (Chanel's 'No. 5' dates from 1921 and Lanvin's 'Arpège' from 1927). Given the example of the perfume 'No. 1' of their competitor LaCloche, Cartier's had to create their own scent. The inspiration for the attempt was, once again, Jeanne Toussaint. Her personal favourites were Poiret's 'Aladin' and 'Coupe d'Or', and it was with these in mind that she entered into contact with the perfumer Pinaud. Unfortunately their plans were interrupted by the Second World War. The names of famous precious stones, such as 'Nassak' and 'Cumberland' were registered and the 'Jubilee' diamond, disposed of by Cartier's at this time, provided the outline for a faceted perfume bottle, which regrettably was never made.[20]

Chinese motifs began to set the style in *haute couture* at least as early as 1923, the year of the Paris Opéra Chinese Ball. Egyptian modes found themselves challenged by 'coolie' coats and 'mandarin' hats. Molyneux and later Mainbocher declared themselves for China and in 1927–28 Lucien Lelong created his 'Confucius' model.[21] Cartier's evening bags of Oriental brocade provided the ideal matching accessories for the new styles which transformed elegant Parisiennes into *princesses lointaines*.[22] These evening bags, together with a range of gift items, were the creations of 'Department S' at the rue de la Paix, also under the creative direction of Jeanne Toussaint. The Department, like the boutique established by the couturier Jean Patou, was a forerunner of the fashion and jewelry boutiques of the 1950s. The trendsetters of the 1910s, such as Princess Zenaïde Youssoupov or Mrs Leeds, had favoured evening bags in gold weave (*maille d'or*) or embroidered in seed pearls. But Jeanne Toussaint established new forms and colours which suited both the clothes and the 'atmosphère morale', or ambience, of the fashionable world: simple elegance now began to give place to 'chic', with its characteristic blend of erotic daring and stylish vitality. Wherever Mme Letellier, wife of the mayor of Deauville, Elsie de Wolfe or the Cole Porters were to be found – visiting the races at Auteuil, discovering a new jazz band at the Boeuf-sur-le-toit, or proclaiming the dawn of the age of the cocktail in the Ritz Bar – their fashionable *tout ensemble* was sure to match the occasion. (In 1922 couturiers like Patou even began presenting sport collections.)

But the essential accessory was the bag. As a rule, Cartier's models were more refined than those by Poiret, Ruzé & Babani on the boulevard Haussmann or Duvelleroy. The firm bought costly materials from Wagner in the Place des Victoires, Worth, Worms or Johny. They were often valuable embroidered brocades of the Renaissance, from China or Persia and permitted only very sparing adornment. On the other hand, with ribbed taffeta or reindeer leather, the full art deco colour range could be brought into play and the results could compare with the most expensive vanity cases of the period. The bag with pharaoh clasp made for Mrs Clarence Mackay, and other models for Mme Martinez de Hoz, Mrs Blumenthal or Mrs Harrison Williams, were quite simply the most elegant of their time. The rectangular *pochette*, carried casually under the arm, represented a simpler version, and the models in crocodile or red calf leather which Hermès produced for Cartier's from 1922 were adorned only with the owner's monogram. In 1926 Cartier's patented a special handbag clasp.

The international monetary crisis of 1929–30 brought about a restructuring of the market which could be seen reflected in the development of Department S; Cartier's 'democratic' department adapted itself to the new social conditions and the changes in pricing (reduced wages for the craftsmen and reduced profits for the firm). Its practical and functional range – smokers' requisites and desk accessories, watches, bags and vanity cases suited a newly price-conscious clientele.

Between 1928 – the year before the Wall Street Crash – and the end of 1930, a shift occurred in the turnover of stock in the department. Turnover in the lower end of the range – gold and silver cigarette lighters, for example, retailing at about Fr890 – rose by some 50 per cent, but the sales of really expensive and exclusive items such as cigarette cases of jade, lacquer and precious metals, fell by the same amount. The more sophisticated vanity cases gave place to powder compacts in black lacquer embellished with the Chinese character for 'Long Life', selling at about Fr1500.

Around 1930 no object was too insignificant to be enriched by the Cartier treatment: Louis Cartier used a Yale key decorated in the finest available Peking enamel, while the New York branch launched writing paper in ocean blue for Palm Beach fanatics. At this time the Department S at Cartier's New York had an especially enthusiastic clientele and after the Second World War, when the Paris Department S was only a memory, Louis Devaux, president of the New York firm between 1946 and 1949, was to set up similar boutiques in the department stores of Saks Fifth Avenue, Neiman Marcus, and I. Magnin in New York, Dallas and Los Angeles.

After 1930 there was an increasing trend towards justifying the luxury article by its function. The multipurpose gadget had a novelty value which might be thought to make the expense worthwhile. A magnifying glass was adapted for use also as a letter opener and might even incorporate a watch, a fountain pen would write at both ends and even contain a calendar. A complicated desk set of jade, lapis lazuli and agate combined inkwell, penholder, vase and table clock. In the 1930s it was rare to find a functional item decked out in the formal repertoire of chinoiserie: the epoch favoured the pragmatic Modern style, and a desk set of 1931 in the form of a Japanese temple garden was the last great example of the type and uncharacteristic of its time.

'Our age is one of invention, machinery, industry, science and commerce,' wrote Paul I. Frankl in *New Dimensions* in 1928. It was a creed which worshipped the machine – 'beauty is speed' achieved the status of an aesthetic canon among a privileged upper class for whom the automobile and the aeroplane were the fashionable means of transport. With Pierre Frondaie's bestseller, *L'Homme à l'Hispano*, the automobile even became the hero of a novel. Derain and Paul Morand with their Bugattis seemed to be celebrating the dictum of Marinetti the futurist that a racing car was more beautiful than the *Victory of Samothrace*. As early as 1914, Cartier's had created a *cantine d'automobile* in royal blue enamel for Elsie de Wolfe and in 1930 they produced a cigarette box in the form of a miniature car. André Citroën commissioned a car brooch in the form of the firm's famous trade mark in coloured stones.

Still more lavish were the fittings of the great yachts of the period, such as the Duke of Westminster's *Flying Cloud* or the Vanderbilts' *Alva*. Yachting was so popular that the rue de la Paix shop exhibited special yachting gifts in the Green Salon. The 1930s were not only the age of fashionable picnics and cocktails – Cartier's produced shakers engraved with recipes and also ivory champagne swizzle sticks – but the age of the sporting trophy. Cartier's made countless trophy designs in silver – for the fastest boat, the tennis champion, or the polo champion – in conjunction with the Linzeler -Argenson workshop.

In 1933 Cartier exhibited a trophy made from platinum and crystal at the 'Century of Progress' Exhibition in Chicago which was assumed to represent the most massive piece of platinum ever worked by a jeweler. It was a time when symbolic trophies and official commemorative presents went hand in hand. When the Atlantic liner *Normandie* sailed on her maiden voyage in 1935, her passenger list included Ganna Walska, Walt Disney, Mrs Jay Gould, and Pierre Cartier. To commemorate the event, the wife of the French president was presented with a Cartier cigarette box, incorporating a clock, and with the ship's route engraved on the lid.

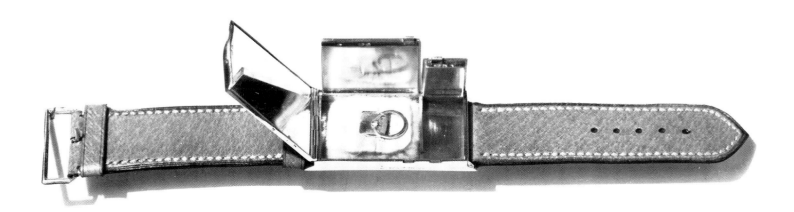

119. Miniature vanity case with 2 compartments, on leather strap. Commissioned by Mrs Evalyn Walsh McLean in 1930 (Actual size)

C ARTIER'S JEWELRY DESIGNERS did not pay much attention to the theories of the Bauhaus, the German design school directed from 1919 by Walter Gropius. This was partly a matter of personal inclination and partly because they realized that the formal principles of architecture and industrial design, no doubt adaptable to table clocks, boxes or desk sets, could not so readily be transferred to the realm of jewelry. Two competitors, Gérard Sandoz and, to a degree, Raymond Templier, did indeed make the attempt. Both liked to create jewels in cube, triangle or disc shapes, with surfaces broken up by colourful and dynamic patterns of linear perspective. Their geometrical forms, ideally suited to cigarette cases and other utilitarian objects, were strictly sculptural in effect, and it is significant that Sandoz later turned to abstract painting and Templier to jewelry with strongly sculptural tendencies. In fact their jewelry derived from an aesthetic diametrically opposed to that of Cartier's, being unrelated to the female form and having a solid weight and character completely incompatible with the diaphanous textiles of the mid-1920s.

At Cartier's, by contrast, Louis Cartier and Charles Jacqueau, an ideal partnership of creative imagination and technical expertise, adapted the contemporary geometrical style with understanding. Their decoration was 'modern', but never forced jewelry into 'mechanistic' forms, thus they restricted the geometric idiom to border ornamentation on brooches or cigarette cases or pendant supports. The focus of a Cartier *objet d'art* was the often figurative ornamental motif; the focus of a jewel was the precious stone. The principle was practical as well as aesthetic, since the Cartier *objet d'art* was often of considerable size. The firm's 'mystery clocks', among its largest creations, might reach a height of 40 cm; to cover such a surface with a network of geometric patterns would not only have made severe technical demands but would also have produced an unacceptably monotonous effect. By contrast, a valuable eighteenth-century jade statuette or an inlaid piece of Chinese lacquer provided a central coordinating element.

The Orient – the world of myth and fairy tale – provided the themes for Cartier's vanity cases, table clocks, scent bottles and other decorative objects. For the three young Cartier brothers, Persia, India and above all the limitless steppes of China seemed to be landscapes pregnant with myth and domains between heaven and earth where the imagination sought in vain for certainties. Yet the legends and sagas were fascinating, and their symbolism, deriving from secret and ancient origins, could, at least, be understood in decorative terms.

Cartier's achievements in integrating the fairy-tale world of myth and saga into the context of contemporary decorative arts marked a clear break with the course taken by his competitor René Lalique. Through the early 1900s Lalique's work had seemed to breathe the pine-laden air of the ancient world of Germanic saga; however, after he opened a glass factory at Combe-la-Ville near Paris in 1909 and put on his last jewelry show in 1912, he banished all such

Chimaeras, dragons and great cats

14

Colour plates 49 — 63

49 *Top left:* Brooch, the semicircular coral mount with cabochon emerald and circular-cut diamonds. Pear-shaped and cushion-cut diamond tassel. 1925. Cartier's New York

Top right: Onyx brooch, the onyx circle inset with diamonds and flanked by tubular coral and onyx motifs. 1923. Cartier's London

Centre: Pendant brooch, suspending a pear-shaped emerald of 19.45 cts from a coral and onyx tube below an onyx and scrolled diamond hoop. 1922. Sold to Mrs W. K. Vanderbilt

Below left: Jabot pin, designed as an umbrella in striped onyx, coral, diamonds and pearls. 1923. Cartier's New York

Below right: Chimaera pin, the coral head with cabochon emerald and gold eyes, holding an emerald bead with pearl, on onyx and cabochon emerald mount. 1923. Offered to Madame Louis Cartier

50. Art deco vanity cases: *above left:* vanity case in rose gold, enamel, purple and green mother-of-pearl, coral and pearl flowerheads, 1925; *above right:* vanity case in onyx with gem-set Chinese vase, 1927; *below left:* 'Panther' vanity case in mother-of-pearl, ruby, turquoise and enamel, 1925; *below right:* vanity case with Taj Mahal in emeralds, sapphires, diamonds and mother-of-pearl on black onyx, 1927

51. *Top:* Love-bird brooch, designed as 2 parrots in cabochon rubies, onyx and diamonds. Similar brooches were made in 1928 and 1929. Cartier's New York

Centre: Coral stomacher, the vase lined by diamonds and onyx and displaying a diamond, coral and onyx garland. 1922

Below left: 'Chinese' vanity case, the gold mount enamelled red with black enamel and cabochon sapphire borders, the lid with cabochon sapphire and emerald crane amid mother-of-pearl 'Chinese' clouds on black enamel. Interior with compartments. 1925

Below right: Design for above vanity case

52. Jade screen clock, mounted with 2 engraved jade screens (Chinese, eighteenth-century) within coral and onyx frame. The rear with trailing enamel dragon. Onyx, mother-of-pearl and gold base with lateral lion mask supports with cabochon emeralds. 33 cm high. 1927. Sold to Mrs George Blumenthal. Musée des Arts Décoratifs, Paris

53. Jade carp clock, the jade carp (Chinese, nineteenth-century) amid mother-of-pearl and emerald waves carrying the rock crystal fan clock with diamond numerals and sea-horse hour hand. Interior minute dial in mother-of-pearl and red enamel. The fish on frosted rock crystal sea. Onyx, coral and gold base. 22.5 cm. 1925. (See p. 253)

54. Temple gate mystery clock, the twelve-sided rock crystal, diamond, gold and black enamel face with diamond hands suspended within a rock crystal, onyx and black enamel gate. The entablature with seated rock crystal Buddha, coral beads, onyx, rock crystal and gold base. 37 cm. 1924

55. *Above left:* Desk clock, the rock crystal arched mount with gold, blue enamel, cabochon ruby, jade and diamond dial, with stylized jade and gem-set flower vases at the base. 1929

Above right: Desk clock, the circular rock crystal mount with gold, blue *guilloché* enamel and rose-cut diamond dial. White enamel chapter ring and diamond cipher. 1916

Below: Desk clock, the arched rock crystal mount with gold, diamond and rock crystal dial engraved from behind with doves below the Altar of Love. Diamond rosettes at the base. 1919

56. Temple gate mystery clock, the 12-sided rock crystal, mother-of-pearl, pearl, diamond and enamel face with diamond dragon hands suspended within rose quartz, black enamel and onyx columns and entablatures, with 'shou' sign for long life in mother-of-pearl. The column bases with enamelled buddhist lions. On onyx and rose quartz stand. 1924

57. *Above:* The Jade Elephant Mystery Clock of 1928. 19.5 cm. Contemporary watercolour

Below: 'Jade buddhist lion mystery clock', the jade animal with its cub (Chinese, nineteenth century) set with cabochon rubies, emeralds and enamel and supporting, by means of a coral bead, the citrine, rose-cut diamond, enamel and pearl clock. Coral and jade tree. On onyx and coral base. 16.5 cm. 1929

58. *Left:* Desk clock, the dial in marquetry of mother-of-pearl, with rose-cut diamond numerals and hands, reeded coral bands. On onyx, red enamel and gold base with lateral semicircular onyx supports. 1925

Right: Mystery clock, the rock crystal face with white enamel and rose-cut diamond chapter ring and hands, on square rock crystal and rose-cut diamond mount, with reeded jade bands. On jade, onyx and gold base with lateral semicircular onyx supports. 1923

59. 'Chinese' desk clock, the gold mount with mother-of-pearl marquetry, gold and enamel Roman numerals, the face as a lacquered mother-of-pearl plaque depicting a Chinese garden scene (nineteenth century). With rose-cut diamond hands and coral baton and black enamel borders. 1929

Bandeau, designed as coral, diamond and onyx 'Moorish' arcs below a gallery in olive-shaped coral, black enamel and diamonds. On tortoise-shell comb. 1922

60. *Left:* Mystery clock, the octagonal rock crystal face with rose-cut diamond hands within black enamel and coral border with rose-cut diamond chapters. On onyx, coral and gold base applied with 'F' for King Farouk. 1930

Right: Mystery clock, the rectangular rock crystal mount encasing the platinum chapter ring with platinum frame, rose-cut diamond hands and chapters. On onyx base with diamond crowned monogram of King Farouk. 1936. Sold in 1937

61. *Above left:* Pocket watch, the gold case with shutter enamelled with a horse. The shutter operated from the winding button reveals the silver dial. With Syrian coat-of-arms of Prince Nashret el Sultaneh. Commissioned by the Prince in 1919

Above right 'Mystery' pocket watch, the cut-cornered platinum case with Roman numerals. 1931. The only 'Mystery' pocket watch made by Cartier

Below: Mystery clock, the hands inset in a square aquamarine, within a platinum chapter ring with coral Roman numerals and border. The base in fluted coral with lapis lazuli corners. 1931

62. *Left:* Mystery clock, the octagonal rock crystal face with diamond hands within turquoise enamel chapter ring. Rose-cut diamond border. On onyx, enamel and gold 'Chinese' column. Gold and onyx base. 1921

Right: Repeater clock, the gold case applied with onyx panels, the dial with marquetry of kingfisher feathers. Rose-cut diamond hands. Gold and enamel chapter ring. Onyx push-piece. On gold base. 1927

63. Turtle clock, the rock crystal turtle (Chinese, nineteenth century) with cabochon ruby eyes and gold and enamel saddle cloth. The dodecagonal rock crystal clock with gold and gem-set chapter ring, on square gold, enamel and cabochon sapphire plinth. Gold, mirror and gem-set base. The turtle flanked by rock crystal statues of Gautama the Buddha and Krishna playing the flute, on similar stands. The turtle clock 1925, the two statues commissioned in 1926. The turtle is the second incarnation of God Vishnu, of whom Krishna is the 8th incarnation. The god appeared as a turtle (*kurma*) in order to act as the pivot of the churning rod when the gods and demons churned the ocean to retrieve precious objects lost in the flood

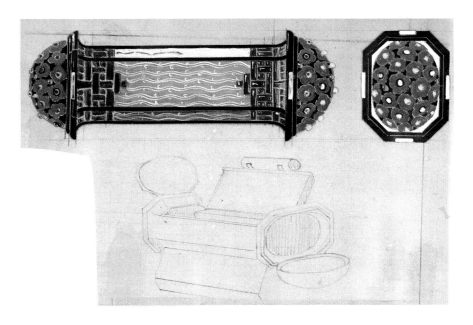

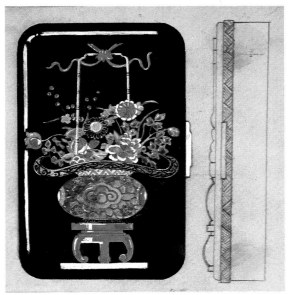

51

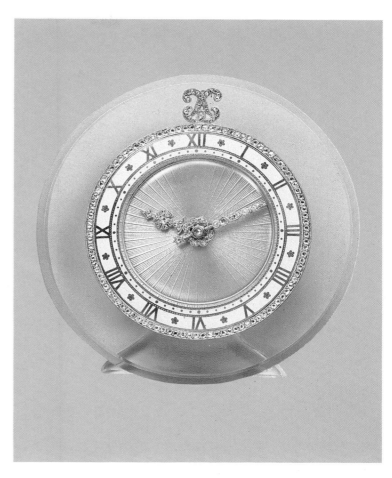

58

62

64

narrative symbolism from his work. His ideas turned to a demythologized art whose key lay in the imitation of rock crystal in glass. The symbolism which survived into this new creative dimension achieved its effect not in narrative but in starkly hieratic terms. Cartier, on the other hand, did not regard rock crystal as a perfectly translucent material in the service of a new factual reality. Apart from a few 'mystery clocks' it was seldom used alone but usually for contrast effects in combination with onyx and coral.[1]

The chimaera, a fabulous and gruesome monster of eastern legend, inspired one of the motifs in Cartier's design vocabulary. Its importance in Cartier's *oeuvre* consisted less in the iconography of the monster itself than in his inspired use of it for the bangles or armrings in the antique style, terminating in animal heads, which are the most original arm ornaments of the art deco period.

Animal bangles were discovered in the Elburz mountains in Iran from the eighth–seventh centuries BC. Represented on Assyrian reliefs with King Assurbanipal as lion-head bangles, these were popular in Lydia and Cyprus from the sixth and in Greece from the fourth centuries BC. The principal types were bull-, ram-, deer-, and snake-heads which were taken over by Roman and Etruscan jewelers and also found their place on earrings and necklaces.[2] In the modern epoch, animal-head bangles came back into fashion during the 1870s thanks to the work of the Italian jeweler Fortunato Pio Castellani (1793–1865) and the Frenchman Eugène Fontenay (1823–87), both of whom had returned to ancient themes and techniques within the Napoleon III style.

The chimaera of Greek mythology is depicted as a fire-breathing monster, with the forequarters of a lion, the body of a goat and the hindquarters of a dragon, which was slain by the hero Bellerophon on the winged horse Pegasus. Even in antiquity, however, there was no agreement as to the exact form of the beast and over the centuries it became simply a synonym for 'monster' like the terrifying Gorgon or the enigmatic sphinx. We encounter the chimaera on nineteenth-century jewelry in the work, for example, of Joseph Fannière (1820–97) and Alphonse Fouquet (1828–1911), with his chimaera tiara of 1878. The motif became so popular that by the end of the century the Paris jewelers Plisson & Hartz were producing little series of chimaera brooches made of gold. It was in this late-Romantic tradition that Cartier produced a chimaera pendant in 1883; it depicts the monster, complete with wings and a scaly comb, within a crescent moon of diamonds. In a sequence of smaller and less fearsome chimaera brooches which run up to the year 1904, the attributes of the chimaera combine with those of the equally mythical griffin.

In the 1920s the chimaera enjoyed a renewed vogue, and Cartier's, breaking free of ancient Greek iconography, turned to a type deriving from various Oriental forerunners. One influence was undoubtedly provided by the Indian sea-monster bangle, the *makara*, which remained virtually unchanged from the sixteenth to the nineteenth centuries. The two animal heads touching each other with open jaws derived from the Indian crocodile *Gavialis gangeticus* depicted in art since the third century BC either as fish or reptile.[3]

64. Comet clock, the circular agate bearing concentric enamel dials for the hours, indicated by a fly-back diamond star, and for the minutes a diamond 'comet' hand on star-studded enamel sky. With Latin motto 'Horas non numero nisi serenas'. Similar clocks are dated 1920 and 1921

Below: Desk clock-cum-photograph frame, the gold mount enamelled blue and white, the minutes on the outer border indicated by the hour numerals which pass in succession through the arched aperture, the reverse in ebonite. The photograph shows a member of the Romanian royal family. 1922

With time, the monster's jaws became extended into snouts or trunks so that the original resemblance to the crocodile was lost. Cartier's did not adopt the iconography of the *makara* armband head endings in their chimaera jewelry, although it was much discussed in the studio and pure examples of later *makara* bangles were produced. They did, however, take up the Indian enamelling on the inner surface of the bangle while replacing the original flower design with abstract scale patterns. The actual animal heads as such became streamlined stylizations of the Chinese chimaera, the *kilin.* Only the dragon head remained of the scaly cloven-hoofed monster.

In China the dragon itself (*lung*, standing for positive protective forces and the male principle) was venerated as a natural force and early became the personal symbol of the emperor, protecting him in full face on the chest and back of the imperial robe. According to legend, the dragon was originally a wingless sea creature which had soared up to heaven and, far from being punished for its presumption, had been received into the heavenly regions. Thus the Chinese dragon, despite its double nature, is not, like the chimaera or dragon in the western Christian tradition, a symbol of evil which has to be defeated, but rather a power of nature to be honoured. The five-clawed dragon adorned the imperial standard. From the seventeenth century onward the dragon was carved on jade bangles and buckles, mostly depicted in pairs, together with the heavenly pearl, the legendary object of the dragon's quest.

Cartier's chimaera bangles thus combined the tradition of animal-head bangles of the ancient Mediterranean, the Indian *makara*, the Chinese dragon, and even African variants. (In the firm's records the bangle form is described as Sudanese.)

The firm's production for 1922 started with a bangle ordered by Louis Cartier, which was to prove decisive for future examples of 1927, 1928 and 1929. Two chimaera heads of carved coral with 35 bejewelled combs are shown playing with two carved spherical emeralds, an apparent allusion to the legend recorded by the Indian poet Bhartrhari of the pearl or precious stone, which the monster *makara* carried in its jaws, and which is possibly related to the Taoist legend of the dragon being fed pearls by Guanyin.

This bangle, followed by a chimaera fibula in 1923 also ordered by 49 Louis Cartier for his wife, represents one of the most convincing ventures into sculpted jewelry in the 1920s. It is true that LaCloche produced a little series of dolphin bangles of frosted rock crystal, enamel and precious stones, but they do not bear comparison with Cartier's chimaeras. The chimaera bracelet, with its sculptural surface, exploded the framework of traditional jewelry design. As a precious small piece of sculpture it belonged to that borderline category of *objet d'art* which Cartier's cultivated on a level with jewelry during the art deco period. So it is not surprising that this motif was built into a special standing clock design in which the dial was framed by a chimaera bangle in the closed form of the Indian *makara* model. The workshops produced clocks of this type in 1925 and from 1928 to 1931. For the first time the entire hoop of the bangle, and not merely the figurative upper section, was of carved stone, generally bright green or white jade, or even crystal.

Nineteenth-century travellers mistakenly applied the term chimaera or 'Fō-dog' to the Buddhist lion, the symbolic animal of the Buddha Sakyamuni (*Fō* being the Chinese for Buddha). This creature stood guard over houses and temples throughout China as the protector of the Buddhist faith. However, since lions were unknown in China, the carvings took on the contorted features of a fabulous monster, part dog part lion. Cartier's used the Buddhist lion in another clock type, with a frame of two crystal pillars which suggest an Oriental temple gate with two lions crouching as guardians. The pivoted clock dial is in black Tonkin enamel, which emphasizes the black–white contrast of the overall design.

The chimaera motif was subject to much freer development on the complex structures of the 'mystery clocks' than in the context of the arm bangle. It appeared on two clocks of 1924 and 1926 as a giant carapace with ringed beard and tail. Three years later the monster lies in wait for its prey on the rim of a jade bowl or, belching fire, coils itself round a coral tree stump.

In 1954 the chimaera style enjoyed a renewed vogue under the inspired direction of Jeanne Toussaint, but now its terrifying aspect was banished and it was transformed into a comical, spaniel-eyed pet. The entire bangle consisted of either coral or lapis lazuli, and Toussaint preferred the bright salmon pink coral to the intense red 'moro' coral of earlier days. Chimaeras entirely set with precious stones – generally rubies, emeralds and yellow and white diamonds – were produced as novelties. In 1959 a yellow and white dolphin bangle was introduced; it is a curious fact that in ancient mythology the dolphin played a symbolic role similar to that of the Indian *makara*. From the distribution of the few examples of the chimaera bangle it appears that the style appealed to women of self-assurance as well as refinement; in 1928, for example, Ganna Walska, the Polish singer, selected the bangle with the two largest emerald beads of 48-carats. In the 1960s the Hon. Mrs Fellowes and Baroness d'Erlanger became devotees of the chimaera, associating themselves with a tradition which continues down to the present day.

The chimaera bracelet was the product of collaboration among a number of Cartier workshops. The lapidaries had the most time-consuming job. The large coral stalks from which the hoops were cut came only from Japan; they were imported to Europe via Italy, and were available in Paris from the Italian coral specialist dealer Borelli. Lapis lazuli, on the other hand, still known in the early years of the century as 'matière russe', was obtained by Cartier's from the Russian dealer Isaharoff, who had branches in both London and Paris. But in later years the Paris market was principally supplied by travelling Afghan merchants.

Louis Bozzacchi's workshop in the rue Turenne was entrusted with carving the chimaera forms. Bozzacchi (1860–1922) was a native of Milan whose lapidaries, such as the Miseroni, were already famous in the sixteenth century. About 1900, Bozzacchi trained for a time with the well-known cameo cutter Lemaire, and his facility with cigarette cases, small animals and statuettes brought him commissions from as far afield as Russia and from Fabergé. His workshop, employing between fifteen and twenty craftsmen, including some

Vietnamese, was already doing work for Cartier's at the turn of the century. The workshop was taken over on his death by his daughter Josephine, one of the few women stonecarvers in Paris, and her husband Henri Durand; in 1941 her fourteen-year-old son Claude began his initiation into the secrets of the family business. Cartier's designers supplied precise working drawings for the chimaeras and often wooden hoop models, after which Durand mounted plaster models of the required design for Cartier's approval. Between 250 and 300 man-hours of painstaking craftsmanship went into the production of a single finished coral or lapis lazuli chimaera bangle. Once the chimaera heads were ready, the job was taken over by the Lavabre workshop and ended only when the assembly was complete.

Whereas the chimaera had its imagined lair in the jaws of hell, the panther or leopard roamed the bush of Africa, the jungles of India, the steppes of Central Asia and China, and Asia Minor. The panther, unlike the lion, was a great rarity in mediaeval and Renaissance Europe. 'Panthera', the panther, was differentiated at this time from 'pardus', the leopard, and was considered a gentle beast loved by the entire animal kingdom save the dragon ('all animals love panthera', wrote Spenser in one of his sonnets). But it was first actually seen at the spiritual and temporal courts of Renaissance Europe: in 1479 Louis XI of France expressed his thanks to the Duke of Ferrara for the present of a splendid panther, and his successor Louis XII returned from victory at the Battle of Milan with Lodovico Sforza's cheetah, with which he hunted in the forest of Amboise. The panther was presented in art as a valuable hunting animal, a famous example being the frescoes in the Medici Chapel at Florence by Benozzo Gozzoli (1420–1497); and two gambol delightfully in the foreground of Titian's *Bacchus and Ariadne.* Painters who had not had the opportunity to study the animal's anatomy contented themselves with its pelt: leopard skins, like crocodile skins, were lovingly preserved in the curiosity cabinets of the sixteenth century. In the seventeenth, the panther skin formed part of the triumphal standards carried in victory processions. In the eighteenth century, as attitudes towards nature and life in the wild changed under the influence of Rousseauism, the pelt of the great cat prompted thoughts of the paradisal innocence of a Robinson Crusoe life untouched by civilization: idealized paintings of Europe's distant colonies depicted the 'noble savage' clothed only in his leopard skin. The French painter Nattier (1685–1766), when he apotheosized the beauties of Versailles as the goddesses of antiquity, included the panther skin among the attributes of their boudoirs.

As a motif, the panther was much in the air at the time of the First World War. In Paris, Princess Elsa de la Tour d'Auvergne and Cécile Sorel, actress at the Comédie-Française, introduced the leopard skin into interior décor. Above all, however, the motif was established by Elsie de Wolfe (1865–1950), who made her debut as an amateur actress in her native New York and, after her brilliant décor for the Colony Club in 1907, became the preferred interior decorator of the fashionable world. As Lady Mendl, this talented woman was a famous hostess in the postwar years and one of the pillars of the

Cartier image, both in Europe and in America; as early as 1919 the gallery at her Villa Trianon in Versailles was decorated with leopard velvet and zebra skins. The style was followed by Paul-Louis Weiller in the staircase of his residence, 'Le Noviciat', in tiger-chintz curtains for Condé Nast, publishers of *Vogue*, and a good deal later, but still under Elsie's influence, in the leopard skins and zebra upholstery in the Paris salon of Mainbocher, the couturier. In the meantime, the panther motif became universally accepted and entered the vocabulary of many interior decorators: the Pavillon de l'Elégance, where Cartier's exhibited in the 1925 Exposition des Arts Décoratifs, was decked out with panther skins (fashion house Jenny) and zebra skins (Soeurs Callot), while the wrought-iron balustrades of the pavilion glorified the prowling panther.

As early as during the First World War Cartier's designers found the modish panther skin a fruitful source of inspiration for abstract designs in onyx and diamond. The first panther-pattern appeared in 21 1914 on a wrist-watch and in 1915 Cartier's offered a watch pendant whose leopard-spot pattern was wrongly described as 'tiger skin'. Two years later another wrist-watch, the model called 'turtle' because of its bellied shape, was decorated with the dot pattern.

But Cartier's had yet to produce a representation of the panther as such. As in interior decoration, the fashion was still only for small surfaces flecked in black and white. Once again, the elaboration of the idea is traceable to Charles Jacqueau; two designs in his pattern book, one relating to the watch pendant of 1915, illustrate the point.

Abstract dot-patterns appeared again between 1922 and 1927, this time in a floral context with an orchid tiara of 1925 for the exhibition of that year, as well as on a little tree brooch with the novel feature of a diamond mounted with the point upwards. Later still, flecked patterns in the form of onyx thorns on a diamond ground were free of any conceivable association with the panther. How far this dissociation from the great cat could go is clearly illustrated in the 13 Egyptian 'sarcophagus box' of 1925 where the two sphinxes of cut emeralds are overlaid with a flecked pattern.

As the years went by, however, the panther was to become one of Cartier's favourite motifs. About the year 1900 the bold image of 'Lady with Panther', reminiscent of the mediaeval image of the Virgin and the Unicorn, emerged as a new subject in European art. But whereas her forerunner represented an allegory of chastity and courtly and heavenly love, the Lady with Panther enters the subtly charged field of demonic eroticism. The ambivalent character of the Lady-Panther combination was expressed by the Belgian artist Walter Sauer in his *Femme devenue panthère* of 1919 and the Belgian symbolist Khnopff in his picture *La Caresse*.

Reality mimicked art: after her triumph as Napoleon's son in *L'Aiglon*, Sarah Bernhardt received her admirers holding a panther on the leash, the Marquise Casati appeared at the Longhi ball in Venice as an animal tamer, with Negro slave and panther, and Boni de Castellane fantasized about Indian slave girls strolling with panthers in the gardens of Château Le Marais. American *Vogue* presented Ida Rubinstein with a leopard in 1913 and the sequence continues in the arts with statuettes by Chiparus and of Diana the

Huntress with Deer by the Swedish porcelain factory Orrefors, down to Erté's *Lady with Leopard.*

In 1914 Louis Cartier commissioned a *Lady with Panther* from George [19] Barbier as a display card.[4] The picture, later used in the firm's advertising, showed a lady in a fashionable Poiret gown with a black panther crouching at her feet.

Jeanne Toussaint, involved in a discreet friendship with Louis Cartier, had the pet name 'Panther', and her apartment was not only adorned with panther carpets but also with an onyx panther vanity case (probably made about 1917) from Cartier's – the firm's first representation of the entire animal. It was the first vanity case in a series with decorations in miniature (probably the smallest zoomorphic motifs of the entire art deco period) based on designs by Barbier and presented in balanced symmetry between two emerald [21] cypress trees: a stalking panther, dogs at play, or a leaping gazelle. Jeanne Toussaint also had a vanity case in black and gold stripes with applied panther in onyx and diamond, and a matching cigarette case.[5] Later examples of the panther motif were to show the animal in all positions – lying, at play and fighting.

The most significant of these panther vanity cases, a miniature masterpiece of colour, appeared in the year of the Exposition des Arts Décoratifs. Its style is again related to George Barbier but also to Paul Jouve (1880–1973), whose fascination with elephants and big cats had produced the illustrations for Kipling's *Jungle Book.* The vanity case depicts a black enamelled panther prowling in a fairy-tale garden beneath a ruby sun.

In 1931 the great Colonial Exhibition was held in the grounds of Vincennes. The frescoes by Ducos de la Haille and the lacquer panels by Jean Dunand depicted the jungles of the French colonies filled with tigers and elephants, and the exhibition's reading room was dominated by a picture of a panther stepping into water. There was a display of French jewelry made of the claws and teeth of the great cats, to which Cartier's contributed Jacqueau's necklace with tiger-paw motif.

Many years went by before, in 1948, the Duke of Windsor placed an order for a panther brooch as a present for the Duchess. It consisted of a cabochon emerald of 116.74 carats on which there was an outstretched golden panther flecked with black. This was the firm's first fully three-dimensional treatment of the motif. Two years earlier the Duchess had lost jewelry valued at £20,000 in a robbery at Ednam Lodge in England. The replacement pieces were of artistic rather than obvious material value, and the panther brooch fitted excellently into the new range. The following year the Windsors took delivery of a cabochon sapphire of 152.35 carats with a crouched panther of diamond flecked with onyx, and three years after that they completed this suite of panther jewelry with an articulated bracelet in the form of an outstretched panther.[6]

The Hon. Mrs Fellowes, daughter of the fourth Duke Decazes, who often entertained the Windsors on her truly royal yacht, the *Sister Anne,* and shared with the Duchess of Windsor the title of the world's best-dressed woman, is known to have commissioned a panther brooch of sapphire and diamond. This jewel is clearly modelled on the pendant emblem of the Order of the Golden Fleece, founded 1430 by Philip the Good, Duke of Burgundy. Jeanne Toussaint replaced the hanging ram's fleece of the order with the drooping form of a leopard entwined with an ornamental band of baguette diamonds which recalls the pendant form of the original ornament.

In 1957, a new panther enthusiast appeared at Cartier's: Princess Nina Aga Khan, the beautiful consort of Prince Sadruddin Aga Khan, who was to acquire within a few years the most extensive parure of panther jewelry. First came a jabot-pin with outstretched panther, similar to the Duchess of Windsor's; the lower clasp was formed by a 30-carat sapphire, but that was replaced with a round cabochon coral. The next year the Princess added an articulated panther pendant, another variant on the Golden Fleece emblem, also to be worn as the frontal clasp of a multistrand pearl necklace, and an exceptional open panther-head bangle, reminiscent of ancient Mediterranean animal-head models. In 1960 she acquired a second bangle of fluted gold; the panther-head terminals also served as earclips, while the gold bangle provided the handle of one of Cartier's most original evening bags. A ring with crouching panther completed the series.[7]

By contrast with Princess Aga Khan, Barbara Hutton, then the world's richest heiress, settled for the tiger variations in Jeanne Toussaint's menagerie. The striped pelt was represented by canary-yellow diamonds and onyx in a pair of earclips on the Golden Fleece theme, and these were followed by a spectacular tiger bracelet and an evening bag with enamelled tiger ornament.

Jeanne Toussaint kept a close eye on the whole panther range and was fortunate to find congenial collaborators like Peter Lemarchand, the designer whose pencil established the panther silhouette of the 1940s. Like many of Cartier's designers, Lemarchand (1906–70) studied at the Ecole Boulle in Paris from 1919 to 1924. He worked with Roger Sandoz, the jeweler on the rue Royale, before joining Cartier's in 1927. In 1935 he began a five-year stint in the London firm, which led him in 1939 to the Indian courts of Jodhpur and Bahawalpur. From there he returned to Paris and worked freelance at the rue de la Paix. He was so quick at putting his ideas down on paper that only a few hours a week at the drawing board were required; but even this brilliant designer was not allowed to miss Jeanne Toussaint's Tuesday conferences. He spent most of his time painting in his Montparnasse studio where he gave lessons to Pierre Cartier's daughter, Marion.

Lemarchand was divided from Jacqueau not just by a generation, but also by a new design awareness of nature and wildlife, free of the stylization of art deco. Whereas, in the last analysis, Jacqueau's animal figures worked in terms of symbolism and myth, Lemarchand maintained an anecdotal approach. In a tribute to him in 1948, Jeanne Toussaint spoke of 'our common love for animals and birds'. From their shared dream-world emerged fairy-tale forms of great cats and shimmering Oriental birds — endearing toys to match the mood of Europe and the United States after years of austerity. Lemarchand's animal figures have vigour, plasticity and an inimitable sense of movement – thanks, it must be said, to the virtuoso technique of the Cartier craftsmen who executed the designs and who could capture the articulate litheness of a great cat or emphasize the tail of a bird of paradise with a flexible platinum setting. According to his colleagues, Lemarchand spent hours in the zoo at Vincennes registering every nuance and reflex in the movements of the cats. In the Louvre he was fascinated by the Egyptian bronze cats of the goddess Bastet, and her playful poses were to be revived in his panthers.

In harmony with the austerity of the war years, Lemarchand created a delightful image whose symbolism was clear to friend and foe alike – a caged, silent songbird. In a second version made in 1945, after the signing of the German surrender at Rheims, the little bird is chirruping blithely at the open door of its cage.

THE YELLOWING PHOTOGRAPH ALBUMS of around the year 1900, with their princely wedding groups, court balls and diplomatic receptions, reveal an astonishing uniformity among the types of jewelry allowed by both fashion and protocol. The close-fitting dog collar, extended by giant ropes of pearls, provides a stylistic complement to the stomacher; the two together dominate the fashion silhouette so completely as to leave no room for large necklaces as such. Apart from the popular *lavallières*, necklaces designed as overall ornaments for the bosom consisted of radiating gemstone motifs in the eighteenth-century style or, like the necklace of Mrs Cornelius Vanderbilt, were in a form adapted from the stomacher – half corsage, half neck ornament.

The great necklaces – The London workshops – Dealers

As the Oriental taste in fashion and jewelry took over from about 1910, the dog collar was considered dated, and the long diamond chain, harbinger of the heavy sautoir of the late 1920s, began its triumphal progress. Lina Cavalieri, the most beautiful opera singer of her day, made a sensation at the Manhattan Opera in New York with a frivolous chain of this kind which fastened at the shoulder seam of her dress. Those who could afford it flaunted a handsome diamond drop on the sautoir. Cartier's set 40-carat stones as pendants of this type for Baroness Henri de Rothschild in Paris and Mrs Rita Lydig in New York, while Grand Duchess Cyrill was conspicuous with a cabochon sapphire of more than 300 carats.

During the austerity years of the First World War, the ostentatious parade of high society gave way, for a time, to the socially more acceptable ideal of charitable works and care for the suffering, exemplified by the Duchess of Marlborough and Countess Greffulhe. But in 1916, when the Paris Bourse reopened, the Assembly resumed its sittings and the Opéra took up its repertory again after a lapse of one and a half years, the curtain rose once more on the round of pleasures which the Parisians reckoned they had too long denied themselves. Lord Derby's reception for the King and Queen of England at the British embassy heralded the spring awakening impatiently awaited by the jewelers and fashion houses.

There were conflicting fashion trends in the immediate postwar years. While Chéruit sketched out his elongated line in gowns for Mme Errazuriz, Lanvin launched his 'period'-inspired *robes de style* which so enchanted Cécile Sorel. The jewelers enlisted followers from both camps. The vertical hipless line, which reminded Poiret of an undernourished switchboard operator, finally won the day, and the long pearl sautoir was seen as its logical accompaniment in the field of jewelry. Anything that looked like pearls was permitted: even the wealthy Mrs Stotesbury extended Cartier's great emerald necklace with artificial pearls so that, in the words of one Paris fashion writer, an observer could never be sure where 'Cartier stopped and Woolworth's began'.

After 1925 the diamond sautoir again took over from the pearl. At the Théâtre Daunou in Paris, the actress-director Jane Renouardt nightly dazzled her worshipping critics and admirers with hers. In fact, the diamond sautoir completely usurped the role of the classic necklace, while eastern-inspired bead necklaces or Cartier's coral and onyx Fuchsia necklace for Ganna Walska encompassed the vague realm of fashion or fantasy jewelry. In this field the couturiers gradually ceased to be dependent on the jewelers; indeed, as the 1920s advanced, they became competitors. Coco Chanel took the young jewelry designer Fulco Verdura under her wing and in 1932, encouraged by Paul Iribe, launched her own jewelry collection.[1] A necklace terminating in a comet was the Iribe-Chanel reply to the 'traditional' style of the rue de la Paix, which was not felt to be sufficiently 'barbaric'.[2]

Yet the large necklace remained the province of the jewelers. It was Cartier's sensational creations which provided the focus of the Autumn Show at San Sebastian in 1919, when the firm's most valuable piece was exhibited at the Hotel Maria Cristina, occupied by wealthy Cubans and Argentinians. The jewel comprised a long diamond chain from which hung the world's largest cut sapphire, a drop of 478 carats;[3] the history of the stone is illustrated by the following sketches:

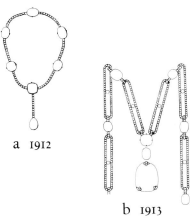

a 1912

c 1913

b 1913

d 1920

a) This shows the original diamond necklace which Cartier fitted with six cushion-shaped sapphires and a drop-shaped sapphire of a total of 224.10 carats. But the sapphires were unmounted and sent to New York where an identical diamond necklace was made to receive them. They were replaced with onyx in the Paris necklace but this was again broken up in 1914.

b) The New York necklace was reworked in Paris and a great 478-carat drop sapphire added to the seven original stones.

c) Next, the seven sapphires were removed and the great drop attached by a pendant ring of *calibré*-cut sapphires.

d) The sapphire drop was transferred to a diamond necklace that had been sold to Mrs Leeds in 1911. At its centre was a great diamond drop and a pink diamond of 6.83 carats; Cartier bought back the necklace, without the two central stones, in 1919. The diamond drop was transferred to a new diamond necklace that Mrs Leeds wore on the occasion of the marriage of her son William B. Leeds to Princess Xenia.

The Cartier display in San Sebastian became the talk of the town: the Queen of Spain, Victoria Eugenia, Queen Mother Maria Cristina and the Princess of Bourbon arrived from the nearby Palace Miramar. The queen tried on the sapphire jewel and remembered it the following year. It was King Alfonso's custom to buy two new diamonds each year for his wife's antique diamond sautoir; but he was not tempted to purchase the Cartier piece. 'Only the *nouveaux riches* can afford such luxuries,' he observed, 'we kings are the *nouveaux pauvres* of today!'

At about the same time, as Louis Cartier was to recall later, the giant stone was to clear the name of a Parisian dealer in precious stones. The case concerned the theft of a sapphire from the Polish Count Branicki. The stone had been stolen from its hiding place, the

121. Queen Mary of Serbia wearing her Russian cabochon emerald tiara and her Cartier emerald sautoir necklace. 1923

120. Queen Marie of Romania wearing her pearl and diamond tiara and her 478-ct sapphire drop necklace. 1921 (See p. 236)

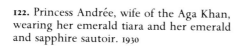

122. Princess Andrée, wife of the Aga Khan, wearing her emerald tiara and her emerald and sapphire sautoir. 1930

count's tobacco jar in his Warsaw residence, and all the evidence suggested that it had found its way to Paris. There it had been acquired in all innocence by a dealer who had it cut because of its great size. He was hauled before the courts, accused of having cut the stone, knowing it to be the largest of its kind, so as to destroy all trace of it. But Louis Cartier, whose grandfather had once handled the stone, was convinced of the dealer's honesty. Called as an expert witness, he astonished the court when he unwrapped the firm's own giant sapphire. It was obvious that the stolen stone had not been unique and Louis went on to prove the dealer's innocence.

Two years after the exhibition in Spain the sapphire drop was to be bought by King Ferdinand of Romania. But he too appears to have approached the purchase with caution. First Cartier's had to pledge to cancel the sale should 'serious and unforeseen events' intervene. (Was the king, perhaps, thinking of his bleak exile in Iasi during the First World War?) The purchase price of Fr11,375,000 was to be paid in four installments up to 1924. Ferdinand's beautiful consort Queen Marie was at that time forty-six, at the height of her fame and the ideal ambassador for Romania's interests. When in Paris she lived at the Ritz, which flew the Romanian flag, and the public followed her every move. But large jewelry had not yet excited her interest; there was nothing in her collection to match the Russian ruby pieces of her recently dead mother, the Duchess of Saxe Coburg-Gotha. Marie preferred to wear a Greek cross or, when she visited the Paris Opéra, her pearls. At about the time she received the sapphire drop she also acquired a Cartier pearl tiara which she liked to wear in the 'Byzantine' manner with a band of pearls framing her face. However, the great sapphire necklace was the perfect companion-piece for the magnificent sapphire tiara the queen had bought from Grand Duchess Vladimir when she fled from Russia. Marie wore them both at her coronation receptions and when she sat for her portrait to Philip de László.[4]

During the year of her coronation in Bucharest, the marriage of her daughter Marie (Mignon) to Alexander I of Serbia also took place. The king, who had recently ordered 350 pairs of cufflinks from a jeweler, entrusted the major commissions to Cartier's, and Farinès, the firm's star salesman, hurried to Belgrade with designs for tiaras and emerald bracelets. Queen Marie, as obsessed with emeralds as her mother was with sapphires, had bought a Russian tiara of cabochon emeralds from Princess Putyatin who formerly, as Grand Duchess Marie, had done Russian embroidery for Coco Chanel. Following the strict Empire style of the tiara, Cartier created a sautoir out of eighteen magnificent emeralds from the Serbian crown jewels which, for sheer splendour, bore comparison with the Romanian sapphire jewels. It was created six months before the birth of Queen Marie's son Peter (1923); his wife Alexandra was to wear it at their wedding; and later, unfortunately, it had to be sold.

The newspaper reports of Cartier's monumental exhibition of the reconstructed Patiala jewels – 'Paris Amazed By Oriental Gems' – gave the Aga Khan the idea of selling unwanted stones from his collection through an exhibition at Cartier's. Revered by twelve million Ismaili Shi'a Moslems as the forty-eighth Imam,[5] the Aga

Khan had been born in Karachi in 1877 and had followed the development of Cartier's, both in the Orient and in Europe, from his youth. His first purchase, in 1902, had been a stomacher with a heart-shaped diamond, shortly followed by a wheat-ear and a laurel-leaf tiara. Later, like Cornelius Vanderbilt and J. P. Morgan, he was an admirer of Cartier's art deco productions, brilliant and colourful masterpieces that appealed to his own pronounced colour sense.

The diamonds which the Aga Khan was proposing to sell comprised thirty-eight round stones, and three drops of 40, 38 and 35 carats respectively. Pierre Cartier set them as a gigantic necklace which was first displayed at the French Exhibition in Cairo in 1929. At the official opening they were admired by King Fuad who, however, bought his Queen Nasli a diamond tiara. Another exhibition followed immediately at Alexandria, and two months after that the piece went on display at the International Exhibition in Barcelona's Montjuich Park. The Aga Khan's necklace, modelled by a mannequin from the fashion house of Callot, proved a sensation — but failed to change hands. Part of Cartier's Barcelona exhibit also featured at the Ibero-American Exhibition in Seville, where the Colombian government had erected a 'Temple of Emeralds'.

The necklace went on its travels once again, this time by the Orient Express to Belgrade, for inspection by Queen Marie. But the city was on the verge of war: tensions between Serbs and Croats were smouldering in the provinces and the constitution had been suspended. That autumn the country was renamed Yugoslavia and a new constitution promulgated by the farsighted king. It was hardly a propitious moment for the sale of a major piece of jewelry. Thus, on the eve of the American Crash, the great necklace was broken up again into its constituent parts. Cartier's bought the 35-carat elongated drop and attached it to a necklace destined for the New York firm. The 38-carat drop was returned to the Aga Khan[6] and the 40-carat one provided the centrepiece of a necklace for his son, Prince Ali Khan. In the meantime, Cartier's of London sold the remaining round stones to the King of Nepal.

123, 124. The Aga Khan diamond necklace (photo: Vogue Studio Paris)

The dispersal of what had perhaps been the largest private jewel collection before the First World War — that of Grand Duchess Vladimir — took place in the early 1920s. The duchess had fled Russia in late 1919 and died in France the following year. According to the chroniclers of high society, she used to put everyone else in the shade when she appeared, bristling with emeralds, at Boni de Castellane's balls in the Palais Rose. After her death, the jewels were divided among her four children, with whom both Pierre and Louis Cartier had personal connections. From her son Boris, Louis acquired the 107-carat emerald[7] and the magnificent emerald necklace of nineteenth-century Russian work.

Two years after the grand-duchess's death, Louis Cartier was showing the legendary emeralds to King Alfonso of Spain, who may have recalled his ironic outburst over the San Sebastian sapphire drop, when he thought that the time for buying such treasures was past. In one sense, Alfonso was right: from now on the world's great jewels were destined to find their home not in Europe but in the United States.

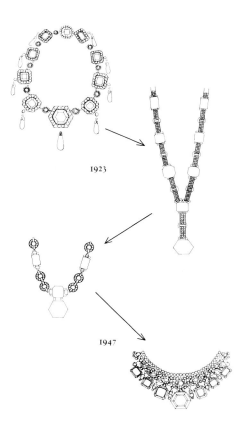

125. Sea-monster necklace, the heads in circular- and baguette-cut diamonds holding a tubular engraved emerald, the necklace mounted with 2 strings of tubular engraved emeralds and circular- and baguette-cut diamonds. Cartier's London. 1930

1923

1947

Cartier's 'American jewelry parade' had begun with a necklace of nine large emeralds ordered in Paris by Eva Stotesbury, the spoilt wife of 'Morgan's man in Philadelphia'. With its hexagonal centre-piece, the necklace could almost stand comparison with Grand Duchess Vladimir's. Thanks to the swelling fortune of her banker husband, Eva could realize her dream of a 1920s Versailles. At their mansion, Whitemarsh Hall, crammed by the dealer Duveen with his most expensive furniture and works of art, the word 'excess' required redefinition. A radical remodelling was prescribed for the emerald necklace; the work was done in New York, in 1923, by Pierre Cartier. The number of emeralds was increased to nineteen and a matching tiara was added. In a similar manner, two years before, Pierre had created a giant emerald parure for Mrs Leeds by combining an epaulette with a necklace. When it was completed, the widow of America's tin king sat to the Hungarian portrait painter László, just as Queen Marie had done in distant Romania.

No wonder that in due course the Vladimir emeralds also found their way to America, mounted in the severe form of an art deco necklace for Edith Rockefeller McCormick. The daughter of John D. Rockefeller senior, founder of the family fortune, she had married Harold Fowler McCormick, son of the Chicago Reaper King, in 1895; but the marriage ended melodramatically in divorce in 1922. Edith sought refuge with C. G. Jung in Switzerland and spent the rest of her life absorbed in a fantasy project to build the futuristic town of Edithton — a project prematurely terminated by the 1929 Crash. Three years after her death, the emerald necklace was once more broken up in Chicago and the stones handed over to Cartier by the executors for the asking price of $480,000.

By this time Barbara Hutton had inherited her $42 million and become Countess Haugwitz-Reventlow. It was apparently her sister-in-law Roussy Mdivani, the new Mme Sert, who drew Barbara's attention to the Rockefeller emeralds.[8] 'There is an emerald necklace at Cartier's that came from the Romanovs, and I can get you a special price.' But the 'special price' did not long remain a secret: 'Countess Buys Emerald Collection For Over A Million Dollars', ran the headlines, without making any notable contribution to Barbara's popularity. The emeralds were sent across the Atlantic in two shipments, the first liner carrying a consignment of ten packets, the second just the precious 100-carat stone. From her Palladian mansion in London, Wingfield House, Barbara had Cartier's of Bond Street make up the emeralds as a pair of earrings, a necklace and a ring. The necklace consisted of a heavy chain with the 100-carat stone at the centre in the massive style of the 1930s.[9] After the Second World War its design was obsolete again.

Barbara, who had in the meantime become Princess Troubetzkoy, was now a devotee of India (which had often provided a refuge) and of yellow gold. Her enthusiasm, together with that of the Duchess of Windsor, the Hon. Mrs Fellowes and the Countess of Surmont, did much to promote the popularity of the metal. Once more the emeralds were returned to Cartier's, where André Denet, the principal salesman, and Lucien Lachassagne, the designer, supervised the creation of a jewel in the Oriental style which Barbara

126. Ruby and diamond necklace, mounted with 31 briolette-cut diamonds of 101.60 cts, baguette-cut diamonds and 280 rubies of 199.06 cts (including the 27.32-ct centre stone). Cartier's London. 1929

127. Emerald and diamond necklace, the 6 lower emeralds weighing 224.08 cts (including the 70.24-ct bottom stone), on circular-, half-moon- and baguette-cut diamond mount. Cartier's London. 1926. Sold to the Maharajah of Nawanagar

128. Emerald and diamond necklace, the rectangular pendant in circular-cut diamonds with 3 engraved emerald flowers lined in black enamel, the necklace in diamonds, pearls and partly engraved emerald beads, the rear as a seed pearl and onyx rope. Cartier's London. Commissioned in 1930

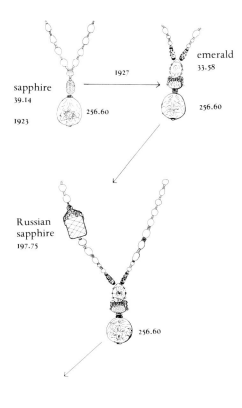

sapphire
39.14

1923

1927

emerald
33.58

256.60

256.60

Russian
sapphire
197.75

256.60

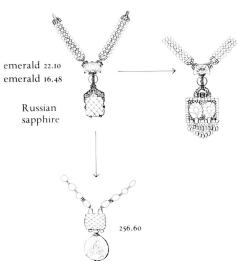

emerald 22.10
emerald 16.48

Russian
sapphire

256.60

Mrs McCormick's
necklace

could use either as a necklace or as a tiara, and which she wore latterly in Morocco.

Another relic of the days of the tsars, spirited out of Russia by an unexplained route, was a 197-carat briolette-cut sapphire which brought Cartier's together again with the McCormicks. Harold McCormick had barely been divorced from his first wife before he married the Polish opera singer, Ganna Walska. She had already extracted from her former husband Alexander Smith Cochran, known as 'the richest bachelor in the world', a wedding present very much to her taste – the choice of whatever pleased her best at Cartier's. Ganna Walska was driven by her ambition, not only to be marvelled at for the splendour of her jewelry, but to be famous for the pure gold (so-called) of her voice. McCormick, who had already brought the singer Mary Garden to the Chicago Opera, advanced his wife's ambitions out of conjugal infatuation and by the expenditure of considerable funds. For Ganna McCormick, who resided in her château near Versailles and was later to buy the Théâtre des Champs-Elysées, Cartier's created a necklace, combining the Russian sapphire with a 256-carat engraved Indian emerald whose step-by-step transformations were even more chameleon-like than the Queen of Romania's sapphire necklace.

During the 1930s Cartier's London house quite overshadowed the Paris firm in the production of large necklaces. Most of them were diamond or coloured stone sautoirs, of which an astonishing number were sold in England. Between 1933 and 1938 London produced approximately 280 necklaces, including forty-five examples of coloured bead sautoirs.

One of the most original designs was a magnificent necklace of 1937, which consisted of fifteen emeralds with a cross pendant cut from a single 45-carat emerald. The 4-cm-long gem belonged originally to Queen Isabella II of Spain (1830–1904), who gave it to the Empress Eugénie. From her it passed via Queen Victoria and Princess Beatrice to Queen Victoria Eugenia of Spain, from whom Cartier bought it and sold it to Mme Patiño.

The stocks of the Bond Street shop were never so extensive, nor its designers and workshops so busy, as during the later years of the reign of King George V and Queen Mary. The king died in 1936, but the epoch really came to an end only with the outbreak of the Second World War in 1939. Cartier's of London had become independent of Paris in 1919, and set up its own workshops two years later. At first, while the goldsmiths and stonesetters were all British, the designers were predominantly French. Up to 1929 there was a daily traffic in gemstones between the Paris and London firms; the then London director, Arthur Fraser, recalled later how he frequently carried cases full of precious stones between the two companies, without any customs formalities. The practice came to an end in 1929 when the Chancellor of the Exchequer imposed a duty. Jeanne Toussaint, who never went to London, later had photographs of the Paris creations sent to Bond Street so that the current styles of the rue de la Paix should not be forgotten.

Cartier's London distributed the production of jewels and clocks among their three subsidiaries: Sutton and Straker, a goldsmiths' workshop in Clarendon House, Bond Street, under the direction of George Straker; Wright and Davies, directed by Sam Mayo, in Ormond House, Rosebery Avenue, which produced cigarette cases, vanities and clock cases; and English Art Works. Directed by Felix Betrand and specializing in large necklaces, English Art Works was one of London's largest workshops in platinum jewelry, and had begun in Cartier's premises before moving to 105 New Bond Street. The company's name itself made it absolutely clear that there was no question of foreign labour competing with native craftsmen. Even before the First World War, Cartier's New York branch had had to defend itself against criticism on these grounds, and in the English crisis of the 1930s, when 60 per cent of the goldsmiths were unemployed, Cartier's London seemed especially liable to the same accusation. It was only when Queen Mary, during the Depression years, visited English Art Works, where sixty skilled English craftsmen earned their living, that the critics fell silent. With regard to designers too, Jacques Cartier was careful to give preference to native designers over French. Peter Lemarchand was the great exception. He came over from Paris in 1935 and up to the outbreak of war was working in London, where his naturalistic style, his tropical birds and flowers, were a lasting national influence. Later visits by French designers, such as Jacqueau's in 1947, were shorter and usually for specific jobs. Like the Bernard Palissy, Boulle and Germain Pilon design schools in Paris, the Chiswick School of Arts and Hampstead's Central School of Arts and Crafts taught jewelry design and other branches of the trade. George Charity, who joined Cartier's in 1925, was trained at Chiswick, as was Rupert Emmerson, the designer of seventeen snuffboxes for the collector Peter Wilding (now in the British Museum).

On the other hand, the rigid geometric style, which appears so often in London's output during the 1930s, and which is so different from the contemporary style in Paris, was mostly the work of Frederick A. Mew, who occupied a position almost comparable to that of Jacqueau in Paris. Just as in Paris the most imaginative creations generally sprang from the joint inspiration of Louis Cartier and Jacqueau or Lemarchand and Toussaint, so in London Jacques Cartier regularly discussed things with Mew and the Frenchman Massabieaux who, though no designer himself, skilfully directed the design studio. Mew designed charming bird brooches like his friend Peter Lemarchand, dahlias and other flowers made of citrine, and in 1953 the diamond tiara for Queen Elizabeth the Queen Mother. A fellow designer with Mew in the commissions department was Ernest C. Frowde, though his work tended to be somewhat dry and academic and lacked Mew's rich imagination. In 1933 the two worked on designs for a crown for the Gaekwar of Baroda, which, however, was never made.

Protocol and etiquette at the court of St James had changed little since the First World War. Tiaras were still obligatory at receptions and balls; sautoirs of geometric pattern took the place of the stomacher which, with the changing dress line, had become dated.

129. Emerald cross necklace, mounted with 15 square, rectangular and hexagonal emeralds weighing 134.45 cts, circular-cut diamonds, and suspending a 45.02-ct emerald cross. Cartier's London. 1937

Generally the sautoir had two strands at the front, with a pendant hanging down the low-cut back. Bandeaux, sautoirs and bracelets were interchangeable in form and structure and multipurpose: thus sautoirs and bandeaux might be worn as brooches and bracelets, and Lily Damita and Gertrude Lawrence demonstrated on stage and screen how five or six might be worn to chic effect on gathered black evening gloves.[10]

Rubies and emeralds were favoured among coloured gems, but if they proved too expensive the acceptable substitutes were amethyst, topaz or aquamarine, the last being a special favourite with Englishwomen for sautoirs and tiaras. Amethyst, from which large crystals were easy to cut, provided massive purple sautoirs. One of these was ordered in 1926 by the Duchess of Marlborough (the former Gladys Deacon), and another, a little later, by Lady Cunard, the feared and famous Emerald. Both of these American-born ladies had their sautoirs admired and copied from Palm Beach to the Riviera.

By contrast, aquamarine was most often used in close-fitting dog collars, from which earclips and the so-called double clips could be detached. In England double clips in characteristic buckle shape were made popular by the Rani of Pudukota and Lady Cunningham-Reid, and represented the 'find' of 1930s jewelry. But aquamarine was also cut in five-pointed, six-pointed and rhomb shapes, unusual forms which livened up the monotonous sequence of stones in the sautoir. Moreover, aquamarine seemed to hold distant memories of that strange, azure-blue stone, the eerie blue diamond.

Fancy-coloured diamonds cropped up now and then at Cartier's from old Indian collections, but they had no statistically-based value equivalents in the European-American market. One of the earliest fancy-coloured diamond sautoirs found its way from Cartier's Paris to Kiev in 1914. Surely the shimmering palette of the ballet *Schéhérezade* inspired the names of its pastel graded stones – narcissus yellow, lemon yellow, aquamarine blue, sultan green, topaz, gold, shrimp pink and lilac. In 1930 Mme Gaston Fournier, the daughter of the last of the Tiffanys (d.1902), was to acquire a necklace of no fewer than seventy-one fancy-coloured diamonds and the following year Cartier's London created a necklace from six pink diamonds, of which two came from the collection of the Maharajah of Nawanagar, and the clasp from the Gaekwar of Baroda. The jewel was later broken up again.

One of the two Nawanagar stones, however, of 9.50 carats, found its place in that most precious cascade of colour diamonds known to history, the ceremonial necklace of the Maharajah himself. Jacques Cartier, who assembled the piece, called it 'a really superb realization of a connoisseur's dream' and confessed that in no other epoch could a comparable jewel have been created. The necklace consisted of two strands of round diamonds linked on both sides by a fancy-pink stone. The 9.50-carat pink diamond formed the first stone of the pendant. Below it hung an azure-blue stone of 26.26 carats[11] and below that 'the world's most beautiful pink stone' of 22.97 carats which, according to Jacques Cartier, came from a world-famous jewel. The centrepiece of the pendant was the 'Queen of Holland', the blue-white diamond of 136.32 carats which came from the same mine as the 'Cullinan' and was cut in Amsterdam in 1913. It was exhibited at the 1925 Exposition des Arts Décoratifs in Paris by the Dutch diamond dealer F. Friedmann, who had branches in Paris and New York.[12] The pendant terminated in a green diamond — 'a rare stone indeed', exclaimed Jacques Cartier admiringly — and a light rhomboid pink stone of 15.26 carats.

20   Before this extraordinary piece was sent to India the London branch, as a playful improvisation, combined the blue and pink stones with the Polar Star diamond (see p. 286) into a temporary necklace which was put on display. It was only when Cartier's acquired the 'Queen of Holland' that the idea of the definitive, spectacular colour combination, now known to history as the 'Nawanagar Necklace', was born.

Cartier's discovered the world's most remarkable stones not only in old collections, but also in the stocks of the leading diamond and gemstone dealers all over the world. The latter entrusted their remarkable treasures to Cartier's the more willingly since, as dealers and lapidaries, they were interested in bulk sales of new cuts. With Cartier's they were guaranteed that daring cuts, represented since 1900 by the trapeze, the obus, the unstepped square and later the baguette, would find optimum application in the wide spectrum of their international production.[13] It is hard to say whether technical or aesthetic considerations came first in determining the new cuts of the period. But it is certain that the new geometric cuts stimulated jewelry designers to the bold formal combinations of art deco. In 1902 the American David C. Towsend evolved a cut which, in the ebullience of the dawning era, was called 'the twentieth-century cut' ('jubilee cut'); the upper and under sides of the stone each had forty facets. But this cut was expensive and furthermore 'round' diamonds were less in demand than the new geometrical forms which matched the contemporary feeling for the cube.

The great pioneer among the diamond dealers around 1900 was Atamik Eknayan (1847–1925). When he was young, the important dealers were located at the Bosphorus, Aden and Cairo, where they brought their wares from India on the way to Venice, Frankfurt and Lithuania. It was only the discoveries in Africa, exhibited in Paris from 1867, that disturbed this network. Napoleon III had already made every effort to establish Paris as the centre of the diamond working industry;[14] and in 1872 the young Armenian Eknayan moved there. He opened his first cutting house on the boulevard de la Villette in 1893; it moved to Neuilly, where experimental cuts were to be developed. But Eknayan was as influential as a dealer in Paris and New York as he was as a lapidary. It was from him, in 1909, that Cartier acquired the historic 90.38-carat Briolette diamond, as well as the heart-shaped 'Blue' of 30.82 carats.

Similarly, when the sons of Isaac Joseph Asscher of Amsterdam, Joseph and Louis, set up a diamond-cutting business in Paris in 1899, it supplied Cartier's from the start. In 1908 the Amsterdam head office was commissioned by Edward VII with the cutting of the 'Cullinan', at that time the largest diamond ever mined. In 1919 the Asschers moved their cutting house to Versailles, where they philanthropically provided work for war wounded and war orphans. Relations between Cartier's and the Asschers remained friendly well into the modern era. Thanks to Cartier's, Asscher's were spared harassment by the Vichy regime during the Second World War and there were to be 150 cutters and 50 apprentices back at work at Versailles by 1948; Louis Cartier's son Claude received his first instruction in diamond expertise with Asscher's of Amsterdam.

The Armenian Carlo Sirakian (1885–1976) was another Cartier supplier. After the Turkish massacres, he left Constantinople through Bulgaria and began business as a diamond dealer in Romania. About 1913 he settled in Paris and went into partnership with Manouk Mezbourian, who worked for Eknayan. Sirakian's speciality was the cutting of diamonds as hexagon, obus, kite, pentagon and rhomb, almost exclusively for Cartier's.[15]

But Cartier's most personal association was with Raphael Esmerian (1903–76). His father Paul (Bobros) began life as a lapidary in Constantinople before he set out on the trail for the 'Golden West', settling as a twenty year old in Paris in 1890. Unlike Eknayan, he specialized in coloured stones, a field in which the small Armenian colony in Paris, with Esmerian's uncle Margossian at its head, held the lead. In 1919 Paul introduced his son Raphael into the secrets of his profession. During the 1920s the Esmerians were the leading gemstone dealers in Europe and for fifteen years they maintained a branch in London, which brought them into close contact with Jacques, the youngest of the three Cartier brothers. Later, at the invitation of the jeweler Raymond C. Yard, Raphael Esmerian, as much aesthete as dealer, went to New York where, as friend and near-neighbour, he was to supply Pierre Cartier with often spectacular coloured stones over a period of some thirty years.[16]

130. 'Dinner Hour in the Grand Restaurant of the *Queen Mary*': advertisement for Cartier's London, c.1935

16

'The jeweled flight of time'

URING THE NINETEENTH CENTURY, Cartier's stock comprised not only jewelry and goldwork, but the entire range of *objets d'arts* of a specialist antique dealer. The first watches are mentioned in 1853. At this period, these were not timepieces from Cartier's own workshops but bought-in pocket-watches of gold, silver, copper and steel, often ornamented in Second Empire style with onyx, pearl and enamel inlay. The principal work of this period was the Egyptian watch of 1873 decorated with rubies and rose-cut diamonds (see p. 151).

To meet the demand of connoisseurs for collectors' pieces in the great tradition of French horology, Cartier bought at auction and from specialist dealers. These acquisitions included a Louis XIV silver pocket-watch; a watch by Lépine decorated in painted enamel; two pieces by the greatest of the French watch-making dynasties, Bréguet; and a watch in the form of a seal, fitted with musical box, made in Geneva about 1820. The most interesting models were sold on richly ornate châtelaines of different colours of gold and enamel in Louis XVI style. These traditional-style pendants were decorated with the conventional motifs of the late eighteenth century, such as quivers and arrows, turtle doves and flower garlands. A châtelaine watch of 1874 was ornamented with urns and a little temple of love; but besides watches, seals and charms were also hung on the châtelaines which were sometimes called *breloquets* (French *breloquet*, 'charm'). In 1875 we find an entry for a châtelaine watch in peacock-eye enamel, an eighteenth-century technique revived by Boucheron; fitted with seals and charms, it was sold to the Prince of Wagram.

In the 1890s, Cartier's were supplied by the greatest watchmakers of the period, chief among them Vacheron & Constantin of Geneva (founded 1736).[1] They delivered a number of pieces between 1893 and 1899, when Cartier's moved to the rue de la Paix. Among them was a simple steel bicycle-watch, a model with neo-Gothic designs and a valuable pocket-watch decorated with *scènes galantes* à la Watteau. In 1896, Cartier bought a watch decorated with enamel birds and flowers from Ferdinand Verger of Paris, father of the brilliant Georges Verger, whose work was again to appear at Cartier's in the art deco period.[2] Barely three years later Cartier's produced their first platinum pocket-watches. One of the earliest, a heart-shaped model embellished with pavé diamonds, was selected by J. P. Morgan.

Between 1872 and 1892, Cartier's inventory records no fewer than 408 watches and châtelaines. The range of stock increased still more dramatically when the firm moved to the rue de la Paix and Louis Cartier, associated with his father since the previous year, contributed his expertise.[3] His involvement in the watch department had three objectives: to add table clocks to the range of pocket-watches; to build up in-house production; and to explore the market possibilities of the wrist-watch, of whose future he was convinced.

Table clocks

The firms of Brédillard, in the rue Jean-Jacques-Rousseau, and Dagonneau, rue des Petits-Champs, with their factories in Geneva, were among the first suppliers of movements for Cartier's table clocks (*pendules* or *pendulettes*). From 1904 Cartier's were using movements made by Prévost on the boulevard Sébastopol, and this workshop was soon undertaking the bulk of Cartier's commissions. In 1911 they supplied a table clock with an electrically illuminated dial, bought by the Aga Khan. The enamelled cases for these Prévost movements were provided by the Dubret workshop in the rue d'Hauteville. In a few instances Cartier's bought cases from Yahr, the Moscow enameller, who worked from detailed designs. Many different workshops could be involved in the production of a single table clock, as a glance at a pyramid clock of 1906 will demonstrate. The marble-like thulite was furnished by the lapidary Varangoz to Cartier designs, Dubret's provided its enamel settings, Brédillard the movement, and Prévost made the accompanying barometer, thermometer and compass as well as the three dials with their hands. The glasses were fitted by a small workshop called Charbonnier. In other instances Lavabre the jewelers enamelled the casing, the Bako workshop was coopted for crystal cases and Haas in the boulevard Sébastopol looked after the dial ornamentation.

Just as the firm's contemporary garland-style jewelry was inspired by eighteenth-century décor, so from 1901 onward table clocks took the form of garlanded urns in pure Louis XVI style. With bodies of marble, hardstone or porcelain, they were clearly related to the *pendules à cercle tournant* as illustrated by Jean-François Forty's copper engravings of 1771. The clock movement, set horizontally in the body of the urn, drove a rotating 'band' dial. Fabergé had created similar clocks, the Serpent clock in 1889 and the Lily of the Madonna Egg in 1899, while his Vase Egg of 1902 for the Duchess of Marlborough was contemporary with Cartier's urn clocks. In 1907 Cartier returned to the form with a miniature egg-shaped version in which a diamond star pointed to the time on the revolving band.

A further model, a silvergilt pillar clock incorporating a barometer, referred back to a design by the Louis XVI ornament designer Jean-Charles Delafosse. Cartier also employed the neo-classical motif of a fluted half-column in a table clock with horizontal dial; when pressed, it rang a little bell to summon a dilatory servant.

At this time, the application of enamel to these eighteenth-century forms was the preserve of Fabergé. Cartier lavished the riches of Fabergé's enamel palette on his own table clocks, using lavender blues, violets, pinks, empire greens or stripes. Bold colours were enamelled on silver, delicate pastel colours, by contrast, on gold. The patterns engine-turned on the metal ground and visible through the transparent enamel were variously described as 'Russian' (ray patterns), 'moiré', 'scaly', 'barley corn', or 'Louis XVI'. At first these table clocks, among the most favoured gifts of the Edwardian period, were square, then, from 1908, circular and from 1909 arched. Mottoes traced in diamonds, such as 'le temps passe, les pensées restent' or 'l'amitié vous l'offre', were designed to express for 55 all eternity the feelings of the donors despite the remorseless advance of time. Edward VII, Lady de Grey, Constantin Radziwill and Zenaïde Youssopov were among the enthusiastic devotees of these early Cartier timepieces.

It was about this time that Maurice Coüet (1885–1963), a young man in the Prévost workshop, was developing a talent which was later to raise Cartier's table clocks to the highest levels of inspired craftsmanship. Coüet's grandfather was a regulator of table clocks for Bréguet and may have been identical with the Coüet who was working at about 1850 in the Place Dauphine, and who exhibited ring watches at the 1867 Paris Exhibition. Even earlier, in 1806 and 1820, there is evidence of yet another clockmaker by the name of Coüet. Maurice learned the basics of his craft in his father's small workshop in the cathedral city of Evreux, then moved to Prévost's in Paris and subsequently set up in business with five assistants in the rue Saint-Martin. From 1911 on, the little workshop was supplying table clocks exclusively to Cartier's. Coüet was a clockmaker of inventive genius in the great tradition of the craft established in the Renaissance. Since the sixteenth and seventeenth centuries, clockmaking had evolved, along with its sister disciplines of mathematics, physics and optics, to the status of an art. Armed with the expertise inherited from the Bréguet tradition, Coüet began to change the Cartier collection with a series of delightfully conceived designs firmly grounded in mathematics.

His first inventions under commission to Cartier's were a series after 1912 of 'planet' or 'comet' clocks in round, square or arched cases. Their star décor showed a remarkable similarity to the Islamic-style jewelry that Cartier's were producing at the same time. The first model consisted of two superimposed dials. The lower one, of sky blue enamel, rotated to give the illusion of a diamond star gliding across the heavens. A crescent moon in diamonds indicated the ensuing hours of night. On another model the central 'sky zone' carried a comet tail along the dial while the minute pointer, set beneath the circle of the hours, circled the outer ring.

64 Since 1919 a third 'abstract' variant harked back to the chronoscope of the seventeenth century. The hour chapters were carried on three hidden arms, each bearing four numerals, which, revolving on their axis, appeared each hour in turn on the left-hand side of the dial quadrant. As it glided across the scale it simultaneously marked the minutes, and then disappeared off the right-hand side. This series of clocks also served as photograph frames and as truly regal gifts adorned the most famous salons of the period. The donor's portrait was often that of one of the monarchs of Europe.

53 The fan-shaped dial of the Jade Carp clock of 1925 operated on a different principle. The minutes were marked by a rotating disc and the hours on an outer semicircle of crystal across which an hour hand moved from VI to VI, being snapped back to its starting position by a spring mechanism.

It is a matter of personal judgment whether these early 'illusion' mechanisms count as true 'mystery clocks'. Coüet loved baffling mechanical illusions and must have studied their imaginative application by the Lyonnais clockmaker Nicolas Grollier de Servières

131. Chronoscope in black and white enamel on gold, the reverse in ebonite. With photo of Queen Mary. 1920

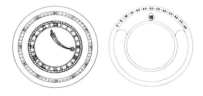

132, 133. 'Turtle' clock, the nephrite turtle on onyx and gem-set base supporting on its back a desk clock with mother-of-pearl, turquoise and lapis lazuli face, and lapis lazuli numerals. Hinged enamelled lid, set with a ruby and rose-cut diamonds. 1928

134. 'Chimaera' clock, the jade (?) carved animal lurking on the edge of a jade bowl filled with water, in which a leaf-shaped motif driven by a magnet indicates the hours. Materials and colours unknown. 1929

(1593–1685/86), whose inventions, later called *horloges mystérieuses*, were hailed in his own lifetime as miniature wonders of the world.[4] The mechanism of Coüet's Jade Carp clock was ultimately derived from Servières' Fan clock as, indeed, was the Turtle clock of around 1927, whose main feature was a turtle swimming in a hardstone bowl filled with water. In place of hands, the mechanism operated a magnet under the bowl which moved the turtle around the bowl to mark the hours.[4] The most sophisticated example of the Turtle clock was a jade version of 1929 which had a chimaera crouching on the rim. 67

Another original creation, the Jade Drum clock of 1938 can also be traced to the inspiration of Grollier de Servières. Within the mechanism, an appropriately balanced weight revolved to counterbalance the drum carrying the 'dial'. 69

Three large table or mantel clocks were made between 1926 and 1928 with Chinese carved jade panels on front and back. An onyx pedestal concealed the lever movement, which drove the hands by a shaft through a hollow stone ball, and along a Chinese dragon climbing up the back panel. The restricted colour range of black, red and green, the dragon pointer, and the jade panels engraved with Chinese landscapes give these clocks the fashionable chinoiserie appearance already discussed in connection with Cartier's vanity cases. Tardy, in his book on French table clocks, classifies these three jade clocks under a group of *sémi-mystérieuses*, a term which can be suitably applied to the comet clocks mentioned above and the models inspired by Grollier de Servières. 52

The pillar clock, called by Tardy 'pendule à gravité', also belongs to the *sémi-mystérieuses* group; its slender shaft of lapis, cornelian and turquoise rests on a mother-of-pearl and coral base.[5] With the passage of time, the clock slides down the pillar controlled by a system of cogwheels; at the bottom of the run, it is moved to the top again by hand, and the process is repeated. Coüet's application of gravity has a certain similarity to a model by Grollier de Servières, in which a drum clock rolls down an inclined track. Cartier's made two pillar clocks with Egyptian finials, one of which was bought by the Maharajah of Patiala. The idea was taken up again in 1927 in the shape of a slender jade portico.

Made of stones of strongly contrasting colours, these clocks gradually displaced the table clocks enamelled in the Russian style. Coral, onyx, jade, rock crystal and ivory expressed the new aesthetic of art deco, and incorporated in their design elements from the arts of China, Japan and India.

A technique known in ancient China was the application of kingfisher feathers on paper or metal for use as hair ornaments or as picture backgrounds. From 1920, Cartier's used kingfisher feathers for clock dials, the shimmering turquoise-violet mosaic gently contrasting with the colours of jade, coral and onyx. Particularly elegant examples were designed for the clock department by Jacques Andrey (b. 1896). 63

An addition to the art deco programme, prompted by Louis Cartier, was the production of a tall mantel clock fitted with a handle. It was in the tradition of the nineteenth-century officer

clock and was often reduced in scale to a miniature carriage clock.
Another new production was the simple globe clock of 1925, made of
lapis lazuli, enamel or gold, which could be turned on its base. It
remains an open question whether Coüet had in mind the sphere
clocks of Jacques de la Garde, the sixteenth-century French
clockmaker.[6]

In 1919 Maurice Coüet set up a Cartier workshop at 53 rue
Lafayette, which employed thirty specialists, as well as freelances like
the lapidary Fourrier.[7] Watchmakers made cases and movements,
which were decorated by enamellers, *orfèvres-boîtiers*, stone setters and
guillocheurs; but the workshop produced other art deco masterpieces,
such as vanity cases, which spread the fame of Cartier's throughout
the world. Although Coüet worked exclusively on the clocks, the
whole workshop bore his name. His colleagues included his brother
René; from 1922 to 1926 René Bourdon, who had been trained by
Verger and Bréguet; and Félix Laumonier, who had patented an
electric regulator. The clock workshop had its own designers such as
Alexandre Diringer, who had joined Cartier's as a seventeen year old
in 1910 and was attached to the clock division in 1922. Three years later
Coüet was joined by Alfred Loquet (b. 1884). Important clock designs,
notably 'mystery clocks', were supplied by Charles Jacqueau and
Georges Rémy, though their major work was in jewelry.

135. Cartier's clock workshop at the rue
Lafayette, headed by Maurice Coüet. On
display is the 'Egyptian' temple clock. The
crystal Chimaera clock is in the process of
being made. 1927

London and New York maintained their own workshops for the
manufacture of simpler clock types. From 1919 the export of the Paris
models was handled by the European Watch and Clock Company, a
Cartier subsidiary with offices in Paris and New York. The collector
will often find the initials 'E W C' alongside the workshop and stock
numbers on Cartier's export pieces.

A model patented in 1937 had claims to be a 'mystery clock' in the
wider sense: the Prism clock by Gaston Cusin. Born in 1897, Cusin
had made his first clock when he was fourteen and had been
working with Maurice Coüet since the move to the rue Lafayette. It
was the underwater periscope which gave him the idea for a clock
with a dial reflected through prisms, and the principle was also
applied to a few wrist-watches. In 1984 Cusin's invention enjoys a
revived popularity.[8]

Less significant for the future were the expensive electric watches
experimented with at the same time. Although some four hundred
electric watches left the workshop on the rue d'Argenson between
1935 and 1938, and a special company, 'Delvicar', was founded, the
models were unwieldy and too expensive. The electric watch which
Louis Cartier took to Budapest, but which in fact stopped working
before he left the Gare de Lyon, may have convinced Cartier's of the
unprofitability of the project, which the Second World War soon
brought to an end.

Jeanne Toussaint, at the urging of Louis Cartier, had presided
over the *haute joaillerie* (since 1933); from 1937, however, she increasingly
devoted herself to the creation of clocks. She was a woman of taste
and was in direct contact with a buying public who, under the
impact of the Front Populaire with its economic crises, devaluation
and unemployment, were less interested in large commissions than
in gold purchases and original presents. Convinced of this, Toussaint

took over the charming ivory and black enamel Domino pocket watch from the London workshop, and promoted it as the gift idea for 1939.[9] The elegant Mme Martinez de Hoz ordered four of them straight away at Cartier's exhibition in Deauville.

Jeanne Toussaint was also the inspiration behind an inclined table clock in mother-of-pearl mosaic, embellished either with ancient Egyptian faience, or with her favourite animal, the panther. Her other symbolic animal, the turtle, gave rise in 1962 to a table clock of three turtles, one above the other, in lapis lazuli and gold. The fact that Gaston Guillemart, the craftsman entrusted with the work, wrestled with its technical problems for two years was of little concern to Jeanne, who was prepared to impose her ideas on the workshop. In the same way, she must be credited with the successful completion of the 1960 Bottle clock: Jeanne had come across the bottle, fitted with a gold Russian stopper in an antique shop; it was Maurice Coüet who achieved the *tour de force* of getting a clock through the narrow neck.

Cartier's clock department had long been at the service of eccentric customers whose quirks not infrequently found their way into literature. Among these clients was the idiosyncratic Prince Constantin Radziwill, who, obliged to give a Christmas present to a hated relation, commissioned Cartier to produce the ugliest object in the world. To his entire satisfaction, Cartier made him a clock in the shape of a Swiss chalet in gold and diamonds, with a cuckoo to strike the hours.[10]

But the clocks which ultimately satisfied the most eccentric customers also incorporated Cartier's most famous invention, a perfect balance of the technical and aesthetic, the legendary 'mystery clocks'.

The 'Mystery clocks' (pendules mystérieuses)

'Marvels of the clockmaker's art,' the *Gazette du bon ton* called them in 1925, 'unreal and seemingly woven from moonbeams, they veil the mystery of time in the shadow of an ancient divinity of jade, between two pillars of rose quartz, enamelled with black dragons.'[11]

It was not simply a matter of the name; the 'mystery clock' contained a secret that was supposed never to be revealed. Over-inquisitive salesmen at the rue de la Paix, who tried to force explanations from the craftsmen, were rebuffed. The wonder clocks guarded their secret like the Sphinx, and Cartier's protected them from the eyes of prying admirers. At the virtually private exhibition in Biarritz in 1922, the Queen of Spain was able to admire three examples (later sold to New York), whereas not a single one was shown at the great 1925 art deco exhibition.

Maurice Coüet was twenty-eight when he presented the first of his 'mystery clocks' to Cartier. It is not known how many years of theoretical preparations lay behind the project. Coüet knew the *pendules mystérieuses* of earlier periods, such as those by Robert-Houdin (1805–71), the Blois clockmaker, who settled about 1835 in the Paris Marais and later, like Mathieu Planchon, devised mystery clocks and automata, or the clock by Guilmet displayed in the Paris Musée National des Techniques.[12] The fascination of Coüet's invention is based on the principle of an adroit optical illusion. The hands seem to float in space apparently without any connection to the movement. In fact they are each fixed onto a separate crystal disc with a toothed metal rim which is driven by worm gears disguised in the frame of the case. Coüet's first 'mystery clocks' relied on a lateral double-axle system. In 1920 he devised another model using a single, central axle and subsequently both principles were to be applied. The movement was sometimes housed in a massive base of onyx or jade, above the saddle of some fabulous monster (Turtle clock), or else, as in the Portico model, in the pediment above the clock.

Since every part was hand-made, production of a 'mystery clock' took between three and twelve months, and even in the 1980s their manufacture requires up to seven months. In 1925 each clock passed successively through the hands of six or seven specialists; besides the watchmakers, there was the designer, the *orfèvre-boitier,* the enameller, the lapidary, the setter, the engraver and the polisher. As already stated, the designs for the cases were often by Charles Jacqueau or Georges Rémy. But as many of the 'mystery clocks' were produced according to an established format, the designer's job was often merely a matter of combining the valuable animal sculptures, usually mounted within the framework, to the base, and consulting the clockmaker in order to establish the ideal position for the dial of the clock, in relation to the movement. The great rock crystals for the pillars of the Portico model, the onyx for the base and the little Buddhas and Buddhist lions for the 'roof' were cut and polished by the Fourrier workshop. Rock crystal was not only used for clock cases but also for the dial. Generally it was rock
61 crystal, occasionally citrine, once only (1931) aquamarine — but always materials whose transparency did not detract from the illusion of the hands being trapped inside. These hands were works
56 of art in their own right, created by enamellers and stone setters together, and gave the appearance of a writhing dragon as they revolved, which contributed to the chinoiserie effect. Diamonds, however, were used only sparingly in the whole ensemble of the clock; most common were cabochons and eight-cut diamonds, less sparkling than brilliant cuts.

It is not certain how many 'mystery clocks', which were exclusive to the Paris firm, were made during the peak production period between 1913 and 1930, though the number may have exceeded ninety. Production after the Second World War continued up to 1970, and was resumed in 1977 with motifs from the 1920s.

The following types of 'mystery clocks' can be distinguished:

60   The first is 'Model A', a rectangular model with which production commenced in 1913. The movement operated on a double-axle

system, housed in a vertical frame often embellished with laurel branches or mother-of-pearl. The base was of onyx, pale agate, obsidian or nephrite; in later models of ribbed gold (1949) with a cabochon ruby on the axle pin of the hands. A version dating from 1944 has a domed base and an arched crystal case.

According to the firm's archives, the first model was sold in 1913 to J. P. Morgan, Jr. Cartier's records show that there was a gap in the production of Model A clocks between 1913 and 1919, which is inexplicable except in terms of the disruption caused by wartime conditions.

A model went to Queen Mary in 1924 and in 1940 Goering bought one with an onyx base. Five years later General de Gaulle, by then head of the French Provisional Government, together with Gaston Palewski, presented a model with a lapis lazuli base to Stalin.

A second model was created in 1920 and went through nineteen variations up to 1931. For the first time a single central axle was used, which ran through the shaft or, as in later versions, through a hollow coral sphere. The bases were mostly of onyx and the hexagonal dial framed in coral, turquoise, lapis lazuli and enamel. This second model was subject to three variations from 1920–21:

An octagonal model with an 8 cm 'Chinese' shaft   60
A model with a dial of circular citrine, on an enamelled pillar   66
with lateral struts
A model in the form of a rectangular cartouche with Japanese corners of ebonite (a hard vulcanized rubber), with a dial of cushion-shaped citrine; also a similar rectangular model with bevelled corners.

A third model, the 'Ecran', in the form of a rectangular panel, appeared in 1923; seven variants had appeared by 1928 and the model continued up to 1954. The motive power was carried by a central axle system through a hollow sphere on the base. Stylistically, this type was characterized by horizontal coral bands (one example had jade   58 bands), which framed the circular dial. Lateral crystal struts connected with the base. The same casing had already appeared in 1922, though not in connection with a 'mystery' movement. In this case the dial was not transparent, but was decorated with mother-of-pearl marquetry, Chinese lacquer or kingfisher feathers.

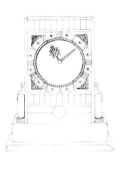

A further category of 'mystery clocks' comprised those using the central axle system with a pendant dial. However, at its first appearance (1920), in the form of a Chinese gong in a white enamelled frame, the idea was simply a matter of optical illusion, as the mechanism still consisted of a movement fixed in the base and a double axle drive.

Subsequently, the six famous Portico models were characterized by pendant dials and transmission to the hands via a central axle. They were designed as a freestanding Oriental-style 'portico' or gateway, its pillars resting on a massive onyx base and crowned with a simple ledged roof that contained the movement:

1923   model in crystal with twelve-sided dial: crowned with a billiken (see p. 95)
1924   model in crystal with octagonal dial, square pillars and vase   56
motifs

1924   model in pink quartz with twelve-sided dial with mother-of-pearl, square pillars and two Buddhist lions

1924   model in crystal with twelve-sided dial; crowned with a Buddhist lion (head to the right)

1924   model in crystal with twelve-sided dial; crowned with a Buddha

1925   model in crystal with twelve-sided dial; crowned with a Buddhist lion (head to the left).

Contemporary with the Portico models was a series of twelve animalia or figure clocks, in which the clock dial either rested on supports or was suspended from above. Stylistically they derived from the Louis XV and Louis XVI *pendules à sujet* in which the clock movement rested on the back of an animal. The bull, horse and rhinoceros, generally of bronze, were then the most popular supporting beasts. Cartier's produced an elephant clock inspired by a silvergilt example of 1620 by Tobias Kramer, and the Louis XV elephant clocks occasioned by the visit of Siamese envoys to Paris.

Although they lacked the symbolism of dynastic commissions and the ceremonies of present-giving associated with Fabergé's Easter eggs for the tsars, these figurative 'mystery clocks' enjoyed comparable prestige in Cartier's production and are today considered the most valuable of all collectors' items with the Cartier signature.

The mystery clocks appeared in the following chronological sequence:

68 1922   The Mandarin Duck clock of Chinese jade, with vertically mounted twelve-sided dial and blue enamel frame. On an onyx base. The duck from around 1800

1924   The first Chinese agate Chimaera clock, vertically mounted with hexagonal crystal dial. On a gold base with enamel motifs. Chimaera nineteenth century

53 1925   The Chinese jade Carp clock, with vertically mounted fan-shaped crystal dial. On an onyx base. The two jade fish eighteenth-nineteenth century. (As mentioned above, the Carp clock follows a concept of Grollier de Servières and thus lies outside Coüet's optically transparent 'mystery clocks'. However, insofar as it is a figurative model, it belongs here.)

1925   The Chinese jade Vase clock with jade bird and rose quartz and sapphire flowers. On an obsidian base. The Chinese carving nineteenth century

62 1925   The Chinese crystal Turtle clock; with vertically mounted twelve-sided crystal dial. On an onyx base. The turtle nineteenth century

57 1926   The second Chinese agate Chimaera clock; with vertically mounted round citrine dial. On a nephrite base. The chimaera similar to the one on the 1924 model

1926   The Chinese goddess Kuan Yin holding a branch of flowering *ling-shi*. The twelve-sided clock next to her on an onyx base. The goddess early nineteenth century

1927   The Chinese crystal Chimaera clock, its twelve-sided dial hanging in the jaws of the chimaera. On a rose quartz and lapis lazuli base. Chimaera nineteenth century. In 1937 the clock was exhibited in Egypt, where Princess Chivekiar, Prince Fuad's former wife, showed an interest in it. Dismantled in 1953

1928   The Chinese jade Elephant clock, the dial in the form of an   57 onyx howdah on the back of the animal. On an onyx base. The elephant from about 1800, presumably acquired from the London dealer and Indian expert Imre Schwaiger. The only 'mystery clock' with arabic numerals. The saddle cloth of mother-of-pearl marquetry and coral beads, the work of the stonesetter Bouillet, was allegedly the most time-consuming ornamental detail on any of the 'mystery clocks'

1929   The Chinese jade Buddhist lion; with vertically mounted, round citrine dial and coral tree. On an onyx base. The two animals from the nineteenth century

1930   The Chinese coral Chimaera clock with vertically mounted   72 octagonal dial in mother-of-pearl frame. On black lacquered silver base. Chimaera nineteenth century

1931   A clock with the Chinese goddess Kuan Yin in jade, with jade chimaera, coral trees and jade vase. Movement with striking chimes. The hardstones nineteenth century.

Pocket, pendant and wrist-watches

Dagonneau, Brédillard and Prévost, who from 1900 provided movements for table clocks, were also Cartier's first suppliers of movements for pocket and pendant watches, including the then fashionable *remontoirs de dames*, ladies' flat pocket-watches. Up to the First World War ball watches of *guilloché* enamel, recorded at Cartier's from 1889, were popular. Worn on a chain from the Duparc-Lenfant workshop, they won admirers as far away as Russia and the United States. Princess Lobanov had one in rare, orange-coloured enamel (1902) whereas the Queen of Portugal sported a model in blue and white banded enamel (1904). Expensive models might be pear- or egg-shaped and set with diamonds; hexagonal pendant watches with *calibré*-cut ruby frames; or the charming flower-basket watch in diamonds (1909) which Nellie Melba selected.

Among the watchmakers employed by Cartier's, Joseph Vergely, though forgotten today, proved indispensable with his talent for gold-coin watches.[13] Born in the Auvergne in 1872, he completed three years in the watchmaking school in Cluses, joined Cartier's old firm on the boulevard des Italiens as watch salesman and repairer in 1896 and mastered his technique there. Twenty-dollar, hundred-franc and five-pound gold coins were sawn in two and inset with an ultra-flat movement of 1.5 mm thick, with a Bréguet overcoil balance spring. The coin was opened by a little thumbpiece, and when closed revealed nothing of its contents. Queen Alexandra presented King Edward with one made from a coin issued to mark his coronation. Vergely, whose patriarchal mien earned him the soubriquet of 'Père Vergely' at Cartier's, subsequently headed the Paris office of the European Watch and Clock Company mentioned above, where he furthered the experiments with electric watches. Yet his first and most important service was to introduce into the firm the man who, like Maurice Coüet in the clock department, was to revolutionize the manufacture of small watches: Edmond Jaeger.

Born in Andlau in Lower Alsace, Jaeger (1850–1922) learned his trade with Lebert in Epernay and with the chronometer manufacturer Gabriel. But he gained his most important experience with Bréguet in the rue de la Paix in Paris. Back in 1775, Abraham-Louis Bréguet (1747–1823) of Neuchâtel had settled on the Quai des Morfondus, where he made the most refined watches of his time: watches with perpetual calendars, chronometers and automata, with which he supplied the French navy, Marie-Antoinette and the tsars. The company, which employed up to a hundred watchmakers during the Napoleonic period, remained in the Bréguet family, but frequently moved premises in Paris, and in 1855 engaged the services of the Englishman Edward Brown, whose family was to continue the Bréguet workshops. It was Brown who took on Jaeger.

By 1905, however, Jaeger had his own business, employing five workmen, in the rue Saint-Sauveur north of the Paris Marais, for centuries the clockmakers' district. In 1907 he moved to the rue Réaumur and signed a fifteen-year contract with Cartier's, giving the firm exclusive rights to his output.[14] This included Jaeger's chronometers, his anchor watches with the flat Jaeger calibres, and every new Jaeger invention. For their part, Cartier's guaranteed regular annual orders of at least Fr250,000.

Although Jaeger had been one of Cartier's suppliers before the 1907 contract, Louis Cartier did not relinquish his connections with Brédillard, Dagonneau and Prévost. Even in 1907 the last of the three delivered four watches set into parasol handles, all bought by the Russian Countess Ouvarov. One of them may have been intended as a wedding present for Mlle Messéna d'Essling, who was married that year to the Marquis de Montesquiou-Fesenzac. *Vogue* mentioned it on this occasion without naming the maker. In 1907 Jaeger collaborated on the Egg clock already mentioned. Otherwise he concentrated on small flat watches, produced Vergely's coin movements and about 1910 supplied pocket-watches in fashionable rock crystal cases that found an eager public as far away as New York.

Cartier's New York were supplied exclusively with Jaeger watches through Cartier's of Paris. Initially, the New York watchmaker Braun undertook merely repairs, at a salary of about Fr150 per week – compared with the 300 paid to a master *bijoutier* or the 500–600 to a stone setter. In 1910, however, he achieved the creation of an extra-thin rock crystal watch, with invisible diamond setting and winder, which was so much talked about that it was followed by further models in geometric shapes from 1912 on.[15] Among them, Pierre Cartier's own model with a single hand was considered far and away the most stylish. Yet the bulk of New York's stock still continued to come from Paris;[16] and Edmond Jaeger, too, maintained a small agency in New York in his own name.

Like Louis Cartier, however, Jaeger was convinced that the future lay not with the pocket-watch but with the much more practical

136, 137. Diamond egg-shaped pendant watch of laurel leaf design in circular- and rose-cut diamonds. The interior in engraved yellow gold (Actual size)

Colour plates 65 — 79

65. 'Chinese' desk clock, the two rock crystal columns with Chinese lacquer, coral, diamond and enamel base surmounted by two rock crystal buddhist lions which flank the octagonal onyx and coral clock with lacquered mother-of-pearl dial (Chinese, nineteenth century). Rose-cut diamond hands and chapters. On rock crystal base. 1928

66. *Left:* Mystery clock, the cut-cornered citrine face inset with diamond hands. Onyx and red lacquer border with mother-of-pearl chapters. On onyx, coral, carved jade and gold base. 1927

Right: Mystery clock, the circular citrine face inset with diamond hands. White enamel and diamond chapter ring. On onyx, black enamel and gold 'Chinese' column. White enamel buttresses. Onyx and gold base. 1921

67. Chimaera clock, the carved agate chimaera with turtle carapace (Chinese, nineteenth century), emerald eyes and black enamel crest supports the circular citrine clock inset with diamond hands. Black, red enamel and pearl chapter ring with 'Chinese' numerals, and similar saddle cloth. On nephrite ground with two coral frogs. Gold and onyx base. 16.5 cm. 1926

68. Mystery clock, the jade mandarin duck (Chinese, *c.*1800) with cabochon rubies supports the dodecagonal citrine and gold clock with inset diamond hands and blue and white enamel chapter ring. On onyx and gold base. 26.5 cm. 1922

Jade belt, mounted with 21 gold-mounted jade medallions with cabochon ruby centres, carved to simulate bronze coins (Chinese, late nineteenth century). 1930. Cartier's London

69. *Above:* Desk clock, the octagonal clock with mother-of-pearl face, red and black enamel Roman numerals, and gold and black enamel centre with diamond hands. Flanked by 2 jade buddhist lions. On onyx, coral, diamond and gold base. 1930

Below: 'Drum' mystery clock, the revolving gold drum applied with 2 jade discs engraved with fish (Chinese, nineteenth century). Gold and black enamel chapter rim. The axle pivoted on gold fluted columns. Onyx base. 1938 (see p. 248)

70. *Above left:* Desk clock, the gold case with floral red and black enamel. On onyx and gem-set stand. 1928

Above right: 'Altar' desk clock, in gold, with boldly enamelled blue and black doors, and white chapter ring with Arabic numerals. The doors spring open to reveal interior with Arabic chapters. A similar clock is dated 1928

Centre: 'Altar' desk clock, in gold, with blue and black enamel and rose-cut diamond doors which open to reveal the rectangular

dial with enamelled chapters. On onyx base. 1928

Below left: Desk clock, the gold and black enamel case with nephrite top on fluted coral columns. Onyx base. A similar clock is dated 1929

Below right: Desk clock, the gold rectangular case enamelled red and black with enamel handle. On onyx base. A similar clock is dated 1928

71. 'Stalactite' watch, the gold and platinum mounted watch inside the fluted lapis lazuli, diamond, pearl and emerald bead mount. On silk cord with diamond sliding motif. 1925

Original worksheet for the above, signed by watchmaker Joseph Vergely

Below right: Desk clock, the gold mounted horizontal clock boldly enamelled in blue with cabochon rubies and flanked by tiered onyx steps. 1928

72. *Left:* 'Chimaera' mystery clock, the octagonal rock crystal and mother-of-pearl, coral and pearl tambour with diamond hands supported by a carved coral chimaera with frog (Chinese, nineteenth century) with diamonds, emeralds and black enamel. On black lacquer, coral and mother-of-pearl base. 21 cm. 1930

Right: 'Chimaera' mystery clock, the carved coral turtle-chimaera with baluster-shaped coral vase (Chinese, nineteenth century) supporting the openwork coral and agate clock with interior rotating diamond star indicating the hours. On white agate base. 21 cm. 1943

73. *Above:* 'Billiken' the 'God of Happiness' carved in agate with diamond eyes, chained to an ivory peg, on circular agate base. 10.7 cm (see p. 95)

Similar Billikens are dated 1910

Below: Agate bird clock, the gold clock with lapis lazuli dial, diamond hands and numerals within an agate bowl carved with birds in flight (a Chinese brush washer, nineteenth century). On lapis lazuli stand. 1927

74. *Left:* Brooch, the agate and gem-set maharajah in front of a turquoise and diamond screen, with gold, diamond and turquoise base containing a seal. 1937

Centre: Hand mirror, gold mounted and set with lapis lazuli, the handle with cabochon citrine finial, the reverse with gold and mother-of-pearl monogram. Commissioned by Mrs J. P. Donahue in 1927

Right: Blackamoor brooch, the carved tortoise-shell blackamoor with gold, turquoise and diamond collar, headdress and aigrette. 1957

75. Brooch, the carved coral branch (Chinese, nineteenth century) with diamond and enamel motif, and jade bead

and diamond clusters. Commissioned in 1938

Coral necklace, the string of coral beads with black enamel and diamond shoulder motifs suspending 13 carved coral bells with onyx, coral, diamond and emerald clusters. 1940

Coral bracelet, mounted with three rows of coral and diamond beads, with oval clasp of circular and baguette-cut diamonds and coral 1955. Sold to Mrs J. P. Donahue

76. Ruby and diamond necklace, the front mounted with two rows of cushion-shaped rubies, surrounded and flanked by navette-, baguette- and hexagonal-cut diamonds. Ruby and diamond shoulder motifs. The rear as a single chain. Weight of rubies: 147.92 cts. 1930. Cartier's London. Sold to Mrs Marshall Field

The Thibaw ruby, of 26.13 cts, mounted as a ring (see p. 292)

77. Pendant necklace, set with a cluster of cabochon rubies and sapphires, a briolette ruby of 4.25 cts, and lozenge and circular-cut diamonds. On diamond chain. Commissioned in 1933

'Palm-Tree' brooch, set with 7 cushion-shaped rubies of 23.12 cts on circular- and baguette-cut diamond mount. 1957. Designed by Georges Rémy from an idea by Jean Toussaint

'Parrot' brooch, set with emeralds, rubies, fancy-yellow diamonds and onyx, in gold and platinum. 1962

78. Emerald and diamond necklace, set with 24 emeralds within circular-, baguette- and square-cut diamond clusters. Total weight of emeralds: 123.72 cts (centre stone: 15.29 cts). 1938. Cartier's London. Sold to Mrs Horace Dodge

Emerald and diamond brooch, the square-cut emerald of 37.00 cts within 20 navette-cut diamonds of 10.94 cts. Commissioned by Prince Sadruddin Aga Khan in 1960

79. *Left:* Lapel watch, the florally engraved emerald of 33 cts encasing the dial and suspended from emeralds of various cuts, surmounted by a mitre-shaped rose-cut diamond of 2.68 cts, with briolette-cut diamond tassel of 2.63 cts. 1924

Centre above: Pendant watch, set with a pear-shaped emerald, cabochon sapphires, diamonds and black enamel, the horizontal watch at the base. 1926. Cartier's New York

Centre below: Lapel watch, of stirrup design, in diamonds, onyx, coral and black enamel, the gold mounted watch at the base. With interior Persian enamel swivel. 1925

Right: Lapel watch, set with an engraved emerald of 30.31 cts, cabochon rubies, onyx, black enamel and diamonds, the horizontal watch at the base. 1927. Cartier's New York

68

69

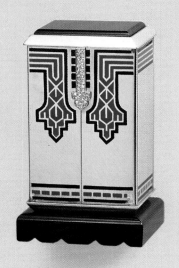

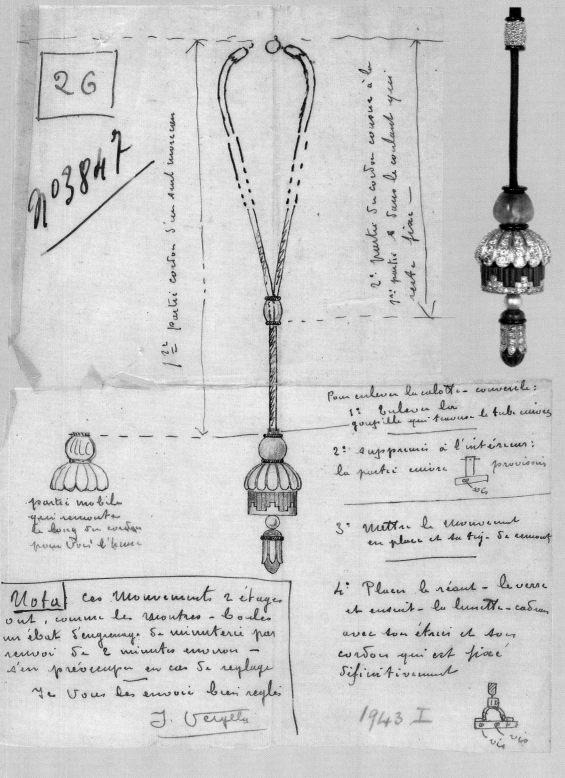

71

72

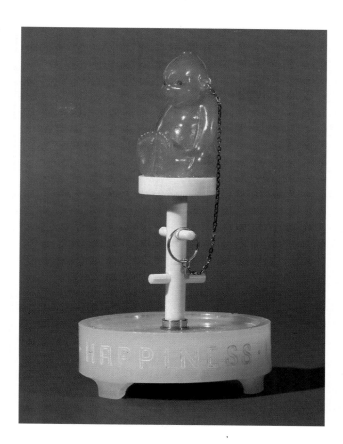

74

75

76

80

wrist-watch. This presented no technical difficulties; but it was a matter of convincing Cartier's exclusive clientele of the 'modernity' of an article which only a short time before had been tried out by soldiers in the trenches.[17]

As early as 1888 Cartier's had offered three ladies' wrist-watches with rose-cut diamonds, and gold link bracelets. But these must have been ahead of their time since other models did not appear until 1892 and 1894, the last having to wait until 1901 for a buyer. Like the jeweled bracelet, the wrist-watch only began to come into its own when, after 1901–02, fashion ceased to dictate long sleeves, and long gloves were no longer required for evening-wear. Cartier's saw this as a remarkable opportunity to establish a new form of wrist jewelry.

In 1906, Cartier's produced a series of wrist-watches with Brédillard movements, finished in platinum, and already fitted with a jeweled winding button – of cabochon ruby, cabochon sapphire or pearl – for which Cartier's later became famous. The series that followed was based on collaboration with Jaeger: fitted with a white leather strap, they were framed with diamonds, and their attachments embellished with cabochon emeralds. The new element of colour was enchanting, and the model was chosen for gifts by Eduard de Rothschild and the Vanderbilts as well as by Pierre Cartier himself; sapphire, ruby and amethyst lug embellishments soon followed. This model initiated the following series of technical and aesthetic innovations far into the 1920s and – besides the still fairly small number of wrist-watches – also embraced the pendant watch known as 'Régente':

1906   The *tonneau* model in the shape of a little cask
        Ladies' models were equipped wih a pearl bracelet threaded on metal wire. The process was patented by the Godefroy workshop and later taken up by the Duparc-Lenfant workshop

1908   Ladies' models with moiré straps of ribbed black silk and sliding rose diamond buckles
        Long moiré sautoirs carry diamond-set pendant watches
        Onyx is the rage. Onyx ball watches much prized as mourning jewelry

1910   The *deployant* gold buckle (*boucle déployanté*) appears. The visible part of the fastener consists of a rectangle set with rose diamonds, ornamented with an acanthus tendril, the initial of the owner or with the buckle pin. In 1913 Joseph Vergely gave it its definitive 'D' shape. One model of 1910 had a double buckle
        Bracelet lugs take the form of ornamental buckles
        The creation of a square wrist-watch with rounded corners
        Production of a hexagonal watch with 'double-Z' lugs
        A round case is devised for the *tonneau* model
        A wrist-watch is made with a strap of *calibré*-cut sapphires
        The creation of a diamond watch with lunette, lugs and strap of square-cut diamonds; the model is still being made today with stones of various cuts

138. Hexagonal 'Islamic' pendant watch in gold and white enamel, with pearl winder. The reverse with diamond in 'illusion setting'. On black silk cord. 1913 (Actual size)

139. Pendant watch, the reverse in polished platinum with 2-diamond 'B', pearl diamond surround, on silk moiré strap with diamond motif. 1913 (Actual size)

80. 'Snake' necklace, the articulate mount set with circular-, baguette- and tapered baguette-cut diamonds, the inside enamelled green, red and black, with emerald eyes. Weight of diamonds: 178.21 cts. Commissioned in 1968 by Maria Felix, the Mexican film actress, after a design by Gabriel Raton

'Alligator' necklace, the articulate gold bodies set with 1023 fancy yellow diamonds of 60.02 cts, 1066 emeralds of 66.86 cts, and 2 cabochon rubies. Commissioned in 1975 by Maria Felix, after a design by Gabriel Raton

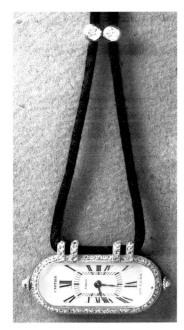

140. Pendant watch of oval shape with rose-cut diamond surround, on black silk cord with twin diamond motifs. 1913 (Actual size)

141. Rock crystal bracelet watch, the engraved rock crystal mount within diamond surround, on black silk moiré strap with *deployant* buckle. 1913 (Actual size)

142. 'Turtle' bracelet watch set with circular-cut diamonds, with cabochon sapphire winder, on black silk moiré strap with *deployant* buckle. 1913 (Actual size)

143. *Tonneau* bracelet watch, the curved dial within circular-cut diamonds, on black silk moiré strap with *deployant* buckle. 1913

1911 The 'Santos Dumont' model goes on sale to the public — named after the Brazilian pioneer aviator Alberto Santos-Dumont (1873–1932). From 1897 he kept the Parisians in suspense with flights in his own balloons and flying machines, and in 1901 he received the Deutsch Prize for the return flight between Saint-Cloud and the Eiffel Tower. Louis Cartier knew Santos Dumont at that time both socially and as a client. Starting from 1906 Santos Dumont made brief flights in a heavier-than-air machine and appreciated a watch which was easier to use than a pocket watch and which also matched his elegant style. (There is a photograph of him in his balloon basket, sporting a carnation in his buttonhole!) Long afterwards, in 1911, Santos Dumont agreed to have the watch commercialized. When we recall the numerous clocks, snuffboxes, fans and so forth *à la montgolfière*[18] which followed the balloon ascent by the Montgolfier brothers in 1783, it is no surprise that Santos Dumont's name should have been given to a watch

A small egg-shaped watch with stirrup outline fixed on the watch bracelet

Pendant watches influenced by Oriental forms dominant in contemporary jewelry

Production of ring watches with rose-cut diamonds. A ring watch appeared in the Cartier archives as early as 1878. The style returned to popularity about 1933

1912 Crystal pendant watches in invisible *serti illusion* diamond setting

The appearance of an oval wrist-watch as the starting point for the *baignoire* model

The creation of an octagonal pendant watch

The creation of a pendant watch hidden in a pearl tassel, sold to the Maharajah of Indore

The creation of a square pendant watch in onyx and diamond, framed in an open circle

Completion of a pocket-watch showing local times in Paris, London and New York; sold to Mrs Stotesbury

1913 Creation of a watch with a moiré strap and a central lug attachment

The Turtle model appears as a further development of the *tonneau* model. The gold case and lug attachments made from a single casting (*modèle à pattes*)

Creation of a wrist-watch with engraved crystal case

Pendant watches in the form of tasselled lanterns as well as in Islamic star shapes

A gold chronograph with hour-hand and date

Production of a 'mystery' pendant watch with a round crystal case, on a moiré ribbon

1914 A further development of the Santos Dumont model with straight outline

An oval wrist-watch with onyx and diamond 'panther' decoration on the lunette. Lateral lugs as *anneaux de la marine*

Further models with panther decoration appeared up to 1917

| 1915 | The Turtle and Santos Dumont are the most popular models, followed by the *baignoire* type |

1915   The Turtle and Santos Dumont are the most popular models, followed by the *baignoire* type
        Pendant watches in onyx, crystal and diamond enjoy great popularity

1919   Following the First World War the Tank model goes on public sale, having been designed two years before by Louis Cartier with golden bars reminiscent of the tanks used by the Allies

1920   Completion of a Tank watch with scrolled lugs
        Following a suggestion by Louis Cartier, a diamond watch is set into a pearl, worn on a platinum chain

1921   Creation of a bell-shaped wrist-watch (*Cloche*) in vertical or horizontal form
        Horizontal disc pendant watches (*montres cachet*) and, a little later, stalactite watches make their appearance. According to *Vogue* the pendant watch had become all the rage. Around 1925 it was the latest fashion and the wrist-watch correspondingly retreated into the background

1922   Creation of a wrist-watch with a royal blue enamel lunette and gold numerals
        A wrist-watch with buckle-shaped gold lugs
        Creation of a 'serpent' watch of *calibré*-cut onyx
        The Chinese Tank model, framed on all sides in bars of gold

1923   Creation of a wrist-watch with gold 'grenade' lugs (*obus*)
        Large Tank watches with curved cases (*modèles cintrés*). One of the first models sold to the Maharajah of Kapurthala[19]

1925   A pendant watch was built into a hollowed engraved emerald of 136 carats. Sold to one of the Dolly Sisters[20]
        A platinum watch with second hand, calendar and the phases of the moon
        Creation of a leather wrist-watch, with the glass turned inwards to the arm (for protection in sport, etc.)
        Creation of the ladies' *baguette* wrist-watch, at that time the smallest in the world.[21] The case width of 6 mm was made possible by setting the escapement and movement on different planes. Subsequently the model had golden sliding cover or diamond *baguettes*

1927   The *ceinture* model appears with cut or 'Japanese' corners
        Production of a Golf watch, a decorated cover and gold pencil

1928   A cigarette lighter with built-in watch
        Patent for a wrist-watch clasp that slides over the hinged, rectangular watch case

1929   The appearance of a gold wrist-watch with cover (*savonette*)
        A Tank watch with hour and minute windows (*à guichet*)
        Creation of a watch bracelet of engraved coloured stones, the dial hidden beneath an emerald cover
        Production of a crystal skeleton watch
        Watches on cigarette cases, lipstick tubes, letter openers, money clips, etc.[22]
        Pocket-watch *à éclipse*: the square enamelled case with covered dial opened by pressure on the side

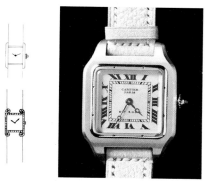

144. The 'Santos Dumont watch' (Actual size)

145. Hexagonal bracelet watch, the case within rose-cut diamonds, surround with central strap attachments, and black silk moiré strap (Actual size)

146. Pearl and diamond bracelet watch, the case within circular-cut diamond surround, with diamond shoulder motifs connected to pearl-strung bracelet. *Deployant* buckle. 1913 (Actual size)

147. One of the workshops where Cartier's elegant time-pieces were created, *c.1927*

1931 A waterproof Tank watch appears
Creation of an octagonal platinum 'mystery' pocket-watch

1932 Creation of a man's wrist-watch with reversible case (*montre réversible*)

1933 A patent for a wrist-watch with central lug attachment (*modèle Vendôme*)
Patent for a wrist-watch clasp, one of whose ends lay across the lunette
Patent for cufflinks-watch, a model that was later sold to King Farouk

1934 Cartier's New York prospectus describes the models then in fashion: clip watches and diamond wrist-watches for ladies; for men, belt-buckle watches, sports watches with covers, electric watches and travellers' alarms

1936 Creation of a ladies' wrist-watch with leather-covered spring bracelet

1938 Creation of an egg-shaped gold pocket watch with compass and sundial
Patent for a wrist-watch without hands by Gaston Cusin

1939 Patent for a further 'mystery' movement, adaptable for wrist-watches. The transparent dial vertically divided in the middle by the axle carrying the hands

1965 Creation of an egg-shaped wrist-watch

1978 Creation of the 'Santos' sports watch with screw motifs on both gold lunette and steel bracelet. As Cartier's best-selling contemporary watch it is exhibited for its exemplary design in the Musée de l'Air in Paris.

17

Swords for Academicians – Cartier's patents – The Second World War

*J*ACQUES-LOUIS DAVID (1748–1825), Napoleon's favourite artist, was responsible not only for the astonishing canvas depicting the emperor's coronation, but also, apparently, for the design of the black ceremonial dress decorated with green olive branches worn by members of the Académie française. Later it came to be supplemented with a sword presented to the new Academician at a private ceremony by friends, admirers or a committee from his home town.

Between 1931 and 1974 Cartier's received twenty-three commissions for these sumptuous ornaments: twenty-three historic commissions, recorded with great solemnity in the annals of the firm. They not only brought Cartier's into contact with artists and scholars, hardly familiar figures in the rue de la Paix, but also with the history of the Académie, one of the most prestigious institutions in the Western world. The Académie originated in a loose association of scholars, organized on a regular basis by Richelieu in 1634 to foster the French language. The great dictionary was the sole fruit of its labours, but that was sufficient to spread its renown throughout France. Dissolved at the Revolution, it was reconstituted in Year III (1794) as a part of the Institut de France, whose five sections survive to this day: the Académie française, the Académie des Inscriptions et Belles Lettres, the Académie des Beaux-Arts, the Académie des Sciences and the Académie des Sciences morales et politiques.[1] Since 1806 it has convened in the so-called Collège des Quatre-Nations, whose semicircular structure, designed on Roman models by the architect Levau, dominates the Quai de Conti. The solemn protocols and ceremonies of the Académies were definitively established under the First Empire. Each year six public sessions are held under the famous dome, one devoted to each Académie and a final joint assembly. The closed sessions are held on Thursday afternoons.

At least since the time of the painter Horace Vernet (1789–1863), whose sword as a member of the Académie des Beaux-Arts carried the emblems of his profession and of his favourite diversion – the palette and the hunting horn – the swords of the Academicians have reflected their work and significance.

As far as Cartier's have been concerned, the moment a candidate for the Académie learned of the intended presentation he visited the firm to discuss the decorative scheme with the designers. The resulting discussions and correspondence offered the designers a rare opportunity to emerge from their imposed anonymity and, like Louis and Pierre Cartier, to make themselves known: the speeches at the presentation ceremonies were among the few occasions when the names of the designers were mentioned in public. Thus Daniel Rops, elected to the Académie in 1956, congratulated Georges Rémy in his speech on 'the magic and the charm of an ornament which, in consequence, spreads the renown of Cartier's across the globe.'

In this context it is interesting to hear what Rémy himself had to say about his preparations for the work. 'I had many serious talks, imaginary and real, over a period of weeks with the future Academician, immersing myself in his personality and his world, and we had many a chat, too, before I embarked on the job.' Such conversations ranged from childhood impressions to the world of nature, from the candidate's homelife to art and religion. Throughout, the designer was alert for easily intelligible yet artistically significant symbols that could be crystallized and transferred to the sword. The themes had to be kept distinct. 'The most difficult thing,' said Rémy, 'is to incorporate the dominant elements into the design and yet remain selective. After all, one has to have a harmonious design and not merely a collection of obvious symbols.' Pierre-Henri Simon, the writer elected to the Académie in 1966, expressed it admirably: 'I wanted simplicity of line, moderation of symbol and restraint of ornament. If there had to be luxury, then I wanted it in the quality of the material, rather than in any kind of ornamentation.'

Over the years, Cartier's developed a special formal vocabulary in the design of these Academicians' swords which should meet both the official regulations and the individual wishes of the candidates. The designers had to be familiar with ancient symbols: for example, the owl as the bird of wisdom, Mercury's staff as the symbol of peace, and two-headed Janus as the tutelary god of gates and doors. But they also had to be able to create new symbols, explicable purely in terms of the Academician's work. Sometimes the juxtaposition of familiar and less familiar images could create formal problems – the 1954 sword of the Academician Duc de Lévis Mirepoix displayed both the Order of the Holy Ghost and an aeroplane!

Of the twenty-three swords produced between 1931 and 1974, the first was for the Duc de Grammont, admitted to the Académie des Sciences for his services to optics and astronomy, and the last to Professor Hamburger, elected for services to medicine. Cartier's entrusted only a few of its designers with the work. Among them was Charles Jacqueau, who designed the sword for André Maurois in 1939; Peter Lemarchand; and, in the case of Hamburger, Pierre Ludwig, who was on the design staff from 1963 to 1977. But the greatest number, fifteen in all, were designed by Georges Rémy (1907–75), who after four years at the Ecole Boulle worked with Cartier's from 1925 to 1973. Although inducted into the spirit of Cartier's ethos by Chenaud and Jacqueau, he was far closer in mood to his contemporary colleagues Lemarchand and Lachassagne. Rémy was not outstanding as a creator of original motifs and, though he continued with Lemarchand's panther and bird of paradise designs after the latter's death, he lacked the true, sympathetic understanding of Lemarchand's dream world. Yet Rémy was second to none in his sense of proportion and the architectonics of a work of art. With his brilliant analytical sense, he could easily have made a career as an art critic. He tackled the complex problems of outline and function presented by his beloved table clocks and desk accessories like an architect. Even his numerous designs for rings breathed the true spirit of the geometer, and it was not by chance that Jeanne Toussaint dubbed him 'the ring king'. It was therefore to be expected that most of the sword designs would fall to him. A typical example of his work, though it was in fact not executed, was the sword design for the architect Guillaume Gillet. The instruments of the surveyor are integrated into the ornamental weapon with an impressive logic, while not a single unnecessary detail breaks the dynamic flow of the design.

In 1966 the historian and novelist Maurice Druon was elected to the Académie; the following year Rémy produced his design for the sword. The hilt took the form of a 'D' monogram supported, like an architectural abutment, by a bull, Druon's birth sign. In a veritable *tour de force*, the hammered pure gold setting was inset with chrysolite, the author's bright green birthstone, while the figure '4', sacred to the god Zeus, referred to Druon's work *Les Mémoires de Zeus*. In 1963 Rémy had produced similarly symbolic designs for the sword of the novelist Joseph Kessel: the lion's head on the pommel, for which the chief of the atelier, André Gagniand, contributed the terracotta maquette, had originally been designed as an all-too heraldic lion rampant.

Rémy's sword design for Professor of Medicine Cordier came from the world of Renaissance anatomy. Since the sixteenth century, wax, bronze or wooden models of the skinless body of a flayed man, with sinews and muscles exposed, had served as demonstration figures. In the masterly drawings of Michelangelo, Leonardo and later Houdon, they evolved into an artistic genre in their own right. In his original design Rémy first envisaged a freestanding bronze of a flayed man, which would have expressed his artistic vision more clearly than did the final flat silhouette relief. Unhappily, but perhaps not surprisingly, there was often a certain artistic discrepancy between preparation and execution in these sword designs.

But surely the most original design for these swords came from a 'poet laureate', Jean Cocteau (1889–1963), who entered beneath the dome of the Quai de Conti in 1955. The Cocteau commission provided at a late stage an encounter with one of the original collaborators with Diaghilev.[2] Leon Bakst had stumbled on a folio of Cocteau's drawings while he was drawing-master to the children of Grand Duchess Vladimir. As a result the twenty-two year old received a commission for two posters for the ballet *Le Spectre de la rose*, followed by work on the unsuccessful ballet *Le Dieu bleu* and in 1917 *Parade*. In constant scintillating orbit round the Ballets Russes, Cocteau had come to know Louis Cartier and the style of the house. Moreover, at the time when the choice of the sword was being made, he was acting jointly with Jeanne Toussaint, as artistic adviser to the banker's wife Francine Weisweiller in her choice of Cartier's jewels. She was to contribute the rubies and diamonds for Cocteau's sword while Coco Chanel parted with an emerald of 2.84 carats. Cocteau himself designed the silhouette of the sword. Over the years he had worked under the aegis of Orpheus, the mythological poet and musician – in 1927 his poem *Orphée*, in 1950 the film of the same name, and still later, in 1960, his film *Le Testament d'Orphée*. The hilt of the sword depicts the poet's flowing profile surmounted by his lyre. The pillar entwined with a ribbon denotes the theatre (especially tragedy) and the horizontal chalk pencil Cocteau's graphic art. Other symbols were more concrete: the ivory ball grasped by a hand at the point of the sword signifies his play *Les Enfants terribles*, and the lances stand for the grille of the Palais-Royal where Cocteau lived as a neighbour of Colette. Like his writings, the sword was signed with a six-pointed star in diamonds and rubies.

Cocteau's sword remains unique in the Cartier *oeuvre*; in many other cases the swords are hidebound by traditionalism and convention. But it should not be forgotten that official commissions were happy to rely on the symbols and allegories that had been appearing on coins, memorials and charters since the nineteenth century, and Cartier's designers often had no option but to follow suit. Furthermore, most of the designs date from after the Second World War, when the art of the goldsmith was searching for new sources of inspiration.

More than any other historical event, the Second World War placed the whole Cartier enterprise in a critical situation. The fact that platinum was virtually unobtainable mattered little, since it had been displaced in public favour as early as the 1930s by the fashion for yellow gold. But in 1940 the wholesale trade in gold was expressly forbidden by the Banque de France. If a customer commissioned a piece in gold, he had to supply the full weight of metal required himself: in the case of platinum it was 135 per cent. If gold and platinum were melted, the State had the right to 20 per cent of the fine content.

Even before the war Cartier's had been experimenting with new precious metal alloys at their workshops in the rue Bachaumont, with the collaboration of Professor Cotton of the Sorbonne, among others. The new alloys were to be both lighter and better value than the traditional precious metals. One of the alloys favoured at the time by Cartier consisted of gold with small quantities of cobalt and chromium. Two gold alloys were patented in 1930 and 1934, the latter containing beryllium, which yielded a particularly hard metal. Another one, much prized by the public as *l'or Cartier*, was no less than the classic yellow gold, launched at a time when the rose-tinted gold, achieved through increased copper alloy, had lost its noble appeal. In London, the Worshipful Company of Goldsmiths decided in 1932 that 14-carat gold should replace the 12- and 15-carat varieties, while in New York Pierre Cartier suggested that the local Battelle Institute should experiment with palladium – not even recognized in France as a noble metal.[3]

At this time, the most important man in Cartier's technical department was Georges Bezault, who had been born in 1888 and joined the firm at the age of twenty-three. In 1937 he inaugurated some interesting experiments with the new alloy, platinix, almost as pliable as platinum but easier to obtain. Like the watchmaker Gaston Cusin, Bezault embodied the inventive spirit of the firm in the 1930s. Basic to the present Cartier repertoire are his necklace clasps, stone settings (*châtons*) and hinges.

Although a committee comprising Louis Cartier, Edmond Forêt, Charles Jacqueau and Gérard Desouches used to consider the latest proposals from the design studio, the question whether an aesthetically satisfying jewel also met technical requirements could only be answered after tests conducted by Georges Bezault. In 1935 the committee was joined by Jeanne Toussaint, who from two years before had presided over the *haute joaillerie* and whose first job was to launch crystal jewelry in the massive style of the 1930s.

No period was so rich in Cartier patents as the decade preceding the Second World War. In 1927 and 1934 the firm patented its clip system for brooches. Apparently, Louis Cartier conceived the idea while examining a clothes peg, and its technical realization was achieved by Georges Bezault. In 1933 Cartier registered a patent for *serti mystérieux*, a technique for invisibly setting *calibré*-cut stones in a mosaic pattern, by securing the undersides of the stones by parallel metal rails. However, Louis Cartier considered that the method damaged the *calibré*-cut stones and it was not much used. Cartier's Paris patents were supplemented by numerous inventions (*modèles déposés*) in the New York branch. Here Jules Glaenzer and Edmond Forêt were especially inventive, the latter conceiving a flower brooch of quivering blooms *en tremblant*. For many years a narcissus brooch with reversible petals enjoyed popularity; set with yellow gold on one side and gemstones on the other, it was designed for both afternoon and evening wear.

On 10 May 1940 the German armed forces occupied Paris. By the following August eleven leading members of Cartier's staff were in prison. They included Louis Devaux, who was nominated chairman of the firm on his release, Pierre Claudel, and the designers Lachassagne and Rémy. Jeanne Toussaint was in Ciboure at that time and the Jacques Cartiers in Saint Jean-de-Luz, while Louis Cartier was in Lisbon waiting in vain for a visa to the United States. The rue d'Argenson workshop was temporarily closed, and the shop in the rue de la Paix carried on with a much reduced stock of valuable pieces. The firm's principal concern was not to fall foul of Reichsmarshall Goering, quartered with the German general staff in the neighbouring Hôtel Ritz. The essence of the problem was that the firm, which had already had to open its books to German inspection, might be saddled with a German commissar and its stock, which included 50 million francs worth of jewelry deposited by customers, might be taken off to Berlin. So the most valuable pieces were secretly transferred in boxes and cases to Biarritz where a provisional Cartier operation opened in the summer of 1940 with fifty-four employees. Yet that same summer the exiled firm, together with the Bourse and the banks, returned to Paris.

In England at the same time, the bombing of Southampton highlighted the danger which threatened Cartier's of London. Shortly before he died, Louis Cartier was to instruct Etienne Bellenger, the London sales director, to shift the London stock to safety on the Kintyre peninsula in the Scottish Highlands. Bellenger had already placed office rooms in New Bond Street, his home, and the firm's Rolls Royce at the disposal of General de Gaulle, leader of the London-based Free French Government. De Gaulle used the opportunity to inspect Cartier's English Art Works, which, under the war emergency, was producing aeroplane parts. The designers Rupert Emmerson and Georges Charity were honoured at that time with commissions to design the insignia and medals for de Gaulle's enterprises which were to end triumphantly in 1944 with a victory parade through the streets of Paris.

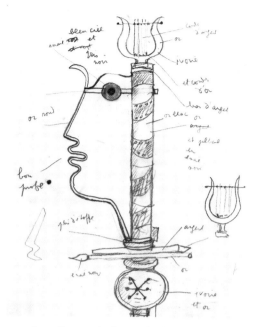

148. Jean Cocteau's design for his own sword, on his election to the Académie française

149. Mrs Evalyn Walsh McLean wearing the Star of the East diamond as an aigrette and the Hope diamond on a pearl necklace

150. Prince Felix Youssoupov dressed as a Russian Bojar for the revived Eglinton Tournament at Earl's Court, London, in 1912

151. The Bolsheviks discover the Youssoupov hoard of treasures in their Moscow Palace in 1925. Cartier's wedding tiara in rock crystal can be seen in the centre

18

The great transactions

N 1910 CARTIER'S HAD AT THEIR DISPOSAL the two most spectacular historic diamonds then on the market: the 'Star of the East' and the 'Hope'. Even today it is still not clear exactly where the first, a drop-shaped diamond of 94.80 carats, originally came from. Legend attributed it, like so many others, to the former treasures of the Turkish Sultan Abdul Hamid II (deposed 1909). But the fact is that the stone was already in the possession of Cartier's of Paris in 1908, the year of the Turkish military revolution, where it was seen by Evalyn Walsh McLean, daughter of the gold prospector Thomas F. Walsh. Spoilt since childhood, when she had been driven to her Washington school in a coach, she had just married Edward Beale McClean, heir to the dollar millions of the *Washington Post*. Furnished with $100,000 each, the pair were on their honeymoon in Paris when Evalyn suddenly remembered that she had still not chosen her father's wedding present to her. She betook herself to the rue de la Paix.

'We have just the thing for you,' said the salesman at Cartier's, as Evalyn recalled later. 'Then', she went on

he hypnotized my by showing me an ornament that made bright spots before my eyes.... A line of diamond fire in square links of platinum where it would touch my throat became a triple loop and from the bottom circle was depended on entrancing pearl. It was the size of my little finger-end and weighed 32¼ grains. The pearl was but the supporting slave of another thing I craved at sight – an emerald. Some lapidary had shaped it with six sides so as to amplify, or to find at least, every trace of colour. It weighed 34½ carats. This green jewel, in turn, was just the object supporting the Star of the East. This stone, a pear-shaped brilliant, was one of the most famous in the world – 92½ carats. All lapidaries know it. With fingers that fumbled from excitement I put that gorgeous piece around my throat.

'Ned,' I said in mock despair, 'It's got me! I'll never get away from the spell of this.'

'A shock might break the spell,' said Ned, 'Suppose you ask the price of this magnificence'.

'Well,' I said to the man at Cartier's as I put my index finger in my ears, 'how much?'

He whispered, 'Six hundred thousand francs, madam.'

'You mean a hundred and twenty thousand dollars?'

He cocked his head to one side so that his nod was made obliquely.

'After all,' I said to Ned, 'this is really an investment. Besides, this is 15 December and I can tell my father it's a double gift to cover both my wedding and Christmas present.' So we signed the bill and Cartier's sent us kids out into the world with the Star of the East.[1]

Was it merely coincidence that the McLeans turned up in Paris again just two years later when the 'Hope' diamond was awaiting a buyer at Cartier's?

'Pierre Cartier', Evalyn McClean continues,

came to call on us at the Hotel Bristol in Paris. He carried, tenderly, a package tightly closed with wax seals. I suppose a Parisian jewel merchant who seeks

152. The 94.80-ct Star of the East diamond below a hexagonal emerald of 34 cts and a pearl of 32 grains, mounted on a diamond chain. Piece of unknown manufacture sold by Cartier in 1908 (Actual size)

trade among the ultra-rich has to be more or less a stage manager or an actor....

'You told me' [he said] 'when you bought from me your wedding present, the Star of the East ... that you had seen a jewel in the [Sultan's] harem [in Constantinople], a great blue stone that rested against the throat of the Sultan's favourite'...

'I guess I did'.... It was too early to argue and, after all, I had seen jewels on Turkish ladies that made my fingers itch.

'Of course you did,' Cartier replied, and after this masterly introduction history did the rest. Originally, Evalyn was told, the stone had been part of a blue diamond of $112\frac{3}{16}$ carats, which Tavernier had sold to Louis XIV in 1669. In 1673 it was recut to $67\frac{1}{8}$ carats and was known thereafter as the 'Blue Diamond of the Crown'. In 1749 the French court jeweler Jacquemin set it together with the dragon-shaped spinel, the *Côte de Bretagne*, and a hexagonal diamond of $31\frac{3}{4}$ carats as the 'Golden Fleece'; in 1792 this, and a number of other pieces from the French crown jewels, were stolen from the Garde-Meuble in what is now the Place de la Concorde. Apparently, the 'Golden Fleece' was broken up in England, and in all probability the stone of just $45\frac{1}{2}$ carats which turned up in London again was the 'Blue Diamond of the Crown'. It is recorded as being in the possession of the gem dealer Daniel Eliason in 1812, and in 1830 he sold it to Henry Philip Hope of the famous banking family. Hope died in 1839. The stone went to his nephew Henry Thomas, who exhibited it in the Crystal Palace in 1851, and it remained with the family down to Lord Francis Hope, who in 1894 married the American actress May Yohe and the following year went bankrupt. In 1901 the 'Hope' was auctioned in London and went to the New York diamond dealer Joseph Frankel's Son.[2] Here it was apparently offered to W. K. Vanderbilt at a price of \$500,000. In 1909 it appeared unexpectedly at the auction of just eight diamonds by the collector Salomon Habib in Paris, and was knocked down for Fr400,000 (\$80,000) to Rosenau, the dealers from whom Cartier's acquired it.[3]

Yet for all Pierre Cartier's salesmanship, Mrs McLean was not at first attracted by the stone. After she returned to America on the *Rotterdam*, he let her have the stone on approval for a weekend. 'For hours', she recalled, 'that jewel stared at me. The setting had been changed completely to a frame of diamonds and there was a splendid chain of diamonds to go about my neck. At some time during the night I began to want the thing.'

But the initial negotiations spanned several months and involved a lawsuit which took until 1912. The selling price was \$180,000, which included \$10,000 for another setting in the form of a diamond bandeau.[4] There was to be an initial payment of \$40,000 and Cartier's agreed to discount \$26,000 against the return of the emerald-pearl necklace of the 'Star of the East'. The balance of \$114,000 was to be settled within three years.[5]

And the legendary curse? Evalyn McLean received warnings from May Yohe, from her mother-in-law and even from Mrs Goelet, who was later to wear Prince Youssoupov's black pearls without a care. Cartier had wisely inserted a clause in the contract – 'customer's privilege to exchange goods in case of fatality' – and when Mr McLean, fearful of the curse, refused a medical examination, his wife returned the 'Hope' forthwith. But Cartier's sent it back promptly. Now, Evalyn had another idea.

We set out in my electric victoria for the church of Monsignor Russell.

'Look, Father,' I said to him, 'this thing has got me nervous. Would you bless it for me?'

We were in a small side room of the church and Monsignor Russell donned his robes and put my bauble on a velvet cushion.

As he continued his preparations the storm broke. Lightning flashed. Thunder shook the church ... [but] Monsignor Russell's Latin words gave me strange comfort. Ever since that day, I've worn my diamond as a charm.

Any troubles the 'Hope' brought were generally of a financial nature. Mrs McLean wore it on the same necklace as the 'Star of the East', but the maintenance of the stone cost $24,000 a year and it was frequently pawned. But she never thought of selling. 'At the moment it is impossible to put a value on the stone,' she wrote in 1944 to Pierre Cartier, who had just spent New Year's Eve in the McLeans' circle. 'These ignorant fools [the Internal Revenue] think you can walk in with the Hope diamond or the big white diamond and get a million dollars case over night on them.'

No doubt the most eccentric figure ever to feature in Cartier's records, Mrs McLean died in 1947. Her seventy-four-piece collection, including the 15.46-carat 'Star of the South' (another historic diamond bought from Cartier's) was acquired by the jeweler Harry Winston in 1949.[6] In 1958 the 'Hope' found its final setting in the Smithsonian Institution, Washington.[7]

The dealer Salomon Habib, however, remains an enigma to this day. Was it true that his diamonds, which included the 70.20-carat 'Idol's Eye', had once been fleetingly in the possession of Sultan Abdul Hamid? Did Habib know the sultan, and what sort of relationship did he have with him? It appears that Alfred Cartier was summoned to Constantinople in 1909, the year of the Habib auction, to make a valuation of the sultan's treasure.[8] At a further auction held in Paris in 1933, Habib's unsold diamonds from 1909 were again put up for sale, together with 'Le Golconde Doré', a 95.40 diamond also said to have belonged to the sultan, which remained unsold. In 1938, however, Habib approached Cartier's for assistance in redeeming the stones pawned in Paris and London.

Over the years Cartier acquired many historic jewels at the Paris auction, the most famous being the 'Thiers Pearls' (see p. 127). Another unique acquisition was a rose brooch, 15 cm wide and set all over with diamonds, which came from the 1904 auction of the property of the late Princess Mathilde. That same year, Louis Cartier sold the great flower to one of the company's firmest supporters, Mrs Cornelius Vanderbilt of New York. For the thirtieth birthday of the Prince of Wales (later King Edward VIII), Mrs Vanderbilt held a ball at Spencer House, London, at which a giant cake was carried in. When cut, it was revealed to be packed with 'surprises' which she had selected at Cartier's. The prince, however, arrived late and in a bad mood, and merely greeted the spectacle with a sullen 'How vulgar!' The next day Mrs Vanderbilt returned the whole lot.[9]

In 1920, a six-day auction was held in Lausanne to dispose of the jewels of Princess Vera Lobanov de Rostock (née Dolgourouky), who had died at Vevey. She had been a customer of Cartier's since 1900 and had named Louis Cartier in her will as one of three jewelry experts. The auction drew all the major buyers and experts to the shores of Lake Geneva and the prize items were a three-rope necklace of pink pearls, originally in the possession of Tsar Nicholas I, and a 118-carat diamond.[10] Louis Cartier bought the tsar's necklace for Fr553,000 and received congratulations on such a valuable acquisition from Queen Olga of Greece and Princess Dolly Radziwill. In Cartier's opinion the auction, which realized a grand total of Fr3,470,000, initiated the steep upward trend in jewelry prices which set in with the 1920s, despite massive sales by ruined Russian aristocrats.

In addition, the news of the discovery in 1925 of the jewelry cache in Prince Youssoupov's Moscow palace haunted the international press. Allegedly the hiding place had been betrayed by the son of the mason who devised it in 1917. Secret passages from the picture gallery led to two underground dungeons, from which were recovered 255 brooches, 13 tiaras (among them Cartier's wedding tiara of 1914), 42 bracelets and 210 kilos of assorted *objets d'art*. By this time, however, Princess Zenaïde and her son Felix had already got the historic pearls and diamonds out of the country (see p. 132). After an unsuccessful American journey, in which he had planned to raise money by selling his precious stones, Felix approached Pierre Cartier in 1922 and offered him the diamonds listed below.

The 'Ram's Head': a 17.47-carat stone, light rose in colour and cut in the shape of a flattened octahedron. This diamond had apparently been given by Catherine the Great to her favourite, Potemkin. Cartier's bought it in 1927 and sold it to the Hon. Mrs Reginald Fellowes. It was stolen from her in 1939 and has not been seen since.

The 'Sultan of Morocco': a steel-coloured diamond of 35.67 carats, said to have been in the possession of the Youssoupov family since 1840. In 1924 Cartier's debated whether to display the stone at the great 1925 Exhibition. In 1926 or 1929 (the records are not clear) the diamond was sold to America. As late as 1969 Cartier's was to arrange to exhibit it in the World of Gems Exhibition held in the New York State Museum. In 1972 it passed into the possession of the jeweler F. J. Cooper of Philadelphia.

The 'Diamond Earrings of Marie Antoinette': with two drop diamonds of 34.59 carats, which had allegedly belonged to the Youssoupov family since 1802. When and to whom Cartier's sold them is unclear.[11]

The 'Polar Star': a cushion-shaped diamond of 41.28 carats, originally the property of Joseph Bonaparte, Napoleon's elder brother. Its second owner was Princess Tatiana Youssoupov (1769–1841). The name comes from the eight-point star cut on the pavilion. As early as 1924 the stone was lodged, with interruptions, with Cartier's London, and was then pledged along with other Youssoupov jewels with the London firm of T. M. Sutton until Cartier's redeemed it. In Paris in 1928 they sold it for £48,000 to Lydia Lady Deterding, the wife of the Dutch oil magnate.[12]

Other Youssoupov treasures included the 'Blue Venus', carved out of a light blue 11-cm-high sapphire on a base set with a ruby with Medusa-head engraving; a ruby carved Buddha from the Summer Palace near Peking, and a statuette of Jupiter ascribed to Benvenuto Cellini.

Another Russian treasure to find its way to Cartier's was the marriage crown of the princesses of the imperial house. It was a delicate piece of six diamond arches surmounted by a simple diamond cross, and both the Grand Duchess Helen, daughter of Grand Duchess Vladimir, and the Grand Duchess Marie, daughter of Grand Duke Paul, who both owned magnificent Cartier tiaras, had worn it at their weddings. In 1927 it was auctioned by Christie's in London on the instructions of a Soviet syndicate, and shortly afterwards Pierre Cartier ran it to earth in a Paris antique shop. Like the Lobanov and Thiers pearls before it, the crown was sent to New York, where the demand for historic jewels was greater than in Europe. Later, Prince Christophe of Greece was to give a melancholy account of an unexpected encounter with the crown:

At the time I was in New York, visiting Pierre Cartier in his office. Suddenly he said: 'I would like to show you something.' He took a velvet case from his private safe, laid it on the table and opened it. Within lay a diamond crown with six arches rising from the circlet and surmounted by a cross. 'Do you recognize it?' he asked me. I nodded wordlessly, seized by a sense of melancholy that rose from the depths of my memory. It was the crown of the Romanovs. My mother had worn it and her mother before her; it had adorned all the princesses of the imperial house on their wedding days. All at once, it seemed to me the room was filled with shades of long-dead brides.'[13]

The silver service ordered by Napoleon from Biennais and Cahier on his return from Elba also found its way to New York. Its 919 pieces were laid out as if for a banquet for all the world's crowned heads, in Cartier's Louis XVI rooms on Fifth Avenue. After Napoleon's fall, Louis XVIII (1815–24) had had the service decorated with his own arms. Evidence of royal etiquette is provided by the engraved *bouche du roi* casserole, used to serve food reserved for the king. The service passed via the Comte de Chambord, the last of the senior Bourbon line, to Don Jaime de Bourbon, who disposed of it to Cartier's.[14] It was exhibited in 1923, not only in New York, but also in Boston and Pittsburgh museums.

Apart from isolated historic *objets d'art*, Cartier's main concern, ever since it had first established itself in the rue de la Paix, was with the valuation, resetting, display and sale of precious stones. In this area Louis Cartier had an art collector's eye, and his father and brothers deferred to his unerring instinct. Louis was later to recount how he held the last remnants of Marie Antoinette's necklace in his hand, that string of twenty-two diamonds owned by the Duke of Sutherland which Louis described as 'the largest antique chain of diamonds I have ever seen'. In addition, Louis bought a cross pendant and a ring in the possession of Pope Benedict XV (1854–1922), pieces whose fascination went far beyond their value as stones.

In New York, by contrast, Pierre Cartier often had the task of building an historic stone into a Cartier jewel. Examples included the drop-shaped diamond the 'Star of South Africa' of 47.75 carats, whose discovery in 1869 had unleashed veritable diamond fever in South Africa,[15] and the drop-shaped Morgan diamond of 35 carats, which J. P. Morgan had given as a wedding present to Mrs Stotesbury, and which she had set in one of her Cartier tiaras.[16]

The series of historic stones handled by Cartier's as brokers offers a glimpse into a slice of cultural history which tells of private destinies, shattered hopes, ambition and tragedy and, sometimes, fleeting happiness. The series began with the drop-shaped cabochon emerald of 75 carats belonging to an Indian maharajah, which Cartier began negotiating for in 1901. In the same year we read of a 15–16-carat fancy-pink Golconda diamond which came from a famous necklace – possibly the stone Cartier referred to in a letter to W. K. Vanderbilt as 'a splendid stone of antique cut from a necklace of the Portuguese royal house'.

Two stones recalled the generous legacy of eighteen diamonds bequeathed by Cardinal Mazarin (1602–61) to the French crown. Two Mazarin diamonds, one of $18\frac{11}{16}$ carats, the other $16\frac{9}{16}$ carats, were exhibited at the International Exhibition of 1900 and set the following year by Cartier's for Mme Hériot.[17]

In 1909 Cartier's received the 90.38-carat drop diamond, later known as the 'Indian briolette', from the great dealer Eknayan who had cut it shortly before. Initially set as a pendant with a 126-grain pearl, the splendid stone was combined the following year with two 22-carat emeralds and the same pearl to form a brooch, which was sent to the New York branch. In 1911 the diamond returned once more to Eknayan, before Cartier's sold it to George Blumenthal.[18]

Among the largest of all the stones set by Cartier was the 1910 cushion-shaped *La Tour d'Auvergne*, owned by the princess of the same name. Four years later the Princesse de la Tour d'Auvergne led the 'Diamond Ballet' at the 'Gemstones Ball' adorned with her historic diamonds, among which not the least eye-catching was the $116^3/34$-carat diamond.[19]

In 1910 Cartier's bought the Dudley emerald of $6\frac{7}{8}\frac{1}{64}$ carats from the New York dealer Joseph Frankel's Son, and at almost the same time sold the valuable 30.82-carat blue heart-shaped diamond also cut by Eknayan in a lily-of-the-valley corsage to Mrs Unzue of Argentina.[20] If the blue of the Hope diamond was described as 'indignant indigo' or steel blue, the Unzue heart diamond glows a deep sea blue and is still among the most remarkable blue diamonds in the world.

The sensation over the Hope diamond had barely died down, and the final instalment had still to be paid by the McLean family, when Cartier's got hold of another piece from the former Hope collection – the 52.17-carat Hope spinel. Bought from the London dealer Peake's, the rectangular red stone first adorned a simple brooch by the Picq workshop, before being set by Cartier's in a necklace.

These great transactions suffered an interruption with the First World War, though it was during the war years that Pierre Cartier was to achieve his spectacular coup of exchanging his two-rope pearl necklace for the Morton Plant palace on Fifth Avenue.

In 1921 we find an important pair of earrings – part of the historic

153. The 90.38-ct 'Indian briolette' diamond, mounted below a square-cut diamond and a pearl of 126 grains. 1909 (Actual size)

Leuchtenberg emeralds – at Cartier's New York. They comprised two emerald drops, each framed in ten diamonds and each fitted to a hexagonal emerald and thirteen diamonds. The complete parure originally belonged to the Beauharnais family before it passed to the Russian ducal family of Leuchtenberg; from them it was bought by a Paris syndicate to which Cartier's belonged.[21] Except for the earrings, the jewels were broken up in Paris, despite a subscription organized by the Louvre to prevent this. The following year Cartier's took the emeralds to Spain to show to the Queen and Queen Mother. However, this did not lead to a sale at the time because, as the salesman Farinès reported back to Paris, the Queen Mother merely 'pouted significantly'.

In 1924 Cartier's acquired another historic pair of earrings, this time descended from the Empress Maria Theresa and until 1918 preserved in the Treasury at the Hofburg in Vienna. In 1921, together with other Habsburg treasures, they were offered for sale in Lucerne. The earrings themselves, through mysterious circumstances, reached the dealer Bienenfeld, who passed them on directly to Cartier's. Set with diamond drops and described as of the 'very finest quality, of unheard-of beauty and absolutely white', they allegedly found a buyer in India.

In 1933, as the waves of the economic crisis spread ever wider, Cartier's transactions began to extend to particularly famous stones, many of which had been in private collections for centuries. Some negotiations foundered on the unreasonableness of the owners, who refused to accept offers which were in keeping with the new economic realities. Thus Cartier's turned down the offer of the blue 35.32-carat Wittelsbach diamond, even though the firm already had plans to show the stone to the King of Nepal. In 1928 negotiations were in hand for the historic diamond briolette necklace presented by Napoleon to his consort Marie Louise on the birth of the King of Rome. Even in 1937 there was still talk of its being taken over by Cartier's London with a view to the approaching coronation of King George VI. But here too the negotiations foundered on the owner's indecision.

Up to the Second World War the London branch was the arena for many important transactions. It was here, in the 1920s, that the 20-carat Cambridge diamond, called after Lady Mary Cambridge, was set into a necklace, and in 1930 the 69.67-carat diamond drop, the 'Excelsior', spent some time in the London shop.[22] The stone was procured, like the Maria Theresa diamond drops, by the dealer Bienenfeld. Used by Cartier's to embellish a three-strand diamond necklace, the 'Excelsior' was the largest of twenty-one stones yielded by the cutting of the original rough stone in 1903.

In 1931, Cartier's London received one of the most remarkable diamonds ever, a sparkling olive-green brilliant of 12.86 carats. Other green stones known to exist by this time were the apple-green drop diamond of Augustus the Strong in Dresden, and a 6.40-carat stone owned by the King of England. Jacques Cartier had been offered the olive-green diamond by the wife of the Cairo jeweler, Buchinger. Originally an oval stone of 17.5 carats, it was said to come from the collection of the Nizam of Hyderabad. Through one of his friends it

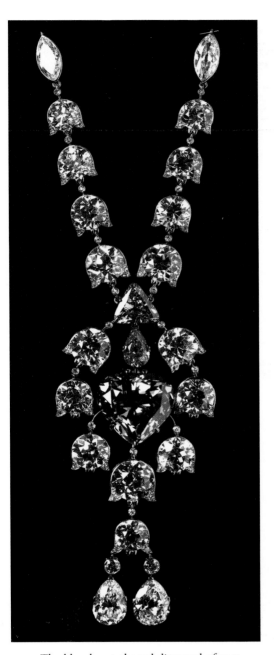

154. The blue heart-shaped diamond of 30.82 cts and a blue triangular diamond mounted on a circular, navette and pear-shaped diamond corsage ornament of lily-of-the-valley design. 1910 (Actual size)

was sold to the Princess Nathalie Narishkine; after the war it came back onto the market and was recut in Antwerp to 12.86 carats. In 1931 Jacques Cartier attached it to the great necklace for the Maharajah of Nawanagar, where, together with the pink diamond, it formed the lowermost tip of the cascade of coloured diamonds which remains unique in the history of jewelry to this day.

In 1933 the talk was of three other legendary diamonds — the 'Pasha', the 'Nassak' and the 'Porter Rhodes'. In 1848, Ibrahim Pasha of Egypt had evidently bought the diamond that was to bear his title for £28,000. How and when it left Egypt we do not know but in 1933 the London company of T. M. Sutton offered it to Cartier's. The trail vanished, however, until the 'Pasha' turned up in Egypt again, and was later bought from King Farouk by the Italian jewelers Bulgari and sold to Barbara Hutton. However, the slightly octagonal form of the stone did not appeal to this capricious customer. She had it recut at Cartier's to 38.19 carats and set in a ring, which sparkled on her finger in India, Palm Beach and Monte Carlo.[23]

The 'Nassak' (still called the 'Nassuck' in the nineteenth century) was, like the 'Idol's Eye', supposed to have been taken from the eye of a temple god. The stone belonged to the family of the Duke of Westminster for nearly a century before he sold it to the jeweler Georges Mauboussin, who exhibited it in America in 1926. In 1933 Cartier's were preparing various designs for a crown and a turban at the request of the Gaekwar of Baroda. Jacques Cartier suggested that the prince should buy the 'Nassak', which had come onto the market, so that it could be introduced as the centre stone in the turban ornament. The Gaekwar let the crown project lapse, but all the same the 'Nassak' found its way to Cartier's London, where the designer Frederick A. Mew used it to embellish a five-string pearl and diamond necklace. In 1936 Cartier's exhibited the 'Nassak' at their Monte Carlo branch, opened the year before, and in 1937 the 80.60-carat triangular stone was recut as a rectangular stone of 47.41 carats.[24]

'The most precious square diamond in the world', Cartier's called the 'Porter Rhodes' while it was on their premises in 1933. The original 73-carat diamond was apparently sold by the Duke of Westminster, and recut to 56.60 carats by the London firm of Jerwood & Ward. Cartier's acquired it from the estate of Solly B. Joël, the diamond mine owner, with the King of Nepal in mind.[25] In the event, however, it was sold to Sir Ernest Oppenheimer, passed later to the Maharajah of Indore, and was bought back from him by Harry Winston in 1946.

In December 1935 Cartier's of Paris mounted a great display of historic diamonds, among them the 'Jubilee'. This stone had been cut to 245.35 carats in 1897, the year of Queen Victoria's jubilee. It was displayed at the World Exhibition of 1900, at which time it was already valued at Fr7,000,000 ($1,400,000). In 1935 this diamond, the world's fourth-largest cut, was sent for sale to Cartier's London by the heirs of Sir Dorab Tata, a rich Parsi of Bombay. Again, the firm looked first to the Gaekwar of Baroda, who in 1928 had appointed Cartier's 'the only adviser for purchases of precious stones in the whole world'. The firm's representatives were prepared to hand over the 'Jubilee' to the Indian ruler in a Wiesbaden hotel at an asking price of £75,000. But the Gaekwar, who wanted the diamond for the state treasury, sought authorization for the purchase from the treasury department in Baroda. Although in 1937 he was still receiving the department's vigorous encouragement, the ruler considered himself too old and declined to buy, as in 1933 he had declined the crown. So in 1937 Cartier's sold the 'Jubilee' to Paul-Louis Weiller. The original dramatic setting as a turban aigrette, conspicuous against its background of white heron feathers, was transformed by Jeanne Toussaint into a baguette diamond brooch, suggestive of either a six-six-pointed star or a stylized turtle.

In 1935 there was talk about a 50½-carat pink diamond which was to be recut at Cartier's as a 30-carat drop. A far more important talking point, however, was the historic 'Cumberland' diamond. Although in the end Cartier's decided not to buy it because of its 'banal colour and shape', this diamond was the subject of a dramatic, yet comic episode in the firm's history. It was given its name because it had been presented, in 1746, to the Duke of Cumberland by the City of London; Cartier's first exhibited it, together with the 'Nassak', in Monte Carlo in 1936. In 1938 Jacques Cartier and the salesman Marcel Marson made a business trip to Albania, where the marriage of King Zog I and Queen Geraldine Apponyi of Hungary was being celebrated. They were startled by the contrast between the brilliant receptions in the Durazzo palace and the 'unimaginable poverty in Tirana'. The bride selected a few pieces of jewelry, while the king appraised the 'Cumberland' and waved a diamond magnifying-glass about, but bought nothing. The trip would have ended in tragedy had Cartier and Marson flown back with the five carefully packed jewel chests, for the plane crashed between Tirana and Brindisi: a large part of the jewels were burnt. The remainder turned up later in the black markets of Rome and Naples.

The accident, however, did not deter Cartier's from returning to Albania in the autumn of the same year for the 'jubilee' celebrations of the tenth year of the king's reign. Marson took more than a hundred pieces, including the 'Cumberland' again and a pair of diamond drops of 35.57 carats, on this new expedition. The temperature in Tirana was 38° C., it was unthinkable to telephone Paris, and the telegraphic connection was constantly interrupted, with the result that the code devised expressly for this journey was quite useless: ANTELOPE = King Zog; EAGLE = the King wants; BEE = the king is favourably inclined; WEASEL = the king's sister; PLUM = tiara; BANANA = gold; DATE = diamond ring; FIG = emerald ring.

The king, however, who was awaiting urgently needed credits from Rome, changed his mind every day and finally made such a risible offer for the important stones that Marson turned his back on Albania with the philosophical comment: 'Cartier does not go a-begging.'

In 1938, the salesman Fernand Teneau was to ask for the 32.82-carat 'Cumberland' for the St Moritz branch, founded in 1930.[26] In the Engadine mountain village Lady Deterding, Countess Haugwitz-Reventlow (Barbara Hutton), the von Opels and the Harrison

Williams ruled as uncrowned monarchs, and their presence justified the inclusion in Cartier's display of not only the 'Cumberland' but also a magnificent 49.64-carat navette diamond and a rectangular diamond weighing 33.68 carats. Furthermore, the director of the Afghan National Bank was also staying in St Moritz and held significant credits from the King of Afghanistan for the purchase of jewels.

In the Cartier archive for 1937, there is mention of a 38.85-carat diamond in the shape of a spearhead, reminiscent in outline of Prince Youssoupov's Ram's Head diamond. In the same year Annie, Viscountess Cowdray, had her black pearls deposited with Cartier's London and Mrs Horace Dodge (then Mrs Dillman) paid $115,000 dollars for the most sensational ruby of the time from Cartier's New York. The stone, named after King Thibaw of Burma (1878–85), weighted 26.13 carats and had previously belonged to J. P. Morgan, from whose daughter Pierre Cartier had acquired it.[27]

During the Second World War the Canadian geologist John T. Williamson (1907–58) became famous with his discovery in Tanganyika (now Tanzania) of what was then the world's largest diamond mine. In 1947, after tough negotiations, he sold it to Sir Ernest Oppenheimer. That same year the mine yielded a rose diamond weighing 54 carats in the rough, which Williamson gave as a wedding present to Princess Elizabeth. The remarkable stone was recut in London to a rose-coloured brilliant of 23.60 carats and inspired Frederick A. Mew of Cartier's to design an edelweiss brooch with the diamond set in its heart.[28]

In 1961 Cartier's bought the emerald jewelry of the Empress Eugénie at Stuker's auction house in Berne. Consisting of nine emeralds, the collection comprised a necklace, ring and brooch, and was in the form of a later, somewhat clumsy Madrid setting of the twentieth century which may have re-used the nine emeralds of the tiara once made for the empress by the jeweler Lemonnier. Eugénie had bequeathed the emeralds, hidden in a fan case, to her goddaughter the Queen of Spain, who did not at first realize its value and casually put it aside. Cartier's set the emeralds as the pendant motifs of a large diamond necklace.[29]

Four years later Cartier's New York sold the Vega navette diamond, a 14-carat stone named after the star. In 1971 Rosemarie Kenmore, wife of the then president of the firm, discovered a 38.71-carat cushion-shaped, canary-coloured diamond in India. Named after her, it was to feature in many subsequent exhibitions.

The interest in these stones, however, paled before the publicity surrounding the 69.42-carat diamond drop associated with Elizabeth Taylor. In 1967 the stone was sold by Harry Winston to Mrs Harriet Annenberg Ames, and it turned up in 1969 as the centrepiece of an auction at Parke-Bernet, New York. Then the 56th largest cut diamond in the world, it challenged its admirers to find a fanciful name for it after Parke-Bernet promoted it as the 'No Name Diamond' and flew it out to the film star in Switzerland. However, at the auction on that memorable 23 October, the stone was bought not by Miss Taylor, but by Cartier's, for $1,050,000. Four days later they sold it on, at a nominal profit, to Richard Burton for $1,100,000.

Before it was handed over to Burton's representative, however, Cartier's exhibited the million-dollar stone in New York and Chicago – one of the biggest publicity successes of the 1960s, which provoked the *New York Times* to make the malicious comment that peasants were forming lines to gape at a 'diamond as big as the Ritz'. It has been known ever since as the 'Cartier' or 'Taylor-Burton' diamond.[30]

For the time being, the last in the long line of illustrious gems which have passed through Cartier's over the past eight decades is the 107.07-carat flawless drop-shaped diamond cut in 1976 and subsequently sold to a European collector. Symbolically, it was christened with the name of the man who had instilled in the firm its standard of perfection: 'Louis Cartier'.

155. The Duke and Duchess of Windsor at their home in the Bois de Boulogne. The Duchess is wearing her flamingo brooch (1940)

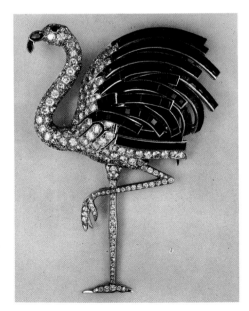

156. Flamingo brooch in rubies, sapphires, emeralds, a citrine and diamonds. Commissioned by the Duke of Windsor in 1940 (Actual size)

NOTES

Introduction

1. This incident, which took place in Paris in 1907, is retold here in Glaenzer's own words. In 1908/9 he travelled with the pearl expert Maurice Richard to Singapore, Saigon, Hong Kong, Canton, Shanghai and Bombay. In Bangkok he was granted an audience with the King, to whom Fabergé also showed his wares at that time.
2. *See* The Duke of Windsor, *A King's Story*, London 1951, p. 51.

1. From apprentice to court jeweler

1. The witnesses to the marriage were the seed-merchant J. F. Benard, and the carpenter Jean Tandonnet. Also present were Pierre Cartier's paternal uncle, and Jean-Pierre and Jacques-Noël Cartier, both coach-painters by profession.
2. According to the *Almanach du Commerce*, Picard is known to have worked in the rue Montorgueil since 1834. He should not be confused with the goldsmith and *bijoutier* of the same name who was Jouquoy's successor and who produced silver snuffboxes, lighters, etc.
3. Princess Mathilde's purchases began in 1856. In 1861/62 Cartier sold her a bracelet decorated with the imperial bees. Interestingly enough, the auction of her jewels, held after her death in 1904, may have contained the item in question (No. 141).
4. Princess Cristina Belgiojoso (1808–71) had settled in Paris in 1831, where her salon was the meeting-place for many exiled politicians. In 1848 she hurried back to Milan to help in the uprising against Austria, contributing a battalion of volunteers. During 1855/56 she embarked on a Grand Tour of the Orient.
5. *See* Henri Vever, *La Bijouterie française au XIXème siècle*, p. 108.
6. One of Léonide Leblanc's most valuable jewels was a blue diamond ring, which was sold after her death, ostensibly as an item of historic interest. Her collection of jewels was auctioned between 29 July and 4 August 1891, while the actress was still alive. Her famous four-strand pearl necklace of 212 pearls weighing 3,300 grains fetched Fr181,000. Since Cartier did not sign his jewels, it is impossible to tell which of the pieces may have been his. The only signed items were by Rouvenat.
7. Not to be confused with Duke Charles de Brunswick (1804–73), a connoisseur of jewelry, who lived in a magnificent mansion in the rue de Beaujon in Paris. He moved to Geneva in 1870 and left his vast fortune to the town; it was here, too, that his collection of jewels was auctioned.
8. *See* American *Vogue*, December 1917.
9. *See* Henri Vever, *op. cit.*, p. 252.
10. In a letter dated 25 August 1873 to his son Alfred, Louis-François Cartier wrote: 'Prosper [. . .] is drawing in the sales ledger, just as you would do.'
11. The term 'galvanoplasty' derives from the name of the Italian physiologist Luigi Galvani (1737–98), who in 1791 developed his theory of animal electricity on the basis of an experiment on frogs' legs. The galvanoplastic process is a technique by which a layer of silver is dissolved in a chemical solution and then fused on to a metal base by means of an electric charge.
12. *See* Geoffrey Munn, *Castellani and Giuliano, Revivalist Jewellers of the Nineteenth Century*. 1984.
13. The French sculptor Jean-Baptiste Carpeaux (1827–75) designed the group *Dance* for the front of the Paris Opéra in 1869. The building itself was the work of Charles Garnier (1825–98).
14. The jeweler Robin was one of Cartier's suppliers and was the first to popularize matt gold in France, a fashion that was already known in England at the time. The gold was dipped in an acid bath, which caused a thin layer of chemically pure gold to form on the surface, thus producing the desired matt effect.
15. Girandoles were originally candelabra with several arms, but during the seventeenth and eighteenth centuries they became a popular motif on brooches and ear jewelry in the form of three pendant drop-shaped stones.
16. One of the jewelers who took up the fashion for animal jewelry was Hubert Obry (1808–53), who specialized chiefly in animals of the hunt.
17. The firm of Plisson et Hartz produced chimaeras, lizards, crabs and turtles, while Charles Marie, Jr. produced dragonflies, frogs and crabs.
18. *See* Marie-Noël de Gary, *Les Fouquet, bijoutiers et joailliers à Paris, 1860–1958.* 1984.
19. *See* Henry Vever, *op. cit.*, p. 706.

2. Rue de la Paix

1. The planned marriage between Princess Victoria, who was a daughter of Edward VII, and Prince George of Greece came to nothing, as did subsequent plans for her to marry the Earl of Roseberry. Prince George married Marie Bonaparte in 1907; Roseberry did not remarry, and Princess Victoria remained a spinster. In 1902 she bought a tiara from Cartier's.
2. Described by the novelist and travel-writer Louis Enault (1824–1900) who was also the author of *Les Diamants de la Couronne.* 1884.
3. Most of the buildings in the rue de la Paix have a central main entrance leading to an inner courtyard, with shops to the left and right of the entrance. This explains the otherwise rather confusing fact that two shops regularly have the same number.
4. Following Boucheron's move to the Place Vendôme in 1893, the square became Paris's second most important centre for jewelry. Lalique established himself there in 1905 (No. 24), the same year as Chaumet (first at No. 15 and, from 1907, at No. 12). They were joined in 1906 by Van Cleef & Arpels (No. 22) and by Cardeilhac (No. 24) and in 1945 by Mauboussin (No. 20).
5. In 1190 Philippe Auguste granted perfume-makers common statutes with glove-makers, which is why their guilds' coats-of-arms contained three gloves. The two guilds remained associated until the end of the eighteenth century, and as late as 1815, on the eve of the Battle of Waterloo, Napoleon received a pair of perfumed gloves from Houbigant.
6. Jacques Doucet, the 'poet of the cravat', famous as a patron of the fine and decorative arts, entered his father's firm in 1875, the year of Louis Cartier's birth. He later added a fashion department.
7. Although the interior decorations of the salesrooms were in the style of Louis XVI, various changes were made between 1926 and 1937 to bring them more into line with contemporary tastes. One such alteration was the introduction of display cabinets in the cubist spirit of art deco. They were supplied by the firm of Fred Sage, which had branches in both London and Paris.
8. *See* Anita Lesley, *Edwardians in Love*, 1974, p. 18.
9. In 1924 Cartier's New York were to buy Dreicer's stock for $2.5 million. Dreicer's collection of paintings went to the Metropolitan Museum of Art.
10. Cartier's New York stock was valued at Fr6,325,183 in 1911, a figure made up as follows: jewels: Fr4,152,477; gemstones: Fr1,472,272; gold and silverware: Fr700,434.
11. During the 1920s the New York workshops became known as the 'American Art Works'. Housed in Cartier's premises in Fifth Avenue, they employed up to seventy jewelers and goldsmiths working under the supervision of Paul Duru (1871–1971). The chief stone-setter was Paul Maîtrejean (1883–1975), who set the Hope diamond. At a later date, his son Philippe Maîtrejean (b. 1914) designed a golden hand bell set with a 970-carat aquamarine. The jeweler Dominik Sala was regarded as New York's leading expert in his chosen field. The number of employees was reduced to around twenty-five following the outbreak of the Second World War; and in 1941 the workshop was shut down completely. After the war, Cartier signed an exclusive contract with the independent firm of Wors & Pujol, which was housed under the same roof as the jewelers. They were taken over in 1974 by Henry Larrieu, who had been Pierre Cartier's last apprentice between 1938 and 1941. In turn, Larrieu's father had been the American Art Works' *donneur d'or*, in other words, it was his responsibility to distribute the amounts of precious metal required by the various goldsmiths.

A second workshop known as the 'Marel Works' was housed on the opposite side of the road in 52nd St. and specialized in goldware such as picture frames, trophies and vanity cases. It was taken over by Cartier's in the 1950s.
12. Maurice Duvallet left Cartier's New York in 1920, George Genaille remaining behind as their principal designer. Duvallet then worked for Charlton (1933–39) and for Van Cleef & Arpels (1943–63). He was responsible for the ballerina brooches which Van Cleef & Arpels launched in the 1940s.

The most talented of Cartier's designers in New York, however, during the 1940s and 1950s was Maurice Daudier. He had previously worked for Cartier's Paris and London and designed jewelry for Mrs Merryweather Post and Mrs Donahue, among others, before his retirement in 1963.

Alfred Duranti (b. 1940) was engaged as a designer by Claude Cartier in 1956, at a time when the workshop employed six designers. He designed the pearl and ruby necklace for the Peregrina pearl as well as a diamond necklace for the engraved Mogul diamond, both of which were bought by Richard Burton for his then wife, Elizabeth Taylor.
13. In 1935 Paul Iribe published *Rue de la Paix, Place Vendôme, vitrine de la France.* Cartier's neighbours in the 1930s were the antique dealer Jacques Seligmann et Fils, to the left, and the fashion house Martial et Armand to the right. Of the jewelers of the nineteenth century Mellerio, Chocarne, Aucoc, Fontana and Vever remained. At No. 2 was the jeweler Rozanès. No. 4, the building which housed Alfred Cartier's office, was also the address of René Linzeler, the gold- and silversmith. Cartier sold his silverware, cutlery and candlesticks, some of which were designed by Paul Iribe with his characteristic rose motif. At the rue de la Paix, Linzeler went into partnership with Marchak from Kiev, while his second workshop at 9 rue d'Argenson was taken over by Cartier at the outbreak of the Second World War.

LaCloche, at 15 rue de la Paix (founded in 1897 and until 1901 at 28 Place Vendôme), had by then gone into liquidation. At No. 17 was the jeweler Morgan, also Berlioz Leroy 1, successor of Paul Hamelin. At No. 18 was Polak, and at No. 19 Albert Janesich, who closed down in 1932. Marzo, who had associated with Eugène Laillet in 1911, was at No. 20.

Tiffany remained at No. 25, but the New York branches of Spaulding and Charlton had closed down.

3. The garland style

1. *See* Henri Clouzot, *Le Style Renaissance en France au XIXème siècle*, Paris 1936.

2. *See* Rudolf Berliner and Gerhart Egger, *Ornamentale Vorlageblätter des 15. bis 19. Jahrhunderts*. Munich 1981.

3. Cartier bought an ornamental fibula in 1873. Louis Cartier's library, which contained one of the foremost collections of eighteenth-century illustrated books, was looked after from 1929 by Louis Devaux, Fernand Teneau and François de Bolvary. Devaux (b. 1907) was the president of Cartier's Paris branch from 1942 to 1946 and of the New York branch from 1946 to 1949, when he became French president of Shell.

4. Between 1900 and 1910 a number of designers engaged by Cartier had been trained in wrought-ironwork: Henri Chenaud, for example, who had previously worked for Baguès. Olivier Baloche had worked in tapestry design, which, like lace-making, was one of Louis Cartier's particular interests.

5. In New York, pearl lace was still a great novelty on jewels as late as 1910.

6. Eve Lavallière made her debut in 1891 at the Théâtre des Variétés, having previously worked in a hat factory, tying ribbons. The cravats which were produced in this way were called *lavallières* and provided a stage-name for the actress, whose real name was Eve Ferroglio. She died in a convent in 1929.

7. The lovebirds motif is found in Cartier's designs as early as 1881. In 1900 he produced a pendant with an altar and doves. In the eighteenth century there had been a fashion for engagement rings with doves, which were symbols of love and fidelity.

8. Shoulder knots were known in the eighteenth century. An important example dating from 1768 may be found in the Green Vault in Dresden.

9. Nancy Leeds' emerald epaulette was reset in 1921, when it was combined with the emeralds from a *lavallière* dating from 1911 to produce the large emerald necklace worn by Mrs Leeds in László's portrait of her. In 1926, after her death, Cartier was commissioned by her executors to resell her jewelry, and a number of her emeralds were bought by Lady Deterding.

10. Gilles Légaré (b. *c.* 1610) was a Paris goldsmith and enameller whose clients included Louis XIV. His book *Livre des ouvrages d'orfèvrerie* became the most important seventeenth-century work on ornamental design for jewelers and goldsmiths.

11. *Sévignés* are also referred to as *dauphines* and *cravates dauphine* in Cartier's records.

12. *See* A. E. Fersman, *Les Joyaux du trésor de Russie* (1926), plates LIII, LVIII, LXI.

13. Curved, three-dimensional bow-knots were a speciality of French workshops. As late as 1910 Cartier had difficulty introducing to New York the techniques involved in making them.

14. *See* Fersman, *op. cit.*, plates XLV, LVII.

15. By around 1830, lace from Flanders, Venice, England and France had begun to suffer the effects of competition from the new machine-made variety. As a result, the numbers of young lace-makers entering the profession fell to the point where it was feared in Normandy that the famous *point d'Alençon* would disappear altogether. The situation was saved by Queen Margherita of Italy, who established a workshop on the island of Burano; both the Empress of Austria and the last Tsarina of Russia lent their support to the ailing craft.

16. Platinum is one of a group of six metals comprising iridium, osmium, palladium, rhodium and ruthenium. Small additions of iridium produce an alloy of the required hardness.

17. The backing of silver with gold in the eighteenth and nineteenth centuries was intended to strengthen the soft silver setting and to prevent the oxidizing metal from coming into direct contact with the skin or with clothes.

18. *See* D. MacDonald, *A History of Platinum*. London 1960.

19. In 1782 Antoine Laurent Lavoisier (1743–94) oxidized platinum, an experiment observed by Benjamin Franklin; but the commercial production of platinum still lay some way ahead.

20. It was not until 1804 that the English scientist William Hyde Wollaston (1766–1828) successfully produced a practicable form of malleable platinum. It was also Wollaston who discovered palladium and rhodium.

21. Jean-Baptiste Fossin was the head of François Nitot's workshop. He later took over the business and established himself in the rue de Richelieu. In 1845 he handed over the firm to his son Jules, who in turn sold it to Prosper Morel in 1854. Joseph Chaumet (1854–1928) married Morel's daughter.

22. As against an annual production of only 5,900 kilograms. The difference was due to melting down old pieces. Ninety per cent came from Russia, the rest from Colombia and the United States. The price per kilogram in 1895 was Fr3,000, compared with Fr10,000 in 1822, the year platinum was discovered in the Urals. In 1870 it was as low as Fr1,560, following the failure of the Russian experiment.

At the end of 1900 a gramme of platinum cost between Fr2.95 and Fr3.00 in New York. Every month Cartier's New York workshops required two kilograms of platinum 3mm thick, in addition to 300 grammes of 20 per cent platinum wire and 300 grammes of 15 per cent platinum wire. Although America had its own deposits, Cartier's imported the platinum they required, duty-free, from the Paris-based firms of Lyon Allemand and Caplain Saint-André. New platinum deposits were discovered between the two world wars: South Africa now produces 75 per cent of the world market, the remaining 25 per cent comes from Canada, the Soviet Union, Zimbabwe, Colombia and the United States.

23. In Paris a new, far cheaper alloy, magnalium, was first used in 1902. It was produced by alloying aluminium with 10–25 per cent magnesium, the resultant alloy weighing less than the somewhat lustreless aluminium on its own.

24. Oscar Massin had manufactured aigrettes with lily-of-the-valley settings around 1860/70. The Rosenborg Collection in Copenhagen contains a number of eighteenth-century jewels with this type of setting.

25. A letter dated 3 December 1900 indicates that it was through Worth that Cartier first heard of the Grand Duchess Vladimir's charity bazaars in St Petersburg. The Grand Duchess was later to make it possible for Cartier to set up in Russia.

26. The *directoire* style came back into fashion in 1888 as a result of Sarah Bernhardt's appearances in Sardou's *Tosca*.

27. The 'Récamier' hairstyle was popularized by the actress Marguerite Brésil.

28. According to the 1903 edition of the *Revue de la bijouterie, joaillerie et orfèvrerie*, there was considerable demand for turquoise jewelry at that time, especially in London. Lady Londonderry, the arch-rival of Cartier's regular patron, Lady de Grey, owned a magnificent turquoise tiara, as did Baroness Leopold de Rothschild and Mrs Cavendish-Bentinck. Cravats were a special kind of *lavallière*, a velvet ribbon overlapping at the front and having diamond ends.

29. Cravats were a special kind of *lavallière*, a velvet ribbon overlapping at the front and having diamond ends.

30. Among Marie Bonaparte's acquaintances at an earlier period had been Alexander Graham Bell and Pierre Curie. In 1925 she moved to Vienna, where she became a colleague and supporter of Sigmund Freud's.

Marie Bonaparte was fond of rubies: the engagement ring which Cartier designed for her was set with a ruby of 2.37/ cts. She was given a ruby and diamond brooch by the King of Greece, and from her fiancé she received a ruby cross and, on the occasion of the first anniversary of their engagement, a ruby and pearl sautoir.

31. Cartier had used onyx in items of mourning jewelry as early as 1910; the pieces in question were made for the Widener and McLean families.

32. Four of Cartier's leading customers went down with the *Titanic*: J. J. Astor, George and Henry Widener, and Edgar J. Meyer.

33. Caroline Otéro (1868–1964) enjoyed the patronage of Leopold II of Belgium and was often to be seen 'proverbially decked out' with jewels that had been bestowed on her by Albert of Monaco, the Shah of Persia, Muzaffar-ed-Din, the Khedive of Egypt and Baron Ollestreder of Berlin. She once appeared at the Paris Opéra triply decorated with a necklace of Empress Eugénie's, a necklace belonging to the Empress of Austria, and the famous pearl necklace of Léonide Leblanc. In her hair she wore a glittering diamond tiara, and as ear studs two diamonds each weighing 50 cts.

Cartier also had dealings with the actress Wanda de Boncza of the Comédie-Française. Her collection of jewels was auctioned in 1902 and included twelve 'bodice or hair ornaments' of unspecified origin, together with a black drop pearl from Cartier's weighing 29¼ grains, which was sold for Fr21,700. Cartier's customers included other celebrated actresses, such as Eleonora Duse, Geneviève Lantelme, Gabrielle Dorziat, Gaby Deslys, Gabrielle Réjane, Cécile Sorel, Lillie Langtry, Forzane and Mistinguett. Emilienne d'Alençon, who for many years was a rival of *la belle Otéro*, appears in Cartier's archives between 1903 and 1922. Polaire ordered a diamond belt measuring 42 cm.

34. In 1901 Cartier's dismantled a number of items of Olga de Meyer's jewelry, including twelve brooches, seven bracelets and three necklaces, which were reset as new pieces. That same year they sent a cabochon ruby and diamond brooch to their client in Bayreuth.

35. The album contained texts by Rodin, Jacques Emile Blanche and Jean Cocteau, and was dedicated to Cartier's customer, the Marchioness of Ripon, formerly Lady de Grey. It was she who brought the Ballets Russes to England and received Nijinsky at her family home, Coombe Court.

36. *See* American *Vogue*, December 1917.

4. Tiaras

1. *See* Gabriel-Louis Pringué, *Trente ans de dîners en ville*, Paris 1948, pp. 122, 104.

2. *See* Stephen Birmingham, *The Grandes Dames*, New York 1982, p. 32.

3. *See* Joseph J. Thorndike, *The Very Rich*, New York 1981, p. 53.

4. *See* Consuelo Vanderbilt Balsan, *The Glitter and the Gold*, New York 1952, p. 152.

5. *See* Andrew Barrow, *Gossip*, London 1978, p. 174.

6. What is probably the earliest pictorial representation of a diadem in the form of a helmet band survives in a battle piece depicting Tuthmosis III (1504–1450 BC). The pharaoh can be seen wearing a kind of crown-helmet; around it, as a sign of his rank as military leader, has been wound a diadem fillet, the loose ends of which have been tied together to form a knot. On the later mummy of Tutankhamun (1371–1352 BC), the fabric ribbon and its two loose ends are reproduced in gold for the first time. In spite of its importance in Egyptian culture, the diadem was not an Egyptian invention. It appears contemporaneously in Median cultures, from which it passed to Persia in the sixth century BC, being regarded as a sign of royal dignity from the time of Alexander the Great onward.

One of the jewels to have survived from the Twelfth Dynasty of Egypt's Middle Kingdom (1929–1717 BC) is Princess Khumet's floral wreath of gold, lapis lazuli, cornelian, turquoise and enamel. Garlands such as this one, which were a second source of inspiration for the modern tiara, were further adapted during the Mycenaean period as well as by the Etruscans.

The diadem reappeared as a fillet in 325 during the reign of Constantine the Great, and from now on only the emperor himself had the right to wear it. At the same time, the diadem developed into a closed circlet which no longer needed fastening. Geometrical uprights were first added in 438 by the Byzantine Princess Licinia, a design which was to result centuries later in the medieval open, plated crown. During the reign of Emperor Justinian (483–565), the golden circlet was adorned with arches crossing at the apex, an idea deriving from the military commander's strap helmet. This design culminated in the arched crown familiar in the West, a form reserved for emperors and kings alone. In addition to its function as a symbol of sovereignty, the diadem was also a symbol of any high office in Byzantine and early medieval art. The Ravenna mosaics, for example, show angels wearing white diadem fillets.

7. A painting which for a long time was attributed to Leonardo da Vinci and which depicts Lucrezia Crivelli, the *belle ferronnière* (the beautiful blacksmith's wife), sparked off the fashion for *ferronnières* in France.

5. Art nouveau
1. On the occasion of the 1900 World Fair, the *Revue de la bijouterie, joaillerie et orfèvrerie*, lending its support to the art nouveau movement, complained that 'Messrs Falize Frères have remained all too loyal to the ornaments, bow-knots and aigrettes of Gilles Légaré and Maria & Babel'. It was a criticism aimed at all those firms producing garland-style jewelry.
2. The term 'art nouveau' is derived from the name of an art gallery opened in Paris by the Hamburg art-dealer Samuel Bing (d. 1905) at 22 rue de Provence. It was later run by his son Marcel (d. 1920), and its main rival was the 'Maison Moderne' of the German art critic Julius Meier-Graefe.
3. Goethe's *Faust* was translated by Gérard de Nerval and illustrated by Eugène Delacroix in 1827. Gounod's version dates from 1859. In his *La Bijouterie française du XIXème siècle*, Henri Vever mentions the year 1895 in connection with Le Turcq's 'Faust' bracelet, whereas Cartier's records list it under 1894.
4. Another art nouveau woman's head was produced at the Plisson workshop, which was particularly famous around 1900 for its miniature animal brooches.
5. *Plique à jour* is a form of transparent enamelling in which enamel surfaces of varying colours are outlined in metal. Eugène Fontenay had made a fan using this technique in 1852, following its rediscovery by the enameller Briet. Around 1864 the patent for the *plique à jour* process was held by Boucheron.
6. The superstition regarding opals dates from the nineteenth century when, fearing competition from the newly discovered Australian opals, Hungarian and Slovak mine owners are said to have issued dire warnings about the dangers of opals. Sir Walter Scott's 1829 novel *Anne of Geierstein*, whose heroine was killed by an opal, also influenced popular feeling about the stone.
7. The collection is now in the Musée des Arts Décoratifs.
8. Tiffany & Co did something similar during the nineteenth century, when they bought up the pieces that were left over from the laying of the Transatlantic Cable and sold them in four-inch lengths.
9. During the war, Louis Cartier served in the air corps, Jacques was a lieutenant in the dragoons, and Pierre served in the 23rd Territorial Regiment in Cherbourg.
10. On the inside were inscribed the words, 'authentic belt made from shrapnel shell from the 75 – Arts Union'. In 1918 Nellie Melba gave a charity recital at the Ritz in New York for the benefit of the Arts Union. She also auctioned, at $250 each, a

number of Baron de Meyer's photographs, one of which was bought by Pierre Cartier. Cartier's contribution to the auction was a flag brooch set with gemstones, which sold for $1,000. The total sum raised was $5,000.
11. Marshal Foch was elected to the Académie Française shortly after the Armistice, following in the footsteps of his illustrious predecessor, the Duc de Villars (1653–1734) who, as Marshal of France, had negotiated the Peace of Rastatt and subsequently been elected to the Académie.

6. Under the spell of Fabergé
1. Wooden boxes made of amaranth, ebony and Cape wood, on the other hand, came from Alexander's.
2. Among Cartier's other suppliers in Russia were Lagoutiev of Ekaterinburg (amethyst necklaces, ashtrays and parasol handles), and a lapidary called Sourovi who specialized in carving animals.
3. Svietchnikov, for example, demanded 50 roubles for a nephrite ashtray, whereas Woerffel wanted only 30; he also asked 20 roubles for an umbrella handle, as against Woerffel's 17. One of Svietchnikov's Orletz vases cost 450 roubles.
4. In 1904 Pierre Cartier bought the following items from Woerffel: 8 umbrella handles made of jade, etc., 2 letter openers, 2 ashtrays, a seal in the shape of a mushroom, 2 tomatoes, 2 pears and an apple.
5. Japanese *netsukes* were carved in wood or ivory, or else were made of metal, etc. They were attached to a silk cord and used for hanging various objects of everyday use from the wearer's belt.
6. In 1907 Cartier's inventories listed over two hundred different types of animal.
7. What *Vogue* is describing here is the collection of Duchess Guido Sforza (née Anna Autokolsky), the daughter of the Russian sculptor whose collection of Egyptian, Chinese, Indian and Persian art was housed at Passy near Paris. *See Vogue*, 1 August 1916.
8. Early examples of these gold and gemstone floral bouquets can be found in Central Europe from the Renaissance onward; the Papal 'Golden Rose', for instance, which since the fifteenth century had been bestowed on distinguished individuals by the pope on the fourth Sunday of Lent. The Kunsthistorisches Museum in Vienna has a series of gemstone bouquets dating from the seventeenth century, and the Green Vault in Dresden has an ornamental altar by Johann Heinrich Köhler, dating from around 1730 and surmounted by three coral vases containing enamelled gemstone flowers. The Viennese jeweler Grosser was commissioned by Empress Maria Theresa to produce a jeweled bouquet, which the empress gave as a present to her husband. It is now in the Schatzkammer in the Vienna Hofburg.
9. Even before 1910 Russian goldsmiths were already looking round for new places to settle in Europe and America. In 1906, for example, the brothers Oscar and Nathan Heyman from Goldingen (modern Kuldiga) in Northwest Russia settled in New York. They had been brought up in the Russian tradition of Carl Fabergé, and soon began working for Cartier, being among the first workshops in New York to use platinum.
10. Berquin-Varangoz's workshop reputedly provided Fabergé with flowers to Russia. Writing from St Petersburg in 1914, Sarda described to Cartier a marguerite in a crystal vase which he had seen in Russia. It was inset with cairngorm stone and had a silver mounting; the stem and leaves were of nephrite, and both the flower and vase were housed in a glass case: 'The plant appears to me not to have been made in Russia. It resembles those from the rue de la Paix, except that it is less fussy, simpler and more lifelike.'

11. In 1906 Cartier lent Henri Lavabre Fr50,000. The workshop thereafter worked exclusively for Cartier's, executing their models and designs until 1921.
12. Just as Fabergé was commissioned by Grand Duke Nicholas to design a jadeite statuette of Queen Victoria, so in 1911 Cartier ordered the figurine of a Russian Grand Duke from Denissov-Ouralski. It was later bought by Mrs Cavendish-Bentinck.
13. Information from the Smithsonian Institution in Washington suggests that billikens may not have depicted an Anglo-Saxon deity, but may have been fantastic forms invented and patented by Florence Pretz in 1908.

7. In St Petersburg
1. *See* Ian Vorres, *The Last Grand Duchess*, London 1964, p. 43.
2. Grand Duke Paul (1860–1919) was the son of Alexander II. He was married twice, first to Princess Alexandra, the daughter of King George and Queen Olga of Greece, and then to Olga von Pistohlkors, who later became Countess Hohenfelsen and Princess Paley.
3. Following the Revolution, Grand Duchess Xenia (1875–1960) settled in England, where she disposed of her jewelry in a series of somewhat unfortunate transactions. A pearl pendant which she sold to Lady Deterding turned up at a Christie's auction in Geneva in November 1980 (lot 647).
4. The extent of the retinue which Russian princes took with them on their travels to Europe is indicated by an account of the household that accompanied the wife of Grand Duke Konstantin, sister-in-law of Alexander II, to Montreux. It consisted of four ladies-in-waiting, a French *masseuse*, a lord-in-waiting, hairdresser, jeweler-in-waiting, servants and Cossack officers.
5. Most of the French crown jewels were sold by auction in 1887 in the Pavillon de Flore at the Louvre. The bidders included the firms of Tiffany, Boucheron, Aucoc, Bapst, Garrard, Rosenau and Vever. Some of the items continued to circulate within the trade for years afterwards, while others were broken up. In the case of the present item, it is not clear whether it was taken over by Cartier in its original form, or whether it had already been reset.
6. The latter received Cheyrouze at Tsarskoe Selo shortly after Christmas, and complained about a letter he had received from Cartier: 'I am their customer: my tradesmen do not use that kind of tone when addressing me.' In fact, Louis Cartier was anxious that protocol be strictly preserved. He wrote from Paris, rebuking Farinès for not having gone in person to present Grand Duchess Vladimir with a bouquet of flowers. One recalls in this context that Fabergé went in person to the palace to deliver his Easter eggs to the tsarina, while those for the dowager empress were delivered by his closest assistant and, at a later date, by his children.
7. Gatchina (modern Krasnogvardeisk) is situated fifty miles to the west of St Petersburg. The palace dates back to the time of Prince Orlov but was extensively rebuilt under Paul I.
8. According to a decree of Paul I dating from 1796, the crown jewels belonged to the imperial family, whereas all other heritable items were the property of the dowager empress rather than the tsarina, who on state occasions was required to walk behind her mother-in-law, on the arm of the emperor.
9. Boucheron had opened a branch in Moscow in 1899, furnishing the building with the original wood panelling from his very first shop in the Palais-Royal.
10. Consuelo Vanderbilt recalls her visit to St Petersburg in 1902, when she bought a pink enamel snake's egg from Fabergé: 'After dinner the Grand Duchess showed me her jewels, set out in glass

cases in her dressing room. There were endless parures of diamonds, emeralds, rubies and pearls, to say nothing of semiprecious stones such as turquoises, tourmalines, cat's-eyes and aquamarines.' See Consuelo Vanderbilt Balsan, *The Glitter and the Gold*, New York (1952), p. 160.

11. Cartier tried to remain in contact with his customers in Russia even when he himself was no longer on one of his regular visits to the country. Farinès, for example, was sent off to Kiev in midsummer, travelling via Vienna, where he made an abortive attempt to call on the actress Katharina Schratt, who was an intimate friend of Emperor Franz Joseph. Unfortunately, the interest in large pearls which Kiev's wealthy sugar manufacturer Teretschenko was reported to have expressed turned out to be no more than a rumour. He had already ordered items from Cartier's while in Cannes, and had discovered a pearl necklace which LaCloche had on display.

12. In February 1912 St Petersburg's newspapers carried the following announcement: 'The business community of St Petersburg intends to file an official complaint about foreign competitors with the Ministry of Trade and Industry. The individuals concerned have been involved in illegal private transactions (in hotel rooms), have not paid taxes or patent annuities, and their merchandise has not been cleared through customs.' This announcement, it must be said, was directed at traders in general, not simply at jewelers.

13. That same year the tsarina organized a bazaar in the Palais Kleinmichel, when the grand duchess was also in charge of one of the stands. Among those who took part was Sarah Bernhardt who, the very next day, was led in triumph to Tsarskoe Selo.

14. Dr Emanuel Nobel, the Stockholm oil tycoon, was one of Fabergé's leading customers, ordering presents and luxury items for himself and his staff. The following spring he bought a pearl necklace and a pair of fir-cone pendants from Cartier's.

15. Lorgnons such as this now have no practical function and are popular collectors' items. But for Cartier, the commission meant that he had to obtain the Grand Duchess's prescription from her eye specialist in St Petersburg and forward it to Paris.

16. The jewel subsequently passed into the possession of Queen Frederike of Greece, who sold it in New York after the Second World War, the proceeds going towards the Hellenic Red Cross. It was bought by the Swiss collector Maurice Yves Sandoz.

17. The egg later found its way from Russia to America in somewhat mysterious circumstances, though it may have been included among paintings and furniture from some of the finest private Russian collections which were being sold to America at that time. In 1930/31 Andrew Mellon and Samuel Henry Kress began building up the National Gallery's collection in Washington and acquired a number of Russian works in this way. The Cartier egg was acquired by the Metropolitan Museum in New York in 1951, as part of the estate of Laird Shield Goldsborough. The stand, which was originally 2 cm in height, was replaced by a wooden base which is too narrow and which foreshortens the base of the egg.

18. Felix Elston, the son of Friedrich Wilhelm IV of Prussia and Countess Tiefenhausen, married Helene Soumarokov. He was the grandfather of Felix Youssoupov and his family's last male descendant.

19. See Léonard Rosenthal, *Au jardin des gemmes*, Paris 1922, p. 274.

8. Pearls

1. *Le Pavillon de l'Elégance*, 1925, No. 10.

2. Marriages between Europeans and Americans which made the headlines at this time were those of Miss Goelet and the Duke of Roxburghe;

Consuelo Vanderbilt and the Duke of Marlborough; Miss Grant and the Earl of Essex; Miss Jerome and George Cornwallis West; Miss King and the Marquis of Angelsey; Miss Longworth and the Comte de Chambrun; Miss Field and Prince Brancaccio; and Miss Coudert and the Marquis de Choiseul.

3. See Stephen Birmingham, *The Grandes Dames*, 1982, p. 41.

4. Eva Stotesbury's pearl necklace, which prompted the purchase of the Dodge pearls, consisted of 77 pearls weighing 2,225.52 grains. She had previously bought a smaller necklace from Cartier's, made up of 49 pearls weighing 656 grains.

5. The price of the Dodge pearls was exaggerated by newspapers at the time and a figure as high as $1.5 million was quoted, whereas the actual price was $825,000. Horace Dodge bought them in 1920 following the successful outcome of a $40 million lawsuit involving the Ford Motor Company.

6. According to Vever, Empress Eugénie that same year sold a 3-strand necklace of 121 pearls weighing 4,260 grains, which was bought by Loew, a former colleague of Baugrand's, for Paiva. On her death it was sold to Kraemer and then to Boucheron, who made several necklaces from it.

7. See Alphonse de Sondheimer, *Vitrine XIII*, 1966, p. 41. Caroline Otéro, who owned a strand of these pearls, no doubt acquired them through Cartier.

8. Thiers' collection included a Pietà attributed to Michelangelo, two angels by Verrocchio, bronzes, ivories, etc. By 1924 the necklace, which also incorporated pearls belonging to Mme Thiers' sister, Mlle Dosne, had come to comprise 3 strands of 145 pearls weighing 2,140 grains. Also among the collection were an Indian necklace, a cross pendant, and a diamond, ruby and sapphire châtelaine.

9. The clasp was later acquired by Pierre Cartier for his wife Elma, who wore it as a brooch.

10. See Paul Claudel, *La Perle*, Paris 1965, p. 351.

11. Morton F. Plant (1852–1918) was vice-president of the Plant Investment Co. and from 1931 to 1944 vice-president of the National City Bank of New York.

12. In 1970 the Landmarks Preservation Commission placed a preservation order on both this building and the one by Charles P. H. Gilbert at 4 East 52nd St.

13. Following the death of her first husband, Mrs Mae C. Plant married John E. Rovensky. She died in 1956, and on 23 January 1957 the two pearl necklaces and their accompanying case were auctioned by Parke-Bernet Galleries (lots 114–116) for $151,000, a price which reflects the market's slump in the 1950s as a result of the increased popularity of cultured pearls. Whereas at the turn of the century, pearls had commanded the same prices as Old Masters, a major work by Rembrandt could now fetch $2,300,000 at auction, which was the price paid in 1961 for his *Aristotle Contemplating the Bust of Homer*.

Mrs Rovensky had also bought from Cartier's a spectacular pearl and diamond pendant with a 15-ct triangular diamond and 5 Oriental pearls weighing 472 grains in addition to the legendary Rovensky diamond necklace. The last of these had a 46.5-ct pear-shaped diamond from Tiffany & Co as a pendant. Necklace and diamond together were sold for $385,000 at the same auction.

14. 'The world's most expensive pearl necklace' was for a time owned by Cartier and offered to Edward VII, the German emperor and the King of Portugal, among others. It may possibly be identical with a necklace recorded in Cartier's archives in 1910, made up of 37 pearls weighing 947 grains. Was it perhaps offered by Mrs Leeds in part payment of the much more expensive necklace that she bought from Cartier's that same year?

15. Every Easter Mrs Alice Keppel, close friend of Edward VII, would spend three weeks in Biarritz, at the Villa Eugénie, as guest of Sir Ernest Cassel. Her regular visitors included the king.

16. On the occasion of the marriage of her son William in 1921 to Princess Xenia of Greece, Mrs Leeds (who was now Princess Anastasia of Greece) bought the ruby diadem from Cartier's as a wedding present. It had been made in 1908 for Grand Duchess Vladimir and bought back again following the Revolution. It incorporated the Beauharnais ruby weighing 5.22 cts.

17. 'La Régente' was an egg-shaped drop pearl weighing 337 grains which Nitot set as part of a tiara for Empress Marie Louise in 1811. In 1853 it was reset by Lemonnier as a stomacher for Empress Eugénie and sold at the 1887 auction under the buyer's name 'Rossel'. According to G. F. Kunz in *The Book of the Pearl*, Fabergé bought the pearl for the Youssoupovs, and a surviving photograph confirms their ownership of it.

18. According to Lord Twining in his *History of the Crown Jewels of Europe*, the Azra pearl was part of the Russian crown jewels until 1783. Following the Russian Revolution, it was acquired by Lydia Lady Deterding, presumably through Cartier's mediation. Cartier's dismantled the original pearl necklace of 110 pearls, of which the 'Azra' had been the centrepiece, resetting it as a diamond band. Lady Deterding lost the Azra pearl in Paris. The remainder of the necklace, together with an exceptional black button pearl and a triangular diamond, formed part of the Deterding Auction held by Christie's in Geneva in November 1980 (lot 648).

19. The necklace consisted of 30 black pearls weighing 937.84 grains, the largest being 73.28 grains. Catherine the Great had three children by her liaison with Prince Potemkin, the Demoiselles d'Engelgardt, one of whom married a Prince Youssoupov, and another Count Branicki. The necklace, having been handed down to Count Branicki, subsequently passed into the hands of Princess Radziwill, formerly Countess Bichette Branicka, who bequeathed it to Felix Youssoupov's mother.

20. Black pearls are found on the islands of Touamotu, Gambier, Fiji and the Marquesas Islands, as well as off the coast of Panama and Mexico. Certain mineral salts present in sea-water, together with the type of plankton on which the oyster feeds, apparently combine to produce the black coloration of the pearls.

Among the most famous of black pearls were a necklace made up of 30 pearls weighing 1,040 grains in the Austrian crown jewels; a necklace with 7 additional drop pearls belonging to Princess Mathilde and sold in her auction in 1904 (lots 16–22); the necklace of Annie Viscountess Cowdray made up of 43 pearls weighing 882 grains, together with a spherical pearl weighing 105.6 grains. The German royal house of Anhalt-Dessau owned some of Europe's finest black pearls. Equally famous were the black pearls of Empress Eugénie, who kept them to the end of her life, when they passed into the hands of Princess Clothilde, the daughter of Prince Napoléon Victor.

Nina Dyer, wife of Baron Heinrich Thyssen and later of Prince Sadruddin Aga Khan, owned a 3-strand black pearl necklace made up of 49 pearls weighing 787.44 grains, 49 at 644.72 grains and 53 at 979.52 grains. It was auctioned by Christie's in Geneva in May 1969, together with the black pearl earclips which she had received from Cartier's (lots 101 and 102).

21. See Alex Ceslas Rzewuski, *A travers l'invisible cristal*, Paris 1976, p. 189.

22. 'La Pelegrina' was the name given to a perfectly spherical pearl of silvery lustre weighing 111½ grains. In 1818 the vice-president of the Imperial Russian Academy of Medicine, G. Fischer de Waldheim, described it as being in the possession of the Zosima Brothers, Greek antique-dealers in Moscow. It was presumably the same pearl as the 27½-ct 'Reine des Perles' which had been stolen from the Garde Meubles in 1792. In turn the pearl was stolen from the Zosima Brothers, although it

may have reappeared briefly in a Moscow convent shortly before 1840. It is now missing, presumed lost.

The Youssoupov pearl, on the other hand, is slightly oval in shape and weighs 133.20 grains. The family is said to have acquired it in 1826. There is no truth in Felix Youssoupov's claim that the pearl in question is 'La Peregrina' and not 'La Pelegrina'. The former was handed down through the Spanish royal family from the time of Philip II, until taken out of the country by Joseph Bonaparte in 1813. Hortense de Beauharnais gave it to her son, who was later to become Napoléon III, and he sold it to the Marquis of Abercorn. In 1969 it was sold at auction at Parke-Bernet Galleries, New York, to Elizabeth Taylor. The catalogue weight of 203.84 grains coincides exactly with that given by Lord Twining in his *History of the Crown Jewels of Europe*. Twining also puts forward the view that 'La Pelegrina' rather than 'La Peregrina' was the sister pearl of the one belonging to Karl II, which was last heard of in 1734. It would have been this pearl which Philip IV of Spain gave to his daughter Maria Theresa on the occasion of her marriage to Louis XIV, and which was later bought by Tatiana Youssoupov. Since 'La Pelegrina' and 'La Peregrina' have frequently been confused in the course of history (even the son of the Marquis of Abercorn erroneously speaks of 'La Pelegrina'), the riddle will probably never be solved. However, since the name 'La Pelegrina' demonstrably refers to a spherical pearl in the piece by Fischer de Waldheim, it can only have been at a much later date that the same name was applied to the Youssoupovs' oval pearl. According to G. F. Kunz's *Book of Pearls* (1908), Mr Henry Hiller of New York made enquiries about 'La Pelegrina' in St Petersburg and was shown two magnificent drop-shaped pearls.
23. See Paul Claudel, *La Perle*, Paris 1965, p. 352. Claudel's son Pierre, who was a diplomat, married Pierre Cartier's daughter Marion.
24. John William Mackay was born in Dublin in 1831 and emigrated to America in 1840, where he became one of the four silver barons of Comstock Lode in Nevada, the richest ore deposit ever discovered (1859). In 1883 he founded the Commercial Cable Company in order to break Gould's monopoly both in that area and in telegraphy. The wife of his son Clarence, Katherine Alexander Duer, was, together with Mrs Rita Lydig, one of the wealthiest of Cartier's patrons in New York.
25. Having divorced Misia in 1927, José-Maria Sert married Roussy Mdivani, Alex Mdivani's sister. 'He adores parties, the spectacle of life, but never entertains formally by way of reciprocity. Instead he sends to his hostess some exquisite bibelot chosen at Cartier's', *The Boulevardier* said of him in 1932.
26. See Philip Van Rensselaer, *The Million Dollar Baby*, London 1979, p. 177. In 1935 Cartier valued the pearl necklace at $500,400.
27. Following the First World War, the Austrian dealer Jacques Bienenfeld established himself in the rue Lafayette in Paris, at the same time opening branches in Bahrain, New York and London. His Paris office employed a staff of eighty. Bienenfeld invented a machine for drilling pearls and from 1924 to 1932 edited the journal *La Perle*.
28. Pearls had been revered in India for many thousands of years as holy beings associated with the gods of the Hindu pantheon, and as such are mentioned in the epic poems of the *Ramayana* and *Mahabharata*. According to the *Atharva-Veda* IV, 10, the pearl is the offspring of the moon. 'There is not a single Indian who does not regard it as his sacred duty to drill at least one pearl on his wedding day,' wrote Caire and Dufie in *La Science des pierres précieuses* in 1833.
29. 1 grain = ¼ carat. In order to calculate the price of a pearl on the basis of its weight, the grain weight is multiplied by itself. The resultant figure is then multiplied by a factor of x according to the beauty of the individual pearl. For example, a pearl weighing 5 grains at a value of 3 × : 5 × 5 = 25 × 3 = 75. G. F. Kunz traces this formula back to Anselmus de Both's *Gemmarum et Lapidum Historia* of 1609, though he suspects it to have been Oriental in origin.

Just as the seeds of the carob tree (*Ceratonia siliqua*) determined the carat as a unit of weight, so the reddish-black seeds of the *Abrus precatorius* fixed the Indian *rati* as a measurement for pearls. The Indian *rati* = ⅞ carats = 3½ grains. The pearls were weighed in *rati*, which was then converted into *chows*: 60 *chows* = 36 grains. To make the situation even more complicated, a Bahrain *chow* equalled 4 Basra *chows*, which were the same as 5 Poonah *chows*, the only measurement valid in Bombay. In contrast to natural pearls, cultured pearls are weighed in carats.

Prices were calculated in Indian rupees (70,000 rupees = 116,000 francs). In the course of the voyage, a great deal was heard about one particular pearl, an exceptional specimen weighing 10 grains and selling at 1,200 rupees per *chow*. Because of its rarity, it fetched ninety times its weight.
30. For an eighteenth-century *bayadère* see G. F. Kunz's *History of Pearls*, illustration facing p. 346. *Bayadères* are mentioned in Cartier's records from 1891 onward.
31. A possible model may have been the strands of pearls found in Byzantine-inspired Russian costumes, where they hang down from a hair ornament or headdress and frame the wearer's chin. See G. F. Kunz, *The History of Pearls*, illustration facing p. 174. In addition, Oscar Massin produced head jewelry with feathers and pendant chains 'en esclavage' during the second half of the nineteenth century.
32. An early form of the modern cultured pearl was produced in China in the thirteenth century, and the same process was again attempted by the Swedish naturalist Carolus Linnaeus (1707–78) but abandoned as being unprofitable.

The method which is used today was invented by the Japanese researchers Tatsuhei Mise and Nishikawa, who created their first cultured pearls independently of each other in 1904. The much more famous Kokichi Mikimoto (1858–1954) acquired his patent for cultured pearls in 1916, having previously dealt in natural pearls. His technique was the same as had been used in China, but it is no longer employed today. However, Mikimoto played a more important part in the commercialization and spread of cultured pearls than any of his other competitors.

9. Charles Jacqueau

1. Emile Sedeyn, *La Bijouterie, la joaillerie, la bijouterie de fantaisie au XXème siècle*, Paris 1934.
2. At the same time Alfred Cartier took on Suzanne Ricaud as a pearl-threader. During 1914/15 she worked for a time as Louis Cartier's secretary, but then left the firm. She was one of the most sought-after pearl specialists in Paris, joining the firm of LaCloche in 1921. She married Charles Jacqueau in 1942.
3. The earliest contact with the Ballets Russes may well have come about through the mediation of Louis Cartier, who knew Diaghilev and thought highly of Leon Bakst, the company's leading set and costume designer. It was Bakst, more than anyone else, who was responsible for a style which is still generally thought of as typical of the Ballets Russes. Cartier's chief contact, however, was with the designer George Barbier who was both a chronicler and a spectator of the Ballets Russes in Paris.
4. In 1909 Nijinsky wore a choker in *Le Pavillon d'Armide* and, according to his wife Romola, 'Nijinsky laid aside the choker, which Benois had designed for him: he failed to notice that in doing so he had launched a new fashion. At first the jewel-studded ribbon was worn low around the neckline of his costume, but he did not like it that way and so he wrapped the jewel more tightly round his neck. Cartier quickly took note of this novel idea, and socially ladies in Paris and London were soon wearing close-fitting "dog collars" of black moiré silk, diamonds and pearls *à l'Armide*.' 'Nijinsky developed a genuine passion for sapphires, and each time they were in Paris, Sergei Pavlovitch [Diaghilev] bought him a sapphire ring from Cartier's. Vaslav claimed that he owned the finest sapphires, and he soon came to be known as the "King of Sapphires".' See Romolo Nijinsky, *Nijinsky*, London 1970, pp. 73, 151.
5. According to Harold Acton, '[…] for many a young artist "Schéhérazade" was an inspiration equivalent to Gothic architecture for the Romantics or Quattrocento frescoes for the Pre-Raphaelites.'
6. Fokine's relationship with Diaghilev was similar to that of Jacqueau with Louis Cartier. In both cases there was a lively exchange of creative ideas, Diaghilev and Cartier both playing the more active of the two roles.
7. The greatest influence here, for Fokine and for Poiret, came from the Persian miniatures in Victor de Goloubev's collection. In 1911 the painter Valentine Serov designed the stage curtain for *Schéhérazade* to look like a Persian miniature.
Louis Cartier owned a valuable collection of Persian miniatures which were exhibited in London in 1931, and in 1933 at the Exhibition of Islamic Art at the Metropolitan Museum in New York.
8. Writing in 1930 in his autobiography *En habillant l'époque*, the fashion designer Paul Poiret, like Louis Cartier, asserted the prior claims of his own unrefracted colours above those of the Ballets Russes. The influence of the Ballets Russes did not, in any case, date merely from 1909/10. The Russian artists Valentine Serov and Mikhail Vrubel had been awarded gold medals at the 1900 World Fair, where their Oriental use of colour had caught the imagination of all who saw their work. In 1906 Diaghilev organized an exhibition of Russian art at the Grand Palais which came as a revelation to many people; and his 1908 production of *Boris Godunov* caused a sensation, thanks to the designs of Alexander Golovine and Alexandre Benois.
9. *Calibré*-cut gemstones had existed in the eighteenth and nineteenth centuries (see, for example, Cartier's Egyptian watch of 1873), but they became the height of fashion in Paris around 1902. Lapidaries who specialized in this technique were Dubois and Gouspeyre. Picq's workshop used *calibré*-cut gemstones from 1899 in many of the smaller items of jewelry, such as tie pins, which they produced for Cartier.
10. In the 1870s Boucheron made a green and blue iridescent enamel bracelet which he called 'Peacock's Fan'.
11. See Peter Hinks, *Nineteenth-Century Jewellery*, London 1975, illustration facing p. 81.

10. Pharaohs, sphinxes and pyramids

1. Howard Carter (1873–1939), the British Egyptologist. In 1899 he was appointed General Inspector of Egyptian Antiquities by the Egyptian administration. From 1902 he supervised the excavations in the Valley of the Kings by Theodore M. Davis and afterwards worked for Lord Carnarvon.
2. The family of George Edward Stanhope Molyneux, 5th Earl of Carnarvon, effected small purchases through Cartier from 1898, at first only at the boulevard des Italiens, among them a round brooch, a trinket pendant, a pink enamelled cane handle, a cigarette box and a large stomacher.
3. Isis, consort of the god Osiris, whom she restored to life after his death. In pictorial representations she appears as a woman with a throne on her head. Her cult spread to Greece and Rome after Egypt came under Roman domination.
4. Jean-François Champollion (1790–1832), a

French Egyptologist, appointed to a professorial chair as early as 1809 in Grenoble. In 1824 he became director of the Egyptian Museum in the Louvre. In 1828 he made an expedition to Egypt and in 1831 was appointed to the Chair of Egyptology in the 'Collège de France'.

5. The scarab is a kind of dung beetle. The comparison of the sun with it was based on the observation of the little ball of dung which the scarab pushed along the ground. It was posited, analogically, that a similar force moved the sun across the sky, day after day.

6. The Egyptian lotus, a white waterlily (*Nymphaea lotus*), was a symbol of both fertility and the sun. In the latter aspect, it was sacred to Horus, Lord of the Heavens, and to Nefertum, God of the Morning Sun, who arose each morning from a lotus blossom.

7. A similar necklace, consisting of seven strings of flat, disc-shaped beads of blue faïence and gold, was later to be found in Tutankhamun's tomb.

8. Auguste Mariette (1821–81), French Egyptologist. In 1850 he discovered the ruins of the Serapeum at Memphis (today in the Louvre), in the course of an expedition supported by the French government; as a result, he was called to Cairo by Ismail Pasha to be curator for ancient sites. Later he was to excavate the temples at Dendara and Edfu and inspire the foundation of the Bulaq Museum in Cairo.

9. Gaston Maspero (1846–1916), French archaeologist who was appointed as General Director of Excavations and Antiquities in Egypt after Mariette's death in 1881. He continued Mariette's excavations at the Pyramid of Saqqara. He published numerous basic works in Egyptology, among them *Egyptian Archaeology* (1887).

10. Ancient gems were being reset as early as the twelfth and thirteenth centuries, often to reinterpret their theme when it no longer dealt with actual religious representation. Later, a thirteenth-century Hohenstauffen eagle cameo was given a new context in a Viennese onyx and gold casket of about 1720 (Residenz Museum, Munich). Some time before 1722 Melchior Dinglinger mounted a Roman cameo of the Emperor Claudius on a baroque pedestal (Green Vault, Dresden) for the Saxon court. More daring still, in the manner of Louis Cartier's syntheses, a Mexican-Olmec mask of green pyroxenite and onyx was enlarged to a half-length figure with robe and diadem in German baroque style and set in a bronze niche (Residenz Museum, Munich).

11. In a special Tutankhamun number of 26 January 1924, *The London Illustrated News* put together a series of 'archaeological' jewelry pieces from Cartier's London.

12. Sekhmet had a double role as the tutelary divinity of warriors and the protectress of temples.

13. As the protector of wild animals, Ched rode on a crocodile and held snakes in his hand.

14. In 1917 Hollywood produced the film *Cleopatra*; in 1923 *The Ten Commandments* with décor by Paul Iribe, in which twenty-four sphinxes adorned the city of Ramses II.

15. Black and white colour contrasts are found only rarely in Egyptian jewelry, mostly in silver contexts. Queen Nefert-ari, *c.* 1280 BC, owned two silver bracelets with black inlays.

16. See the apron of Senebtisi, Metropolitan Museum, New York, Reg. No. 08.200.29, Ill. no. 9 in Cyril Aldred, *Jewels of the Pharaohs*, London 1971.

11. Les Indes galantes

1. It is interesting that though Lady Curzon ordered her state trousseau from Worth of Paris, she had it embroidered in India according to local patterns, which were not without their influence on design before the First World War.

2. Further points of contact, still not fully explained, can be traced as early as the sixteenth century. Besides stylistic traits that point to Flan-

ders and even Italy, the late-sixteenth-century 'Canning Jewel' reveals Indian details such as a lotus engraved ruby and an Indian pendant motif (Victoria and Albert Museum, London).

It is equally unclear whether the Indian aigrette (*sarpech*) was influenced by gifts from Europe (*see* Chapter 4).

3. In 1852 the Koh-i-Noor was reduced from 186.06 cts to 106$\frac{1}{16}$ cts in a rose cut by the Dutchman Voorsanger. Queen Victoria wore it in a brooch, in a bracelet or in a hair circlet. Queen Alexandra wore it in her crown. In 1911 it adorned the crown of Queen Mary and it is now in the crown made for Queen Elizabeth the Queen Mother for her coronation in 1937.

4. Boucheron displayed pierced diamonds, the work of the cutter Bordinckx, at the 1867 Exhibition. In 1880 he created a ring from a block-shaped diamond, and in 1889 he (and Legrand) produced diamond rondelles. Boucheron showed diamonds engraved with flowers at the 1900 Exhibition.

5. *Champlevé*, literally 'raised field'. An enamelling technique in which the design was engraved in lines or cells in the metal base (copper) then filled with powdered enamel of various colours and fired to fuse the enamel. In Europe the technique flourished principally during the twelfth and thirteenth centuries. Later, enamel 'à basse taille' was used in India; in this the engraved motif was covered with transparent enamel of various colours.

6. The mango tree was revered in India and its fruit known as the king of fruits.

The palm-frond motif on the Persian *mir* and *serabend* carpets is called *mir-i-bota*. Even today, the mango or Kashmir motif is known in Bengal as *kalka* or *kolka*, which probably derives from the Turkish *kalga* (leaf). *See La Mode des chales cachemire en France*, exhibition catalogue, Palais Galliera, Paris 1982. *See also* Emma Pressmar, *Indian Rings*, 1982.

7. Jade was used under the Persian Timurids, ancestors of the Mogul rulers of India; a great jade monolith, for example, adorns the tomb of Timur (d. 1405) in Samarkand. Today it is assumed that jade-working in eighteenth-century India was done by Chinese craftsmen. The jadeite used in India came from north Burma.

8. Egyptian emerald mines were systematically worked from 330 BC to 1237 AD. Forgotten after 1740, they were rediscovered in 1816 by the French researcher Cailliaud. In 1899 Edwin Streeter, author of *The Great Diamonds of the World*, attempted a renewed exploitation of the mines, but without any great success. Egyptian emeralds were small and of low quality.

9. Colombian emeralds first became known in the West when Hernando Cortez, who had received magnificent emeralds from Montezuma in Mexico and in Tenochtitlan since 1519, returned to Spain with cut stones. In 1537 Jimenez de Quesada conquered New Granada (Colombia) and so discovered Chivor. The mines of Muzo were first discovered in 1567 and rediscovered in 1895. In 1925 the mines of Chivor were reopened. Chivor emeralds, with their characteristic pyrite inclusions, are basically yellower than the Muzo stones.

10. Jean Baptiste Tavernier (1605–89), the French jeweler and stone dealer who undertook six Indian journeys from 1638 to 1668. He returned with important stones, among them one later to be cut to 45.52 cts, the Hope diamond. Cardinal Mazarin and Louis XIV were among his customers. In 1676 his famous travel journal, *Les six voyages de Jean-Baptiste Tavernier*, appeared. By the time he died, this had been translated many times. A further English translation of 1889 contributed to a deepening interest in India and her precious stones.

11. Emerald is a beryllium-aluminium-silicate, deriving its green colour from traces of chromium oxide. It belongs to the beryl group, together with

aquamarine, Morganite (pink beryl), heliodor (golden beryl), etc. In ancient times emerald and beryl were regarded as two distinct minerals. Pliny the Elder distinguished twelve subspecies of 'emerald' which were distinct from 'beryllus'.

12. Indian manufacture of beads dates back to the fourth millennium BC; turquoise, lapis lazuli and cornelian were the stones most commonly used. In Roman times the city of Ujjain was the principal exporting centre. India was also known for the production of glass beads, the industry being centred on Arikamedu (Pondicherry). *See* Peter Francis, 'When India was Beadmaker to the World', *Ornament*, Vol. 6, No. 2 (1982).

13. The De Beers diamond was found as a stone of 428 cts in South Africa in 1888. It was exhibited in Paris in 1889; afterwards it probably went directly into the possession of Patiala. The stone, a light yellow colour, follows the 245.35-ct 'Jubilee' as the world's fifth largest cut diamond.

14. Jeanne Toussaint loved to wear bunches of pearls or gemstones, hanging in glittering cascades of colour from brooches or pendants. The idea derived from the Indian *turah* and found an echo in Cartier's supple gold-bead jewelry of the postwar years, which also took up the motif of the butter beads of Krishna. These last symbolized the essentials of life and are specially featured on rings with four pierced beads and a pale Ceylon ruby.

Both Indian and surrealistic sources were combined in the popular 1938 brooch of a black lacquered hand holding a coral flower, which recalled the gesture of the flower-holding emperors in the finest Mogul miniatures of the seventeenth century. Toussaint and Louis Cartier both collected such miniatures.

12. '1925'

1. Technical innovation in the 1920s was represented by the new baguette cut known for a time as the 'diamant bâton'. A contrast to the fashionable triangles and rhombs, this cut, which involved a comparatively large wastage, first appeared about 1909. As late as 1912/13 the early baguettes still had rounded corners and had to be firmly integrated into the geometry of the jewel.

2. During the second half of the nineteenth century artists and designers had been stimulated by impressions from the French North African colonies. Chassériau, Delacroix and the so-called Orientalists had depicted the desert, the eastern market and other scenes. Charles-Edmond Duponchel (1795–1868), among others, produced Arab-style jewelry. The Moorish bathroom of the Païva on the Champs-Elysées and also the Arabic hall in the London house of Frederick Leighton (1830–96), the painter, inspired by the La Zisa palace in Palermo, are further instances of Moorish influence.

3. In the 1925 Exposition the motif of the fountain was to acquire almost the importance of a leitmotif. It featured in plaster at the main entrance, in wrought iron, and in Lalique's glass waterfall in the Perfumerie Section. Mauboussin's fountain tiara, which permitted an exemplary use of baguette diamonds, was well known.

4. Misia Godebska (1872–1950), who appears in different chapters, married Thadée Nathanson in 1893. Between 1905 and 1909 she was married to Alfred Edwards and from 1920 to 1927 to José-Maria Sert. Since in the Cartier context she features most interestingly as Mme Sert, this fourth name is retained throughout for simplicity. The case is similar with Elsie de Wolfe who is referred to by her maiden name though she became Lady Mendl when she married Sir Charles Mendl in 1926.

5. Iribe collaborated on *Le Témoin* and also on *Schéhérazade*, the review founded in 1909 by François Bernouard and Cocteau. On one of the title pages he set a sultana wearing an aigrette within the décor of the Diaghilev ballet of the same name. *See*, for Iribe, the outstanding work *Paul Iribe* (1982) by

Raymond Bachollet, Daniel Bordet and Anne Claude Lelieur.

6. See *Les Robes de Paul Poiret racontés par Paul Iribe* (1908). In 1911 *Les Choses de Paul Poiret vues par George Lepape* appeared, which Iribe answered with *L'Eventail et la fourrure chez Paquin*, with drawings by Barbier and Lepape.

7. As early as 1909 Iribe had designed advertising for the jeweler 'Maxima', for 'Novelty' pearls and also for the pearl specialist Juclier.

8. Iribe married the actress Jeanne Dirys, who in 1911 appeared in *Comoedia Illustré* wearing a hat by Chanel. All the jewelry was by Iribe, among it the emerald aigrette.

9. See *Vogue*, September 1925.

10. In 1910 *Le Témoin* devoted a special issue to the Ballets Russes in which Iribe illustrated *Schéhérazade*. It was followed by a number featuring Vaslav Nijinsky, with graphics by Iribe and verses by Cocteau. In 1914 Iribe published the album on *L'Après-midi d'un faune* compiled by Baron de Meyer.

11. In 1912 Louis Süe, the interior decorator, had opened L'Atelier Français. After the war, with André Mare, he renamed it 'Belle France' and from it, in 1919, arose the Compagnie des Arts Français, in the Faubourg Saint-Honoré. Flower garlands and baskets of fruit achieved almost the status of leitmotifs in its products. In 1912, one year before his American tour, Poiret opened his École Martine, followed by Atelier Martine where, for a time, Dufy was a collaborator.

Paul Follot (1877–1941) enjoyed importance in a similar connection. Coming from Meier-Graefe's Maison Moderne he had already been designing jewelry in new forms between 1910 and 1914. From 1923 he headed the Pomone workshops in the department store Au Bon Marché, designing as its symbol a fruit-laden tree. His furnishings designed in 1913 for Germain Lubin employed the cornucopia as motif. In 1928, together with Serge Chermayev, Follot was appointed to head a department for the decorative arts with Waring and Gillow of London. They popularized in England such motifs as the bowl of fruit, cornucopia and garland. In 1928 René Prou, the representative of rational modernism, took over from Follot at Au Bon Marché in Paris.

12. Apart from Lubin, Iribe also worked for Jeanne Lanvin. He designed the firm's golden trademark of Jeanne Lanvin with child for the 1927 'Arpège' scent bottle (the bottle itself was by Rateau).

13. Lucien Vogel, whose importance is still not properly recognized, was the publisher of *Femina* in 1906 and later of *L'Illustration des modes* which became *Le Jardin des modes*. From 1912 to 1925 he published *La Gazette du bon ton* and from 1928 *VU*, a weekly photo-magazine from which *Life* developed in 1936.

14. George Barbier published the albums *Nijinsky* (1913) and *Karsavina* (1914) with poems by Vaudoyer and also *Modes et manières* (1914). He created the décor for *Casanova* (1919), for *Lysistrata* by Maurice Donnay, *La dernière nuit de Don Juan* by Rostand and *Manon* by Henri Bataille. Barbier's depictions of Harlequin recall Nijinksy in *Le Carneval*, in which he first appeared in 1910 with Karsavina and which influenced many *Vogue* title pages, among them the crinoline ladies by Helen Dryden (American *Vogue*).

15. He is described in Jean-Louis Vaudoyer's *Georges Barbier* (1929) as *un peintre vraiment grec*.

16. The watercolour comes from the 1913 *Nijinsky* album and is now in a private collection in London. *See La Renaissance de l'art français et des industries de luxe*, 1918, no. 5, p. 162.

17. For Iribe's tiara *see Art et décoration* (1908), footnote 4, p. 105 mentions Iribe; and *Femina*, July 1912.

18. In 1864 the Union Centrale des Beaux-Arts Appliqués à l'Industrie was founded, under English influence. It was to organize, with others, the exhibitions in Paris (1867), London (1871 and 1874), Vienna (1873) and Philadelphia (1876). In 1882 the

Union merged with another association which in 1877 had independently founded the Musée des Arts Décoratifs on the model of the South Kensington (now Victoria and Albert) Museum in London. Renamed the Union Centrale des Arts Décoratifs, it was to mount its exhibitions in the Palais de l'Industrie. In 1890 the Société d'Encouragement à l'Art et à l'Industrie was founded. The review *Art et décoration* was launched in 1896 and *L'Art décoratif* which continued to appear up to 1914, two years later. The Société des Artistes Décorateurs was founded by Grasset, Guimard, Follot and others in 1901 following the success of the international exhibition of the previous year. The important exhibitions held at the Musée Galliera included the following: book binding (1902) and *La Parure précieuse de la femme* (1908). *See 'La Bijouterie, la joaillerie, la bijouterie de fantaisie au XXème siècle'*, Paris 1934.

19. See *L'Exposition internationale des arts décoratifs et industriels modernes* (Imprimerie Nationale, 1923): 'Admitted to the exhibition are works of new inspiration and genuine originality, by artists, craftsmen, industrial and fashion designers and publishers, as long as they are in tune with the decorative and industrial arts of today.'

20. See *L'Exposition internationale des arts décoratifs et industriels modernes* (1923).

21. The Committee for the 'Parure' group comprised M. Dausset as president, Fouquet-Lapar as president of the chamber of trade, Georges Fouquet as additional president, Louis Aucoc, Louis Boucheron and Louis Cartier as vice presidents (which explains why Cartier's could exhibit without competition). The committee members were Paul Brandt, Hughes Citroën, Dusausoy, Linzeler, Raymond Templier, and Van Cleef. The jury included, among others, Georges Fouquet and the writer J. L. Vaudoyer (*see* note 15).

22. *See op. cit.*, note 20.

23. *See La Renaissance de l'art français* for 1925: the magazine referred to the participants as 'four incomparable couturiers, the leading jeweler in Paris and doubtless in the whole world, a great ironworker and a fine leather worker'.

24. Jeanne Lanvin became one of Cartier's customers about 1922 when she ordered a necklace in pearls, diamonds and crystal rondelles.

25. The Cartier exhibit cost Fr178,000. Cartier's participation amounted to Fr125,000. After the exhibition, Rateau made a buy-back proposal to Louis Cartier.

26. *See Paul Léon, L'Exposition des arts décoratifs et industriels modernes — rapport général* (1927).

27. *See François Carnot, 'Rapport de l'exposition internationale'* (1921).

28. The great couturiers regularly bought from Cartier's, both on their own account and for their customers. Callot featured in the sales records from 1908; others included Chanel, Doucet, Doeuillet and Mme Paquin.

29. The shoulder ornament, composed of pearls, diamonds, emeralds and onyx, was adorned with three engraved emeralds of 153, 88 and 141 cts. It yielded three brooches, one of which was bought by the Glaoui from Morocco.

30. Only fifteen watches and table clocks of little interest were exhibited. Both 'mystery clocks' and the richly decorated boxes in the Chinese and Egyptian styles were absent.

31. *See Eugène Fontenay, Les Bijoux anciens et modernes*, 1887, p. 120.

32. The Empress Eugénie's link necklace featured in the auction of 1887 as No. 28. For an example of a Renaissance necklace of the same type, *see* Yvonne Hackenbroch *Renaissance Jewellery*, London 1979, p. 222.

33. *See op. cit.*, note 23.

34. *See Eugène Fontenay, op. cit.*, pp. 338, 339.

35. *See* museum in Saint Germain-en-Laye, I-17, 716.

36. Important Scottish fibulas were found, for

example, in 1854. Between 1840 and 1860 a revival of Celtic forms was observable, also in the later productions of the English firm of Liberty's.

37. *See Eugène Fontenay, op. cit.*, p. 439.

38. *Le Métal* (no date), published by Ed. Longuet, had four volumes: I: *Le Fer*; II and III: *Le Bronze, le cuivre, l'étain et le plomb*; IV: *Les Métaux précieux*.

13. Vanity Fair

1. *See Le Pavillon de l'Élégance, numéro spécial de la Gazette du Bon Ton*, no. 10, 1925.

2. Abbreviation for 'vanity case'. The expression is to be found, for instance, in Paul Léon, *L'Exposition des arts décoratifs et industriel modernes — rapport général* (1927).

3. *See Vanda Forster, Bags and Purses*, London 1982.

4. *Boite-à-mouches*, English 'patch boxes', held the patches of black taffeta which were gummed to the face as artificial beauty spots.

5. A letter of 1749 by Mrs Montagu.

6. Sir William Chambers published his *Designs of Chinese Buildings* in 1757 and his *Dissertation on Oriental Gardening* in 1772.

7. The dealer Jean Dupuis began his voyages of discovery up the Red River in 1860, the year in which French and British troops stormed the Summer Palace near Peking. The French expedition to Indo-China under Doudart de Lagrée and Francis Garnier took place in 1868; in 1883 France asserted a protectorate over Annam and Tonkin; in 1886 Tonkin became a French colony. Siam (now Thailand) became a French protectorate in 1867. In 1876, Korea opened her ports to European trade.

8. The London International Exhibition of 1862 included a display of Japanese bronzes, lacquers and porcelain and the Paris exhibition of five years later showed French faïence following Japanese patterns (the 'Rousseau service'). At the Paris exhibition of 1878, the dealer Bing showed his Japanese bronzes and lacquerwork, while the ethnographical exhibition in the Trocadéro presented the Far-Eastern finds of Guimet and Régamey. (The Musée Guimet was opened in Lyon in 1878, but moved to Paris the following year.) The Japanese Exhibition followed in 1883, with loan exhibits from Bing, Camondo and Sarah Bernhardt. Whistler had already stumbled on woodcuts by Hokusai in Paris in 1856 and by 1880 the department store Au Bon Marché was selling albums of Japanese woodcuts. The London firm of Liberty's founded in 1875 introduced such artists as Morris, Ruskin and Rossetti to Japanese wares while the architect Godwin designed houses for himself and Whistler in the Japanese style.

The Milanese politician Henri Cernuschi who, like Emile Guimet, travelled to Japan in 1871, bequeathed his collection to the city of Paris in 1896. Two years before, the Louvre had received the great Grandidier Collection (now in the Musée Guimet).

9. Edmond Goncourt published *Outamaro* in 1891, *L'Art japonais* in 1893 and *Hokusai* in 1896.

10. Jade jewelry became popular in the wake of the rising fashion for things Chinese. In the 1920s Cartier's jade jewelry for Mrs Wellington Koo, wife of the former Chinese ambassador to London, became renowned.

11. The word 'lacquer' derives from the Portuguese *lacca*; in the eighteenth century it was called 'shellack'. The terms refer to the sap of the lacquer tree, the most important species of which, *Rhus verniciflua*, is found throughout China south of the Yellow River. *See Sir Harry Garner, Chinese Lacquer*. London 1979.

12. Far-Eastern lacquer, mostly Japanese, had proved a stimulus to a number of eighteenth-century box designers — Adrien-Jean-Maximilien Vachette, Pierre-François Drais and the German Heinrici, to name but a few.

13. According to Sir Harry Garner the term *laque burgauté* (from 'burgau' for mother-of-pearl mussel)

should be avoided; it was first used in 1862 for porcelain with mother-of-pearl lacquer.

14. C. T. Loo (1880–1957), the greatest dealer in Chinese art of his time. Some time after 1902 he opened a business in the Place de la Madeleine and ran branches in Shanghai and Peking. In 1926 he built the Chinese pagoda on the rue de Courcelles as his business premises.

15. He Xiangu was one of the Eight Immortals. His emblem is a lotus stalk, often surmounted by a peach.

16. *See* James Gardner, *Elephants in the Attic*. London 1983.

17. Mother-of-pearl, widespread in the cheaper synthetics of nacrit and nacrolack, was part of an industry which included ivory, horn, etc. and their derivatives, such as xylonite. Further synthetics were galalith, celluloid and Bakelite, invented in 1917. Cartier used ebonite, a black vulcanized rubber, in his fine cigarette boxes.

18. Lucien Gaillard was employing Chinese craftsmen as early as 1900, and they were to introduce their French colleagues to the art of lacquering. However, the Chinese left France before they had established their own school.

19. Jean Dunand (1877–1942), creator of the examples mentioned, had been initiated into the technique of lacquer by the Japanese Sugawara; he himself made lacquer with forty layers. At the same time he supplied Madeleine Vionnet and Mme Agnès with belt-buckles and handbags, which were shown at the 1925 Exposition. During the artist's lifetime, Cartier's assembled the first show of his work in the United States, on the sales floor of their Fifth Avenue branch.

20. The 1930s saw further contacts between Cartier's and the cosmetic firms: in 1931 two vanity cases were fitted with Patou's new lipstick. In 1935 Cartier patented a new lipstick cartridge that could be opened with one hand and was taken over by Elizabeth Arden for a popular model. There were, too, relations with the firms of Coty and Houbigant, whose lipsticks and powder compacts were built into the vanity cases. In 1948 Louis Devaux granted the firm of Lenthéric a further lipstick licence.

After the Second World War, since the major impetus for the cosmetic industry was flowing from Hollywood (for example Mary Pickford became president of 'Mary Pickford Cosmetics'), Cartier's New York became the principal pioneer in this field.

21. Poiret had already designed a model of the same name in 1905.

22. On the occasion of the exhibition in the Palais Galliera of 1929, as was apparent from the colour choice of materials, the influence of Oriental styles was less dominant than had been the case in 1925. Whereas then the predominant colour combination had been green-black-white (emerald-onyx-diamond), in 1929 diamond alone dominated, above all the baguette cut, and critics spoke of the 'grand silence blanc'.

In 1929 artists like Fouquet and Templier joined the Union des Artistes Modernes, a group devoted to a strict geometrical style. These tendencies were dominant in the Colonial Exhibition held in the Park of Vincennes in 1931: the strongest formal influences were cubist experiments and the art of the African colonies such as negro masks and ivories. The stylistic debt to the Far East had disappeared: 'We have no more to learn from the techniques of either the Orient or the Far East.'

14. Chimaeras, dragons and great cats

1. Rock crystal differed from diamond in that it gave rise to softly modelled transitions. Its glimmering transparency had prompted mystical associations since Ezekiel's vision of 'the likeness of the firmament [which] was as the colour of the terrible crystal' [1:22].

Cartier's first used rock crystal in its new style in 1910 in spear, palm and disc shapes on hatpins. A technical tour de force which the New York company patented was the setting of diamonds in rock crystal. The surface of the crystals was engraved with Oriental arabesques by the Berquin-Varangoz workshop.

2. *See* John Boardman, *Archaic Greek Gems*, London 1964; K. R. Maxwell Hyslop, *Western Asiatic Jewellery c. 3000–612 BC*, London 1971; E. C. de la Ferté, *Les Bijoux Antiques*, Paris 1956.

3. *See* 'An Indian Crocodile', *Bulletin of the Museum of Fine Arts*, XXX, IV, 26.

4. *See* 'Exposition d'une collection unique de perles et de bijoux de décadence antique chez Cartier', 27 May–6 June 1914.

5. Jeanne Toussaint received a number of pieces of panther jewelry over the years, among them a wrist-watch, a pearl fastener and a panther shoulder brooch.

6. In 1954 the Duchess of Windsor received a *face-à-main* with tiger decoration, two years later a tiger bracelet. Bracelets in the form of stretched tiger skins were a Boivin speciality after the Second World War.

7. The Princess Aga Khan's panther collection was auctioned after her death on 1 May 1969 by Christie's Geneva.

15. The great necklaces

1. Other couture houses which produced fashion jewelry were: Jean Patou with imitation necklaces; Madeleine Vionnet with necklaces of green feathers and crystal; Lucien Lelong with wooden bead bracelets; and Coco Chanel, who in 1928 launched a range of diamond paste jewelry designed by Count Etienne de Beaumont.

2. Coco Chanel was an occasional customer at Cartier's from 1919, choosing, among other things, an emerald ring and a brooch with sapphire, ruby and topazes.

3. Among the world's largest cut sapphires are the 423-ct Logan sapphire (Smithsonian Institution, Washington) and a cushion-shaped sapphire of 337 cts, which Harry Winston bought in 1948 from a private collection and presented to an Eastern potentate.

4. The sapphire sautoir passed into the family by inheritance via Queen Helena. The diamond necklace was broken up in Paris and Harry Winston sold the sapphire drop in the 1960s to a Greek collector who presented it to Queen Frederika.

5. Ali, son-in-law of the Prophet, was the ancestral founder of the Ismaili Shi'a Moslems.

6. The stone has recently been reduced to 33.13 cts and designated with colour 'E' and as 'flawless' by the Gemological Institute of America.

7. Subsequently, Cartier's displayed the 107-ct emerald at exhibitions on a long diamond sautoir. In 1947 Raphael Esmerian acquired important emeralds from the Payne Whitney family and with these and two additional stones he created a necklace which he sold to Pierre Cartier; Cartier attached the 107-ct stone as a pendant. In 1954 the emerald was reduced to a drop of 75.63 cts on the advice of Esmerian. The necklace, sold meanwhile to the Rockefellers, reappeared one last time in November 1971 at a Sotheby auction in Zurich.

8. Roussy Sert, who embodied the chic of the 1930s, owned a Cartier bracelet of rock crystal and diamonds, which Barbara Hutton had copied. A similar model belonged to the Rani of Pudukota, and two further models to Gloria Swanson.

9. About 1938 the fashion for classical necklaces with radiating stone motifs on the eighteenth-century model came back into vogue. Mostly they consisted of seven stones increasing in size towards the middle; Barbara Hutton had an especially valuable example of the type which stayed in fashion up to the 1950s.

10. In 1923, Cartier's London lent jewels valued at £400,000 to the actress Alice Delysia for her 'Radiant Diamond Dress' in *Topics*. Her entrance on stage was watched over by four dogs, six policemen and three detectives.

11. In 1927 Cartier's created a necklace of onyx tubes and diamond rondelles and suspended from it three stones from London: a square, canary-coloured diamond of 2.46 cts; an oval, amber-coloured diamond of 2.48 cts; and, below that, the 26.26-ct blue diamond.

12. In 1933 the Maharajah of Nawanagar was succeeded by his nephew Jamsaheb Disvijaysinhi. In 1938 he bought from Cartier's a red diamond of 2.32 cts, a brick-coloured diamond of about 3 cts and a golden diamond of about 3.75 cts.

In India, the 'Queen of Holland' was re-christened the 'Ranjitsinhji'. Today the stone weighs 135.92 cts and in 1978 was designated as 'D' and 'internally flawless' by the Gemological Institute of America. As the world's largest flawless cut diamond, the 'Queen of Holland' is second only to the 'Premier Rose', a drop diamond of 137.02 cts which, in 1978, belonged to the New York diamond dealer William Goldberg and was designated as 'D' and 'flawless' by the Gemological Institute of America.

13. Some of the noteworthy forerunners of the geometric cuts so popular after 1900 included the hexagonal diamond, reportedly of 31.75 cts, in the 1749 'Golden Fleece' – in the then French crown jewels, which later also included the Hope diamond. Also, in 1909, a hexagonal diamond of 16.25 cts featured as lot 4 in the Habib auction in Paris; it could be traced back to Somaviva, a general under the First Empire. In 1933 the stone passed at another auction to Cartier's customer Baronne de Forest.

14. For example, Napoleon III honoured the lapidary Grosfillex for his services in the diamond import trade. Two diamond cutters, Roulina's and Goudart's were already established in Paris at the time of the 1878 exhibition.

15. After the Second World War hexagonal diamonds were recut in the fashionable navette shapes and pentagons into drops.

Edouard Sirakian (b. 1915) entered his father's business in 1930. Around 1960 he invented the 'Troidia' diamond, a triangular conforming to the circular.

16. Today the firm of Esmerian, New York, is headed by the fourth-generation Ralph Esmerian (b. 1940).

16. 'The jeweled flight of time'

1. Vacheron & Constantin were again supplying Cartier's between 1951 and 1972; similarly, between 1959 and 1967, Piaget's were supplying movements.

2. Georges Verger (1884–1945), son of Ferdinand, was a jewelry and clock designer. He designed clocks with movements by Vacheron & Constantin, his father already holding the agency for their productions. Verger worked for Van Cleef & Arpels, Janesich, LaCloche, Ostertag, Marzo, Boucheron, Chaumet and Gübelin, and in the United States for Black Starr & Frost, Cauldwell and Tiffany. Together with Cartier, Verger was the only producer of 'mystery clocks' which he supplied to Van Cleef & Arpels, Ostertag and to the United States. In the 1930s, Cartier ordered the *montre radiateur* from Verger, a lamella-covered clip watch which could be attached, for example, to evening bags. Verger invented the *montre captive*, a covered pocket-watch which could be opened like a little 'altar' on a desk.

3. In 1949 Rodanet, the then president of Jaeger, spoke of the importance of Louis Cartier as 'the inspirer of the revolution in the art of the clock', in a paper entitled 'Les Méthodes de fabrication de l'horlogerie moderne'.

4. In 1719 in Lyon *Recueil d'ouvrages curieux du cabinet de M. Grollier de Servières* by Grollier de Servières was published.

5. *See* Tardy *La Pendule française*, 1961–64, ill., p. 266.

6. *See* Ernst von Bassermann-Jordan, *Montres, pendules et horloges*, 1964, ill., p. 194.

7. From 1930 Coüet was accommodated at 37 rue Réaumur in Cartier's associated studio, the Renault Atelier; here his assistants were also entrusted by Cartier with simple gold work. At this time, during the economic crisis, Coüet still employed approximately twenty craftsmen, including nine *orfèvres-boîtiers*, one enameller and one *guillocheur*. In 1931 more workers had to be dismissed. In 1929 Cartier's had opened their own workshop at 17 rue Bachaumont; at the outbreak of the Second World War it moved to 9 rue d'Argenson, where Robert Linzeler had his studio. Later Coüet too moved into the studio in the rue d'Argenson and finally to the other workshops at 13 rue de la Paix until 1956.

8. In 1938 Cusin patented another invention related to the *pendules mystérieuses*. This was a clock for maritime use in which two dials, without hands, and moving at different speeds, represented the minutes and the hours. In 1946 he invented a clock whose illuminated dial could be projected onto the wall at the press of a button.

9. These so-called fetishes of the late 1930s were little items of bargain jewelry or watches, brought out at Christmas for the most part and eagerly sought out by the international clientele. In 1935 it was the ladybird brooch in coral and onyx, in 1937 the Moor brooch which Louise de Vilmorin was so enthusiastic about, in 1938 the Sioux brooch and in 1939 the domino watch.

10. *See* Alex Ceslas Rzewuski, *A travers l'invisible cristal*, 1971, p. 171.

11. *See La Gazette du bon ton*, no. 10 (1925).

12. Various '*pendules mystérieuses*' were shown by Guilmet, Cadot, Rosset and Henri Robert at the 1878 exhibition. The model by Jean Eugène Robert-Houdin was the most famous of its time and was described in the *Dictionnaire encyclopédique* of 1881. There were examples with both one and two hands; the transmission was carried through two griffins on a crystal pillar. One of these Robert-Houdin clocks is to be found in the Château museum at Blois and another in the Museum of La Chaux-de-Fonds in Switzerland. *See* Catherine Cardinal, *L'Horloge dans l'histoire, l'art et les sciences*, 1983, p. 108.

13. Gold-coin watches were already being exhibited in the nineteenth century; perhaps the earliest model was one from 1809 by the Swiss watchmaker Moulinie. Two coins were required for each watch, for the case and for the cover.

14. The 1907 contract was renewed even before it fell due in 1919. By that time Jaeger had been at the rue du Louvre for two years and associated in a joint stock company with Cartier's. In the new contract the annual value of the purchases by Cartier was raised to Fr1,500,000. But Cartier's also had the exclusive rights to Jaeger's production both in Paris and in Switzerland (the firm of LeCoultre).

15. We find an entry for an octagonal crystal pocket watch in the Cartier archive as early as 1876, however not as yet with the ultra-thin movement of the 1900 model.

16. The European Watch and Clock Company looked after its exports to New York, where Louis Roehrich, with eight assistants, headed the clock department. Even after the company closed, *c.* 1950, most watches and clocks came from Paris. However certain models in 18-ct yellow gold (though not in enamel) were produced in New York. Quite recently Walter Kroehnert (b. 1899), the German watchmaker at Cartier's New York, once again made his mark. A contemporary of Gaston Cusin's, he had, like Cusin, made his first watch at the age of fourteen. In 1936 he joined Cartier's New York where he produced Cusin's prism clock and, as late as 1977, a series of pocket-watches from various precious stones.

17. In 1572 Queen Elizabeth I received an 'armlet or skakell of golde, all over fairely garnishedd with rubyes and dyamonds, haveing in the closing thearof a clocke'.

The *Almanach du Dauphin* for 1772 mentioned a watchmaker on the rue de Buci in Paris, who made ring and bracelet watches. In 1790 the inventory of Jacquet-Droz and Leschot of Geneva mentions 'une montre qui est fixée sur un bracelet'.

In 1806 Empress Josephine presented her daughter-in-law, Princess Auguste Amelie of Bavaria, with two bracelets of gold, pearls and emeralds made by Nitot of Paris – a watch was mounted in one of them.

In the 1867 exhibition the jeweler Rouvenat showed a wrist-watch with its dial concealed beneath an emerald. In 1868 Patek Philippe sold the first Swiss wrist-watch.

In 1880 the German Ministry of Marine ordered watches with metal straps for naval officers in La Chaux-des-Fonds in Switzerland.

18. In later years, Pierre Cartier was greatly interested in aviation. In 1928 he held a reception in the Ritz Towers New York for Dieudonné Coste and Joseph le Brix, who had made the first crossing of the South Atlantic in 1927. In 1930, together with Maurice Bellonte, Dieudonné Coste made the first non-stop flight from Paris to New York (Lindbergh's Atlantic crossing in the opposite direction), in the Bréguet biplane 'Question Mark'. In the following year the two were officially received in twenty-two American cities, whose mayors were later guests at an official reception given by the French President Doumergue in the Elysée Palace, Paris. Afterwards came the presentation by Bellonte at Cartier's of a silver model of 'Question Mark' (made in-house by Albouse and Watte from a wooden model). In 1933 it came to the Rockefeller Center, New York, as a gift from the French government.

19. The Maharajah of Kapurthala was reputed to have owned 250 clocks, the majority made by Cartier's. One of his servants was engaged exclusively in winding them up.

20. A hexagonal emerald with a watch mounted in it was found in the 'Cheapside Hoard', a collection of Elizabethan and Jacobean jewels, now in the Museum of London.

21. Princess Elizabeth received this wrist-watch, still the world's smallest, in a presentation by President Lebrun in the Elysée Palace, on the occasion of her parents' state visit to Paris in 1938. The British royal couple held a reception at the Paris embassy for representatives of the 'Vendôme' Committee, among them Mme Ritz, Mme Charvet, Mme Boucheron and Mme Jacques Cartier.

22. In 1929 Cartier's sold 626 watches and 86 *pendules* in Paris. In 1930, even in the wake of the economic crisis, the figures were 423 and 69 respectively.

17. Swords for Academicians

1. The five Académies that make up the Institut de France have the same regulations as to dress and ceremonial swords. Most of the swords designed by Cartier were for candidates to the Académie Française.

2. Diaghilev died in 1929. In 1931 René Blum and Colonel de Basil founded the Ballet Russe de Monte Carlo, but they separated after three years. Blum and Massine retained the name 'Ballet Russe', but appeared mostly in America. De Basil's group became the Royal Covent Garden Ballet Russe and, later, the Ballet Russe de Colonel W. de Basil. In 1945 Serge Lifar founded the Nouveaux Ballets de Monte Carlo which was taken over, in 1947, by the Marquis de Cuevas.

3. Palladium is the lightest of the six members of the platinum group of metals.

18. The great transactions

1. *See* Evalyn Walsh McLean, *Father Struck It Rich*, London 1936, pp. 155ff.

2. *See* Susanne Steinem Patch, *Blue Mystery: The Story of the Hope Diamond*, Washington 1976.

3. According to the catalogue for the auction of 24 June 1909, the 'Hope' was acquired by Habib in 1908 direct from Frankel. The Habib Auction comprised:
   1) A cushion-shaped, rose-coloured diamond of $\frac{5}{16}$ cts.
   2) A drop-shaped 'blue-white' diamond of 24 cts.
   3) A cushion-shaped 'blue-white' diamond of 23 cts.
   4) A hexagonal diamond of 16.25 cts. The original provenance was traced to Princess Mathilde, but this was later carried back to General Somaviva in the early nineteenth century.
   5) An 'aquamarine-coloured', pale triangular diamond of $70\frac{1}{16}$ cts. This is the diamond known today as the 'Idol's Eye'; present weight 70.20 cts.
   6) A cushion-shaped, rose-coloured diamond of $30\frac{1}{2}$ cts.
   7) The 'Mi-Regent', a drop-shaped diamond of 58 cts.
   8) The Hope diamond.

4. The 'Star of the East' was also worn as an aigrette (see ill., p. 282), just as the 'Hope' could be worn on either a necklace or a bandeau. Subsequently, Cartier's New York created an additional diamond necklace on which both stones were worn alternately.

5. A later payments calculation of 1918 shows that in the end the transaction developed rather differently. The first payment amounted to only $20,000 and in addition to the emerald-diamond necklace a further diamond necklace (*cravate*) was taken into account. Furthermore, the payments were still not complete in 1918.

6. The 'Star of the South' is not to be confused with the 128.80-ct stone of the same name, said to be in a private collection in Bombay. The 15.46-ct 'Star of the South' had been set by Cartier's in a bracelet with sixteen rubies and sixteen diamonds. Later, Harry Winston had it recut to 14.37 cts.

7. Harry Winston sold the 'Star of the East' to King Farouk.

8. The sultan's jewels were auctioned during his lifetime between 27 and 29 November 1911. Catalogue numbers 234, 240 and 294 were from Cartier's.

9. *See* Alex Ceslas Rzewuski, *A travers l'invisible cristal*, 1976, p. 250.

10. This was bought for Fr1.4 million by the stone dealer Jacques Bienenfeld to prevent a further auction of the remaining Lobanov jewels in April.

11. Unfortunately the archives do not record to whom Cartier's sold the earrings. Later Mrs Merryweather Post bequeathed them to the Smithsonian Institution, Washington.

12. The 'Polar Star' was auctioned by Christie's in Geneva on 20 November 1980 as No. 653, together with other jewels belonging to Lydia Lady Deterding.

13. *See* Prince Christophe de Grèce, *Le Monde et ses cours*, 1939, p. 59. The prince was the son of King George I of Greece and married Mrs Nancy Leeds (Princess Anastasia) as his first wife, and Princess Françoise of France, as his second wife.

The crown later came into the possession of Helen M. de Kays and was auctioned by Parke Bernet in 1966. Today it is in the Merryweather Post collection in Hillwood, near Washington.

14. In 1898, when Cartier's business was still in the boulevard des Italiens, he had other pieces of historic silver at his disposal: a tankard and beaker by Thomas Germain once in the possession of King Joseph of Portugal.

15. It is alleged that the 'Star of South Africa' was acquired from a young herdsman on the Zendfontein farm on the Orange River for ten oxen and a horse. It was then cut by Louis Hond who sold it

to the Countess Dudley. From her it went to the family of J. P. Morgan. In 1971 it was sold in Geneva by Christie's.

16. For the Stotesbury wedding the Morgan diamond, 'as big as a robin's egg', was attached to a necklace. Only later did Cartier's mount it in a tiara.

17. In 1928 Cartier's were to be shown a further Mazarin stone of 15.88 cts.

18. Later Harry Winston was to sell the briolette to an Indian Maharanee who wore it in an aigrette. Winston later bought it back and sold it once more in Europe in 1971.

19. The 'Ball of Jewels' (Bal des Pierreries) was held by Princess Jacques de Broglie in her palace on the avenue de Messine. Seven ballets were presented, one under the sign of each of the most valuable precious stones.

20. The Unzue Heart was sold by Van Cleef & Arpels in 1953 and bought back by them in 1960. In 1964 Harry Winston sold it in a ring to Mrs Merryweather Post who bequeathed it to the Smithsonian Institution, Washington. The Unzue Heart had nothing to do with the Empress Eugénie.

21. Eugène de Beauharnais, Duke of Leuchtenberg, son of the Empress Josephine by her first marriage, had eight children. The youngest son, Maximilien-Eugène, married Marie, daughter of Nicholas I, in 1839. Their children called themselves the Princes Romanovski. The Leuchtenberg emeralds were bought in 1920 from the antique dealer Seiler's of Vevey by Bienenfeld.

22. The Diamond Dictionary of the Gemological Institute of America gives the weight of the drop as 69.80 cts.

23. Today the 'Pasha', after a further recutting, weighs 36.22 cts and is in a private European collection.

24. Subsequently, Harry Winston acquired the 'Nassak', recut to 43.38 cts (colour 'D', pure) and sold it to Trabert & Hoeffer-Mauboussin, the New York jewelers. In 1944 Mrs William B. Leeds, daughter-in-law of Mrs Nancy Leeds, bought it. Edward Hand bought the stone at Parke Bernet in 1970 and sold it later to Bulgari's. They then sold it to a private buyer.

25. In 1912 Solly B. Joël, nephew of the diamond mine owner Barnato, had ordered a large diamond corsage from Cartier's; it contained a drop diamond of 34.25 cts and a navette of 23.54 cts (See Ill. 38, p. 52).

26. The St Moritz branch was called 'JacNel' after Jacques and Nelly Cartier. At first it opened for three months in the winter and then for two months in the summer as well. In 1929 Carl Nater, son of the mayor of St Moritz, represented the branch. Etienne Bellanger, later sales director in London, worked with him. The branch was closed in 1945. In that year Nater, who had married Jacques Cartier's daughter Alice, became director in London.

27. The Thibaw ruby was auctioned by Christie's in Geneva on 27 May 1971 and was subsequently recut by Van Cleef & Arpels.

28. Cartier's designed a similar flower brooch of rubies and diamonds to a commission from Dr Williamson for Princess Margaret. The jewel was later reshaped by the designer Dennis Gardner.

29. The ring and brooch of the emerald parure were signed by Cartier. See Lanllier-Pini, Cinq siècles de joaillerie en occident, 1971, p. 266.

30. In 1980 Elizabeth Taylor sold the diamond drop for $2 million to the New York dealer Henry Lambert.

BIBLIOGRAPHY

Abd-ul Hamid II, Sultan. Catalogue de bijoux, Paris, 1911.

Abeler, Jurgen. Kronen, Wuppertal, 1976.

A la Vieille Russie. The Art of the Goldsmith & the Jeweler. New York, 1968.
Fabergé. Exhibition catalogue, 22 April–21 May 1983.

Anni Trenta. Exhibition catalogue, Comune di Milano, 27 January–30 April 1982.

Armstrong, Nancy. Victorian Jewelry. London, 1976.

Bapst, Germain. Histoire de joyaux de la cour de France. Paris, 1889.

Barten, Sigrid. René Lalique. Munich, 1977.

Beaton, Cecil. Cinquante ans d'élégance et d'art de vivre. Paris, n.d.

Biehn, Heinrich. Alle Kronen dieser Welt. Munich, 1974.
Juwelen und Preziosen. Munich, 1965.

Birmingham, Stephen. The Grandes Dames. New York, 1982.

Blakey, George G. The Diamond. London, 1977.

Brij, Bhusan Jamila. Indian Jewellery Ornaments and Decorative Design. Delhi, 1964.

Brunhammer, Yvonne. 1925. Paris, 1976.

Cartier. Retrospective Louis Cartier: One Hundred and One Years of the Jeweler's Art. New York, 1976.
Retrospective Louis Cartier: Masterworks of Art Deco. Exhibition catalogue, Los Angeles County Museum, 1983.

Castle, Charles. La Belle Otéro. London, 1983.

Charles-Roux, Edmonde. Le Temps Chanel. Paris, 1979.

Chaumet. Une Pléiade de joailliers: 1780–1930. Paris, 1930.

Christie's Geneva. The H. Robert Greene Collection of Art Deco. Catalogue, 16 November 1978.
A Casket of Magnificent Jewels: The Collection of the late Lydia Lady Deterding. Catalogue, 20 November 1980.

Demoriane, Hélène. 'Les Most de Cartier 1925', Connaissance des Arts, April 1974.

Desaultels, Paul E. Gems in the Smithsonian. Washington, 1965.

Le Diamant. Paris, 1979.

Fabergé 1846–1920. Exhibition catalogue, Victoria and Albert Museum, 23 June–25 September 1977.

Finestone, Jeffrey. The Last Courts of Europe. London, 1981.

Flower, Margaret. Victorian Jewellery. London, 1963.

Fontenay, Eugène. Les Bijoux anciens et modernes. Paris, 1887.

Forster, Vanda. Bags and Purses. London, 1982.

Gaal, Robert A. D. Diamond Dictionary. Santa Monica, California, 1977.

Gary, Marie-Noël de. Les Fouquet. Paris, 1983.

Gautier, Gilberte. Rue de la Paix. Paris, 1980.

Gere, Charlotte. Victorian Jewellery Design. London, 1972.

Gernsheim, Alice. Victorian and Edwardian Fashion. New York, 1963.

Gold, Arthur and Fizdale, Robert. Misia. London, 1980.

Golish, Vitold de. Splendeur et crépuscule des maharajas. Paris, 1963.

Habsburg, Lothringen von Geza. Fabergé: Court Jeweller to the Tsars. London, 1979.

Heiniger, Ernst A. Le Grand Livre des bijoux. Lausanne, 1974.

Hendley, Thomas Holbein. Indian Jewellery. London, 1906–1909.

Hinks, Peter. Nineteenth-Century Jewellery. London, 1975.

Howarth, Stephen. The Koh-i-Noor Diamond. London, 1980.

Hughes, Graham. Modern Jewellery. London, 1963.

Ileana, Princess (of Romania). I Live Again. New York, 1951.

The Indian Heritage: Court Life and Arts under Mughal Rule. Exhibition catalogue, Victoria and Albert Museum, 21 April–22 August 1982.

Jenkins, Marilyn. Islamic Jewellery in the Metropolitan Museum of Art. New York, 1983.

Jourdain, Margaret. Chinese Export Art in the 18th Century. London, 1950.

Jullian, Philippe. Robert de Montesquiou. London, 1967.

De Meyer. New York, 1976.
La Belle Epoque. New York, 1980.

Kochno, Boris. Diaghilev. New York, 1970.

Kchessinska, Mathilda. Souvenirs de la Kschessinska. Paris, 1960.

Kunz, George F. The Book of the Pearl. London, 1908.

Lanllier, Jean and Pini, Marie-Anne. Cinq siècles de joaillerie en Occident. Paris, 1971.

Latif, Momin. Bijoux Moghols. Exhibition catalogue, Société Générale de Banque Bruxelles. 21 January–31 March 1982.

Letson, Neil. 'Cartier, Sovereign Jeweler', Connoisseur, November 1982.

Lobanoff, Princesse de. Joyaux de.... Sale catalogue, Lausanne, 1920.

Marie, Grand Duchess (of Russia). The Education of a Princess. New York, 1930.

Masters, Brian. Great Hostesses. London, 1982.

Mathilde, Princesse. Catalogue de bijoux. Paris, 1904.

Menzhausen, Joachim. A la cour du Grand Moghol. Leipzig, 1965.

Munn, Geoffrey. Castellani and Giuliano: Revivalist Jewellers of the Nineteenth Century. Paris, 1983.

New York, Museum of the City of. The Gilded Age: 1860–1968. Catalogue of the Worth exhibition, New York, 1983.

Nijinsky, Romola. Nijinsky. London, 1970.

Nou, J. Louis. Les derniers Maharajahs. Paris, 1980.

Paley, Princess. Souvenirs de Russie. Paris, 1923.

Parke Bernet. The Magnificent Jewellery of the late Mrs John E. Rovensky. Catalogue, 23 January 1957.

Poiret, Paul. En habillant l'époque. Paris, 1930.

Ponsonby, Sir Frederick. Collections of Three Reigns. London, 1951.

Pressmar, Emma. Indische Ringe. Frankfurt am Main, 1982.

Princely Magnificence: Court Jewels of the Renaissance. Exhibition catalogue, Victoria and Albert Museum, 15 October 1980–1 February 1981.

Pringué, Gabriel-Louis. Trente ans de dîners en ville. Paris, 1948.

Quennell, Peter. Customs and Characters. London, 1982.

Rensselaer, Philip von. Million Dollar Baby. London, 1979.

Reselle, Bruno du. La Mode, Paris, 1980.

Rosenthal, Léonard. Au royaume de la perle. Paris, 1920.
Au jardin des gemmes. Paris, 1922.

Ross, Ishbal. Silhouette in Diamonds. New York, 1975.

Ross, Marvin C. The Art of Karl Fabergé and his Contemporaries. Oklahoma, 1965.

Seebohm, Caroline. The Man who was Vogue. London, 1983.

Sinkankas, John. Emerald and other Beryl. Radnor, Pa., 1981.

Smith, Jane. Elsie de Wolfe. New York, 1982.

Snowman, A. Kenneth. The Art of Carl Fabergé. London, 1955.

Sondheimer, Alphonse de. Vitrine XIII. Hamburg, 1966.

Spencer, Charles. The World of Diaghilev. Harmondsworth, 1974.

Steinem Patch, Susan. The Blue Mystery: The Story of the Hope Diamond. Washington, 1976.

Taburiaux, Jean. La Perle et ses secrets. Paris, 1983.

Taylor, Gerald and Scarisbrick, Diana. Finger Rings from Ancient Egypt to the Present Day. London, 1978.

Twining, Lord. History of the Crown Jewels of Europe. London, 1960.

Vente des diamants de la couronne. Catalogue, 1887.

Vever, Henri. La Bijouterie française du XIXème siècle. Paris, 1906.

Vorres, Ian. The Last Grand Duchess. London, 1964.

Ward, A. La Bague de l'antiquité à nos jours. Paris, 1981.

Wartski. A Thousand Years of Enamel. Exhibition catalogue, 18 May–5 June 1971.

White, Palmer. Poiret. London, 1973.

CARTIER FAMILY TREE

Louis-François Cartier
1755—1793/94
|
Pierre Cartier
1787—1859
|
Louis-François Cartier
1819—1904
|
Louis-François *Alfred* Cartier
1841—1925

Louis-Joseph Cartier
1875—1942
1 = Andrée Worth
    daughter of
    Jean-Philippe
    Worth
|
Anne-Marie Cartier
= René Révillon
|
René-Louis
Michel

2 = Countess
    Jacqueline Almassy
|
Claude Cartier, 1925—1975
= Rita Salmona
|
Alain
Véronique

Pierre-Camilla Cartier
1878—1965
= Elma Rumsey
|
Marion Cartier
= Pierre Claudel
|
Violaine
Dominique
Elma
Marie
Michèle
Pierre

Jacques-Théodule Cartier
1884—1942
= Nelly Harjes
|
Jacqueline
Alice
Jean-Jacques
Harjes

Suzanne Cartier
= Jacques Worth,
    son of Gaston Worth
|
Roger
Hélène
Maurice
Gérard

CHRONOLOGY

Cartier History	*Cartier Jewels and Fashions*	*Historic Events*
1819. Birth of Louis-François Cartier		
		1822. Platinum discovered in the Ural Champollion deciphers hieroglyphs
		1831. Obelisk on Place de la Concorde, Paris
1841. Birth of Louis-François-*Alfred* Cartier	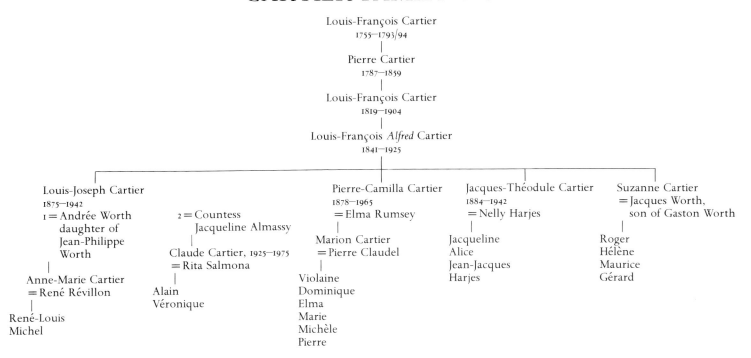	
1847. Foundation of Cartier's, 29 rue Montorgueil, Paris		
1850. Birth of Edmond Jaeger		**1851.** World Exhibition, London
	1852. 'Egyptian' scarab bracelet in stock	
1853. Transfer of Cartier's to 5 rue Neuve-des-Petits-Champs First American client	**1853.** First mention of platinum First mention of watches	**1853.** Marriage of Napoleon III to Eugénie de Montijo
	1854. First hair ornament (pearls, enamel) in stock	
	1855. Countess de Nieuwerkerke is client	**1855.** World Exhibition, Paris Death of F. D. Froment-Meurice Fontenay creates blackberry tiara in platinum
	1856ff. First purchase of Princess Mathilde Duchess of Fitz-James buys pearl and ivory brooch	**1856.** Birth of the Prince Impérial Whistler discovers Japanese wood-prints in Paris
	1857. Count de Nieuwerkerke buys Imperial eagle	**1857.** Longchamp racecourse established
		1858. C. F. Worth established at 7 rue de la Paix Boucheron founded
1859. Transfer of Cartier's to 9 boulevard des Italiens	**1859.** First bandeau in silvergilt in stock Empress Eugénie is client Count Belgiojoso buys amethyst pin Shirt studs in platinum in stock	**1859ff.** Suez Canal built
1860. First Russian client	**1860.** Prince Soltikov buys emerald bracelet	**1860.** Summer Palace Peking destroyed
	1861. Princess Mathilde buys 'Egyptian' earrings	**1861ff.** Campana Collection at Louvre
	1862. Prince Bibesco buys diamond ring	**1862.** World Exhibition, London
		1864. 'Chambre Syndicale de Bijouterie, Joaillerie et Orfèvrerie' founded 'Union Centrale des Beaux-Arts appliqués à l'Industrie' founded
		1867. World Exhibition, Paris Future Edward VII visits India and Nepal First major diamond found in South Africa
1869. Louis-François Cartier's Swiss voyage		**1869.** Empress Eugénie in Egypt for inauguration of Suez Canal

Cartier History	Cartier Jewels and Fashions	Historic Events
		1870. Franco-German War
		Empress Eugénie flees to England
1871–73. Temporary establishment of Cartier's in London		**1871.** Birth of Proust
Cartier's sells Barucci jewels		First performance of *Aïda*
		Insurrection of Commune
	1872. Indian ear-pendants in stock	**1872.** Eugénie's jewels auctioned in London
		Atanik Eknayan settles in Paris
	1873. Creation of 'Egyptian' châtelaine	
1874. Alfred Cartier takes over the shop		**1875.** Liberty's London established
1875. Birth of Louis-Joseph Cartier		**1876.** World Exhibition, Philadelphia
		Peacock Room by Whistler
		1877. Musée des Arts Décoratifs opens in Paris
1878. Birth of Pierre-Camille Cartier	**1878.** Princess de Wagram is client	**1878.** World Exhibition, Paris
		Chimaera tiara by Fouquet
		1879. Fouquet opens at avenue de l'Opéra
		1880. De Beers Mining Co. established
		Rational Dress Society founded in England
	1881. 'Lovebird' brooch	**1881.** Alexander II assassinated in Moscow
		Gaillard studies Eastern lacquers and enamels
	1883. 'Chimaera' pendant	**1883.** Japanese Exhibition, Paris
		Metropolitan Opera House, New York, opens
1884. Birth of Jacques-Théodule Cartier		**1884.** Exhibition of French crown jewels at the Louvre
1885. Birth of Maurice Coüet		
	1886. Count de Paris buys silvergilt frames	**1886.** Tonkin becomes French Colony
	City of Bordeaux buys 155 medallions	
	Vicomtesse de Bonnemain buys pearl bracelet	
1887. Birth of Jeanne Toussaint	**1887.** Lalique sells 5 bird brooches to Cartier	**1887.** Wilson scandal in Paris
	Prince of Saxe-Cobourg buys 2 miniatures	Mariette publishes *Egyptian Archaeology*
	Vicomtesse de Bonnemain buys diamond aigrette	Sale of French crown jewels
	Countess de Turenne buys peridot brooch	Fontenay publishes *Les Bijoux anciens et modernes*
	Countess de Nattes buys diamond ring	
	1888. First bracelet watches in stock	**1888.** Cecil Rhodes controls Kimberley Central Mine
		Sarah Bernhardt appears in Sardou's *Tosca*
		1889. Paris World Exhibition
		Eiffel Tower
		Bapst: *Histoire des joyaux de la couronne de France*
	1890. Prince Pedro of Brazil is client	**1890.** Société d'Encouragement à l'Art et à l'Industrie established in Paris
		Paul Esmerian settles in Paris
		1893. Edmond Goncourt publishes *L'Art japonais*
		Eknayan opens first diamond-cutting factory
		1894. Marriage of Grand Duchess Xenia
	1895. Appearance of ribbon and bow jewels	**1895.** Death of Charles F. Worth
		Anna Gould marries Boni de Castellane
		1896ff. Journal *Art et décoration* founded
		Coronation of Nicholas II
		1897. Cutting of 'Jubilee' diamond
		Vienna Secession
		First flights by Santos-Dumont
		Lacloche Frères established
		1897–99. Dreyfus Affair
1898. Louis Cartier associated with his father Alfred: 'Alfred Cartier et Fils'	**1898.** 'Japanese' and 'Chinese' buckles	**1898.** Hotel Ritz opens
Louis Cartier marries Andrée Worth		Emile Zola publishes *J'accuse*
1899. Transfer of Cartier's to 13 rue de la Paix	**1899.** 'Valkyrie' aigrette	**1899.** Asscher's diamond-cutting factory established in Paris
	'Persian' aigrette	René Lalique: 'Isis and lotus' tiara
	1900ff. *Lavallières*, *sévignés* and *cravates* in fashion	**1900.** Paris World Exhibition
		Fouquet's shop, 6 rue Royale, designed by Mucha
	1901. Pendant 'barbe de cardinal'	**1901.** Death of Queen Victoria
	Prince Alexander Bariatinsky buys 6 diamond bows	Flight by Santos Dumont from Saint Cloud to Eiffel Tower
	'Indian' necklace for Queen Alexandra	Société des Artistes Décorateurs founded
	Urn vase clocks	Birth of Harry Winston
	Duchess of Devonshire buys sunshade	'Hope' diamond sold in London
	Princess Victoria buys belt-buckle	
	Grand Duke Paul buys Wedgwood opera glass	
	Lina Cavalieri buys boa agraffe	
	Duchess of Manchester buys brooch 'Question Mark'	
	First ear-of-wheat tiara	
1902. Cartier's London branch founded at 4 New Burlington Street	**1902.** Marquis of Anglesey buys charm with Santos-Dumont portrait	**1902.** Coronation of Edward VII
Alfred Cartier opens own office at 4 rue de la Paix	Lillie Langry buys fancy-yellow diamond brooch	Sir Ernest Cassel the King's financial adviser
	Duchess of Devonshire buys pearl and diamond tiara	Townsend develops 'Twentieth-century' diamond cut
		Consuelo Vanderbilt visits Russia

Cartier History	Cartier Jewels and Fashion	Historic Events

<table>
<tr><td valign="top">

Cartier History

C & A ◇ 1903

</td><td valign="top">

Cartier Jewels and Fashion

Nellie Melba buys diamond and pearl stomacher
Countess Essex buys diamond tiara
Lady de Grey buys diamond tiara
1903. Princess de Polignac buys laurel wreath
  tiara
Countess Warwick buys emerald tiara
Mrs Keppel buys diamond tiara
Grand Duke Alexis buys serpent monocle
Princess Amédée de Broglie buys ruby heart
  brooch
Duchess of Roxburghe buys diamond bracelet
Duke of Westminster buys ruby and diamond
  tiara
Caroline Otéro buys tassel necklace
Nellie Melba buys opal heart pendant
Chinese jade pendants in fashion
Anna Gould buys laurel leaf tiara

</td><td valign="top">

Historic Events

1903. Paris Exhibition: 'Des Arts Musulmans'
Bicentenary of foundation of St Petersburg
Bojars' Ball at Winter Palace, St Petersburg
Poiret opens shop in rue Pasquier, Paris

</td></tr>
</table>

1904. Warrant of King Edward VII
Death of Louis-François Cartier
Pierre Cartier travels to Russia
Warrant of King Alfonso XIII of Spain

1904. Santos Dumont buys 'Merovingian'
  brooch
Geneviève Lantelme buys diamond ring
Princess George Radziwill buys statue of St
  Antony
Mrs Mackay buys diamond and sapphire tiara
Countess Greffulhe buys laurel wreath tiara
Mrs Burns buys 'Louis XVI' thermometer
Cornelius Vanderbilt buys Princess Mathilde's
  rose-brooch
Eleonora Duse buys pearl ring
Vincenzo Florio buys black diamond pendant
W. K. Vanderbilt buys necklace with 5 black
  pearls
J. P. Morgan buys first sun-tiara
Queen Alexandra buys ruby necklace
Queen Alexandra buys *résille* necklace

1904. Death of Princess Mathilde
Vever moves to 14 rue de la Paix
Chaumet's 'Via Vitae' exhibited at St Louis,
  Missouri

1905. Warrant of King Carlos of Portugal

1905. Lilian Nordica buys briolette diamond tiara
K. Vanderbilt buys 5 diamond combs
The Aga Khan buys 6 'Louis XVI' brooches
Bandeau 'Maria Stuart'

1905. Outbreak of revolution in Russia
Paris Exhibition of Fauvist Painters
Lalique moves to Place Vendôme
Chaumet moves to Place Vendôme
World Exhibition in Liège
Einstein creates Theory of Relativity
Caruso and Melba sing at Covent Garden in
  honour of Alfonso XIII

1906. Jacques Cartier in charge of London shop
Louis and Pierre Cartier associate: 'Cartier Frères'

1906. First attempts at art deco jewelry
'Renaissance' tiara in emeralds and diamonds
New series of leather strap wrist watches
King of Sweden buys pearl necklace

1906. Edward VII in India
World Exhibition in Milan
Paris Exhibition of Russian Art by Diaghilev
Van Cleef & Arpels to Place Vendôme
Marriage of King of Spain
Vever: *La Bijouterie française du XIXème siècle*

1907. Fifteen-year contract with Edmond Jaeger
Pierre Cartier travels to New York
Dowager Empress Marie Feodorovna visits rue
  de la Paix shop
First Cartier exhibition at Hotel d'Europe, St
  Petersburg
Warrant of the King of Siam
Warrant of Tsar Nicholas II of Russia

1907. 'Chinese Cloud Head' pendants
Enamelled 'Egg' clocks
'Parasol' watches
Baron Henri de Rothschild buys key pattern
  tiara

1907. Norwegian state visit of King Haakon VII
  to Paris
Fabergé models Sandringham animals
Marriage of Princess Marie Bonaparte to Prince
  George of Greece
Picasso paints *Les Demoiselles d'Avignon*
Elsie de Wolfe decorates the Colony Club, New
  York

1908. Temporary Cartier branch at 28 quai de la
  Cour, St Petersburg
Cartier received at Gatchina Palace by Dowager
  Empress Marie Feodorovna
Cartier received at Tsarskoe Selo Palace by tsar
  and tsarina

1908. First circular clocks
Fashion for onyx
Grand Duchess Vladimir buys briolette diamond
  tiara
Nellie Melba buys 'Greek' bandeau
Grand Duke Paul buys pear-shaped diamond
  tiara
Egyptian choker with lotus motifs
'Star of the East' diamond sold to Mrs McLean
King George of Greece buys amethyst necklace
Duc d'Orléans buys 'Greek' bandeau
Sultan of Zanzibar buys cigarette holder

1908. Ayrton discovers royal tomb at Thebes
Boris Godunov staged in Paris
Exhibition: 'La Parure Précieuse de la Femme'
  (Galliéra)
Poiret opens Boutique 'Chichi'
Asscher cuts the 'Cullinan' in Amsterdam
George F. Kunz publishes *The Book of the Pearl*
Death of Grand Duke Vladimir

1908/09. Jules Glaenzer's trip to the Far East
Pierre Cartier marries Elma Rumsey
1909. Warrant of King George I of Greece
Alfred Cartier appraises Abdul Hamid's jewels in
  Constantinople
Charles Jacqueau joins Cartier's
Transfer of London branch to 175/76 New Bond
  Street
Cartier opens at 712 Fifth Avenue, New York
1910. Louis Cartier and Andrée Worth divorced
Louis Cartier in St Petersburg
Cartier participates at Christmas Bazaar in St
  Petersburg

1909. Grand Duchess Vladimir buys sapphire
  kokoshnik
Queen Alexandra buys fleur-de-lys tiara

1910. Epaulettes fashionable
Onyx and diamond jewels
Crystal and diamond jewels
Persian influence. Aigrettes

1909. Blériot crosses the English Channel
Ballets Russes in Paris
Lalique opens glass factory in Combe-la-Ville
State visit of King Manuel of Portugal to Paris
Lace exhibition at Musée des Arts Décoratifs
Proust begins *A la recherche du temps perdu*
Auction sale of 'Hope' diamond in Paris
1910. Death of Edward VII
State visit of Spanish sovereigns to Paris
Ballet *Schéhérazade* in Paris
Poiret invents the hobble skirt

Cartier History	Cartier Jewels and Fashions	Historic Events

Cartier History

First recorded Cartier locking 'C' on seal

1910/11. Louis Cartier and Jacqueau travel to Moscow and Kiev
1911. Exhibition of 19 tiaras at Cartier's London
Birth of Marion Cartier in New York

1911/12. Jacques Cartier's trip to the Persian Gulf (repeated 1912/13)
1912. Paris City Council presents Nicholas II with Cartier egg in Russia
Cartier adds 11 rue de la Paix to No. 13
Cartier exhibition in Canada and Belgium

 1912

1913. Warrant of King Peter of Serbia

1914. Warrant of the Duke of Orléans

1917. Transfer of Cartier's New York to 653 Fifth Avenue
(Exchange of two-row pearl necklace for the Morton Plant Building)

 1919

1919. Warrant of King Albert I of Belgium
Cartier's London independent of Paris
Cartier exhibits 478-ct sapphire necklace at San Sebastian
Coüet transferred to Cartier-owned workshop at rue Lafayette
European Watch and Clock Company (E W C) founded
1920. Warrant of King Victor Emmanuel III of Italy
Warrant of Prince Albert of Monaco

1921. Warrant of the Prince of Wales
'Cartier Frères' becomes 'Cartier S.A.'

 1922

1922. Louis Cartier travels to Spain (Granada)

Cartier Jewels and Fashions

Mrs Leeds buys pearl necklace for Fr2,850,000
Extra-flat crystal pocket watches fashionable
Deployant buckle invented
Sale of 'Hope' diamond to Mrs Walsh McLean
Blue heart-shaped diamond of 31 cts sold to Mrs Unzue
Marcel Proust buys opal plastrons

1911. Mr Blumenthal buys briolette diamonds of 90.38 cts
Mrs Lydig buys 43-ct pear-shaped diamond
'Santos Dumont' wrist-watch
Mr Stotesbury buys 10.44-ct ruby ring

1912. Torpedo pendants
Mrs Leeds buys emerald epaulette
Queen Elizabeth of Belgium buys diamond tiara
First aigrette with 'Indian' *sarpech*
First baguette-cut diamonds in geometric outline
'Comet' clocks
Princess Nicholas of Greece buys pearl and diamond necklace

1913. Mrs Leeds buys pearl and pear-shaped diamond tiara
First 'Mystery' clock
'Mystery' pendant watch
Remounting of 14 bracelets for Gaekwar of Baroda
1914. First panther motif on watch
Coloured diamond sautoir sold to Kiev
Elsie de Wolfe buys 'Cantine d'automobile'
Lady Randolph Churchill buys diamond pendant
Jacques Doucet buys sapphire pendant
Mistinguett buys pearl bracelet
1916. 'Hope' spinel mounted on necklace

1917. Emilienne d'Alençon buys ruby ring
Henry Clay Frick buys 4 diamond brooches
Vanity case with first entire panther

1918. 'Bâtons de Maréchal' for Marshall Foch and Pétain
King of Belgium buys 3 brooches with royal cipher
1919. Lady Curzon of Keddleston buys diamond bandeau
Caroline Otéro buys 10-row pearl 'écharpe'
Arthur Rubinstein buys ring
Necklace with 21.18-ct heart diamond
'Tank' watch

1920. Cartier purchases Tsar Nicholas I pearl necklace at Lobanov auction in Lausanne
Lady Granard buys diamond tiara
Queen of Spain buys pearl and diamond tiara
First kingfisher feathers as clock dials
'Mystery' clocks with central axle
1921. King Ferdinand of Romania buys 478-ct sapphire necklace
Lady Granard buys sapphire necklace
Queen Sophie of Greece buys arrow brooch
Frieda Hempel buys diamond ear-pendants
Queen Mary of Romania buys pearl and diamond bandeau
Serge Diaghilev buys black pearl plastron
Prince of Wales buys 'Egyptian' bracelet
Mrs Leeds buys emerald necklace
Historic Leuchtenberg emerald ear-pendants at Cartier's New York
1922. Queen Helen of Italy buys 2 diamond brooches
Jeanne Lanvin buys crystal, pearl and diamond necklace

Historic Events

1911. Auction sale of the jewels of Abdul Hamid in Paris
Franco-Egyptian exhibition at the Louvre
George Barbier's first exhibition in Paris
Coronation of George V

1912. Persian Ball of the Marquise de Chabrillan
Persian Ball of the Comtesse de Clermont-Tonnerre
The *Titanic* sinks
Auction of Doucet's collection of eighteenth-century art
Lalique's last jewelry exhibition
La Gazette du bon ton founded
Stotesbury marriage in Philadelphia
Dunand taught Japanese lacquer by Sugawara
Borchardt discovers head of Nefertiti
1913. *Le Sacre du Printemps*
Chanel invents sport fashion
Celebration of Romanow tercentenary
American Vogue: 'Ida Rubinstein with panther'

1914. First World War
Marriage of Prince Felix Youssoupov
Crinoline Ball of Duchess de Gramont
Bal des Pierreries of Princess de Broglie
Mosaic Egg by Fabergé
Woman with Panther by George Barbier

1916. Mikimoto's patent for cultured pearls
Murder of Rasputin
1917. Invention of Bakelite
Garçonne hairstyle
Hollywood film *Cleopatra*
Ballet *Parade* by Diaghilev
Ironwork collection 'Le Secq des Tournelles' exhibited at Rouen
1918. French franc at half its prewar value

1919. Treaty of Versailles
Torkowsky develops brilliant cut
Leopard motifs at Villa Trianon
Compagnie des Arts Français opens

1920. Death of Empress Eugénie
Russian fashion starts at Chanel's
Vogue cover by Bakst
Marriage of Misia with José-Maria Sert
Death of Peter Carl Fabergé
Death of Grand Duchess Vladimir
1921. 'Chanel No. 5'
Marriage of William Leeds to Princess Xenia of Greece
Habsburg Jewels for sale in Lucerne
Exhibition 'Salon du Goût Français' in Paris

1922. Death of Marcel Proust
Discovery of Tutankhamun's tomb
Poincaré is president

Cartier History	Cartier Jewels and Fashions	Historic Events
	First coral 'chimaera' bangle First figurative 'mystery' clock	
1923. Exhibition of Napoleon silver service at Cartier's New York, Boston Cartier received by King Alexander of Serbia in Belgrade	**1923.** 'Egyptian' lotus bandeau Mrs Stotesbury buys emerald necklace and tiara First Temple Gate 'mystery' clock Lady Cunard buys 'flower vase' necklace Madame Paquin buys emerald and diamond necklace King of Serbia orders emerald necklace and diamond tiara	**1923.** Death of Sarah Bernhardt Steichen photographs for *Vogue* Death of Lord Carnarvon 'Chinese Ball' at Paris Opéra
1924. *London Illustrated News* mentions Cartier's 'Egyptian' jewels Cartier's New York acquires jeweler Dreicer's stock for $2.5 million	**1924.** Princess Helen of Serbia buys diamond necklace 'Egyptian' vanity case with flute player Cartier buys Thiers pearls Trinity rings and bracelet Fashion for long diamond sautoirs Cartier buys historic Maria Theresa ear-pendants First Chinese mother-of-pearl lacquers on vanity cases	**1924.** French Exhibition at Grand Central Palace, New York
1925. Death of Alfred Cartier Cartier exhibits at 'Exposition Internationale des Arts Décoratifs et Industriels Modernes'	**1925.** Zenith of art deco fashion Queen of Greece buys emerald and diamond bandeau Coco Chanel buys sapphire and emerald ring Baronne de Meyer buys vanity case 'Egyptian' sarcophagus vanity case Jeanne Lanvin buys spectacles with lotus motif Pendant watches fashionable Cartier's sells Prince Youssoupov's black pearls	**1925.** 'Exposition Internationale des Arts Décoratifs et Industriels Modernes' in Paris Negro Fashion in Paris. Black Bottom The Bolsheviks discover Youssoupov treasure in Moscow
1926. Cartier patent for handbag clasp	**1926.** Ganna Walska buys coral 'fuchsia' necklace Maharajah of Kapurthala orders emerald head ornament	**1926.** French franc falls to 240 to the pound English fashion starts at Chanel's Elsie de Wolfe marries Sir Charles Mendl
1927. Patent for brooch-clip (also 1934)	**1927.** Madame Enrico Caruso buys handbag with turquoises Rajah of Mandi orders emerald head ornament Queen of Spain buys laurel leaf tiara 'Egyptian' temple gate clock Chinese 'turtle' clock	**1927.** Sert divorces Misia Lindbergh's flight from New York to Paris Lanvin's 'Arpège' First South Atlantic crossing by Dieudonné Coste and Joseph le Brix Boucheron's 'falcon' tiara for King Fuad
1928. Warrant of Queen Mary of Romania Exhibition of Patiala jewels at rue de la Paix shop Pierre Cartier receives aviators Coste and le Brix in New York Gaekwar of Baroda appoints Jacques Cartier as sole adviser on his jewels	**1928.** Maria Barrientos buys emerald and diamond brooch El Glaoui buys pearl and diamond belt José-Marie Sert buys ruby bead necklace State diamond necklace for Maharajah of Patiala Ganna Walska buys coral 'chimaera' bangle 'Polar Star' diamond sold to Lady Deterding Engraved emerald Indian necklace mounted for Maharajah of Nawanagar	**1928.** Death of Dowager Empress Marie Chanel opens at rue Cambon
1929. Cartier branch in Saint Moritz (until 1945) Cartier workshop in rue Bachaumont Cartier exhibits at French Exhibition in Cairo Warrant of King Fuad of Egypt Aga Khan necklace exhibited in Barcelona Exhibition	**1929.** Maharajah of Indore buys pearl and onyx handbag 'Egyptian' vanity case with Goddess Bastet	**1929.** Resignation of Poincaré as president Death of Diaghilev Wall Street Crash International Exhibition, Barcelona Union des Artistes Modernes in Paris French Exhibition, Cairo Exhibition: 'Les Arts de la Bijouterie'
1930. Coüet workshop transferred to rue Réaumur Cartier patents for gold alloys (also 1934)	**1930.** Engraved emerald jewels mounted for the Aga Khan Cigarette case designed as miniature motor car Necklace with 71 coloured diamonds mounted for Madame Fournier	**1930.** First Atlantic flight from Paris to New York Marriage of King Umberto of Savoy to Princess Marie-José
	1931. Coloured diamond necklace with 'Queen of Holland' diamond mounted for Maharajah of Nawanagar Necklace with 6 fancy-pink diamonds First Academicians' sword for Duc de Grammont Vicountess Astor buys 'Peacock' bandeau	**1931.** Colonial Exhibition, Paris Ernest Oppenheimer takes over Diamond Syndicate Ballet Russe de Monte Carlo founded Economic crisis in France
1932. Cartier received by King of Nepal in Katmandu		**1932.** Chanel's own jewelry collection First colour photograph in *Vogue* England legalizes 14-ct gold
1933. Exhibition of Louis Cartier's Persian miniatures in New York Marion Cartier marries Pierre Claudel 'Porter Rhodes' diamond at Cartier's Cartier patent for 'serti mystérieux' Jeanne Toussaint presides over Cartier Haute Joaillerie French Government presents Rockefeller Center with Cartier model of 'Question Mark' biplane	**1933.** Wedding jewels for Barbara Hutton Crown designs for Gaekwar of Baroda New fashion for gold-mounted jewelry Academician's sword for François Mauriac	**1933.** Hitler elected Chancellor Exhibition 'A Century of Progress' in Chicago Death of Maharajah of Nawanagar
1935. Cartier Paris designer Lemarchand works	**1934.** Purchase of white pearls from Youssoupov Massive crystal jewelry fashionable **1935.** First models of electric watches	**1934.** Stavisky affair in France Assassination of Chancellor Dollfuss **1935.** Death of Paul Iribe

(centre emblem: diamond with letters S C C A around a ccc monogram) 1929

Cartier History	Cartier Jewels and Fashions	Historic Events

Cartier History

at Cartier London (until 1939)
Exhibition of Historic Diamonds at rue de la Paix shop
Cartier patent for lipstick holder
Opening of Monte Carlo branch

1936. Cartier's shows 'Nassak' diamond in Monte Carlo

1937. Cartier's makes jewelry using metal, 'Platinix'

1938. Princess Elizabeth receives smallest wristwatch in the world, signed Cartier
Opening of Cartier's Cannes
Jacques Cartier visits Maharajah of Nawanagar
Cartier relation with perfumer Pinaud
Cartier's exhibition in Tirana (Albania) on occasion of marriage of King Zog I
1939. Designer Lemarchand to Jodhpur and Bahawalpur in India
Warrant of King Zog I of Albania

1940. After German occupation of Paris, temporary Cartier shop in Biarritz

1942. Deaths of Louis Cartier and Jacques Cartier

1945. Pierre Cartier President of Cartier International
Jean-Jacques Cartier takes over Cartier's London
1947. Pierre Cartier retires to Geneva

1948. Cartier's New York presided over by Claude Cartier

1956. Cartier opens workshop at 13 rue de la Paix

1959. Death of Elma Cartier

1961. Cartier purchases Empress Eugénie necklace in Bern
1962. Cartier's New York sold by Claude Cartier who remains President until 1963
1965. Death of Pierre Cartier
1966. Marion Cartier sells Cartier's Paris

1969. Cartier buys 69.42-ct pear-shaped diamond at auction and sells it to Elizabeth Taylor
1972. A group of investors organized by Joseph Kanouï acquires control of Cartier's Paris and

Cartier Jewels and Fashions

Ladybird brooches
Indian emerald and ruby necklace mounted for Maharajah of Patna
20.41-ct pear-shaped diamond mounted for Queen of Spain
Emerald and pearl head ornament mounted for the Maharajah of Dhranghadra
1936. Emperor of Annam buys diamond tiara
Baroness Maud Thyssen buys ladybird bracelet

1937. Emerald necklace with cross pendant
Blackamoor brooches fashionable
Sarpech with 'Tiger's Eye' diamond for Maharajah of Nawanagar
Gaston Cusin invents 'prism' clock
Engraved emerald and pearl necklace mounted for Maharajah of Nawanagar
1938. Barbara Hutton buys diamond bandeau
Jade 'drum' mystery clock
Fashion for 'Sioux' brooches
P. L. Weiller buys 'Jubilee' diamond
Laura Corrigan buys 31.45-ct square diamond ring
Mrs Horace Dodge buys 'Thibaw' ruby
1939. Academician's sword for André Maurois
Barbara Hutton buys pear-shaped and navette diamond necklace
Maharajah of Jaipur buys cabochon emerald drop necklace

1941. Silver shoe created for Madame Solvay

1945. General de Gaulle presents Stalin in Moscow with 'Mystery' clock

1947. Diamond necklace and rose tiara presented by Nizam of Hyderabad to Princess Elizabeth on her wedding
Remounting of emerald necklace for Barbara Hutton (Vladimir emeralds)
1948. Duchess of Windsor orders panther brooch

1953. Queen Elizabeth the Queen Mother orders diamond tiara
1954. Academician's sword for Duc de Lévis-Mirepoix
New 'chimaera' jewels created under Jeanne Toussaint's direction
Duchess of Windsor buys tiger lorgnon
1955. Academician's sword for Jean Cocteau
1956. Duchess of Windsor buys tiger bracelet
1957ff. Princess Nina Aga Khan receives panther jewels

1959. Dolphin bangle, inspired by Jeanne Toussaint
1960. Clock in crystal bottle inspired by Jeanne Toussaint
1961. Barbara Hutton buys peacock brooch

1962. Barbara Hutton buys tiger bracelet

1967. Academician's sword for Maurice Druon
1969. Maria Felix commissions her serpent necklace

Historic Events

Atlantic crossing of Normandie
Italian troops invade Ethiopia
Etienne de Beaumont's ball 'Le Grand Siècle'

1936. Léon Blum's 'Front Populaire'
Vogue and Vanity Fair merge
Edward VIII becomes King
1937. French franc taken off the gold standard and devalued
Coronation of George VI
Marriage of Duke of Windsor
International Exhibition 'Des Arts et Techniques' in Paris

1938. State visit of English sovereigns to Paris
Death of Gabriele D'Annunzio
'Mode Gitane' at Chanel's

1939. Outbreak of Second World War
World Fair, New York

1940. German occupation of Paris
French gold trading prohibited
French Armistice under Pétain
Vichy Government (−1944)
De Gaulle escapes to London and founds the 'Free French Movement'
1941. Death of Alfonso XIII
U.S.A. enters war
1942. Barbara Hutton marries Cary Grant

1944. De Gaulle heads Provisional Government
1945. End of Second World War

1947. Dr Williamson sells Tanganjika Diamond Mine to De Beers
De Gaulle's 'Rassemblement du Peuple Français'
Vincent Auriol President
'New Look' by Dior
1948. Slogan 'A diamond is forever' coined for De Beers
Israel's diamond market established
1950. Celebration of 250 years of Place Vendôme
1953. René Coty President

1955. Synthetic diamonds by General Electric

1957. Death of Ernest Oppenheimer

1958. 'Hope' diamond shown at the Smithsonian
Fifth Republic under De Gaulle
World Exhibition, Brussels

appoints Robert Hocq as President
Alain Perrin in charge of Cartier marketing
1973. Creation of 'Les Must de Cartier'
First 'Must' boutiques in Biarritz, Singapore,
  Tokyo
1974. Cartier's London is acquired by the owner
  of Cartier's Paris
Nathalie Hocq joins Cartier's Paris
1975. Death of Claude Cartier
Retrospective 'Louis Cartier' in Paris
1976. Another group of investors acquires
  Cartier's New York and appoints Joseph
  Kanouï as chairman
Sale of the 'Louis Cartier' diamond of 107.07 cts
Retrospective 'Louis Cartier' in New York
1978. Death of Jeanne Toussaint
1979. Birth of 'Cartier World' through the
  merger of the groups owning the Paris,
  London and New York stores
Death of Robert Hocq

1975. Maria Felix commissions her alligator
  necklace

 1980

A chronology of clocks and watches is given in Chapter 16. 'Cartier Jewels and Fashions' is a subjective and selective list of some important clients, important purchases and trendsetting fashions. It does not differentiate between orders and purchases from stock, nor distinguish between the three Cartier branches.

ACKNOWLEDGMENTS

My first thanks go to Mr Joseph Kanouï, President of Cartier, whose understanding, farsightedness and encouragement made this book possible. Equal thanks go to Mr Ralph Esmerian who as a friend and arbiter accompanied the project right from the beginning.

At Cartier's I had the privilege of working with Mme Véronique Ristelhueber and subsequently with Mlle Betty Jais, whose assistance as archivists was at all times invaluable. Mlle Jais followed this work through to the end with practical help at all levels. In New York Mrs Bonnie Selfe opened the Fifth Avenue archives and lent all her support, as did Mr Joe Allgood at Cartier's London. The Cartier designer Jacques Diltoer provided accomplished sketches which accompany the text.

Stimulating help and continued reference to literature came from Mr Frederik Schwarz, Berlin, and from Mr Nicolas Sarafis, Geneva. I am indebted to Mr Antony Derham and Mr Simon Bull who read through Chapters 13 and 16, respectively.

The following have given advice, suggestions and precious information: Jane Lady Abdy, Prince Sadruddin Aga Khan, Countess Carla Albertoni, Mr Jacques Arpels, Mr Louis Asscher, Mr Jean de Beisteigui, Mr Michael Bennett, Mr and Mme Christian Benoist, Prince Lennard Bernadotte, Mr Hans Bichsel, the late Mona Countess Bismarck, Mᵉ Suzanne Blum, Comte Bruno de Boisgelin, Mr Alain Boucheron, Mr Thierry Bousquet, Princesse Jeanne-Marie de Broglie, Mr Frédéric Brun-Theremin, Mr Paul Calmette, Mr François Canavy, Mr Robert Carlhian, Mr Alain Cartier, Mme Marion Cartier, Mlle Véronique Cartier, Mr Paul Casta (La Garantie), Mme Marguerite Carré, Mme Jutta Cassel, Countess Emmeline de Castéja, Mme Catherine Cardinal (Musée des Arts et des Métiers), Mme René Clair, Mr Peter Clayton, Mlle M. C. Commère (Bibliothèque des Commisseurs-Priseurs), Lady Diana Cooper, Mme Gilberte Cournand, Mr François Curiel, Mr Gaston Cusin, Mr Pierre Debofle (Archives de Paris), Mme Pierre Delbée, Mr André Denet, Mr Patrick Descamp, Mr Gérard Desouches, Mr Louis Devaux, the Diamond Information Center New York, Miss Frances Dimond (Royal Archives, Photograph Collection) Mr Jean Dinh Van, Mr Daniel Du Jeannerot, Mlle Marie Du Mesnildot, the Marchioness of Dufferin and Ava, Mr Henry Duru, Miss Diana Edkins (Condé Nast Library New York), Mr Myran Eknayan, Mme Pierre Emmanuel, Mr Rupert Emmerson, La Baronne Edwina d'Erlanger, Mme Simone Eymonaud, Mr Harry Fane, Mr Thomas Färber, Prince Jean Louis de Faucigny-Lucinge, Mr Jean Feray, Mr Christopher Forbes, Mme Claude Forêt, Mr Enrico de Franceschini, Mr Donald Fraser, Mme Tatiana Fruchaud, Mme Axelle de Gaigneron, Mr James Gardner, Mr Guillaume Garnier (Musée Galliéra), Mr Richard Garnier, Mme Marie-Noël de Gary (Musée des Arts Décoratifs) Miss Georgia Gigon, Mr David Gol, Mᵉ Blaise Grosjean, Mr H. Robert Greene, Mr Claude Guerin, Dr Géza de Habsbourg, Mme P. Hebey, Mrs Gloria Hendy, Baroness von der Heydt, Fürstin Charlotte zu Hohenlohe, Mr Hanspeter Hüsistein, Mme Suzanne Jacqueau, Mr Pierre Jeannet, Messrs Johnson, Walker and Tolhurst, Mr Stephen Kahane, Photothèque Kahn, Mr Clive Kandel, Mᵉ Albert Kaufmann, Mr Lawrence Krashes, Mr Jean de Laborde Naguez, Mr Lucien Lachassagne, Mme Nicole Landolt-Sandoz, Mr Henri Larrieu, Mr Fred Leighton, Mme Marcelle Lemarchand, Mr Jacques Lenfant, Mr Jean-Marc Leri (Bibliothèque de la ville de Paris), Mme Levy-Strauss, Comptoir Lyon-Allemand, La Duchesse de Maillé, Mr Philippe Maitrejean, Mr Félix Marcilhac, Mlle Lucette Marson, Mr Georges Martin, Mr Paul Martini, Mr J. Martory, Mr Frederick A. Mew, Mr Albert Middlemiss, Sir Oliver Millar (the Chamberlain's Office), le Comte de la Moussaye, Mr Geoffrey Munn, Miss Mary Murphy, Mr Carl Nater, le Colonel Neuville (Musée de l'Armée), Mme Noetzlin, Mr Eric Nussbaum, Mr Edmond Oxeda, Mr Gaston Palewski, Mr Max Pellegrain, Mr Michel Périnet, Platingilde Frankfurt, Miss Penny Proddow, the Prince of Pudukota, Mr Corentin Quideau, Mr Nicholas Rayner, le Baron de Rédé, Mme Janine Rémy, Mr René-Louis Révillon, Mr Alexandre Reza, Mᵉ Maurice Rheims, Mr John Richardson, Prof. Frank W. Ries, Mr Peter Riva, Mr Jean Rosenthal, Mr Joël Rosenthal, la Baronne Liliane de Rothschild, la Baronne Marie-Hélène de Rothschild, la Princesse Irina de Roumanie, Mme Geneviève Rouvrais, Mr Lionel Rouvrais, Mr Hubert Salmon, Mr Charles Schiffmann, Mrs Diana Scarisbrick, Mᵉ Pierre Sciclounoff, Mr Alexander von Solodkoff, Mr Bernard Solomon, Mme Charlotte Spoerli, H. H. Sukhjit Singh of Kapurthala, Mr Edouard Sirakian, Countess Florence de Surmont, Mr Charles Spencer, Mr Karl-Hans Strauss, Miss Suzan Strong (Victoria and Albert Museum), Mr Robert Thil, Mr Jean Taburiaux, Mr Michael Tree, Mr Michel Turisk, Mr Anthony Thompson, Mr Hugh Tait (British Museum), Mr François Verger, Mr Roger Valentin (Pyramid d'Or), Mrs Diana Vreeland, Mr Gérald Van der Kemp, the Grand Duke Vladimir, Mr Guy Villeneuve, Mr David W. Wright (Pierpont Morgan Library), la Baronne Geoffroy de Waldner, Mme B. Watel, Mr Paul-Louis Weiller, Mr Paul White (Smithsonian Institution), Mr Tjerk Wicky, Mrs Cortwright Wetherill, Mrs Rosamond Wiszniewska, Mrs E. Wynkoop, Mr Maurice Worth, Princess Olga of Yugoslavia.

My final thanks go to Mr Stanley Baron of Thames & Hudson whose taste and knowledge shaped this book.

INDEX